AWAKENING ONE'S LOVENERGY

Our Next Step to Enlightenment

Joseph L. Tolve, Jr.

Book Cover Design by Red Willow Design Studio
www.redwillowdesignstudio.com

ISBN: 978-1-936539-27-7

To my perfect parents, who get more and more perfect the older I get. They taught me the true meaning of love because they have always lived it.

To my always-loving wife Lillian, who is my divine sweetheart.

The most important thing in life is to learn how to give out love, and to let it come in.

Morrie Schwartz

Contents

Eventually you will come to understand that love heals everything, and love is all there is.

Gary Zukav

A Spiritual Conspiracy

On the surface of the world right now there is
war and violence and things seem dark.
But calmly and quietly, at the same time,
something else is happening underground

An inner revolution is taking place
and certain individuals are being called to a higher light.
It is a silent revolution.
From the inside out.
From the ground up.
This is a Global operation.

A Spiritual Conspiracy.
There are sleeper cells in every nation on the planet.
You won't see us on the T.V.
You won't read about us in the newspaper
You won't hear about us on the radio

We don't seek any glory
We don't wear any uniform
We come in all shapes and sizes, colors and styles
Most of us work anonymously

We are quietly working behind the scenes
In every country and culture of the world
Cities big and small, mountains and valleys,
In farms and villages, tribes and remote islands

You could pass by one of us on the street
And not even notice
We go undercover
We remain behind the scenes

It is of no concern to us who takes the final credit
But simply that the work gets done
Occasionally we spot each other in the street
We give a quiet nod and continue on our way

During the day many of us pretend we have normal jobs
But behind the false storefront at night
is where the real work takes a place
Some call us the Conscious Army

We are slowly creating a new world
with the power of our minds and hearts
We follow, with passion and joy
Our orders come from the Central Spiritual Intelligence

We are dropping soft, secret love bombs when no one is looking
Poems ~ Hugs ~ Music ~ Photography ~ Movies ~ Kind words ~
Smiles ~ Meditation and prayer ~ Dance ~ Social activism ~ Websites
Blogs ~ Random acts of kindness...

We each express ourselves in our own unique ways
with our own unique gifts and talents
Be the change you want to see in the world
That is the motto that fills our hearts

We know it is the only way real transformation takes place
We know that quietly and humbly
we have the power of all the oceans combined
Our work is slow and meticulous

Like the formation of mountains
It is not even visible at first glance
And yet with it entire tectonic plates
shall be moved in the centuries to come

Love is the new religion of the 21st century
You don't have to be a highly educated person
Or have any exceptional knowledge to understand it
It comes from the intelligence of the heart

Embedded in the timeless evolutionary pulse of all human beings
Be the change you want to see in the world
Nobody else can do it for you
We are now recruiting

Perhaps you will join us
Or already have.
All are welcome
The door is open

Brian Piergrossi

Introduction

I have recently just joined the human race again. Because I need to protect the identity of myself, the crusade I am working with, and most of all, my beloved eternal soul mate who I am looking forward to meeting again in a few years, I am falsifying names and locations to all of the earthling characters in this book. Because most facts given from this date and on are yet to occur, I've got to prevent anyone from determining our identifications. For we are a protective, loving, healing, and peaceful community who want only to promote those things. In short, we are a threat to all destructive terrorists and people who want to control humanity.

Let me ask you, is what I have written factual, only a figment of my imagination, or is it what I am creating via my imagination? Even after living through all that you will be reading in this book, I am still unsure of what is real and what is illusionary. Perhaps they are the same? After all, everything about us is created by the universal divine imagination of God, who we members of the Cause fondly know as One. "All is One and One is all there is."

The one thing that is real is lovenergy, and I personally know that in this book you will learn an effective method of triggering it as never before possible.

Love is the only sane and satisfactory answer to the problem of human existence.

Eric Fromm

Chapter 1
Crossroads

Life, death, and afterlife experiences are far more than I had expected. For me specifically, my 40 year old life drew to a finish and I moved into what I consider the metaphysical portion.

Only weeks ago, returning back to my home planet, I started writing this story in my newly-acquired, human, teenage body's daily journal. So much happened while I was in that other dimension that it seemed like I had been there for years. I now know that it was only months of Earth time, although I had experienced a whole new and thrilling life while present in that universal utopia. My old earthbound body had been so-called dead for me because I no longer was part of it. Although it was very much alive for another one of our causes, and I had gotten to briefly see it from another plane of consciousness.

Imagine my surprise when only days after this new earthly life began, I ran across my past life sister, Louise, who was doing some planting at our family gravesite. Because I was in the body of a strange young man, she didn't have the slightest inkling of who I was. She did look at me oddly, though, when she found me feeling the Braille label I had placed on Nana's headstone. It had my family name, Tolve, with a space and an extra Braille letter for "o" so that it spelled my favorite words, "TO LoVE".

The words "to love" in Braille.

I had written it myself only days in advance of my own unexpected death. While in that past life I hadn't actually seen my sister for 30 years, yet I had immediately recognized her with my new working human eyes. "Guess I've done a pretty good job of aging my loved ones," I reflected. That was especially true when you consider the fact that I had been 12 and she only six when I had last been able to see.

I now have total recall of all of my lives when absorbed in a special meditation that my masters had taught us while with them in that different plane of consciousness. It conveys me back and forth between metaphysical parts of my many lives as well as reliving any actual pieces of those lives I need to examine. In this book, however, I will limit my adventures to just a fleeting glimpse of my concluded human life. Since the very real plane of consciousness I had just lived is so vital, I will be spending more time reliving it for you and myself. I need it so that I will recall everything I learned and be able to exist at a much higher level of consciousness than we poor humans are presently able to conceive, let alone live.

I also need to examine it so that portions of my "out-of-this-world's existence", are recalled. Being able to have my irresistible eternal soul mate back again depends on it. I had to leave her so that I could experience human life again as I am now doing for the cause. My happiness here on Earth can only occur if I can recall necessary data so that I might locate her. Right now I can't recall her new human name, race, age, or where she might be residing in her also newly-acquired human body. We discovered one another while in the astral plane where our eternal relationship was revealed to us. We are members of a devoted team of both human and heavenly beings who are bent on saving our quickly-failing planet Earth.

Let's briefly analyze the meaning of reality. What I want to ask you is: What is the difference between reality and illusion? I want us both to say and believe that it is the same difference. Like Rene Descartes so aptly said in the 17th century, "Cogito ergo sum", translated as, "I think, therefore I am". Let's clarify it further. "Experience and believe". What you live through you believe. It may, nevertheless, only be fantasy to those who haven't had the same or similar experiences.

I was fortunate to have shared many happy years with caring people during my last earthly life. My parents were or are, not sure at this writing if they are still alive, the greatest. Thanks to them I had a nearly perfect childhood. The only imperfection was a rare disease that struck me at age 10. If I had chosen my parents, which I believe we do, I couldn't have created better. During my healthy years, despite my poor performance in sports, dad attended every event and cheered me on. He was an outstanding athlete, coach, and indulgent motivator. However, putting as much energy as I could into it, I was only a mediocre participant in all of the sports I tried. Then one day during a track meet I crumpled to the ground in excruciating pain and dad ran to me, scooped me up like a doll, put me into the car, and immediately took me to our family doctor. Dr. Hibard examined me and told dad that there wasn't any sign of fluid, but that I most likely had water on the knee. He instructed my parents and me to keep my activities to a minimum. Six weeks later mom took me back for another examination and Dr. Hibard, after not finding any signs of water on the knee, advised her to take me to a hospital where I would be seen by an orthopedic doctor.

I was hospitalized and for the first time in my life was separated from my loving family. My disease was misdiagnosed twice and the second time I was almost killed by my doctor's incorrect conclusion. Dad said that doctors were human, too, and let me tell you that very human man made all kinds of mistakes regarding my disease and me. I was voiding 10 gallons of water daily, and he was restricting my fluid intake! On top of that, he wanted to chip bone and put me into a body cast for a year or more. I would have died within months if that charlatan had been given the okay by my apprehensive parents. Another doctor they took me to misdiagnosed my brutal pain and also my unquenchable thirst and dehydration. However, he did make the correct recommendation. "Take Joey to Colombia Presbyterian Hospital," he told my always present and loving parents. Six horribly-long weeks later I was given massive dosages of radiotherapy and within only days the severe pain had decreased. I was also given a hormone replacement that controlled the drinking and voiding problem. It was discovered that my pituitary gland had been destroyed, which accounted for the enormous thirst and frequent urination. My kidneys were not getting the necessary hormone to stop taking fluid from my bloodstream, thus I was dehydrating relentlessly. I had been home only weeks when this very rare disease struck me a second time.

Two years later at age 12, after having attacks of Hand-Schüller-Christian and having bones eaten away in both hips, shoulders, and in my back, it did its most vicious thing and virtually ate away my optic nerves. This obviously caused me to become sightless and launched me into another chapter of my life.

When I reached age 20, I was transformed by a beautiful-hearted woman coming into my life. She was a born deaf-mute named Claire who I met shortly after she had lost her sight at age 22. I was the only one in West Chester County, NY who knew sign language and Braille, which I taught her. I had been contacted by the Lighthouse. In months she had learned how to read Braille and use a white cane and other necessities that would have allowed her to live a more fulfilling life if only . . . Well, we did live together for nine joyful months. Then after asking her to marry me, I for the first time found out that she was of a different race. In the middle '60s, a salt and pepper couple met with all kinds of problems and was even considered disgraceful by both races. If I were to marry this black woman, my always-fair and accommodating parents threatened to take everything from me including my most-prized family name. Until they had told me of our racial differences, I had been literally and figuratively in the dark. I was madly in love and if my beloved Nana hadn't been with us when I learned this agonizing truth, well, I have to believe that I would have married my darling Claire.

However, fate had other plans for Claire and me. My Nana was crying her eyes out after I had asked, "You won't deny me will you Nana?" She became short of breath and then had a heart attack. As she was being taken from our house by EMS workers, I promised her that our family wouldn't break up because of my infatuation. I told her that I would leave my precious flower, no matter how I felt about her. If not for that unselfishness on my behalf, I know that Claire and I would have been married and had shared a spectacular relationship for many years. Nonetheless, that wasn't in the cards for us and later that night after I had confronted her with the ugly truth of my leaving, she took even more hideous actions and committed suicide.

By accident, although I don't believe in accidents now, years later I found a method of creating heartfelt love. I know now that it would have transformed my life entirely if only I had discovered it sooner. I wouldn't have been able to leave Claire, my parents would have okayed our relationship, and love would have won out!

Chapter 2

Expanding Love

I briefly outlined a few years of that life for you so that you can recognize the differences I created for myself soon thereafter. For months after losing my precious Claire, I tried escaping by overworking. For years I had been a freelance tennis racket stringer for companies like Wilson and Davis and had been stringing my nights away. It wasn't enough so I became an x-ray darkroom technician by day, and a pianist on the weekends in a steakhouse. I was still very lonely as is common for most blind people.

I had to do something fast and only days after that realization had dawned on me I discovered a powerful technique for creating love. It transformed my life enormously and I was no longer nearly friendless. Everyone seemed to suddenly befriend me wherever I went.

Only two months after unearthing this method I was asked by two psychologists to teach it in their family center. I had been discovered by one of them while I played the piano in the steakhouse. Gary, one of these psychotherapists sensed enormous love coming out of me. He and his partner Frank asked me if I would teach my method to the patients in their center and I amiably agreed.

Getting into bed late one night, about six months later, I settled down for a good night's sleep. I moved my mind into my peaceful self-created garden scene and relaxed. I soon imagined a stream babbling, birds of every variety singing, and began visualizing Mother Nature's splendor. With my mind's eye I saw the birds flying overhead, the brook softly gurgling past, gigantic boulders that I longed to climb, and tall majestic trees with their tops thrusting into the blue sky. As always, I was thankful that I had those 12 years of "normal" sight and clear memories to call on now. It enabled me to create these glorious visions so perfectly that it was almost like really seeing them again.

Talking about seeing things, strangest of strange, a never-seen-before man dazed me by suddenly walking into my private setting. *Where on Earth did he come from, and how the hell did he get into my head like this?* I wondered to myself.

He was a small, compact man with a very distinctive red Van Dyke beard. "Hello, Jim. Nice day isn't it?" he asked me, with an experienced twinkle in his large brown eyes. "I really like your garden, it's downright exquisite. Mind if I use it during my own meditation right now?"

For a moment I entertained the idea that I must have fallen asleep, but no, I was able to mentally ask him, "Who are you?" and" how did you ever manage to get into my head like this?"

"I never thought you'd ask," he said to me as I realized I had actually moved into this impressive movie scene that I had been imagining. Unconsciously, I had moved from my bed to this setting, like an actor might move from backstage into a movie scene. In the fullest sense of the words, I was mind traveling and somehow traveling into a portion of my own imagination! Let me interrupt for a second to say that I now know that there is only one supreme Being who is One. "I am Rama, your spiritual guide," he said, extending his hand to me. "Being a spirit allows me the freedom to go wherever I please. Besides, the fact of the matter is that you have now moved your picturesque landscape into my network," he said with a laugh. "In other words, it's *you* who has gotten into *my* head," he said with an even more boisterous laugh.

"Jim," he said, "months after you lost your sight, your mind lost its ability of creating visual dreams. Notice that you are seeing and not just imagining this setting. Now for the purpose of this visit. I am here to prepare you for tomorrow. Because of your priestly growth via your love enhancement technique, you have evolved to another dimension of our Oneness. You have just entered the fourth dimension. You have become a new being founded in love and truth. It is time for you to come with me and begin a two-step cleansing ritual that will inevitably take you to even higher realizations of self."

Feeling mystified by this request and the man who had suddenly appeared in my meditation, I only managed to think, *Okay, Rama.* As soon as the words had formed in my mind, not even reaching my lips, I was zapped to another time and location.

While in this newest level of consciousness, a voluptuous woman slowly approached us. She was attired in ancient garments. Long, blond hair hung to her waist and her blue eyes held the same meaningful twinkle of Rama's brown ones. "I am Marza," she demurely said, beckoning to me. "Come with me, Jim." Taking the lead, she brought me to a stone pool with water trickling from a narrow waterfall at the far end. This pool was nestled between huge, resplendent maple trees whose foliage was luxuriously colored in yellows, oranges, and reds. Yet it had been early summer where I had come from only moments before. *Boy, time really flies here*, I briefly thought.

Even though my heart was soaring with excitement at actually being able to see this fantastic beauty perfectly, her words took me by surprise, "Time is only an illusion."

I somehow managed to ask, "What would you like me to do now?"

"Why, climb in of course," she divinely said, pointing at the slightly rippling pool. I did as she bid and found that the skin-temperature water reached only to my waste. "Now lay down with your head toward me," she instructed. A second later I lay with only my head raised above the water. Placing her hand on my forehead, she said, "Now take a deep belly breath," and pressed my head below the surface. Bending forward, she held it down with her left hand while her right hand pressed downwards on my hip so that the rest of my body was also submerged. She held me there for a minute or two, her lips moving rapidly in a silent prayer. Her ravishing bosoms were only inches from my face and I involuntarily gaped in awe at them, suddenly discerning that I was totally naked. With the stimulation of sight and touch, her amply-shaped breast almost in my face, and her soft, warm hands penetrating deeply into my skin, I pitifully found that my manhood had involuntarily become rigid. Not since before 12 had I seen breasts, and back then it was through the eyes of a non-appreciative child. A shiver of desire moved unwillingly throughout my entire body. *Here you are being purified and you are thinking like a depraved carnal man.* I severely reprimanded myself.

Moments later, with an understanding pat on the shoulder, she tendered our farewells and only a breath after that I was back in my inner garden. "Now that you have undergone the first phase of the purification ceremony, you just go to sleep," Rama said, grinning warmly. "This will empower me to do some housecleaning on your subconscious mind." Compliant with his wish, I drifted off to sleep almost immediately. My words, *What are you preparing me for?* were dutifully repressed.

Needless to say, the following morning I awoke with a new objective to my life. I was going to notify the hospital of my leaving and only finish another week or two in the darkroom. Then I would devote my full attention to my stress reduction and love enhancement meditation classes. Both psychotherapists who I worked for had requested over and over again that I make that my only commitment. My experience with Rama and Marza the night before had enlightened me, and greatly reinforced my desire to help mankind. It was the extra nudge that I had needed to commit myself to this venture.

My seeing eye dog, Tarot and I joyfully caught the 7:11 train out of Port Chester, NY. Reaching the last street crossing before the Greenwich Hospital, Tarot stopped at the curb while I listened for traffic. Knowing that we were between the lines of a crosswalk and not hearing any approaching cars, I commanded, "Tarot, forward," and stepped briskly out following her confident stride. We were right in the middle of the street when I heard the screech of tires on a speeding car. It veered left, turning the corner on what I'm sure was just two wheels, and came directly at us. Tarot drastically jerked to a stop and started to back up in an attempt to get us out of the way, but before I could adequately respond, the car smashed into my bewildered body. Just as suddenly, I was 10 feet above it all. I saw my inert body lying on the street below me. A leg bone protruded through the skin, blood spurted from my left eye and my mouth, as well. I saw a large hole in the car's windshield where evidently my head had gone through it. My face looked like it had been through a meat grinder. Probably because I was no longer a part of my body, I was experiencing no pain—feeling only internally blissful. I then looked for Tarot and saw her lying at the entrance of the hospital that we would have entered. Except for some of my blood on her fur, I was grateful to see that she was in perfect condition. I did feel sorry for her because she was trembling fiercely from the shock. Sensing my presence, she looked up and focused directly on me. I threw her a kiss and said, "It wasn't your fault, Tarot. You tried your best to get me out of the way." Her tail momentarily lifted, wagged, and then dropped heavily back to where it had been. I was drifting upward and further away from her, yet she followed me with her eyes and a slight tilt of her head. I noticed that I was once again seeing everything with my external eyes rather than my imagination. I moaned with happiness as I realized that I was seeing with a renewed and more finely-tuned sight. *Maybe that's why I am noticing that the grass is less green than I remember, the trees less effulgent, and the air actually hazy with airborne pollutants?* I wondered to myself. "Despite these negative defects so evident now, this world is more than just beautiful," I whispered. "I wish only that everyone could see this truth as obviously as I do.

My body had been imperfect, yet I had loved it and enjoyed the pleasures life had afforded me," I declared honestly. "Am I finally able to mind travel or are these eyes those of a dead man?"

I heard a familiar voice and chills of pleasure coursed through my spiritual body. It was a distant voice, yet I knew it also to be only feet away. This male voice joyfully said, "It's Lance, Jim. You are now one of us, too!" The only Lance I had ever known was a childhood friend who, unlike my other classmates, hadn't abandoned me when I had lost my sight. He came to my house to visit regularly right through high school and college, and I was most grateful for his ceaseless friendship. Unfortunately, a kidney disease took him from me only years after he had graduated college. I gazed upwards hoping to grab a glimpse of him and was amazed by the fact that I was not alone; thousands of other bodies floated around me. They were shrouded in various shades of a gray-like hue. Some were a deep gray and I saw a few that had real black light around them, that is if you could really call it black light. "No, down here," came his joyful voice. I looked down and saw my recently abandoned body stirring below me.

"Jim," called another voice from above me. I looked upward and saw a very luminous white body move closer and I soon recognized my visitor of the previous night. He beckoned to me saying, "Come follow me." His voice seemed to be almost musical and unusually sweet to my out-of-body ears. Without a second thought or another glimpse downwards I moved into position beside him. "For now you must eliminate things of your past life. Holding onto earthly memories can only deter your progression," he told me.

Comprehending the meaning behind his words, I suppressed the curiosity about my past life friend, Lance, and asked, "Who or what are these other beings floating around us Rama?"

"They are spirits," he replied. "The white ones like your friend Lance are ready now for new enlightened bodies. The light gray are ready for less-enlightened lives in lower states of consciousness. Some of these grayish souls will have to circle the Earth for many years until they become pure and innocent as little children. Following that period they have to wait for a body to become accessible to them. Purest always come first as expected," he told me with a knowing smile. "The dark gray are entangled spirits struggling to let go of their past deeds or being controlled by Earth-bound humans. The black encased ones are evil spirits who will never be cleansed of their iniquity. They are condemned to be eternally separated from the light and are unable to ever reincarnate," he explained. "That is their eternal self-created hell."

We drifted side by side into a bluer sky than I had ever remembered seeing. Although, like the beautiful sound of Lance and Rama's voices, I was also perceiving these vibrant colors through embellished sight. "You are going to One for total purification. This Universal One is you, me, and every existing object throughout the universe. We enlightened beings know that there is only One. Onenergy, Onexistance, for there is only One energy, that of lovenergy, which is another name for God." Rama paused slightly to allow this concept to sink in and then said, "After that we are going to Tesa, the place of absolute knowledge. There you will learn the truths and gain immeasurable wisdom," he said as we moved toward a dark tunnel. "Fear nothing, Jim. I will not allow these demoralized spirits or anything to hurt you in the least," he said, noting my faltering movement. "As is true with all of humanity, they would like to pervert your honorable morality, but they know better than to try something with me present." Dark forms swarmed all about us, but we glided through and past them without any effort at all.

Moving into the dark tunnel, he said, "I will be with you during your introduction and training in Tesa. I will always be at your beckon call even if invisible: you need only call my name and I will be there with you."

"My body back there," I asked, pointing behind me, "is it dead or alive? You mentioned before that there are spirits waiting for new bodies and I have to wonder if I really heard my old best friend. Is he replacing me maybe?"

"You won't understand this, but let it suffice for now to know that your body is alive and is already inhabited by another more advanced being. It would be decidedly paradoxical for someone you knew to be supplanting you, although, you were blind, and it is going to take a very special kind of person to replace you." After a moment of thought he said, "We want you to know the whole truth, we needed your body for one of our crusaders. You were making advancements, but our goal would be achieved faster and more efficiently if one of our already-trained spirits were to inhabit your body, freeing you to undergo a total awakening with us. Your focus should be on this moment and the rapid changes taking place in you right now! In short," he told me, "you will be a new superior person being now that you are here with us at this time."

I felt calm and at peace. Not even the idea of Lance possibly residing in my prior body perturbed my tranquility. Through the mouth of this interminably long tunnel, I saw a brilliant light and wondered, *Are we going to enter the sun itself or is this all a continuation of the illusions that started last night?*

"Soon, Jim," he said, looking directly into my eyes, "you'll know everything there is to know. Truth and love is all there is now, and within a period of time you will have full wisdom of the depth of this truth. In Tesa, all of the truths will be disclosed to you. In that plane of consciousness, you're inaccurately-perceived transgressions will be erased from your mind and spirit. You will undergo a total reversal of your old ways. Following your clearing of barrios and misconceptions, you will be trained in Tesa to think as a purified spiritual being."

"What is this truth you speak of, Rama?" I asked, desiring further insight.

"Humanity was kept in the dark regarding edification and unity of spirit. Mankind has been brainwashed all of their lives. You've been led to believe in duality, and there is only One." His brown eyes glistened with an inner self-assurance that gladdened my heart. They were looking deep through the windows of my soul when he said those words and I felt them touch me internally.

"I know you are telling me the truth, but what do you mean by brainwashed?" I naively asked. I knew at that moment that I had literally been in the dark for far too long. I now wanted the light of this One who he had spoken so highly of to reach into my innermost being. At the end of my former life, my inner sense of self had begun to get more refined after my transformation. My Catholic church was far too restraining and I was beginning to feel too controlled by its inflexible dogma. I had become a freethinking seeker and had begun exploring other beliefs outside that restraining religion. Here I was now an entirely unknown being brought into a totally new and revealing light, and I couldn't feel more liberated.

"Jim," said Rama with his little red beard accentuating a broad smile. "I do understand your curiosity, but take it easy, You'll have knowledge of everything in a short time." At that moment we exited the dark tunnel. The light was a hundred times stronger than what it had been on Earth. It struck me hard and I blinked several times and then shielded my eyes with my hand so that I could look about me. I also noticed a sound, which simulated one I had heard while alive. This was also a hundred times more powerful than what I had been able to hear during periods of silent meditation. It replicated the sound of bees swarming.

"You are closer now to the pure light and sound of One," said my companion. "That's why the light is so much brighter, and the sound that you are hearing, that's the voice of One on this plane. You probably heard it during moments of stillness while on Earth; some even know it by the name 'sound of silence'. Ask nothing more of me right now, until you have been purified more. In only minutes your inner spirit will be enlightened enough for you to accept more of what I tell you."

"Can you at least explain who or what you mean by One?" I asked.

Following a short-lived pause, he said, "In a word, brainwashing. By your parents and controlling churches you were incorrectly taught to call our One, God. The name God and the belief of his existence in a place called heaven are far too restrictive. When you have become more clear of your spiritual impairments due to those and other inaccuracies, you will discover yourself being the embodiment of One: all of existence."

"There is only One, not Him and us, for that would make two," he said powerfully. "There is no separation, we are all One. In your teachings on Earth, humans were incorrectly taught that God is a supreme being existing far above us and that obtaining Oneness with Him was impossible for us mere mortals. We people of the light fully comprehend One as being present in the past, current, and future. In short, they are all equal parts of the same perpetual moment of our absolute Oneness. He is eternally omnipresent in all stages of development. Everything from the air we breathe to the most enlightened mind is manifestation of His collective essence."

He proclaimed, "This includes even distasteful things like ignorance, criminally-minded people, and love-deprived and nonconforming thinkers. Because after all, One is all there is and there is No More! One's imagination is the vastness of existence: for all is proof of His lovenergy. You and everything that ever takes place are products of the very thought of this universal mind we call One."

"If it makes it easier, think of One as being both your Father the sun and Mother your Earth. We are the seed of this divine union: the very substance of One, our Father and Mother," said Rama. He took a deep breath and slowly let it out. Then he added, "Roses do not produce weeds. Humans are divine at birth; however, they do become defiled by poor conduct, or wrong decisions. But, we are not born in sin for we are divine seeds of a pure Mother and Father."

You were beginning to experience the reality of our Oneness when still on

Earth. When you held an x-ray and became the substance of it as well as the patient who you were sharing love with, you were experiencing Oneness."

"Rama, are you telling me that He is criminal, poverty, blind, crippled or what have you?" I asked.

"It's going to take you a short time longer, but you will soon be comprehending what I am telling you. In short, we are One and the same. Remember," he said with a clever twinkle, "there is only the One, we are not ourselves, for then there would be not One but many. I just told you there is only One and you know what that makes you!"

"Yes, and I'm glad that most earthlings don't realize that about themselves!" Some kings and other people in position of power already control others. I can't imagine the power they would control if they knew themselves to be one with God."

Beneath us, I saw three men standing in front of a building. Right before my eyes, the old structure disappeared and a new one took its place. We moved near the three men and witnessed another miraculous feat. They were discussing plans for a fountain. "Just like you see here in this photograph," one of the men said, showing a picture to the others. He made a mark on the ground and then all three men stepped back and focused on that spot. What occurred next made me disbelieve my own eyes. A beautiful, sculptured whale water fountain, like the one in the picture, suddenly appeared! The whale was shooting crystal clear water high into the sky and the brilliant light of One made colorful dazzling rainbows that drifted into the pure air high above us.

"Your disbelief is a prime example of your brainwashing," said Rama, looking into my dazed eyes. "On this astral plane men have learned to use their imagination to help them achieve whatever it is that they wish. Rather than helplessly wishing for what they desire, they live in their already gained reality. Creation is only a matter of using that given power effectively. Humanity has been given the same powers, but because of their ignorance caused by presumed-right teachers, church leaders, etc. these powers go unrealized. Those men," he said, pointing at the three men, "know that they are One, and as Him, they only need to focus on what they want."

I was bursting to know more, but because of wanting to preserve my vanity, I refrained from my inquisitiveness. Although I was pleased to notice that my aura was becoming less grayish, fear of my questions frustrating him kept me silent. My only exception to being absolutely silent was an exhilarated, "Man, this surely isn't Earth! These people obviously exhibit powers that we humans consider utterly impossible," I whispered in awe.

"No, this sure isn't Earth," Rama said sadly. "You earthlings are brainwashed and thus made incapable of achievements like these. You were endowed with the same competence, but because of your diminished belief of self, brought about by inaccurate teachings, you have become inept. Pragmatically, water in the brook that you dip your hand into isn't necessarily fluid and unable to bear your weight, nor the stepping stones taking you across that stream unyielding, they are only what you/One create and/or imagine them to be." I remained silent while we slowly levitated further into a magnificently clear sky. The light and voice of One became more and more dominant the higher we drifted.

"At the present time we are in the fourth density of the astral plane," Rama told me with reverence in his voice as if he was talking with someone who was more sacred than me. Perhaps it was the fact that we were getting closer to One that created this illusion. "Never diminish your own sanctity he scolded. We'll be moving onto a higher plane after you have gotten better acclimated to this one's intensity of light and sound. The higher we go, the greater we become."

Giving me more time to adjust to the sound and light, we moved lower and were flying only a few feet above the land. Everything looked so clean and orderly that I imagined an enormous landscaping crew keeping it so magnificently pristine. Unlike what I had briefly seen back on Earth, there wasn't anything that detracted from the perfection of this plane. There were no signs of filth, deterioration, or pollution that were commonplace on my home planet. *I'm sure that there isn't any litter to be seen for light years*, I thought to myself with a broad grin.

Then flying low over a large body of water, I remarked, "I've never seen our oceans look so pristine." We flew at almost sea level, and I was able to clearly see tiny fish swimming on the surface of the sea and larger ones deeper. "I sure do wish that Earth could be this beautiful and pure."

"When One created your planet," said Rama sadly, "it was just as pure and orderly as it is here. The human race have all but destroyed her with their pollutants, and all for the sake of futile greed," he renounced, with a shake of his head. "This isn't the first time either!"

His comment about it not being the first time went right over my head, although I did hear later that Earth had been inhabited many times. With consternation, I said, "For temporary comforts in life, humanity is destroying the very ground on which it has been built."

Rama was nodding his head as I had spoken from my heart. "Earth cannot survive if its inhabitants aren't awakened to their destructive behavior." With a wise smile, he said, "You were chosen for your strong love of nature and of humanity. Rectifying their wrong perceptions regarding the permanence of their planet is most important." He then ended the subject by turning and heading upward again. I wanted to learn more, but I knew in my heart that everything would be revealed in time; therefore, I held my eagerness in check and joined him without delay.

I hadn't detected any humor in his voice when he had said that I had been chosen; yet I wondered the true meaning behind those words. First I asked him outright, "Are you mocking what I said, Rama?" To myself I was questioning what he had meant by that particular word 'chosen'. *Does this mean that I was forcefully taken from Earth?* I considered to myself. "No," I said, answering my unasked question that had determinedly weaseled itself into my conscious mind. "I am here for specific reasons and must believe in the truth and goodwill of these people and their crusade!"

"Sorry Jim, I spoke out of turn," he said contritely. "I'll fill in all of your inquiries following a period of greater absolution."

Since our view of the ocean, we had been ascending upwards into an exquisitely blue sky. The light was becoming even more intense as we traveled upward. In only seconds we seemed to have moved to another higher plane and quickly exited it. I only had time to observe the sound of millions of birds singing in bright, clear, shadowless light of one plane and piercing light and angelic voices of another. Both of these planes had huge city-like structures that made patterns similar to happy faces. We rapidly soared even higher and passed by other planet-like spheres. One of them had only a few cities, which were replaced with immaculately kept landscapes. It seemed to me that every time we rose into another higher realm of consciousness that the change of light and sound accompanied a spirit, mind, and heart expansion. My body increased in vibration to the point that my teeth almost chattered.

When we had reached our intended goal, I was shaking from head to toe with a renewed excitement and a previously-inexperienced vibration of spirit. We seemed to be suspended within immaculately pure light and the sound of flutes came from within and all about us. The stark purity and magnitude of this light penetrated my being, which made me virtually transparent. Physically, I was not myself, yet mentally, as far as I could detect, I hadn't changed. Although, come to think of it, I did feel united with a part of myself that I hadn't recognized until now. I was also feeling an ecstatic sensation of indescribable reverence, as if every cell of my body were individually loving the absolute perfection of this One who I was uniting with. For an unfathomable period of time I was actually the flawlessness of this eternal energy of Him. His perfect love my own, light and sound me, and His cleansing forgiveness mine.

"Jim," said Rama, with his eyes radiating passionate love, "needless to tell you, we are now in the presence of One. He is the Universal One, the Father/Mother seeds of all existence. One Love-Energy, Mind, Father/Mother/Creator, Source, Light, Sound, and Power of all of existence! I've brought you here for purification in His absolute authority. Preceding your mind and spirit expansion, you must receive this spiritual, physical, emotional, and mental cleansing/enlightenment. During your tutelage in Tesa, it assists us if you are as clear of impurities as possible. You will be taught corrective measures for removing the enfites—your corrupt beliefs—that have been burned onto your soul and brain during thousands of past lives. These enfites need to be thoroughly extracted from your conscious and subconscious minds so that you can grow fully into the pure being who will assist us in achieving our goals. In Tesa you will learn all that you will need to become a unified being in your future life. For now you need only to accept your cleansing and supreme union."

Breathing in deeply, I forgave and then eliminated my evil past life thoughts and deeds. I completely exposed myself to His galactic essence and became more of Him. Dismal memories of my doubting the existence of One, what I then called God, ran through me and plagued me for a few moments of discomfort. I didn't hear anything per se, but within my being, I felt a desire to let those wicked recollections pass from me. Reality then hit me; I was the one who was holding onto my doubts and my weak and offensive moments. It wasn't the absolute perfection of One who was resenting my iniquities, but me! The necessity of my letting go reached my inner being and I forgave myself for not recognizing my unity of spirit. "Everything is the wholeness of One," I whispered with awe, reaching my very soul. The old man died and immediately a new man was born in me. Instantaneously, I became the entire perfection of One rather than the me who I had been only moments before. His cosmic consciousness and universal knowledge became mine and I loved Him and myself thoroughly, for we were one.

Like the turning of pages of time I envisioned only blackness, the emptiness of nonexistence, yet there was PP (Pure Potential). What would be was present because of lovenergy that was God and that was me. Then in another instant this Pure Potential witnessed the Big Boom and Onenergy expanded everywhere. One's light shown and the seeds of creation were planted, germinated, and spheres of all size and varieties materialized and an always-expanding universe came into being. Then the hands of time pressed forward revealing the Earth's genesis. I witnessed the births of land, sea, air, fire, volcanoes, glaciers, and then the PP became life on it. Vegetation was the first to be seen. Then in another wink, creatures of all kinds quickly followed. The Oneness of me became UFOs, quickly followed by the appearance of mankind. I witnessed the building of pyramids and great sailing vessels. In another flash I was a progressing Earth with combustible engines, an upward swing of humanity, then followed shortly afterwards by scandalous warfare between equally created men who considered themselves superior. These skirmishes were followed by a decline of civilization, family union, and belief in a supreme being. As a result, a ghastly war broke out. Most likely, I reckoned later, a disastrous nuclear war. Immediately followed by furious earthquakes that nearly tore my beloved planet to pieces. Change of Earth's rotation led to a total annihilation of all remaining forms of life. Consequently an extensive ice age that seemed to last for eons encompassed the entire Earth. Like other planets, it had become an empty spinning sphere. After this protracted period of lifelessness, the cycle renewed itself. The Oneness of Father and Mother's seed impregnated the dead planet and life was born again. I witnessed this occurring again and again. It was surprising to see that other planets in different galaxies also had human-like beings. I regrettably noticed that those other intellectually inhabited planets seemed to go through similar cycles of life then absence.

Dimly, as if through a veil, I saw millions of humans living on other planes of consciousness that were in layers surrounding these populated planets. I then realized that there were only three dimensions: height, depth, and width, but perhaps billions of densities within them. I was horrified to find out that these other beings were likewise annihilated whenever life on one of these planets was destroyed. *Not only do we have to protect ourselves*, I painfully realized, *but also these innocent bystanders who also depend on functioning planets.*

"You are all that you are perceiving, Jim. Look at yourself and see the evidence of your right thinking. It is clearly written in your flawless aura. As you can now see, you are truly a part and whole of One," said Rama with a broad unfeigned smile that welcomed me as I immerged from the realer-than-real experiences I had just observed.

Gazing down at myself and my aura, I could hardly believe what I was now. I was as pure and white as the light of One; in fact, there wasn't any distinction between us, we were One continuous pure white light. Inwardly and externally I was aglow with a shining, pure, white light, which had replaced the dull eggshell white I had been only moments before. "You have now reached the perfection of One. However, not until you are totally righteous will you be able to maintain this intensity of light. Only when your tainted thinking becomes unblocked and you are absolutely clear of feelings over imagined past sin and your separate self-image can you retain this purity. As long as you insist on keeping your feelings of division you will not know the reality of our Oneness. That is why you need to receive devout instruction. Every morsel of your enfite-implanted brainwashing has to be eliminated. The minute that you have felt sorry for a misdeed, One/you forgave yourself. However, through treacherous religious teaching, you were made to feel eternally guilty for any transgressions. Now in order for you to be free of this wrong belief and the feelings of evilness that it causes, we've got to release the damage done. These enfites are a reservoir of inaccurate concepts. They are like stains put onto your soul. You've got to be clear of them in order for you to sustain the pure perfection of One."

I realized that Rama shown with the same light that I now manifested. "I guess then," I said without hesitation, "you, too, are One like Rama." We simultaneously laughed with feelings of harmonic comradeship.

"Please rephrase your last sentence," he advised, following our outburst of mirth.

I hesitated only a second then seeing my error apologized, "I'm sorry, Rama. Like me, you are the totality of One."

"Yes, the two of us at this moment are the light, sound, power, and evidence of this Divine One," he stated. "However, there is no We, for One is the same as the Roman numeral one. There is only One and I am that. We are One. I am of the sea of One, and I am the Universal Mind of One. He/She/It is all there is of existence. At this moment you are a person of the light and a part of this reality."

Smiling at him, I asked, "I've heard you say that a few times now, but you are referring to this second and what exists here on this plane. How do we become this Universal One 24/7 on Earth or on other planes of consciousness?"

"Simply, don't defile yourself with doubt. In truth, I mean that everything that is or has ever been present in the entire universe is a part of the unity of One, until you become clouded by disbeliefs. As we have already discussed, you had begun to realize that fact shortly before your rebirth here. Also, I was with you while you visualized the birth of existence a second ago. I know that you truly saw people on all planes, both on our beloved Earth and other planets."

I then remembered that sense of Oneness that I had begun to feel. "You're right, I was experiencing Oneness on Earth, at work and especially in nature. At a nearby park, the rocks, air, and vegetation were all parts of this divine feeling. You can't be suggesting, though, that everything, including sin and wickedness, are segments of our sacred One? How could evil be acceptable to our divine One?"

With another joyous smile, he said, "One is unconditional love which is absolute freedom. One imagines humans and their only duty is to once again become the perfection of Him. Segments of His handiwork may choose evil ways, but their behavior doesn't cause Him to dislike them or to deny them in any fashion. In fact, it is them who, by their neglectful thought and actions, are rejecting their own perfection of One. As difficult as this may be right now, I want you to comprehend this fact: because One is everything, He is even that very act of denial. Unlike you at this precise moment, basically all humans lack knowledge of the truth of their unanimity with Him."

He smiled at a new more enlightened me and said, "We are proud of you, while yet on Earth, you discovered lovenergy and a good means of creating it for everyone who practices that method. It is what our One is, divine unconditional love energy, and that's why, like you, we combine the words love and energy lovenergy. He is the unreserved LovEnergy/LifEnergy/ OnEnergy of everything that is Him. A stone is comprised of His revolving atoms, therefore making even rocks alive. The energy of One is the molecules and subatomic particles, as well as the energy that holds everything together. This zero-point energy is equal to the vacuum of space that holds the universe in sync. He concluded, "One is what everything is made of and the energy of what holds them together. Thus, there is nothing that isn't One's lovenergy!"

Without further ado, he began telling me a beautiful story.

One of my first students asked me, "Master Rama, what exactly is the true self?" I replied, "Ultimately, One is I am, and what I am you are and what we are is what I am."

"I find that hard to believe, Rama," he told me. "The One is great; I am insignificant. The One is powerful; I have but a little strength. The One is unlimited; I labor under many limitations. The One is everywhere; I can only be in one place at a time. As far as I can tell, the One and I are completely different. How can you say that I am ultimately the One and It me?"

Rather than to respond directly, I handed my disciple a bowl and said, "Go to the nearby river with this and use it to bring back some water, then we'll continue the discussion."

He carried out the order, but when he came back, I looked at the bowl and frowned. "Didn't I tell you to fetch the water from the river? This can't be it."

"You're wrong, it is, Master Rama." My disciple was confused by my disapproval. "I collected the water myself. I assure you that this water absolutely is from the river."

"I know the river quite well," I mildly argued. "All kinds of fish swim in it, but I don't see any fish in this water. Numerous animals come to the river to drink from it, and yet I see no animals in this bowl. Many children from the village frolic in the shallows of the river. Well, I see no children here either. Therefore, this cannot be the water from the river."

"Master, it is only a small amount of water, of course it cannot contain all those things!"

"Oh, I see. Well, in that case, I want you to go pour the water back into the river," I told him.

My pupil did so with a puzzled expression on his face. He couldn't help but wonder what had possessed me to act so strangely. He completed his task and returned.

"Is the water back in the river?" My young student nodded. "Good," I told him. "That small amount of water you brought back is now the same water that touches the fish, the animals, and the children. In fact, everything that the river is now applies to the water we were both looking at just a while ago. Think of the river as the One and the water in the bowl as your true self. From a limited point of view, that water seems very different from the river. It is understandable how one can be led to believe that the two are not the same and can never be the same. There is no separation; The river is far greater than the bowl of water, just as the One is far greater than an individual human being. Having carried water from the river, you can now see it from an expanded perspective. The river is the source of the water, just as the One is the source of our true inner selves. You saw this for yourself as you dipped the bowl into the river, so you insisted that the water was the same even when I tried to convince you it wasn't."

Rama smiled at me appreciatively and continued.

I told my apprentice, Ohma, "When you poured the water back, you saw that the separation of the water from the river was only a temporary illusion. It's just like that for the true self. Our physical existence is only a temporary condition brought about by our conception. The eternal truth is that our innermost nature comes from, and ultimately returns, to the Universal One. When all is said and done, we are one with this eternal One. The concept of separation is an illusion, just as the bowl contains the water in this story, we have physical bodies that contain our true selves. Having a bowl is useful in that it allows one to carry water from one place to another. Similarly, having a body is useful in that it allows us to experience the physical realm as a part of it. Sometimes we identify with the body so much, we become attached to it and think of it as the self. That's like mistaking the bowl for the water. The water remains the same no matter what container it occupies. In the same way, your true self remains the essential One/you no matter how your body, mind, or spirit might change."

With only a quick smile he continued again.

"Just as my disciple learned a valuable lesson carrying water from the river and back to it again, we also learn from our experiences and various journeys through the material world. Just as the bowl of water is all by itself as it is being carried around, we can also feel alone and isolated as we move through life, working on our individual lesson plans. This feeling, reinforced by physical perceptions, can make us forget that we are all part of a greater self. The bowl cannot hold water forever. It may be accidentally dropped and smashed to pieces one day, or it may develop cracks and break apart after years of use. Similarly, our physical bodies cannot last indefinitely. I told him as I tell you now, Jim, accidents, injuries, illness or age will eventually render physical bodies unusable. The water must return to the river. Even if the water isn't poured back, but spilled somewhere, it will still flow or seep its way into the river. Similarly, when the body is no longer a suitable vessel, the true self it contains must return to the source. Religious people may call this source God; atheists may call it the laws of nature; we members of this cause call it, One. Whatever its label, it is our point of origin as well as our ultimate destination. Just as the water becomes one with the river, the true self merges with the One. That's when we realize that the feelings of isolation and separation are illusory. You and I are never truly isolated or separated from the divine source of universal creation. We are never truly alone. Oneness that unifies all is the ultimate reality of the true self."

"I love your analogy of our unity with One, Rama, but can you tell me more fully who One truly is? I'd also like to know if there is an idea of His value?" I asked, still feeling a bit confused.

Shaking his head slightly, Rama said, "Let me give you another example, it will be explained better in another story."

When a young disciple, I posed a similar question to my wise sage: Master, what is the value of the One? He then gave me a complete explanation, but I didn't understand it. Knowing that explanations conveyed by words weren't always adequate, and that the best way to cultivate the One was learning by direct experience, he took a rock from his desk and wrote down an address on a piece of paper. "Take this rock and go to this address. When you get there, I want you to ask people how much they would pay for the rock. Don't you dare sell it on me! Just find out how much people are willing to pay you for it." I went to the address and found myself in an outdoor market. There were many merchants hawking their wares and many shoppers browsing and haggling. Beginning with the person nearest me I held up the rock and asked, "Excuse me, how much would you pay for this rock?" Like most people, he ignored me and kept walking. Some glared at me. Some looked at me and sneered. Some laughed out loud. The few who did speak said things like, "nothing," or "no thanks," or "go away." After about an hour of this, a lady took pity on me and said, "Maybe I can use it as a paperweight? Here, I'll give you a dollar." She held out the money, but remembering my sage teacher's admonishment, I shook my head and thanked her.

I returned and reported my experience to my teacher. "Master, most people were not interested in the rock at all. The most I could get for it was a dollar."

"Good," my sage replied, handing over another piece of paper. "Now go to this address with the rock and do the same thing. Ask the people there how much they would pay."

This address was in another part of town. When I got there, I saw that it was a jewelry shop. I entered and saw display cases full of glittering gems. Serious-looking clerks stood behind the counter. Everyone was dressed formally. "What do you want, kid?" One of the clerks closed in on me. "Uh, I want to find out how much you would pay for this." I took out the dirty rock. The clerk looked surprised, and then irritated. "Where are your parents? This shop is no place for children. Out you go. Now scat. Shoo," he said, angrily waving his fingers at me when I didn't respond to his incensed gesture.

"Okay," I thought, "I guess that we are done. The results here are no different than what I got at the market."

Turning to leave, the store manager took notice of the situation and called me back. He had glanced at the rock just as I reached for the door. "Wait," he said, "let me take a look at it son." The manager examined the rock. He looked puzzled, and then his eyes widened. He ordered one of the clerks to fetch the senior jeweler from the workshop in the back.

The old jeweler came out, grumbling about the interruption, but when he saw the rock, his eyes widened, too. He examined it under a magnifying glass for a long while, turning it this way and that. Then he handed it back to me and whispered in the manager's ear.

Suddenly the manager was all smiles. "Son, I like you, so I'll exchange this candy here for your rock. Okay?"

I shook my head: "I need to know how much you're willing to pay for it, sir."

"I see," the manager said considering this. "How about if I give you ten bucks? Is it a deal?"

"No sir. I can't sell it, and now I have to go." I got the answer I wanted, so it was time to report back.

"Wait. I'll give you a hundred dollars. That's a lot of money. Come on, what do you say?"

Again I refused to sell and tried to leave. Again the manager increased his offer. We went back and forth like this until the sum of ten thousand dollars was offered and turned down.

"I'll tell you what, son," the store manager said, maintaining his smile, but starting to sweat. "You tell me how much you want for it. Name your price."

"I can't sell it for any amount, sir. That's what I've been trying to tell you."

The manager had no choice but to let me go, and I made my way back to my teacher.

I was puzzled. "Master, the highest offer I got from the market was a dollar. Now it went to ten thousand and beyond. Why such a big difference?"

"In general, people focus on external appearance," my sage teacher explained. "The rock looks quite plain and ordinary, so everyone at the market assumed it was worthless. However, there's more to the rock than meets the eye. It is, in actuality, a diamond of extraordinary size and quality. Only a few people have the ability to recognize it for what it truly is. The people at the market do not possess that ability."

"But Master, the clerk who wanted me to leave, he didn't recognize it either, and yet he works at a jewelry store."

"Being at the store is no guarantee of real knowledge. He probably knows the value of all the gems on display quite well, because they are all carefully packaged and clearly labeled. When it comes to recognizing a real diamond in its most natural, unrefined state . . . well, he is obviously no better at it than the average person."

"How about the manager and the jeweler, Master?" I asked. "What makes them different from the clerk and everyone at the market?"

"The manager suspected that the rock might be valuable because he had years of experience with all kinds of precious stones. The jeweler had even more experience. He had devoted decades of his life to become an expert practitioner of gemology. That's why he didn't just suspect; he knew the real value of the rock." Rama told me.

Showing me his empty hands, he said, "This story isn't about the rock, me, or my teacher. It's a story about the One in all of existence. The rock appears to be nothing out of the ordinary at first, but if properly cut and polished by an expert, the diamond within would stand revealed in all its sparkling glory. Similarly, the One often appears to be something plain and simple, but when a true master expresses or explains a spiritual truth, the One reveals its brilliant beauty. The world in which we live is similar to the market, which is all about monetary transactions: haggling, buying, and selling. The world is also an overwhelmingly materialistic place, filled with material acquisitions and price tags. True masters of the One are few and far between, so the majority of the people in the world have little understanding or appreciation for the value of the Universal One. In the story, we see this reflected in the reactions of the people toward me, a young disciple. Even though the rock was extremely valuable, people regarded it with indifference and even aversion. People who possess a high level of spiritual refinement recognize a spiritual truth when they hear it because it resonates deeply with them. In the setting of our story, such individuals were rare, and none of them appeared in the market. Most people at the market were still a long way away from this level. They were used to dealing with things they could see and touch, like the tangible goods at the market. The intangible One that arrived without colorful packaging, promotional posters, or a price that could be negotiated, was not something they could readily grasp. There were also people who laughed at the One. These were usually the people at the lowest level of spiritual refinement. As we heard my description of them, it is almost as if I am talking directly about the people we have encountered who regard spirituality as weird. Some of them even express disdain and mockery; 'Oh, you're one of those Oneness movement believers?' They look at everything that way because the material world is full of merchandise for sale, so people often mistake price for value. The easy assumption is that anything with a high price must automatically be high in value, and something with no price attached must therefore have little or no value."

"This is exactly as my wise teacher noted in the story," Rama told me. "Most people relied on external appearance to pass value judgments. The rock looked unimpressive, so they dismissed it as worthless. Only the most discerning eyes could look past the rough facade and detect the diamond within."

Rama cleared his throat and continued. "If the market is the world at large, then the jewelry shop would be a religious institution like a temple or a church. In a jewelry shop, craftsmen cut and polish gemstones, and then present them in settings to be displayed for the buying public. In a similar way, a religious institution takes spiritual teachings, organizes and formalizes them, and presents them to the spirituality-seeking public. The rings and gems on display at the jewelry shop represent the distilled and packaged religious doctrines humans come across in daily life. The Ten Commandments, The Four Noble Truths, The Eightfold Path, and others are commonly recognized and regarded as valuable because they are clearly marked as such; just like the rings and gems with informational labels touting their value. Oftentimes we have a tendency to assume that people in a temple must be knowledgeable about the One, but as we can see in the example of the clerks, this is not always so. The knowledge level of a clerk may be limited to only what he or she can read from the labels—the name of the product and the selling price. Similarly, someone at a temple may know just the basic doctrines and little else. When confronted with a spiritual truth, people at this level will have trouble recognizing it. They may even reject it outright without due consideration, as we see in the story when the store clerk tried to get rid of you. The manager of the jewelry shop represents someone at a higher level of understanding. Such a person has devoted time and effort into studying the One, and the extra learning elevates him or her above the lower levels where people can recite phrases and rules, but have no real understanding of the spiritual teachings behind them. Although the manager seems to be the authority figure from the perspective of the store clerks, he pales in comparison with the jeweler. The manager knows a lot about gemstones, but his knowledge is primarily derived from gemology books and working with finished products. His foundation of book knowledge may seem impressive at first, but when he is confronted by something beyond the scope of his books, he must still turn to the jeweler for help and clarification. The jeweler represents a higher level of understanding. He is the true master because his primary source of knowledge is not books. Instead, he learned from diligent practice, working directly with gemstones from their most unrefined state all the way to polished rings, necklaces, and other jewelry. From this, we can see that action is the critical element that separates a true One master from those who merely possess book knowledge. True masters are not content to read about the One; they cultivate it through direct, hands-on experience. They must experience Oneness, the power of the One within themselves."

Without even a pause for a breath of air, Rama continued.

"Just as the jeweler cuts and polishes gems so they can be made available for the public, the true One master studies, contemplates, dissects, and showcases spiritual truths so people at lower levels can easily understand the truth better. If we keep in mind that the One is simply a generic term for spirituality, then we see that great teachers from the past like Jesus, Buddha, Lao Tzu, Muhammad, Krishna, and many others are, in effect, master jewelers. They note the beauty inside of an uncut gemstone called spirituality. They can see this beauty, but most people cannot, so they work to bring it out in a way that everyone can appreciate.

"The role of the master isn't limited to these great figures from history. For instance, there are many writers like I hope you will be in your next earthly life," he told me. "They can take great spiritual truths and explain them in a simple and fascinating way. They, too, are jewelers. When you read a particularly good book and it opens your eyes about life, you have come face-to-face with the work of a master jeweler. What does all this tell us about the value of the One? The answer varies depending on the level of the individual seeker. At the lower levels, the people at the market could not tell you because they really didn't know. The clerks and the manager could quote you a price for any piece of jewelry you wanted to purchase, but they didn't really know the value of the rock either. The jeweler realized that the rock was not less valuable because of its unrefined state. In fact, it was more valuable than any single piece of jewelry because he could create many diamonds of different sizes from that one rock. This is the real value of the rock, is it the real value of the One, you undoubtedly want to know? That truly depends on the level of the seeker. For the eternal One forces no one to understand or even recognize His infinite value.

"In the story," Rama explained, "the rock was never sold. Why not? You might be wondering. "Because, as I, a young disciple in that previous life told everyone, it was not for sale. My sage alone understood that there was more to the value of the rock than any amount of money. He knew that the rock (One) was not a good that could be marketed. From the perspective of the jewelry shop, it was associated with a certain figure that they would be willing to pay;

from the perspective of my sage teacher, no haggling, buying, or selling was possible because the rock was valueless. It simply had no price tag. It could not be acquired for any amount of money. Unlike all the rings in the jewelry store, no price tag could be affixed to it.

Turning to me again, he said, "To recap, Jim, the universal lovenergy of One is priceless and beyond value! Yet free for all who truly appreciate its fathomless value and seek it with their hearts, minds, and being."

He smiled and said a curious thing. "The Prime Creator (One) only knows Himself via what He creates, for He is fathomless and without form."

I was thrilled with that last sentence; in only a few words it gave me the reason for my existence. Since my discovery of lovenergy transformation, I've lived so that I eventually would realize my Oneness. My comprehension was now broader and my feeling of Oneness more fulfilling. These stories had clearly brought home the reason for my existence. I had been seeking such insight for all of my life. "Then if the One comprises everything, loving a woman is loving One, too?" I asked with naivety displayed by my carnal question. Even though I had confessed and received absolution for my breaking of church rules from my priests, I evidently was still feeling guilt for my past out-of-wedlock affair with my precious black flower, Claire. We had loved one another like there was just the two of us in existence and I had ignored all church rules.

"Since the thought of you represents One and she also Him, you could say that," Rama said with a crafty grin. "That's because the thoughts of One are all there is to life. However, recognized or not, she is One, and if you are forcing her, then you are also breaking karmic laws." He swallowed and added, "Thought, imagined matter, even the smallest particles and zero energy and vacuum of space itself are the wholeness of One. For without His inception, there is nothing. Remember this, One is all, and all is One."

"Rama, who am I?" And I ran my hand from head to toe.

"Now stop denying Him," commanded Rama, "the answers are within. We are not separate entities, but living examples of One Himself. On Earth you have groups and religions that believe in Hinduism, Tao, SGI, and Eckankar. They call One different names, but it is the same One that we members of this cause are becoming a part of. It is the same wholeness whether you call Him Tao, ECK, God, Muhammad, One, or Lovenergy."

"I could find it easy to love everything on this plane, but on Earth, that's another story. How do we love something that is revolting to us?" I asked hungrily.

"You already know the answer, if," Rama said, emphasizing the word 'if', "we can believe that One embodies a person or given thing, which He does, then we can love it no matter how revolting it might be to us. Since it is in our nature to love One, believing a given thing is the perfection of Him allows us to love even the most detestable entity. Neither of us like hatred or greed, but we can easily love the perfect One within the person who exhibits even those traits."

"How about a true atheist? They don't even acknowledge the existence of One . . . a supreme consciousness," I added a second later.

"Even if they deny the reality of His deity, they can't reject Him from their lives. Sound, light, and love of One abounds whether or not He is acknowledged. The vacuum of space doesn't recognize Him, yet it still exists in His flawless creation. Because in reality, it is part of existence, which is the totality of the Universal One." As an after thought he offered, "I've got another good story to better exemplify this for you, but I am led to save it for another more critical moment."

I waved off another story and asked, "Then our Divine One gives these atheists an excuse to be greedy and to hate?"

"The Universal One has given all mankind freedom to act, feel, believe, and think as they choose," he answered forthrightly. "There are no restrictions. We are all free to live as we choose. Remember this, Jim, we are not who we think we are. We are, in fact, like the story of the water in the river and the unavailable rock—all equal parts of One, temporarily residing in human bodies."

"Then there are some behavioral guidelines?" I asked, still thinking of evil beings that do hurt others.

"As simplistic as this may seem, our Universal One basically sees Himself in all of His good, evil, or indifferent selves." Clearing his throat, he proclaimed, "This next concept is above your comprehension right now, but I would be amiss if I failed to inform you that there is only love in the One, and things like evil, good and/or indifference don't really exist."

"Although you did see those black spirits who chose eternal detachment, it is their own decision. On Earth you call them demons and they are trying to corrupt other spirits around them."

He next told me, compellingly, "All who do objectionable things will get other chances. However, their Karma (deeds) will determine their status in that next life and until their slates are totally purified, they will continue to reincarnate on material planes like Earth."

After hearing that, I thought to myself, *What then is the meaning of life? Why do we live on Earth struggling to do good throughout our lives?*

With tenderness in his eyes, Rama spoke softly to me, "All humans contain the spirit of One. We, who recognize Him, try to do His will of loving all that exist. Due to the nature of the humankind, duality is widely taught and felt by most humans. In that state they do not feel their connective-ness to one another thus, One. Our continuously-thinking, brainwashed minds, evil perceptions, and/or deeds do exist. In truth, they demoralize that part of all beings that was once pure. The purpose of living over and over again is so that we can eventually attain the purity and wholeness of ourselves—better known to you now as One," he patiently explained. "It is the free will of some people to cause heartache by their actions, and they do it because of their own voracious appetite for possessions. No matter what they may acquire, their desires are often not appeased. This is because they misinterpret their honest yearning for the perfection of One. Inaccurately thinking that possessing objects can gratify this zeal they are feeling, they may struggle an entire life for naught," he said with finality in his voice.

"I don't consider myself righteous nor do I mean to brag, but the truth is that I have always prized goodness, wisdom, love, and faith above riches," I replied with heartfelt sincerity.

"That is true for this current life, but that's only because you were born at a higher station. Thus, you're devout and steadfast to this path you've been traversing. All of your past lives will soon be revealed, let's see what you think then," he said with a chuckle. Then more seriously, he said, "Jim, One is watching more than 6 billion movies all at once. Believe me, He is pleased by every One of them you humans produce for Him to observe."

His thoroughness in answering my endless questions made me ask, "I hope that I'm not pressing you for too much information, Rama, but why are you willing to explain things now when a few minutes ago—"

"Simply because you're not the same being you were before," he interrupted. "Your having been purified by the power of One allows you to now clearly hear and accept most of my words. Your mind is less clouded with inaccurate concepts, and you do not doubt the validity of everything I tell you. In other words, you are more in the Unified Field of One," he said in explanation. "However, be warned that this is only a transitory moment. Very soon you will be slipping into your brainwashed self again."

The light of One and Rama's amiable character reverberated deep in my heart, making me feel exotically comfortable about myself and totally at peace.

As we had been speaking, I had been searching all around us and reported, "I see only dazzling light and hear only flutes playing Rama, where does One reside?"

Rama pointed to his chest. "One is everything which is lovenergy. How do I explain the truth when you have been blinded by lies of all of your former lives? Without the presence of One's imagination, there is no substance. Like I said before, even a vacuum exists because of One. We are presently in the purity of His spirit, which is the totality of Him. On this plane the light of One equals pure light, as well as the sound of Him equaling pure sound. Only the spirit of One's divine lovenergy resides on this plane. Although, as you will learn later, some of the humans who have previously died are parts of the Universal One. It is impossible for ordinary mankind to reside on this, the highest plane. Only if we become unified beings can we exist here, but then we are not ourselves but the quintessence of One."

Because of his clear description, I found myself beginning to comprehend the true meaning of this supreme being. What a new and alien universe my old one had suddenly become. In comparison to my prior unenlightened reality, this was like relating sight with total blindness. I was now learning the truth and I was at last seeing the true light. Here I had thought myself more spiritually aware, but the grim state of affairs was plainly vivid now. I had been only an inexperienced disciple searching shadows hidden in the dark. "Yes, yes," was all I could reply.

"All that you see and hear is the divinity of One," he said, spreading his arms wide while trying to make all of this clear to me. "The truth is that One inhabits everything and everyone in every density and/or dimension of consciousness. Right now for you and His united spirits to experience the Oneness of Him, He has this particular kingdom. As you know, earthlings would do well to meditate on the pure light of Him and listen to His internal voice coming from their heart," he told me.

Rama must have comprehended my unspoken concentration because he then said with concern written in his eyes, "Jim, we are discussing subjects that you will learn all in good time. Please don't pressure yourself into possessing total knowledge of these new truths this second. The deceptions must be first removed from your subconscious before your conscious mind is capable of accepting everything you learn here. Give yourself adequate time to recognize the differences between light and dark, truth, and deception. Unless you know light and darkness, warmth and cold, truth and lies, doubt and faith, joy and sadness, etc., how are you to know the reality of each? You have been enlightened to some degree during your last few lifetimes. Although, comparatively speaking, you were still very much in the dark ages."

We moved back into the astral plane and I saw homes and people again. Rama said, "Many spirits feel the way you do right now. After purification they want to know every hidden mystery."

"Huh?" I had just been thinking how nice it would be to remain here in the astral world. "Oh, yes, it's so beautiful on this plane. Why would anybody want to live on Earth?" I said, not really hearing his words. "This is what I classify as paradise." Not getting the reaction I expected I said, "I take it that you agree with my supposition?"

After a rather long period of time in complete silence, he gave me a warning that I have always kept in mind and heart, "Don't grow overly comfortable here. You will not be with us very long. You were chosen for an essential task, which you will eventually learn in full. Being in the presence of One has opened your mind to a more full potential, crucial for your future earthly existence. Keep Him in you at all times and you will remain faithful, never deviating from this level of consciousness." Then Rama reiterated, "Keeping One a part of you is especially vital when you are again living as a human. Don't ever deny or denounce Him no matter how badly things might seem to be going for you. Your predicaments will be rectified as soon as you feel you have learned enough from that exclusive episode. We all create problems for specific reasons, and learning from them is our ultimate goal and reason for developing them in the first place. Every future dilemma you will encounter was brought about because of a specific lesson you needed to learn. Acknowledge them for the instruction they dispense and don't curse the darkness, but accept the hidden light in them. When you see the situation for what it really is, a self-created tool, you will have then learned the intended lesson. Live in the moment, knowing that you are the eternal One in it. The second you can actually be the intended One, found in that given moment, you have turned the poison into the intended medicine and risen above that adversity."

I immediately saw that this was an important message meant for me to learn and was trying to remember all of it right here and now. I then recalled how I felt about accidents never happening—that they are all meant to be learning tools for us.

"Minutes ago you had said . . ." I paused, thinking of time as I had previously known it. *Was it really just minutes ago or possibly hours?* I wondered. Somehow my understanding of time had escaped me, and I was no longer even discerning of the day let alone the time span. I started again a little more noncommittal. "A little while ago you said that you would explain what you meant about me being chosen. Also, is it the reason for my being here? You just said something about me returning to Earth. What does that entail and is that the purpose of my being with you now?"

"Your recognition of humanity's slow but definite extermination of Earth's life forces is right on, thus it and your level of spirituality make you a perfect candidate for our cause. We collectively must deter this destruction! Soon you will learn of your gifts and they will be just what we need to aid our cause." He paused while taking in a gulp of air—fragrant with the smell of fresh mowed grass. "Your development of a love enhancement technique will alter the minds and lives of countless earthlings when you make your return. I will inform you only that it is imperative that you learn all of the truths and are free of distortions taught to you humans. As you correctly ascertained, life on your globe is doomed and you are here with us to be taught by the masters how best to assist her to survive. This will require you to inevitably return to your planet so that you can help us best by teaching these truths to future generations. Teaching them your transforming love method: changing hatred, bad habits, and addictions, so that they might overcome their imminent destruction is an absolute necessity."

It took all of my power of will to refrain my desire to question him further. Deep in my heart I wondered how I, an uneducated and insignificant blind man, could be of any assistance to such an essential cause like this? *How am I capable of taking part in saving Earth?* I pondered. "How can I, a dead man, do anything at all to save her?" I ruminated aloud.

"Eliminate your worry about your future," Rama said as we moved into another density. Because of its meticulously-kept appearance it had no resemblance of Earth. It also differed from the others I had passed over in that this domain had only secluded patches of buildings. Despite the fact that this probably meant fewer inhabitants, the structures were much more luxurious and the landscape more elaborately kept. In a strange way I seemed to recognize it. I considered that maybe it was one that we passed so quickly during our ascent to the plane of One? Nevertheless, it did have similarities— especially since it looked so clean and orderly. Like on the other planes, One's light was mighty here. The sound of ocean waves filled me with tranquility. The love of One abounded everywhere I looked. I felt my love expand as I shared my lovenergy (pink light) with its sparse residents.

Seeing heartfelt ecstasy written both in my eyes and on my smiling face, Rama said, "I can tell that you are also feeling the presence of One here, Jim. His love can be found equally on every plane of his consciousness. He is total lovenergy wherever you might move in this universe. Of course, I am including our beloved Earth, although it does have some countries and their people in great turmoil. You now know that One is even the substance of impurity." He turned and smiled knowingly while saying, "You have discovered a working method of creating love and that is where we so desperately need you. Your teaching it here will be helpful of course, but especially necessary when you return home."

We had now moved in front of an immense church or temple. Its huge stained glass windows depicted various scenes filled with different shades of piercing light and color. In one, a young boy looked directly into my soul and his smile warmed my heart. In his hand he held a small green frog that seemed to be smiling at us both. The colors were so vibrant that I thought them made from gems. *That cute little frog looks like it was made from green jade*, I thought. *The blue eyes of the boy resemble turquoise, and his red hair—*.

"You're right," Rama said, interrupting my thought. "It is ruby. As you aptly surmised, gems are the primary substance in these windows." Still smiling, he said, "This is Tesa, our temple of learning. You are going to dwell on this plane for an unspecified period of time during your forthcoming training. This is the training center where you and 149 other newcomers will be learning the truth taught by honest, spiritually-enriched people. There are 309 other classes in various stages of completion simultaneously being conducted here. They are in other densities, thus undetectable by you." Following a momentary pause he explained, "Along with training, all knowledge is kept in this great arena." Seeing a puzzled look in my eyes, he said, "Past, present, and future data is kept in this very establishment. If you desire any bits of history or wish to know what the present or future portends, you will find it behind these eternal doors of knowledge."

"First, you keep saying density, don't you mean dimension?"

"No, there are three basic dimensions, but endless densities within them. It's like having a three by three by three box of Kleenex. There are only those three dimensions, but within that box there might be 500 Kleenex, which are like densities. To complicate it further, if those Kleenex were the size of atoms, there could be billions of densities, and within each atom there are perhaps billions of molecules."

Putting that concept on a back shelf for later contemplation, I asked, "Pyramids, and inventions not yet thought of are here—everything Rama? How can unconceived future facts and inventions be here?"

"Jim, whatever I say is always completely correct and forthright. Everything is kept here. Thoughts of mankind are only reflections of One. Inventions and ideas of earthlings are already perceived bits of the creation of the Universal One. Remember without the thought of One, there is nothing. Existence in every form is only a concept of One, therefore, everything in existence including man is Him/Her/It."

"I, for one, hope that He doesn't ever get distracted," I said with an overwhelming chuckle of gratitude. Then more seriously I said, "I was only asking for clarification before, Rama."

"No need of defending yourself here, my good friend," he said.

Amiably with laughter still lingering on his lips, he said, "We are all the best of friends and I was not judging your words, but trying to enlighten your perceptions. I just wanted you to understand that all of us who are here helping you, desire you to remain free of falsehoods. This includes all of us spirit guides, none of us will ever deceive any of you; we long to only share righteous truths!"

"Sorry, Rama," I said from my heart. "It's just that I am a little jumpy with all of these sensational events occurring all at once." Without uttering another word, we walked into Tesa. The entranceway had two beautiful paintings and I stared at them in awe. My 12 year old eyes hadn't gotten to see many paintings so these two held me spellbound for a long time. The first painting portrayed an Earth-like planet and in the center stood a naked man and woman holding hands and with One's radiant snow-white auras encircling them. Beautiful flowers blossomed at their feet and stately trees overshadowed them. Rings of varying shades of light encircled the planet, becoming more and more gray the further away they got from it. Within each band were small globes, some of which shown with color and others just a lifeless ashen color. The innermost ring encompassing the planet, as well as the ring surrounding the two humans, was the exact resemblance of One's pure light. "Is that Adam and Eve, Rama, standing on Earth?" I moronically asked pointing to the illuminated couple holding hands.

"Your brainwashing is showing again, Jim," he said with a broad smile on his lips. "To answer your question and to enlighten you, as you undoubtedly guessed, their auras show us that they are in the Unified Field of One. The rings of light are different planes and the "planets", to use your vernacular, are the places of habitation on that particular plane. Also, I want you to know that One hasn't put any restrictions on men or women. That was the doing of humans who wrote the book of Genesis. It, as you know, portrays Adam and Eve as evil, untrustworthy children. Its purpose was commendable and the story has taught people good decorum, but the truth is that One unconditionally loves everyone. He created us free—to feel, think, and behave as we choose. Deciding how to live our lives is ultimately our choice to make. With techniques like you've developed, people who use it are brought to a higher plane of love consciousness. At that level they are transformed and everyone near them are influenced by their expanding sensations of love. As a result of loving themselves more, they are better able to love others more. The circle is forever expanding and becoming more and more powerful. As you have proven, people have to practice this method regularly in order to reach an optimal rate of success. The length of time will vary some, as you know; however, from the beginning there will be expansion of emotions. Each of us is the creator of our own lives and love is another component of that life we generate."

Rama indicated the third or fourth shining ring. "This specific band is the astral plane where we are located right now." Pointing to tiny dots floating within that circle he told me, "These represent different planets where people choose to live within this astral plane. At this level, we each have the power to create our own home or planet. Or, if we desire, we can choose to live on already established planets." With a whimsical smile he said, "We hope that you elect to stay with us, but please remember, there is no 'have to' here or elsewhere. If you do stay, you need to know that you will be undergoing vigorous training. When completed, we anticipate your return to Earth and aiding us in achieving our worthy goal. Like I've told you, though," he said with his hand rising to a stop signal, "there are no *must* performances and you owe it to yourself to do as you see fit. You have already earned your position here, so it's totally up to you whether or not you choose to remain with us or find another already developed homestead."

Turning, he pointed at the other painting. This portrait showed a ball of One's light in the center with many planets in various bands of orbit around it. Between them were hundreds of people of all different sizes and growing larger toward the center. The center most men and women had One's white light around them and the others had various shades of gray. Smiling at him,

I declared flatly, "Rama, I won't even attempt to guess at the meaning of that painting."

"Wise decision," he said with a chuckle. "The center light," he pointed out, "is as you correctly surmised and is the pure energy of One. The rows of planets represent all of the spheres and densities of habitation in different galaxies throughout the universe. The people show us that everyone is attempting to reach the reality of their Oneness. Some are close," he began to explain, pointing at the larger ones, "but others have a long ways to go. Perhaps they have even millions of reincarnations before they can reach the absolute perfection of One. As long as a planet is able to support life, there is still hope for it and its inhabitants. That is why your future is so important to us as well as to earthlings at all levels of spirituality." At that moment the meaning of his words escaped me to some degree, but the purpose of them penetrated deep into my heart, mind, and spirit.

"Yes," I agreed from my heart. "As long as there is life, there is hope. We've got to do everything possible to save our planet until all of its inhabitants have gained their level of cosmic consciousness." I looked into Rama's eyes with a growing comprehension of what he was teaching. "The One doesn't mind me changing His name, does He?"

With a conspiratorial smile, he said, "Don't you mean She?" After we had laughed, he pointed to another further extended row of planets a d said, "That's the Milky Way. The small nebulous appearing planets are fourth and fifth density spheres, which also encircle Earth and exist in your galaxy."

Without thinking, I automatically counted the planets in our Milky Way. "There are eleven, not the nine or ten we've been more recently led to believe," I said, pointing at the denser planets in that circle.

"Well, I guess even human astronomers make errors," he laughed.

Following my laugh, I asked, "Rama, why does Earth look so gloomy in this painting? The other planets are nearly black, and I suppose this is because they are lifeless, but Earth?"

His chin fell and the sparkle left his eyes for a moment. "Simply, but painfully," he said, "you're right again. She is sick and dying," he sadly proclaimed.

We moved into the first gargantuan room filled, floor to ceiling, with bookshelves loaded with thousands of books. "Here," he said, indicating this enormous library full of books, "we keep the last few weeks of data our transcribers have received from the Earth." In an adjoining room on other shelves I saw models of all kinds of unrecognized objects resting in front of other books. Most of these toy-like objects were unidentifiable by me. I also remembered that according to Rama, mankind hadn't yet invented many of these sorts of things.

We then advanced through room after room overflowing with books and similar items of interest. After picking up a dusty light bulb I asked, "I guess that Edison was here, huh?"

"Maybe while in a meditative state… Quickly, Jim," Rama said, like a director might, "we're running a little late." We quickly skirted through corresponding rooms stacked high with all kinds of documents and odd contraptions. In the distance I suddenly heard a voice beginning to read off names and greetings.

"You're wrong," said Rama perceptively. "Your intuition has diminished some since we've departed One. Now you're not receptive enough to receive communications from a distance. Your master teacher Swuel has been calling names out for sometime now. The names are alphabetized and he has nearly reached your name. If we don't get in there soon we will definitely be late." He increased his pace a bit.

"So we aren't too late then?" I asked, worried that I might have missed something important.

"Quiet," Rama mentally replied. Because 90 percent of our conversation had been telepathic, Rama was evidently afraid that it would disrupt Swuel. We moved into an immense room filled with people. It appeared to me that every other person had bright white light around them. *Like Rama, they are probably spirit guides*, I correctly surmised. The others had contrasting shades of gray like me. In contrast, I immediately noticed that the speaker had a white aura that matched the brilliance of One.

The lecturer held up his hand in greeting and said, "Welcome, Rama and Jim. Please take your seats." He indicated two chairs near the front of the room. Blue light literally radiated from his eyes that shown with his inner enlightenment. He was a tall, solid man with a very muscular frame. Unlike Rama's neat white-collar clothing, this man was casually attired in leather sandals, blue jeans, and a brightly colored t-shirt. Looking around me as we walked forward, I estimated that there were at least 200 people in attendance. Once we had taken our seats he continued reading the names of the remaining students.

"I am Swuel, your teacher and healer," he announced after concluding with the rest of the roll call. "Although all of you, with the exception of one, have been in the purification light of One; you are here now with me to be healed of more enfites caused by your inaccurate teaching on Earth. To begin with, I will be healing you of your self-imposed beliefs of guilt due to your perceptions of church decreed iniquities. Because you are holding onto these opposing emotions, your auras are already dwindling in their purity of the light of our divine One. Future healings that you will be receiving over the next weeks and months will brake down your mental blocks and negative emotions. As for those enfites caused by that faulty education on Earth, well that might take us months of daily reprogramming." He paused a moment allowing Rama and, I expect, other spirit guides to whisper "brainwashing" into our ears. Swuel then continued. "Our ultimate goal is to get you free of all spiritual defects. We, my friends," he powerfully announced with a wave of hands, "need you, as our great teacher Christ had told us, like little children." He paused a long time then very strongly said one word, which he let hang for a longer period of time—Clear.

"Please stand and form into a large circle, " he instructed us, following that long pause. "We want you to hold hands," he said while stepping down from behind the podium. "Make sure there are no free hands." There was a momentary shuffling of feet as we moved into a growing circle which soon encompassed the large room. Having two people separate hands, he said, "As soon as I grab these two hands my blue healing light will touch all of you. Now open yourselves up and be receptive." He took the two vacant hands and a blue light transferred through all of us assembled. Brilliant blue light flashed through my mind then propelled down my body. Accompanying it was a body trembling vibration, which went through all of us like powerful ocean waves. "In the power and love of One—" he started.

A rather dark spirit on Swuel's immediate right startled us by crying out, "You ass! What the hell do you think you're working on anyway, a butcher's block or something? If you're a healer, I'm a monkey's—"

"Stop it now, Nick," commanded Swuel. "If you weren't so important to our worthy cause and Earth's future, I assure you that we wouldn't have accepted you in this condition. No matter how imperative these jobs really are, we will be asking you to leave if you disregard my leadership like this. This is insubordination and we may have to omit you from associating in this class." He turned away from the assailant and nodded his head once. Nick's spirit guide released his right hand, which had been holding another's, and took the transgressor out of the room.

"I'm sorry for his outburst," apologized Swuel, stepping before the microphone again. "We were aware of his immense problem with anger and his inability to handle it. However, we did think and hope things would be better for him after this powerful healing. Because of his violent nature, we decided not to take him into the light of One. As you know that cleansing energy force would have substantially improved his demeanor, if only..." He shook his head back and forth before saying, "Please take your seats and ask the questions that I know are on your minds. I will respond openly and honestly to all of them."

Swuel looked directly into my eyes before moving onto another person. The second man that Swuel had looked at stood and with a lilt in his voice asked, "If you had known what kind of man he was, why then did you pick him for this job you've spoken so highly of?"

"Simply because he possesses expertise in specific areas that we are in need of procuring for Earth's future," answered Swuel frankly. "He would be a great aid to our cause if only his poor deportment didn't disrupt your training."

Feeling that he had answered that question as much as he intended and wanting more information, I stood clearing my throat and asked, "What is this meaningful cause that we keep hearing about?"

Swuel smiled grimly at us and returned, "As you undeniably know, the Earth is being slowly, but surely, destroyed by her inhabitants. Even more impressive and much more urgent is our awareness of its path of self-destruction. Because of the deterioration of the ozone layer and even more recent, the Greenhouse Effect, Earth has been recently suffering great plights. Violent storms, quakes, simonies, volcano eruptions, floods, heat waves, droughts, and the melting of glaciers are being seen worldwide. Deadly bacteria not encountered by this cycle of humans are being released into the atmosphere. Unfortunately, these are only the beginning signs of Earth's decline; each of these environmental disasters will increase in frequency and severity. Unless, of course, we can change this progression, and in simple terms, that's why you are here. With your enlightenment you will teach others and, combined, you will be better able to subdue these destructive causes".

Swuel paused because many hands were raised in alarm. "Please hold off with any further questions on this subject, everything will be answered in turn." He serenely continued his reply. "During the breakdown of your spiritual and mental impediments, we are going to be training you to rescue our fine planet. Without your input and active participation and indirectly your masters and teachers, Earth is infinitely doomed to total annihilation of all life forms." He shook his head and announced, "That's within the next 50 years if humans don't manage to blow Earth up beforehand," he said grimacing.

As if secretly letting us know a vital truth, he revealed, "First, we people of the light know that all of existence is perfectly balanced, that even the movement of a butterfly's wing in America causes change in the air currents in China."

A troubled voice cried out, "But we're dead, how can we assist in this grand effort?"

Swuel raised his hands and green light was discharged from them. As the light fell upon us, he said, "My peace I leave you." His demeanor had an immediate tranquilizing effect on all of us. Our anxieties immediately evaporated and we became silent listeners to a story, which sounded hopelessly idealistic. "Following your instruction here, you will be returning to Earth in the body of another newly dead person," he quickly said. "For now, please let that suffice; in time you will learn every detail."

The woman on my right stood and nervously asked, "I was studying Reiki healing, what are these lights you keep putting on us, and how do they work so quickly and effectively?" Finishing her questions, she sat down and turned her head slightly toward me for approval. I stared deep into her shyly smiling brown eyes and patted her approvingly on the shoulder. She thanked me with those expressive eyes and a Mona Lisa smile. I knew, although I had no memory of it, that I had known this woman sometime in my life. She was gorgeous with pale white skin, bright red hair offsetting her fair pallor, and delightfully large brown eyes, which seemed to have their own means of communication.

"Well Gail," Swuel started, "if used appropriately, light is the mechanism that everyone can use to improve their emotional, physical, and spiritual problems. As a Reiki healer, we know that you understand how it has been used in healing on Earth for thousands of years. Its origin arrives directly from One who presides within one's spirit. White light, as you might guess, purifies, blue is a healing light, pink is a light that creates feelings of love, and green causes calmness. In the coming days you will be learning to use various colors to change your perceptions and attitudes about yourselves and to change your assumed shortcomings. Until your opinion of yourselves has changed uniformly you can use white light to alter any fatalistic emotions that might come into play while you are here. When you return to Earth, using it and/or other colors we will be teaching you will aid you in modifying living conditions."

"Why," another person asked, "did we physically feel the great power in the blue, but not the green light?"

"Merely because I had accompanied my body energy with the healing blue light. I knew that using my bodily energy in conjunction with the powers of it would have even more of a positive effect on you and specifically on Nick who wasn't able to experience the purification from One."

A man with a very white aura said, "I can see and feel my body right now and it seems the same as when I was alive." Saying that, he then asked, "Are we living, functioning bodies or spiritual beings?"

"In simplified terms, you are right now the same person you were when alive except now you are also a more advanced being. You will find that your new metaphysical body has the same functions, senses, emotional feelings, and even sexual drives as it had before your transformation here. It is exactly as you envisioned, often more flawless than your earthly form had been."

He paused and looked all of us in the eye, "Now that this subject has arisen, it is time for me to inform you that because you will soon be returning to Earth in totally different bodies, we ask that you do not get attached to another person here. We do not know where you will be placed, your gender, age or race. Believe me, neither you nor us want to complicate your futures anymore than necessary." His next words were said slowly, projecting every word clearly. "Guard yourselves at all times against falling in love with a person you might find irresistible. Needless to say, lustful acts will not be permitted on this honorable plane." He emphasized his last words even more with a prolonged pause and a waving of his index finger.

Changing the subject, he said, "In these new angelic bodies you will also discover that you will be able to do things that were impossible to do previous to your conversion into the astral plane. While in your free time you can fly around here or even to other densities. We request, though, that you limit your aeronautics to only this plane for now. We have your own security to consider and leaving this level could be dangerous. In your newfound freedom, you could eternally lose your way in this ever expanding infinity." Allowing that idea to sink in, he said, "Like the densities, the list of differences between your present bodies and your earthly ones go on indefinitely. You are imagination and your thoughts create your reality."

Nick's spiritual guide approached our teacher and healer. They looked knowingly into each other's eyes and Swuel turned to us. "Please examine Tesa until this necessary matter has been attended to; perhaps an hour from now I will call you back. It would be a good idea if you and your spirit guides peruse your living quarters."

Rama stood and took my arm as if to guide me away. Shaking him off and turning to the woman on my right I extended my hand to her and said, "Name's Jim, what's yours?"

She smiled shyly and slowly placed her hand in mine as I helped her get to her feet. "Like Swuel told everyone, I am Gail and very pleased to meet you Jim.

"Oh, yes," I said, feeling like a dummy. "Swuel had called you Gail hadn't he?" Catching my breath that seemed to be escaping me through my open mouth in wistful sighs, I racked my memory trying to recall how I knew her. I was feeling exhilarated by this gorgeous woman and asked, "How bout joining me for a walk around this as yet unknown territory, Gail?"

"I'd like—"

"Excuse me," said her guide who I also vaguely recognized. "It's better for this first time if you stay with your respective spirit guides. We've got to show you your dorm rooms and eating area."

"That's correct," said Rama taking my arm again. "Come with me, Jim."

"I guess we have no other choice," Gail said with her eyes smiling into mine.

"Guess not. For sure, though, I want the next walk with you," I returned. Grinning into her smiling eyes and feeling an indescribable attraction toward her, I added, "Until later then?" and turned and walked toward the doorway with Rama.

As I reached the doorway in this room a very luminous and grinning person stopped me with, "Excuse me, Jamie, but I couldn't allow you to leave without saying hello to you once again. It's been many years since we've last met."

Staring into his face I utterly failed to recognize him. I then closed my eyes thinking that I might have known him during my years of blindness. Neither modes, sight, nor hearing, identified him for me and I wondered to myself, "Who is this man and how is it that he knows me well enough to call me by, my family name, Jamie?" A shiver abruptly ran down my spine, "Lou!" I cried with a feeling of joy and shock. "Swuel had called you Lou a few minutes ago. Around 50 years ago I had a very close cousin named Lou who died when I was in the fourth or fifth grade. Are you by any chance a reincarnate of him?" I asked thrilled with that hopeful expectation.

"I'm sorry for flustering you like this. I guess that my last earthly name was the same as your cousin, but I'm sorry to report that I'm not him. In your just prior life you knew me as Dr. Hibard."

"Oh my One!" I exclaimed with even more chills running up and down my spine. "I can't believe that you and I have met again, and here, too!" Then after a brief momentary pause we hugged each other in an appreciative recollection of our past friendship.

"By your usage of One instead of God, I can see that we've already converted you," Lou replied joyfully.

"Dr. Hibard!" I cried with heartfelt jubilation. "I haven't seen, I mean heard, you since I was 13 or 14 in your summer home on Little Moose Lake. You had invited my family and I to stay with you and your lovely wife Winky for a whole week! By far it was the very best summer of my entire life. You had everything there a kid could dream about having, and you allowed us to use it all, too!" He was now tall and slim, totally different from what he had been in those days. Only his eyes held the veneration of his prior existence. Through enlightened eyes I now saw eternal love and bliss that touched me with their inner tranquility and profound divinity.

I was still feeling unstable when he thoroughly blew my mind. "With my misdiagnosis of your rare disease, I was guilty for your loss of sight. I know that our sharing our summer home with you wouldn't make up for my error, but I had to do something."

"Please," I said from my heart, "don't think or feel that way! It was the four or five doctors I saw after you who allowed the disease to progress. In truth, nothing occurs by accident. I know now that it was meant to happen just as it did." To myself I reveled with my past memory, if I hadn't lost my sight I wouldn't have ever learned deaf sign language or Braille. I then thought of the deaf kids in my school bus who I told stories in sign to, my deaf-blind ham radio friend who helped me get my ticket, and especially the love of my life who was deaf-blind. Claire and I would have never met and fallen in love. If only I had been stronger . . . If only my parents hadn't been so darn prejudice . . ." I moaned under my breath.

Echoing my words, he said, "Everything occurs as it is meant to." With a grateful smile, he changed the subject and said, "Winky and I wished that you could have had sight so that you could have enjoyed our summer resort even more. I remember seeing your true grit at learning how to sail, and you got it, too. You really showed us all up that summer day following my fly casting instruction. You didn't need to be taken out in a fishing boat. You were the first and only person to ever catch a fish off of my pier! What was even more impressive was that you did it only 20 minutes after I had taught you how to fly cast. You were a mighty determined young man, Jamie. That Speckled Trout sure was a beauty and you followed that up with two on the following day! I had tried discouraging you from even attempting such a foolish thing and you had to show this old man how foolhardy he was didn't you? I had never seen fish come that close into shore to eat; it had to be your unique talent that compelled them to think that food was at hand." He smiled and looked off into a distant past. "I can remember my wife Winky cooking them for us. Matter of fact, that picture of her presenting you with the three of them, still steaming from her kitchen, hung on my wall right up to my dying day. I couldn't have been more proud of you, even if you had been my own grandson—"

I was so delirious with his recollection that I succumbed to my enthusiasm and interrupted. "You can remember that, Doc?" Shocked with the revelation of his memory, I further said, "The clarity of your aura tells me you've been here before, how is it possible that you can remember things from another lifetime when I can hardly recall my just past?"

"Your question about our memory acuity is a question that hasn't been yet revealed by medical science. For a more complete answer than I could ever give, you'll have to ask Swuel or your spirit guide Rama," he replied with a smile of unspoken awareness.

By the fact of a special twinkle I saw in his eye, I knew that he knew more than he was admitting to. The clarity and brightness of his aura was also a powerful hint that I couldn't ignore. Dr. Hibard was far more involved with these people than he was divulging. Putting that idea aside, I asked Rama, "Why do our memories differ so and what could cause these dissimilarities?" However, before he could reply, another more urgent question popped into my mind and I impetuously asked, "Please Lou, how'd you recognize me in this body?"

"Frankly, you aren't all that much different from when you were a kid. Furthermore, I've always felt a distinctive link that conjoined us and am now perceiving it as powerfully."

"To begin with," said Rama as if Lou and I hadn't digressed, "in a single word, illusions. I've got to keep it simple, but the life you had experienced on Earth was illusionary in comparison to Lou's. For many lifetimes he has been an enlightened member of this cause and hasn't had the same mental, spiritual, or physical hurdles that you have had to deal with during your last few lives," he explained. "Matter of fact, even though he has lived on Earth many times over, Lou has managed to stay free of detrimental spiritual defects. Every obstacle that we have to overcome hinders and can even prohibit us from recalling events of our present lifetime as well as those of past lives. The most conflicting and inaccurate obstacles are your illusions brought about by your inaccurate parental and church teachings. In fact, they are the primary reasons for humanity being held back for so long."

My past life friend said, "It's those kinds of enfites that our teachers here will be purging first."

"These blocks you speak of sound like mental walls," I said, wanting to comprehend this concept more fully. "Being philosophical, that's over simplistic don't you think, Lou?" I asked, feeling somewhat immature on this more advanced path of enlightenment.

"Nah, for a greenhorn that's a fair analogy," he answered with a laugh. "Brainwashing or negative thinking and emotions build up memory barriers very much like stone walls in your mind. We are here right now to have these opposing causes of memory loss and spiritual imbalances purged. When you have reached Clear you will notice that your memory is vastly better. Total recall won't be too far away for you then. It will also be a faster operating mind and most likely you will be CC (cosmic conscious) in a very short time afterwards. This will give you knowledge of things like time, place, and events happening throughout the universe since its conception," Lou proudly explained.

"I've been meditating for years with the hope of reaching CC, like TM told us we would reach," I told him. "Until now, though, that's only remained an unfulfilled dream."

Lou smiled at me and I remembered that warm smile as if it were yesterday. Even though his physical appearance was totally different, he had still been able to preserve his winning smile as well as the wisdom clearly read in his eyes. I also noticed that his aura was more brilliant than Rama's. It was radiant and clear of discoloration except for tiny specks of grayness that peeped through in various places. "Does Lou's pure light indicate CC?" I asked, looking into Rama's face.

Before he had a chance to reply, Lou offered, "My aura illustrates my union with One. But if you look closely, there are some irregularities there. They represent my recent human life; spiritual intervals of disharmony affect even the best of us," he said with a hardy laugh. I am constantly CC and because of my indispensable desire to aid this cause, I've chosen not to be unified with the Universal One." He looked into my eyes and deciding that I could be trusted. "I am here now for another spiritual cleansing. I've built up a few minuscule barriers that need to be removed before returning to Earth in another person's body. We can perform optimally, but only if we are Clear."

Finding it difficult to comprehend why a person so pure would want to keep going back to a contaminating Earth, I asked, "It is so much nicer here, why are you returning again and again to that unkempt place?"

"Excuse me, Jamie," said Lou with a grimace. "You are being specifically trained so that you can soon be reinstated on Earth as a participant in our cause. However, if you keep on talking and feeling this way about our Earth, then you will be rejected from our society. We will not tolerate anyone who isn't totally faithful to our cause. I know you well and this is only a transitory feeling of apprehension. Notwithstanding, it's causing your uncertainty to cloud your inner feelings. You are now blocking the light of One. Reverse that negative thinking as of this second. Be objective and open yourself to His absolute perfection and allow yourself to be One. Since we have just arrived, it is reasonable for you to doubt the validity of this cause this minute, but your dislike for Earth and wanting to stay away makes you a poor candidate to be aiding us in this worthy campaign. I am sure that when you are yourself and taking part in helping to correct conditions on Earth that you'll understand why I am going back there again. Putting it simply, our home planet is in dire trouble and because my work hasn't yet rectified those problems, I've got to return," Lou replied earnestly. "My comrades need my practical assistance and I am absolutely loyal to them and to this movement."

"I'm sorry, Lou," I said, feeling wounded by his misconstrued meaning of what I poorly attempted to say. "The truth is that I was only denoting the vast contrasts between this plane and the polluted Earth. Like you, I want to be a devout crusader of this effort and desire so badly to participate in this cause. Just tell me how I might help."

"I'm the one who has to apologize then," he said with true sentiment displayed in his voice and his wounded eyes. "I unwisely jumped in with both feet and misinterpreted your viewpoint. That's a prime example of why I need to be here again. It wouldn't have occurred if I was clear of these imperfections," he said, indicating the gray blotches in his aura. "Please forgive me for responding so impulsively."

Just as he had completed his request, I noticed Gail approaching us; she and her spirit guide were headed for the doorway where we now stood. I smiled my most amiable smile at her and asked, "Running out on me now, girls? Where are you off to?"

I felt my body quiver with excitement as Gail gave me her warm, timid smile. The feeling that I knew her persisted and I tormented over my pathetic memory. "My spirit guide Marza is going to show me my living quarters," she answered, indicating her stunning companion.

I had turned and was facing Gail's guide. Although her attire was very casual today, I now knew why she had previously seemed so familiar to me. I recognized her from the proceeding night's OBE adventure. Again I became memorized by the enormous beauty and prominent love that shown in her eyes. "You're uh, uh . . ." I stammered, "the same Marza who had first absolved me of my sins. Rama had met me in my meditation garden and brought me to you for cleansing

"Well, you are almost right. The truth is that we are equal portions of the unity of One and thus your wrong perceptions are forgiven even before they can take place. In simple terms, the One in all of his perfect creation forgives you of every transgression before you can even request it. There is only karma and we will be teaching you about it soon." She smiled into my eyes and I found myself becoming intrigued by her comportment. "You are accurate in that you have seen me before this moment. It is better said, though, that I performed a purification ritual on you."

She paused at that point and I jumped in blurting my spontaneous thoughts. "Oh my One! This was all planned! Even the accident and my death were intentional! The members of this cause . . ." I wanted to finish my accusation, but something deeper in me made me pause a moment. From deep within me came the feeling that this was the bluntness of reality and not a delusion as I would have preferred. I wasn't imagining this revolution; it was all very real and I had to complete my thought. "Marza, you and Rama knew well before time that I was going to come here. Was my death an accident or was it all a part of a strategy for getting me here?"

"You do have qualms about being here," said Lou dejectedly. "I'm afraid they are of the worst kind, too!"

"Please," said Rama with his hand raised again and tension showing in his strained voice, "Yes, we were cognizant of your approaching death, but had absolutely nothing to do with its occurrence. We are righteous beings founded in the perfection and truth of an eternally loving spirit. If you are thinking otherwise, then you are blaspheming us, our cause, and One Himself. As your co-worker Gary had told you shortly before leaving Earth, this is your true calling."

"Then you know Gary and Frank, too. Were they in on this crusade? Did they entice me into teaching that class about love enhancement so that I would personally have spiritual awakenings and be better prepared to come here?" I asked, recalling those very friendly men who I worked with for a short period of time before being taken from the reality I knew and loved. They had found me playing piano in a steakhouse while projecting love to everyone listening. When I told them about what I was doing to attract so much attention from total strangers, they asked me to teach my technique to patients in their mental health facility.

Seeing my agitation, Lou, Marza, and Rama simultaneously raised their hands and projected green light to me. My uneasiness noticeably dwindled. Seconds later, with feelings of appeasement, I openly told them, "If I had desired, I could have blocked your soothing green light with restless red or black light. However, I am honestly seeking the whole truth, so that I can forever release this anguishing thought!" Changing the subject entirely around, I said, "When the truth is known, how perfectly all of the pieces seem to fit. Back on Earth I was afraid that I'd never know my true calling." Understanding the significance of this dynamic revelation, I said, "I knew that darkroom work wasn't what I was supposed to be doing for the rest of my life. Then I discovered the power of love, but where I should be focusing my attention had evaded me until now. For at least the last 10 years I've been a seeker. However, I realize now that I had only been blindly searching for illusions found in faulty religions. Thanks to you members of this unique movement, I am now prepared to take part in my true calling." The good in me was growing more secure with the true me who I'd been before the doubts had temporarily corrupted my innocence.

"You're welcome," said Lou and Rama simultaneously, and then Marza a breath later.

"It's only the occurrence of this alien phenomenon that is knocking me off balance right now. Forgive my backward concept."

Then Marza spoke up, "We accept your apology with joy." Her bright smile was like the light of One falling upon me. "I want you to know that Gary and Frank are invaluable collaborators in our sacred quest of saving Earth," she added.

"Yes," said Rama, picking up from where Marza had ended. "When Frank had informed Gary about the good will and powerful love that you were freely giving to everyone, we collaborated and they took you on as an instructor. They styled that class specifically for you. They soon discovered the virtuous powers of your teaching, and too shortly afterwards of your approaching death. That's when they increased your classes and asked you to leave the hospital."

"At the beginning, however, they didn't have any idea that you would only be with them for an exceedingly short duration—not that it would have affected their yearning need of someone with your gift. As workers in our cause they were glad to find you so that you could teach your love technique to other humans, hence moving them into the light of the truth and thus supporting our cause even further," said Marza with awareness showing in her radiant eyes. "Oddly enough," she added, with that sparkle in her eyes moving to her heart-shaped lips, "your method is so effective that one of your first students, a wife beater, has become a loving person and will be joining us soon."

Forgetting that my thoughts here were common knowledge, I silently deliberated. "It seems like I've been indoctrinated into a dynamic movement whose aims are to help the Earth and the human race. I want so much to cooperate with this charismatic community. I've just got to be an upright member of this society and stop my indecisive behavior. I hate these doubts of mine cropping up like this, and have to find a way of forever ridding myself of them." After an uncomfortable moment of silence, I realized the reason for it. "I'm sorry . . . just thinking . . . forgot you guys are privy to my every thought," I said with great embarrassment. The three of them stared into my impassioned eyes as I realized what I had done.

"Nonsense, Jim," said Rama. "We know your inner most desires about helping Earth with its restoration. Your ambition to bring transforming love to the world is admirable, although too pretentious; we've all got to work on that!"

"Thank you for this revealing glimpse into your true inner self. It is time for you to know that trustworthy self in you and to stop questioning it. As you know best, You are One, and by loving Him unconditionally in others, He is loving you in return. Now that you know about us," he said candidly, "we can see by your thoughts that your desires are evolving in the right direction—"

"No doubt," interjected Lou to Rama, whose mouth was still open. "Like all of you, we want you to know that your path here is not going to be completely flat. There will be high and low points along the way. In fact," he warned me, "there is going to be what we consider a prolonged black period before you are clear."

Picking up the same thread he had been exploring previously, Rama said, "After Gary had discovered you, he asked Frank to join him to the restaurant where you were working. Once we knew of your using lovenergy, the power of One, we told them to do their best to get you into their group, knowing that it would help everyone including yourself spiritually. We were also interested in getting the word around about what you had discovered concerning lovenergy and its life altering effects of creating powerful feelings of love in those who practice it a few minutes daily. To be even more frank, we were hoping that you had time to write a book and thus get more people using your healing method."

"Gary is a great teacher and he kept us abreast of your enormous progress," said Marza. "Besides their psychological work, both he and Frank are engineers working on finding a safe alternative source of energy," she quickly added. "As you undoubtedly understand, that would aid our cause in prolonging Earth's longevity."

"They both approve of you and your willing desire to bring love to everyone alive on your planet. We were told of your unselfishness and willingness to teach your love technique free to the poor and severely sick and disabled. They told us how, on your own, you were going to nursing homes and other special facilities for needy people and teaching it to everyone you could. Gary told us that you were teaching them in groups whenever possible and even one to bedridden patients," said Rama, placing a hand over his heart area and then moving his hand toward me in a gesture of goodwill.

"When you return to Earth, we want you to produce an mp3 file teaching your love enhancing meditation. Secondly, write a full length book informing the world of what it has done for you and everyone else you have taught it to." Rama, with a grin from ear to ear said, "You are learning lots of truths that you can add to your second larger advanced book about us and your modus operandi of energizing feelings of love."

"Put all of this away for now," advised Lou.

"Yes," piped in Marza. "We are jumping the gun and you have only to be in the moment of this eternal now."

"We cannot fail with people like Lou, Gary, and Frank. Your doubts, fears, and misgivings will be gone once you and the others gathered here have more of your negative enfites removed. This process unfortunately takes time and effort. Your willing participation as well as your teacher's coaching will make you great members of our cause. You've got to overcome all of the inaccurate conditioning of many lifetimes. As infants we were all lied to by the leaders of the time. Sure, our forbearers had thought that they were teaching us truths. In reality those instructions were only illusions."

Here in Tesa, you will learn accurate facts, which will correct your erroneous beliefs," said Marza.

"These valuable truths will give you a strong foundation with which you can become a trustworthy member of this affiliation," said Rama with a pleasant smile.

"Your special area of expertise will soon be disclosed in full," said Lou.

I was now standing between Rama and Marza while Lou stood face to face with me. Gail stood a step or two shyly behind her spirit guide watching me closely, as if fascinated with what was taking place before her. Feeling extremely excited about the enlightening doors now opening ahead of me, I said, "I am still very confused. Why was I chosen and for what purpose?" I asked this feeling like a starving animal hungry for vital details that I could really sink my teeth into.

"Like we've been eluding, all of the facts regarding your innate gifts will soon be detailed to us and all of you new students. We've already discussed your writing about your powerful technique of creating love. Nevertheless, after a past lives meditation that Swuel will soon be using, we will know better if that is the only area in which you should be focused. At this point we are only suggesting ideas."

Looking at Rama and getting a nod of affirmation from him, Marza continued, "You were chosen because of your comprehension of the power of light, high spiritual belief in our Oneness, mental capacity, and teaching abilities. To be frank, Gary told us about the enormously successful classes you were holding in their center. With the right tools and the right marketing, your effective method will touch everyone worldwide."

"We don't mean to single you out or to boast about your aptitudes, Jim," said Lou. "You no doubt are recognizing your place in this new reality, aren't you?"

I was no longer having two converse conflicts going on in my head and, at this precise moment, I was seeing the movement as a necessary tool for combatting the evil and destructive paths humanity was traveling. Almost out of breath with the thrill of being part of such an important group, I replied with all the gusto I could muster, "Let's get rolling!"

"Right now you are radiating pure love," continued Rama as if still trying to bolster my ego. "We learned from Frank and Gary that you also win trust and love from whoever and wherever you are instructing."

Marza stepped in and picked up right where Rama had finished. "Because of those potentials you readily exhibit, Frank and Gary had repeatedly tried to get you to dedicate your full attention to helping the people in the classes you were holding. Instead you stubbornly kept your demeaning jobs as a darkroom tech and as a pianist in a bar." Getting a warning look from Rama, she concluded more cautiously, "Coupled with your heartfelt feelings concerning Earth's perilous breakdown, your teaching others how to create overwhelming feelings of love for One, mankind, and themselves makes you a perfect candidate for our cause."

Adding his own feelings, Lou said, "And that's without our direct knowledge of your pending expertise. All of us students will soon have all of our past lives exposed and from them we should know a lot more about our future identities." Immediately cutting himself off and turning to Rama and Marza he asked, "Don't you think that you should show your trainees to their living quarters?"

Taken out of my reverie, I quickly said, "It's too late now, but my One how I only wish I had given more time to love production classes! Frank and Gary had wanted me to devote all of my efforts to my teaching too. Like you said, though, I resisted and stubbornly continued working full-time in the hospital." Feeling suddenly kicked in the head, I exclaimed, "Was that the reason for my being hit by that car?" Wanting them to understand my accusation I angrily spelled it out to them. "Was I sacrificed because I had foolishly denied my devotion to them, One, and this movement?"

"You're back on that wrong track again," warned an unknown radiant bystander who I had noticed standing next to Gail. "Until you've had more of your brainwashing removed you are likely to keep having these rash exhibits of delusion. For you and your peers sake, ignore them and don't give thought or especially voice to them."

"No, Jim!" cried Marza, Rama, and Lou synchronously.

"Now get this into your head; number one, our Universal One doesn't inflict any sort of pain on us for our actions or lack of them!" said Rama, uninterrupted by Marza or Lou. They seemed to know their places, and aware that as my spirit guide, Rama was in command.

"Secondly, as my equally endowed colleague Renny so aptly said, 'You've gone astray again,'" said Lou with a deep furrowing frown creasing his forehead. "Now get that lunatic enfite out of your head!" he ordered.

"The One is perfect, undivided love, Jim, so there isn't even such things as hatred, anger, disappointment, or evil; there is only eternal lovenergy. You've heard us say many times that we are honorable people. You scorn our names and our devout venture when you talk or think that way! We people of the light would never purposefully kill anyone for disobedience or to aid our worthy cause."

"No matter who they were or what they might contribute," said Lou with conviction.

"Like you, Jim, we are a harmonious peace loving people!" added Rama a bit more indulgently." Our Universal One is absolute perfection and flawlessness, for it is the Infinite Presence!" declared Lou's friend Renny with his arms spread fully open.

"Furthermore, and this is essential for you to remember," Marza proclaimed powerfully, "scoreless religions have been wrongly educating earthlings to blame what they mistakenly call Adam and Eve for committing 'original sin'. Can you imagine the damage they've caused by telling humans that they were born in sin? Mankind has evolved much slower because they were limited by these controlling leaders, their retarding dogma, and their institutions. These gross inaccuracies were taught throughout the ages!"

"I and the father are One. You have seen One and you have seen the other," Jesus Christ taught us thousands of years ago.

"Wake up and rejoice mankind, for you are as free as the eagle."

"The One is perfect and couldn't ever create imperfection! One's lovenergy did create the first man and woman, but they were flawless because they were human replicas of One—therefore absolutely divine!"

"Excuse me, Marza, but we are imperfect. However, this is only because we are not currently unified with One," said Lou with great elation in his voice.

Rama nodded in agreement and said, "The only real wrong is believing that there is any separation between us and the utter perfection of Him. That which detaches us from one another is obviously in violation of His commandment to love One another as we love ourselves." Taking a deep breath, he repeated, "Lou's comment, 'Our only sin is our belief of a disconnection,' is so accurate! There is no division between mankind and One."

"There isn't two, Him and us, there is only One divine energy to all of existence," added Marza, shrewdly.

Lou spoke before Marza whose mouth was still agape in an attempt to finish her previous thought, "You were not punished because of perceived or conceived evil, rebellion, bad karma, behavior, or any misdeeds or thoughts. Get those concepts out of your mind once and for all." A second later he added, "Our always loving One didn't cause you to go blind either. Illusions, we as The One create illusions so that we/He can experience the diversions of life. When we have realized our divinity, we are this same perfect One who rejoices with us."

A picture of a helpless squirrel suddenly popped into my mind. He was shot through the stomach by an arrow and pinned to a tree. His little arms and legs struggled to free himself, but my arrow had gone right through him fastening him solidly to the tree. I was 12 years old only days before this hideous act. While tears poured from my eyes, I searched the underbrush for stones that I tossed futilely at the arrow trying to knock it free. Nevertheless the poor little creature remained steadfast and my efforts proved to be unfruitful. "Lou," I said a bit under my breath, "I thought that I was being punished for being an evil boy . . ."

"First, Jim, evil is a wrong concept. You are to know that there isn't such a thing as evil. Our One is only love, and that means that there aren't things like evil, sin, hate, injustice or even heaven or hell; there is only Oneness found in the perfection of universal lovenergy," said Lou.

Renny quickly added, "Lovenergy is a term you will be hearing often around here, for as you've heard, our One is the realization of his lovenergy lifenergy Onenergy force which you are tapping into with your powerful method of enhancing love."

Rama proclaimed proudly, "Jim taught us to combine the words love and energy. Now all of us are calling this divine energy lovenergy. Following his combining the words we are now doing it for lifenergy and Onenergy as well. These are new words for mankind to adopt."

"Not divinenergy?" asked Lou.

"There is only divine Onenergy, for all the energy of existence is One," replied Renny.

Marza said, "Mankind is One, thus Roman numeral I, which we are all. A more powerful cause and affect will be brought about in those who love everyone unconditionally as One supreme being. Lovenergy is the tool to create all that we desire."

Then in a whisper Marza presented an idea that troubled me. "Subconsciously, Jim, you wanted a way out of the hospital job. However, for some odd reason, maybe because of the feelings of independence it gave you, you retained a need to stay there. Being so much in control of lovenergy, the creator of your life, your subconscious mind decided on a tactic of escape, thus the accident, which is an example of cause and effect. Also, Jim, remember your great desire to mind travel? Well, you did at last achieve it!" She, Rama, Lou, and Renny looked me in the face and each in turn nodded their heads in affirmation."

"What Marza has just told you may seem a bit crude or farfetched to you now, but we want you to absolutely know that we had nothing to do with the conclusion of your past life. Being One, we have given ourselves a free subconscious will to select our own living conditions. There is no stipulation that we/One, at any time, cannot change our living status into whatever we personally desire. All it takes is willpower and faith accompanied by lovenergy."

"Being fixed on Marza's radical notion, I asked Rama, "Can you please block my thoughts for a second? After getting a nod from Rama, I said, "Marza, you mean to tell me that I caused that car accident to occur?" In shock, I added, "Imagine what we might achieve in life if we only realized our self-worth seen through the reality of our devout Oneness?"

"We, the people of this movement had absolutely nothing to do with your death. Unless you feel of course, that having prior knowledge and doing nothing to prevent it makes us guilty. We only knew that you were going to die some time today; we didn't know the time nor cause. I did keep an eye on you and when the moment came, I helplessly yelled at you to stop crossing that street. Your Seeing Eye dog did hear me, but you were in command. Besides, One gives us free will to live or die as we decree."

Feeling as if a great weight had been lifted from my back, I realized a moment later that I had just been released from some kind of internal barrier. Marza confirmed it with her next words. "I believe that we have just dissolved our first enfite!"

"Jim, be in the moment and stop your analyzing all of the time," said Renny.

"You are rushing it too much," advised Marza. "Before reacting so passionately, surrender and allow yourself to unite with One."

"Feel your union with One and speak only from the heart," added Lou.

"You are right, and I really should take a few seconds before voicing my opinions." Looking down at my aura I noticed some graying, although since the enfite had been release, it was a lot less blemished. Wanting some time alone I abruptly did an about-face. "Excuse me," I asked with a tilt of my head, "but I've got to go out for a breather."

My eyes suddenly fell on Gail's expressive eyes searching mine. "I know," she said putting her index finger to her full lips. "Don't allow me to detain you. Go while you have the chance!" With a conspiring smile she said, "Go ahead and get that needed time alone. I'll catch you later."

"These last minutes were vital for me to experience, and I can't ever forget what I've learned. However, I can't leave you right this second," I said. Forgive me, Lovie, for temporarily turning away from you."

With a shiver that shook her body, she whispered, "Jim, what is happening to us? I feel something unexplainable is occurring between the two of us and I can't put a finger on what it might be."

"I, too, feel odd about everything that is happening here, especially concerning the two of us. A moment ago I called you Lovie, and it felt like that was your name; it just came out of me. Have we ever met before? Do you recognize me at least? As you heard, I was blind on Earth so I don't have any visual memory of seeing you. Then again, neither is your voice familiar. I feel deep in my heart that we were . . ." I quickly wondered how to say this properly. "Lovers." I decided that was delicate enough. "Yet I have no memory of a relationship between us."

She stared deeply into my eyes and touched my very soul. Her beautiful expressive brown eyes communed with something vulnerable deep inside my being. "I feel the same way, Jim. Although, like you, I have no recollection of our ever meeting. Yet I feel somehow attached to you. When you called me Lovie my heart and body fluttered with joy, which caused chills to run up and down my spine. I really don't have any direct knowledge, but I do have an overpowering sense of familiarity about you" Without saying another word, I took her hand in mine and walked toward the door. Lou, Marza, and Rama were overlooked by our urgent need to discover our past life association.

At the front door of Tesa, Rama touched my shoulder and said, "I'm going to have to separate you from Gail." His hand was still firmly gripping my left shoulder as he tried to propel me in a different direction from where Gail and I had been headed. He was literally pulling me away from her and said, "The men's quarters aren't far from here. Now let's get a move on and go there, I mean pronto, too." He directed me with another tightening of his hand.

Gail's overseer had been talking to her in very much the same vein, and still I had denied abandoning her. "Anyone have a crowbar?" I asked with a giggle. "I think you're going to need it!"

"Until later, Jim," Gail pathetically replied. "I'll meet you when Swuel calls us back."

Getting no objections and feeling right about what I had called her, I used it again. "Later, Lovie."

Turning to Rama, I said, "Excuse me for a while. I've got to be on my own for a short bit." And I left the ground then and there.

Having such overwhelming questions about Gail and my new environment was making me feel a bit punchy. I wanted to just float alone so that I could privately contemplate my rousing emotions and thoughts. If time allowed, I also wanted to examine this powerful information that I had just learned. Magically, I found myself in the midst of lofty treetops. I personally witnessed a mother robin feeding her babies. "Oh my One," I murmured. "How good it is to see with functioning eyes again!" With startling recognition of the truth, I said, "These creatures, and all of your creation, are examples of our universal self! Because you are, I am, ergo they are, too."

After drifting in a clear sky and observing the perfection of nature on this plane for a while longer, I mentally turned and examined some of my most urgent thoughts. "If I and One are one . . . If He didn't cause me to lose sight, what could ever possess Him/me to want to experience life in a blind boy-man's body?" Memory brought back to mind the picture of that helpless squirrel. "I did hate myself at that moment," I painfully recalled. "All the same, we mere humans can't inflict punishment on ourselves like that, or can we?" I pondered.

I found myself drifting in a bluer than blue sky. "Being normal is what I've desired for most of my life," I realized with a smile of reckoning. "Once again I have sight, and at last I have achieved freedom for my imprisoned spirit. Mind travel is now a reality and no longer just a desired fantasy. We really do have greater power in our lives than we had been led to believe."

During my days of teaching love enhancement meditations, I had firsthand experience at what it was like being at a higher plane of consciousness. It also showed me that the majority of humans were really remorseful about their living conditions. In spite of these discomforts they insisted on sustaining the life that they had created for themselves. "Yes," I said aloud, "we do live in the world of our own making." If only I had known that we really have options I could have transformed my lonely life even sooner!" In an afterthought I said, "If only we were taught as kids about the powers of lovenergy and how to use it effectively; every single living person would be living a more perfect life! There wouldn't be greed, poverty, and everything between them."

Smiling to myself, I said, "After my book has been written, I have to get my method taught to every child in every school around the world." Following another short pause I screamed out, "I do want to be present in this dimension so that I can learn even more effective tools to assist this cause in their pursuit of peace and survival for all humanity! Using this great tool of lovenergy, I've got to return to Earth and teach humans the correct methods of feeling, thinking, and acting."

With that revelation in the open, I somehow sensed my aura growing lighter. I looked down at it and sure enough it had changed from gray to a noticeably more luminous white. I threw the robin who I had revisited a kiss. She turned her head up toward me and chirped a farewell. It was so precisely synchronous that I whispered with awe, "We are one, little mama. What I am you are, also. All of us, the Onenergy individual segments of this eternity, are unified in the wholeness of our gracious Universal One." I realized that I had heard Rama and Marza say nearly those same words to me, but now that that sentimentality was my own, I felt even more jubilant.

Chapter 3

Further Teaching

I now flew rapidly around Tesa relishing the beauty of her stained glass windows. I studied each one more and more carefully and felt in accord with every individual setting and their almost-live caricatures. One of them was a Virgin Mary-like woman who held out her two hands to me. In one was a golden sun that seemed to radiate toward me, and in the other was a silver star that twinkled in the light of One. Next came an operating fountain displaying a little girl who had curly, ruby red hair. She poured sparkling water for me from her pail. She seemed to smile at me as I bent and sipped her pure cold water. Another imaginative window showed a double rainbow, over which hung a partly clouded sky. In the upper right corner, a little sunlight seemed to be peeping through the clouds. Resting beneath the effervescent rainbows stood a wishing well filled with gold coins. The coins sparkled with the light of One, which came from a bolt of lightning radiating from the upper left corner. I was fully aware that this window was only a still and totally motionless picture, but it was so real and moving that it took me to a higher level of consciousness. It was really as if the light of One was coming from the lightning and that the gold coins were sparkling in its light. The last window that I viewed was a fat alligator that was resting peacefully next to a turquoise-colored pond. His gigantic mouth was opened wide, showing enormous white teeth. A tiny bird was perched on one of his teeth, contentedly picking out the debris stuck between his sharp molars. "I guess that all of existence is symbiotic," I whispered aloud. "We are taught the truth by these masters who were similarly trained by their masters and then we return to teach to the earthbound humans." With this thought barely formed in my mind, I heard Swuel summoning us to another session.

I started to fly around to the front door of Tesa when I realized that, like always, I was capable of fulfilling all of my aspirations. Without any hesitation, I visualized the seat where I had been previously sitting and sailed peacefully through the wall to it. Unfortunately, for the moment, I discovered myself sitting alone—Gail not yet having returned.

"Glad to see you using your head for more than just a hat rack," said Rama, amiably materializing in the chair that he had formerly occupied. With an understanding smile, he suggested, "You could also have emerged right here, rather than having to focus on it and metaphysically flying through Tesa's wall."

"Well," I said smiling vacantly and putting my hand on Gail's empty seat, "having found my wishing well, I thought that I'd use it for its intended purpose." Then sensing her silent approach from behind me, I said with relief, "Hello, Gail. What kept you so long?"

"How did you know that I was behind you?" she asked me as I slowly swiveled and looked directly into her intriguing eyes with a delighted smile framing my face.

After taking her hand and helping her to the chair next to mine, I told her, "Six months after losing my sight I developed a sixth sense which gives me feedback of nearby obstacles like parked cars, walls, trees telephone poles, and people. It apparently is still functioning as it had before coming here."

She shuddered slightly and asked, "Sixth sense?"

Her words had hardly been spoken when Swuel stepped behind the podium. "Thank you all for being so prompt in responding to my call," he said as the room became quiet. "There are a few of you who are still having difficulties believing and accepting all that has recently occurred. This is not unheard of, nor should any of you feel guilty for it. In case you are one of those insecure people, I am going to send you white light, which will remove some of these annoying negatives that you have acquired because of the changes. They no doubt are due to emotional fluctuations and rigorous shifts of your location. Couple that with your new bodies and lifestyle changes and it's expected that many of you would be feeling a bit ill at ease." Next he instructed us, "Please stand and hold hands as you had done earlier." We complied with his wish and gathered hands forming a large circle. He separated two hands and held them as his One-like white light fell upon us. It felt like gentle ocean waves, which immediately washed away our anxieties and enlightened our minds, hearts, spirits, and auras. While on Earth, during my last few months, I had used white light to protect myself against all kinds of evils. At least twice daily, I would imagine a pure white light entering through my head and exiting my feet. I imagined it dissolving all the darkness that had entered me that day. Conversely, I effectively used black light to cure and shrink skin diseases like moles and warts on myself, and even skin cancer on two of my students.

He discontinued sending us that white light and assumed his position behind the microphone. Without a word being spoken we collectively sat in our chairs and gave him our full attention.

"Lesson one," he announced, "is usage of corrective light."

He then smiled at each of us and, feeling better about what he saw, he continued. "Since arriving here, all of you have personally experienced the power of light and can testify to its corrective potential. The majority of the human race has forgotten its usage. All of the great healers of the distant past knew its awesome capacity and they used it with positive results. Thousands of people in my classes have also sensed the unconditional effects that it has on their psyche, metaphysical bodies, and spirits. Earthling scientists have demonstrated the differences of those who were exposed to many hours of light with others who were deprived of it. Those who receive an ample amount of light feel more awake, have more energy, are emotionally stable, happy, and less argumentative. Conversely, they who were limited had the opposite reactions. I'm sure that you remember feeling more depressed during winters when there was less light. There is even a term for it called log cabin fever. No one is inhibited from using light to correct or enhance their own or another's life. All it really takes is awareness, perseverance, and corrective usage of light. Many of our problems can be alleviated with powers of heart, mind, and spirit, which are all profoundly effected by a stimulating light change. Distance isn't an obstacle to its extraordinary powers either. For instance, Christ, who was a great teacher used blue light to heal people close at hand as well as those more remote."

Changing the subject ever so slightly, he continued. "Comparing differing shades of colored lights and their effects is equivalent to analyzing various drugs. Every light has its own property, and therefore its own modification of correction. Healers on Earth have been using the light energy of Reiki for thousands of years." At this point Swuel raised his palms to us and shot red light throughout the room. An energetic restlessness stirred all of us into various forms of activity. I was suddenly compelled to tap my fingers on my knee, Gail was tapping her feet, and someone behind us was panting as though he had run a marathon. The walls of the gigantic room that we were in actually vibrated from these unaccustomed noises. Then a pale, green ray fell upon us and we immediately became tranquil. "If I had used black rather than green light, you would have suddenly become tired," said Swuel. "Black is a death ray and if used by many, several times daily, it would destroy life. The ancient Inca Indians in South America would surround a live tree that they wanted dead and destroy it using only black light. Every living thing depends on light to keep it functioning. Existence would inevitably expire if not for it. The true light of the One is pure white because it's the genesis of all forms of life itself.

That's why we call your sun Father, for without Him there wouldn't be existence. Nothing can survive in the absence of light. I'm sure that you saw the black spirits that eternally circle Earth; they are really dead and only black, empty shadows of their past. Without the light of One there is only blackness, which is actually interminable hell."

Swuel stood, still looking deep into our eyes, and I actually felt his gentle touch. When he had completed his appraisal of our spiritual standing, he continued, "Because this discipline is so important to the future of earthlings, we will be spending time teaching you the proper usage of light projection. This knowledge will be of great help to you and to mankind in general. We want you to bring pink, loving light into a cold dark world when you return. With enough of us issuing light, the world will become a loving haven for everyone. Teach everyone you can about its assets and freely demonstrate its awesome power. Using light, correct every wrong thing that you encounter. At first it will take a considerable effort to accomplish raising your energy to the necessary level wherein you can amend conditions. However, with frequent daily practice you'll have elevating results. Pink light is a perfect example of a color that you should use frequently—every day. Because it turns you into a powerful magnet, it will attract people to you and after being exposed to you, it will give them feelings of love. Using it daily for weeks brings your and other's inner Gods to life! All it takes is focus. Your Oneness is there, you need only to recognize it. As a result of repeated use, you change and adversaries become allies." Swuel stretched and paced back and forth twice, allowing us to think about what he had said—or so I thought.

When he moved into place behind the microphone he directed with a point of his finger, "Jim, please inform us of your discovery of pink light while on Earth. Tell us about its effects on you, your life, and those around you." I sat rigid, unyielding in my chair for another minute. I was feeling very uncomfortable about being singled out like this, especially on the first day. He smiled patiently and asked again. "Your story is important to us all, will you please share it with us?"

I was very unenthusiastic when I began, but quickly became animated and a detailed explanation poured forth. "I was a darkroom tech and not getting along with other employees of the hospital where I worked. Ten years of all but unbearable loneliness followed me in and out of my workplace. One day I was listening to an audiobook and the author was describing the different properties of crystals. I turned the book off when I heard her say that rose quarts gave off a pink light and feelings of love. I thought to myself, 'If a stone can give us feelings of love, then we humans should be so much better at it!'" I had purposefully raised my voice for my co-workers in Tesa so that I could emphasize those last words. I paused for a long time so that they might gather the importance of them. "Then, without informing anyone in the hospital of what I was doing, I began projecting pink light to my boss and other employees outside the darkroom whenever time permitted. Only weeks later I was being brought coffee when too busy for a break, being offered rides to and from work, people volunteered to help me shop or offered me rides to the laundromat. I was being invited out to lunch and even to some of their homes for dinner. While I developed x-rays, doctors came into the darkroom and discussed their patients or even personal matters. I played piano in a neighborhood steakhouse and my tips went from $20 at best to over $200 every night. The only change I had made is that I was projecting pink light, lovenergy, into the lounge where I was playing.

"Previous to my using this life altering energy, rarely would anyone approach me, a blind man, and start a conversation. In fact, the disabled are normally shunned. But suddenly total strangers were coming over to me and chatting while waiting for a bus or train. Many who I taught it to can testify to its overwhelming powers and all of you can easily learn it. I've even taught it to a six year old boy who changed his molesting uncle into a loving family member in only six to eight weeks of use. That's with using it for only 10 minutes daily, too! He told no one that he was using it until after his uncle stopped his molestations and had turned himself in for rehab. Everyone using it has told me about their personal experiences: new lovers were coming into their lives, unsatisfactory marriages were suddenly improving, abusive partners became best of friends, and commanding habits like smoking, overeating, drinking, and poverty were miraculously corrected. The list of their experiences is endless, for it is ongoing."

Before I could take my seat again, a man in the front row asked me, "Are you still feeling this same degree of love like you did on Earth?"

"Very much the same," I told him honestly. "But like any muscle in our physical body, we do have to exercise it regularly to maintain lovenergy's effectiveness. Like those muscles, the longer and more frequently we use it, the more effective it gets. Besides promoting love, I believe it enabled me to move to higher planes of consciousness and, thus, I am here. I do know that this is a consequence of my expanding love."

Another man said, "You must be missing your wife like I am mine."

A jolly-faced woman called out, "I'm glad to be out of my miserable marriage! That miserable drunk . . ."

Thinking of my lover, Claire, I nodded my head at the man on the right and said, "It was a perpetual honeymoon and man do I miss her!" Smiling at the woman, I said, "If only you had known about use of the pink light you probably would have stopped his overdrinking and made your marriage divinely romantic for you both."

"Him? Romantic? Poo," she scoffed.

Taking a step closer, I said, "It's only a matter of what I call the focus factor. Focusing pink light to surround others loves the One in them. As a result, their inner Lovenergy expands and they will love themselves and you more. Why are our feelings of love so much more powerful during engagements and honeymoons? Simple—we focus intently on that special person during those times. So, if we focus love more often on others, we are creating a transforming love within ourselves and in them as well."

Trying to prevent other questions, I quickly took my seat again.

Swuel smiled at me and I flinched at the recognition he was still giving me, especially from what he said next. "Jim, everyone has been desiring greater feelings of love. You've discovered a powerful way of creating it for everyone. When you return to Earth you've got to write a book about this powerful method. Humans everywhere need to learn your technique and learn how to use it effectively. Since the beginning of human existence, masters have been telling others to love one another as they love themselves. However, not until now have they taught a valuable method of creating love. You shouldn't feel so shy about it; this innovation is a literal lifesaver. If you had remained on Earth, via this commanding method, you would have been one of the first men there to advance humanity's ability to create love. We do know from eyewitnesses that Christ existed in the grace of eternal love. Also, He told us to love our neighbor as we love ourselves. However, until now, the common off-the-street person had no idea how they might achieve that ideal state of consciousness. Your ability to unravel a simple method of expanding our feelings of love is something to be very proud of and you shouldn't feel shy about sharing it with everyone. Because you unveiled and developed this technique, countless humans here and on Earth will learn to use its enormous powers." He then pointed to all of us assembled and said, "When you soon learn to use this technique effectively, you will personally know its awesome power. When you return to Earth again, Jim, we will expect you to also hold classes for other teachers so that they will teach it to humanity worldwide. As a consequence, everyone who gains this skill will be greatly assistive in creating global harmony. Therefore, we must teach everyone, person-by-person if necessary, how to create unconditional love of the self and others.

In a short period of time this technique will bring humanity closer to our ultimate goal for earthlings. Abundant love will generate everlasting peace." Smiling at all of us, he loudly announced as if it were the most profound statement ever, which it was, "No one can have too much love in his or her life. Not having enough, though, causes disharmony and as a result we have disputes and wars. Within the home we find personal, family, marital, and social behavioral imperfections. All of these shortcomings will be corrected by elevated feelings of love. You teach this pink light procedure to let's say 50 people and it snowballs, each of them sharing it with another 50, and you get the idea. My first assignment for each of you as you return to Earth is to search for Jim and become teachers in one of his love enhancement centers."

Turning his attention to me again, he said, "As you have personally experienced and learned from your students on Earth, this awe inspiring power influences everyone else near them. People need only to be exposed to the astounding power of lovenergy and they are transformed. Using your simple method will alter the most criminally-minded people in the world, and we've got to find ways and means of introducing it to every living person!"

"Especially to terrorists who nowadays could kill thousands in one swoop," someone cried out.

"Jim," asked Rama, "how did you ever come up with combining the words love and energy?"

"I told a born-blind friend about my pink light discovery and she asked how she might use it since she had no idea what the color pink looked like. I answered by asking, 'you know what love feels like don't you?' Well, just use the energy of love you feel. In my very next email message to her I signed my closing, Lovenergy."

After a short pause, Swuel said, "Please make yourselves comfortable. I am going to give you a short meditation to reinforce my instructions. Whenever the brain waves are slowed down through relaxation and/or meditation techniques, the subconscious is reached more easily. Now close your eyes and feel as if you were floating on a cloud." He was silent for about a minute. "Now say to yourself *I am totally relaxed* and feel your body responding accordingly. You're becoming lighter in weight. Notice your muscles becoming more and more limp throughout your entire body." Swuel paused as we followed his instructions. "As your brain waves slow, know that you are gaining more control over your entire being. Now relax and feel absolutely in command of yourself. No one has any control over you, unless you freely give him or her that power. Relax and feel your Oneness and know that only you control your existence. Life is as only you desire."

Subsequently, he spoke in a softer tone with a long interval of silence between each sentence. "Now visualize a luxurious pink rose in your cupped hands," he said, followed by a minute's delay. "See its beauty and smell its fragrance. Now sense the rose's vibration of pink light growing stronger and stronger in your hands. Imagine its color becoming even more brilliant." He then lingered for a longer period of time. I noticed the sensation and color intensifying. "Now absorb that loving pink light and its potent vibration into both of your hands. Sense its presence there and feel it gaining more and more strength as the pink light fortifies and moves upwards." Swuel paused again, giving us time to comply with his coaching. "Now allow this energy to advance up your arms and extend into your chest. Bring it into your heart and feel love's enriched light being pumped through the bloodstream to every cell of your entire body. Feel it arousing newly felt emotions in your mind, heart, and spirit." Following a short respite, he said as if from another place, "Be ye One's unifying lovenergy."

After a longer pause he said, "Imagine the palms of your hands facing someone here in this room, or someone special on Earth. See this pink light, or lovenergy if you prefer, exiting your hands, forehead, heart, and entire body as you project it intensely toward that special person. Visualize it encircling them and moving through their total being. Hold this love-energizing light on them for 30 seconds or more. Because you love the One within that person, the Universal One within them is returning that love to you 100 times more powerfully. Now feel that expanding love pulsating through your entire body. Notice your abdomens, the center of emotions, tightening and accept this divine lovenergy joyously." He was silent for a few minutes while we exchanged our newly enhancing love with those we had chosen. "Our ultimate goal for you is for you to be able to maintain this sensation of love 24/7. However, please know that even the best of us are unable to achieve that. As a result of your focusing on love, and frequently sharing it, both you and the person or persons will sense an enhancement of love and have spiritual growth. Jim told you before that he only used it 10 minutes daily and experienced growing feelings of love. He did fail to inform you that he shared it with five or more people. He divided those ten minutes into two or three-minute sessions, so he was doing it 10 to 15 times daily. We all know that the more the better. Unless, of course, you find yourselves becoming overly passionate and it does happen, believe me! In case you do find yourselves becoming too emotional, back off a bit on its usage. This is your tool for bringing more love into your lives; use this transforming power prudently."

Gail was the person who I had chosen, and feeling a more powerful sensation in my gut than ever before, I believe that she had also chosen me as the focal point of her love projection. In any case, the power that we all sensed was most profound and impressive. Despite its very familiar sensation, I enlarged in its glorious feelings of compelling love.

After a long pause and the pink light exchange, Swuel spoke to us again. "I want you to remain in this loving meditative state of consciousness. From your hearts I want you to say these enlightening phrases three times each. Paraphrasing them is permissible. Now mentally repeat, 'I am love energy and I love myself as well as others.'" He waited a few seconds before continuing. "'I am, I am, I am One, the very source of lovenergy. I love life and will make it more fulfilling for everyone alive.'" He paused another moment so that we could repeat it. "'I am the energy of love. I am the purity of One's unconditional lovenergy. I can effectively share loving, healing, and any other corrective light I desire. I am the light energy of lovenergy.'" With emphasis, he said, "With all of your emotions think 'I am' and breathe deeply while feeling these words: 'I am, I am, I am. I am One's divine lovenergy.' Now imagine yourselves unified with One and rejoice in these powerful sensations of love."

Following a long pause, he said, "Please remain relaxed and aware of your heightened understanding of love." Once again he paused before instructing, "At the count of five, you will be completely awake, feeling sharp and alert. One, slowly your brainwaves are becoming more active. Two, you are feeling more aroused with every ascending number. Three, your brain waves are becoming faster and you're becoming more awake. Four, you are virtually awake now and your eyes are slowly opening. Five, you are totally awake and feeling wonderful."

I noticed that I was still feeling this love and wondered if someone was perhaps projecting it still. Then, without even giving it any further thought, an inner knowing informed me that 'exchanging' was the right word for it because I was still projecting it to Gail's Oneness, as she was focusing it on me in return. This lovenergy made all of us One and we all celebrated with our sensations of Oneness. We were many drops of water in the eternal sea of One.

Following another moment of silence, he said, "All of humanity are equal drops of water in the sea of One. When you return to Earth, your most important job is to help mankind realize this truth for themselves. Now if you feel so inclined, you are free to stand, stretch, converse, whatever. We will resume in a few minutes."

Gail and I simultaneously reached out and touched each other. Our eyes embraced the others spirit in camaraderie. I knew, at that moment, that she had decidedly experienced my pink loving light just as strongly as I had felt hers.

I then perceived a peculiar sensation, like I was being observed. Promptly, I turned and saw Rama staring straight ahead. Then, from the corner of my eyes, I caught Swuel's eyes fastened upon Gail and me. I looked directly into his eyes, smiled, and gradually stood and stretched. Gail, I noticed delightedly, had done the same. We accidentally touched again and stared in wonderment at one another. Both of us were evidently having arousing sensations. *I love you, Gail*, I thought. Our eyes met in common knowledge, and nodding wordlessly, her lips separated and a Mona Lisa smile snuck out.

Seconds later, Swuel cleared his throat and said, "Please be seated."

Waiting until the room had become completely silent, he asked, "Are there any questions?"

A hand on the left side of the room rose immediately. "Yes, Lou?" asked Swuel, bowing deeply in his direction.

"Rationally speaking, Master, how do we send an enemy lovenergy? If I feel hatred for them and they for me, how can we exchange divine lovenergy?"

"One doesn't exist within us; all, but the darkest spirits, reside in the wholeness of One," said Swuel matter of factly. You love One, for it is One who is having a human experience."

A man standing behind me followed that question with, "Swuel, you said during that great meditation that we are the creators. I had thought that God—ah, I mean One, was the only creator?"

"One initiated existence, and everything consists of His lovenergy. In fact, all existence is the continuous manifestation of His everlasting energizing spirit. He is the origin of all life forms," Swuel replied with a warm smile. "However, it's His creatures who proliferate their own kind. Being an extension of His eternal spirit, His powers are our own. This means that we have the capacity to create our own lives to our specifications. Because mankind has been in the dark regarding this truth, subconsciously they commonly accept whatever living conditions befall them. As a student of mine, H. P. Blavatsky (1831-1891) aptly said, 'Thou shalt not separate thy being from BEING, and the rest, but merge the Ocean in the deep, the drop within the Ocean are one.' The truth is like drops of water, each of us are part of this eternal sea of One. Therefore, we are equal parts of Him and able to create our own living conditions. We are many parts/cells/atoms in the beingness of One.

By your actions during your lives you can choose to take part in a swift moving undercurrent, be tiny ripples, or huge life altering title waves. Now that you are cognizant of your powers, why not take charge of your lives and direct them as you desire? The Latin interpretation of desire is Father, thus it isn't evil to desire. The concept of evil is an illusion! You don't have to just adopt circumstances as they transpire. Formulate your own life style and live the way that you consciously choose."

"Most importantly," he said, following a slight pause, "we want you to realize that our physical and metaphysical bodies are divinely three dimensional—mind, body, and spirit. All three of which comprise the essence of One. In other words, this genuine Holy Trinity of self really is the unblemished Universal One. Nevertheless, our minds, bodies, and spirits did become defiled by wrong interpretation of evil by teachers and other respectable authorities. They generated a self-imposed feeling of guilt, thus a division between us and the perfection of our beloved One. I want you to understand that in this case I am talking about One as in Universal Spirit. Because we are truly universal as is our creator, His might is made manifest by the degree of belief of our divine sanctity of self. This is to say, mind, body, and spirit. He paused a longer period of time and told us, "I don't mean to be so repetitive, but we do need to raise your minds from the quagmire where they presently reside. We've got years of brainwashing to overcome in nearly all of you, so it is necessary for you to comprehend these new concepts thoroughly. Although, in an attempt to keep your attention, I will be trying to say them in slightly different ways."

He took a few mouthfuls of water and started again. "Most of Earth's religions falsely teach humans that they are born in sin! What a repulsive thing to have to live with," he said with disgust. "No wonder children and adults fall victims to mental illnesses like suicide and criminal behavior! From day one they are taught to believe that they were created by an immoral act, ergo they are evil beings. All of their lives they are taught that they are born in 'original sin', that everything that doesn't meet with their churches version of God's approval is sinful. This misconstrued dogma can only create upheaval and chaos in one's life. That view is so totally unethical and barbaric. No wonder humans are still having wars, killing one another, and hurting each other every way possible."

Another man to my right asked, "Here or on Earth again, will using pink light and causing a desirable woman to fall in love with me be an evil act?"

"For reasons you will learn, we mustn't become lovers here. If we still must define good and evil, virtuous and immoral, we are in trouble," Swuel said with a laugh, which we joined in on. "Well, Greg, if you are unselfishly loving the One in her, you are not being insolent. If, though, you are only trying lustfully to entice her, then you are abusing this gift. We humans are in One and what blemishes others demean is only another view of yourselves." After another moment, he said, "What we must realize is that One is us and we are One; there aren't any deviations from that truth. "Love thy neighbor as thou love thyself."

He called next on a chunky woman who slowly rose to her feet. Her face shown with pink light and she radiated love. "Swuel," she began, blushing profusely, "I really love my husband, but he was unfaithful to me. If we transmit this pink loving light to our spouse, will we have a perfect relationship?"

He prefaced his answer with, "I doubt any two individuals can have a 'perfect' relationship together. However, Rose," he said with a handsome smile, "the love between you both would have been greatly enhanced and he would have been less likely to look elsewhere for love. You both would have also felt happy and consequently coped better with individual feelings and thoughts that undeniably would have otherwise caused contradictory conflicts in your past." Looking me in the eye, he said, "Like Jim told you before, your personal feelings become so heightened that they positively influence those around you. With you practicing this technique full-heartedly, you would have been on a ceaseless honeymoon. Regardless, let go of your past. You are on another entirely different path now, Rose. Along with your colleagues, expand and grow in the glorious light of our Universal One."

A rather small man wearing a large festively decorated turban on his head asked, "When back on Earth again, Master, will we have the same ability of transmitting light and will it have the same effectiveness we are experiencing here?"

"Genuinely believe in your heart that you will have the same powers that you possess here and you will make it factual. Never have any doubts about your creative abilities. Any indecisiveness that you presently possess will leave you soon. Sustain a clear trinity—One mind, body, and universal spirit—and you will preserve all of the powers you gain while here with us. If you allow negative emotions like hatred, envy, anger, or greed back into your lives, your spiritual gains will be squandered. Keep yourself focused on lovenergy and staying constantly positive and all will go as desired. Your abilities and powers will be as forceful here on Earth as on any other plane you might decide to reside," he said with a smile and nod of his head.

"While on Earth, I've had trouble maintaining belief," said another woman bashfully. "Will our faithfulness be bolstered before we leave?"

Smiling directly at her, Swuel said, "Grace, you have always had stronger beliefs than most, but knocking from your loved ones and self-doubts have deluded your value of your faith. Naturally, it will strengthen again as your self-image improves. As far as faith, unlike earthlings, you have witnessed the absolute truth of One and that alone will boost your powers of belief. If uncertainty does occur in your life, you need only bring His pure light into yourself and focus on Him and His omnipresence in you."

"Does that also equate with strengthening our ability to dispatch light?" asked a tall gray haired man with arching shoulders.

"With practice and growing trust every endeavor will be magnified," Swuel said with confidence. "Just as I had said a minute ago, dissolve all of your doubts and with unfaltering belief in your unity, thoroughly believe that all of your desires will be gratified. We are the architects of our lives and we have the necessary power to create them to our own individual specifications. Words to remember: law of attraction, focus factor, and cause and effect. In simple words, what we focus on we cause to occur. Focus on love, your Oneness, your godliness, wealth, health, sickness or poverty, and you will create it."

When all of the questions had been addressed, Swuel announced, "This will end today's session. Whether or not you want to eat, sleep, walk, or fly is totally up to each of you independently. On the bulletin board in the master doorway of this room are a list of classes that will be held in this room between now and 10:00 p.m. It is not mandatory that you attend. We are holding them, however, for people who might be experiencing tribulations about loved ones they have left behind and the transformation they have undergone." After rechecking the time, he said, "We ask only that you keep your communications to a minimum. Also, please confine your activities to this plane."

Wishing in my heart to be able to talk with Gail, I asked, "Excuse me Swuel, but are you telling us that we can't communicate with any of our peers?"

"At this vulnerable moment of your transition," he replied mechanically, "it's much better if you refrain from open conversation. When all of you are at equal spiritual standing, having had some of your enfites removed, your convictions will not be challenged as easily by what someone might say. For now, please avoid lengthy discourses with your new acquaintances. Converse with them only briefly, especially concerning recent events. If dire need should arise, you can discuss any irksome problems with your spirit guide. Conferring with others about transactions that have taken place here today should be absolutely avoided except when addressing your guides." Knowing that he hadn't addressed every reason for us not to exchange words with our neighbors, he more slowly said, "In truth, because of your love enhancement meditation all of you are experiencing greater feelings of love. We must not allow ourselves to get overly friendly, especially with people of the opposite sex."

I stayed in my place, facing Swuel, while the room emptied. Sensing Gail's proximity, I felt joy in my mind and heart. Knowing only that we were following internal voices, neither of us moved nor spoke a word aloud. Without first notifying her, I rose to my feet. Aptly surmising my actions, Gail silently rose beside me. We seemed to be marionettes or rehearsed actors in a play. First we stood, and then in slow motion, turning on invisible strings, we faced each other. In perfect synchrony we both burst into enraptured smiles. As I looked into the depths of her soul through her windows of sight, as if a practiced actress, a tear glistened in her eye and dripped forlornly onto her cheek. Loathing what I was about to tell her, I reluctantly unsealed my lips and whispered, "Have a good night, Lovie."

A moan escaped her compressed lips as she murmured, "Goodnight." Impulsively, and without a moment's hesitation or forethought, I reached out grasping her chin with my right hand and pulled her toward me. I bent forward and kissed her firmly and longingly on her full moist lips.

"Oh, my, Jim!" she cried out in response. "That's just what I wanted you to do!" Her words touched me tenderly. They stimulated a warm place in my mind and heart and I wanted so to take her into my arms and love her right then and there. Our arms started to involuntarily rise, then fell heavily to our respective sides as rationality once again took hold.

Swuel then interrupted our longing contemplation of each other. "Please," he said as a little boy might, "stop this behavior and go your separate ways." Marza stepped in and took Gail by the hand and led her away from me.

Rama had also taken my shoulder, but I stood fast despite his directional twist of hand. "I must speak my mind," I said shrugging off Rama's hold. "Why are Gail and I both feeling this way about one another?" I asked looking into Swuel's eyes. "It's as if we were long time lovers in our past and united after a prolonged period of separation. It is unfair for you to expect us to hold off our long-awaited and overwhelming desires for a joyous reunion!"

"You told us only moments ago," said a retrieving Gail over her shoulder, "that we are the architects of our own lives, that desires are not wrong."

"Let it suffice for me to inform you now that you were most likely lovers. Being born again you often pick familiar people as family members in your new human lives. A whole lot of you will soon ascertain that you have one or more persons here who were close comrades and/or soul mates. Maintaining your composure, however, is mandatory; exemptions are unattainable."

"Swuel," I said frankly and with great feelings of discomfort, "neither of us can contain our enormous attraction to one another. It's inconceivable that we can last another day, let alone until this class ends, and I assume that we are talking about quite a prolonged period of time. We are both feeling a demanding need for expressing our felt desires for one another. I don't know how we can quell these emotions for too long."

Gail and Marza were just turning the corner and heading out of the large room, but Gail's last words reached us, "This desire is too powerful . . ."

"In a very short time, you and Gail as well as your guides and I will know all of your past lifetime affiliations. We will then be aware of the entire truth of your existences and all involvement therein. Don't rush headlong into a love affair that is bound to cause hardships for you both. It will disrupt this class we are all taking part in." Swuel looked me in the eyes and said, "We mustn't allow anything like that to occur. You've just started on a new and enlightening adventure. Why not tarry awhile longer and examine your emotional states in a day or two?"

That did sound fair, but I had to say, "I need—"

Rama stopped me with three words, "Give it time."

I allowed myself to be drawn away this time although I craved to discover the reason for this seemingly restrictive behavior on their part. Inwardly I knew that everything would be revealed; yet I yearned to learn more so that I could combat the opposition that was destined to come between this worthy cause and us. *For now*, I silently thought, *I must allow these crusaders to guide my every thought and action.* I did wonder, though, about what Swuel had told me about Gail and me probably being lovers. "Why don't I have any memories of her? She must have been a lover in a prior past life of mine. In as much as I have no memory of a former lover relationship in this last life, I shrugged it off. *Except, for your beloved Claire*, I was reminded. *In no way*, I argued with this inner voice, *Claire was black!* Lastly I thought, *These people have nothing to gain from deceiving any of us, so we are only to believe.* The idea of knowing all of my pasts, after undergoing some kind of meditation or something, excited me and enabled me to hold off my compelling desires of questioning him further.

Like a puppy, I had permitted Rama to take me for a walk. When rationality brought me back to awareness, I found myself standing in front of a one-story building. Like Tesa, this structure also had superb stained glass windows. Because of the dimming sunlight as well as the increased indoor lighting, the caricatures they depicted had a 3D appearance. They astounded me with their life-like splendor and seemed to be jumping right out at me! One in particular struck me in the heart. It was a voluptuous, naked woman with her arms extended toward me. In her outstretched hands she held a beating pink heart. As she stepped out of the glass in front of me, a dark shadowed spirit simultaneously appeared to move within and about her. I felt at once that this singular window held a message meant especially for me. As I stared at her nakedness, I thought to myself, *That possessed woman is here to warn me not to allow myself to get excessively involved on this plane with someone of the opposite sex. I am to guard myself against getting emotionally, mentally, or particularly physically attached to another person.* I felt deep in my heart that there was an element of danger to my progress if I permitted anything to get in the way of my spiritual expansion and this worthy cause. I mentally told myself, *Just cool your heels.*

"Would you like to have something to eat?" Rama asked me, pausing outside the buildings front door.

"Sure, why not?" I said automatically moving to the open doorway.

A repelling voice reached me as my right foot stepped over the threshold. "You must be extra cautious, Gail." That threatening voice belonged to Marza and I cringed inwardly. Despite what I had thought only seconds before, these words were menacing to me because it could jeopardize a relationship that I desired above all.

A part of me sensed that we were meant to meet on this plane and at this particular moment in our lives. "Why else," I mentally theorized, "would we meet here and end up seated next to each other?" I knew in my heart that this was meant to occur. *I mustn't deny what we both passionately want,* I told myself. Stepping back I whispered, "Isn't there another place we can eat, Rama?"

Piloting me by the shoulder, Rama took me to a bench under a large overhanging oak tree that rested only 30 feet or so from the building. "Jim," he advised, "you can't be running away from Marza. She was only guiding her ward. Nor can you escape the reality of the strong attraction that you and Gail share. You've got to face up to this truth, which in part you have already recognized. Being that you both are here, you've got to restrain your compulsive feelings of passion. I know that while in this dimension it will be days, weeks, and even months of exasperating frustration for the two of you, but know that there isn't any other choice. We cannot allow you to breach the trust we have in you, nor can we permit you to violate our law." He raised a finger and said, "You are the first couple to realize a relationship between you, but believe me, in only days from now we will have others discovering former associations."

"I don't think you know how difficult that task is going to be, Rama" I moronically replied. "Only once had I experienced love of this magnitude and that ended tragically. It is feasible that Gail and I had shared one in a forgotten past life, but who knows. In any case, Rama, how can I possibly tolerate denying my desires and powerful needs now that I have discovered this woman at this time?" My words were coming hard from my heart and my tightened stomach that was aching for the love I was being forced to deny. At this point I was almost ready to call it quits. On the other hand, I had been an unfulfilled seeker for many years and about to have powerful questions answered. I was more than intrigued and just had to learn more!

"In truth, Jim, because you both have shared a strong relationship on Earth, you are experiencing this craving now. So you are correct; you have shared great love in your past. I do understand more than you know," said Rama with true conviction exhibited in his tone of voice. "I, too, was once human. In fact, in the 16th Century, I, Prince Philip of Spain, was in love with Princess Elizabeth of England. Because of our religious differences I married her stepsister Mary, who like me was a Catholic. For the sake of peace, Elizabeth and I had to sacrifice our true desire for one another, even when Mary died. Rather than causing problems between the Catholics and Protestants, I was forced to forego a relationship with my beloved Elizabeth."

"My One," I said covering my mouth in shock. "How did you ever withstand not being with her?" He only replied with a shrug, so I continued. "You and Swuel said that we were past lovers. I would hazard it a guess that there are still unresolved feelings remaining between us today. It makes sense that our loving affiliation is amplified here by that fact alone and that this only increases our need for fulfillment now." Thinking of him and of the controversy that he was forced to accept regarding Elizabeth I said, "Rama, I can't imagine living the rest of my whole life without obtaining the woman I so powerfully desired! How did you ever achieve it?" Since you did experience it, I've got to ask, how do I put finding her now out of my life so that it doesn't effect me to the degree it is now?"

"As you are comprehending, Queen Elizabeth and I had also been past life sweethearts many times over. Like I've just told you, right now you and Gail are the only couple who have discovered a past life union. While on Earth you both were on higher planes of consciousness; therefore, meeting here you recognized your prior affinity sooner than your peers. After a few more mental blocks have been dissolved, several members gathered here will notice an identical correlation with another member. In fact, as unlikely as it might seem, we've had a few third-party homosexual and even bisexual relationships discovered on this plane. Now you want to talk about conflicts, let me tell you that you wouldn't want to experience that kind of contention. Also, the fact that we have men and women staying together in a loving community like this will produce feelings of love and sexual desires. With the breakdown of your disillusionments, we spirit guides will have to waylay several other desiring individuals. Like you, they will have to reject their passions for the sake of our demanding work."

Feeling pressured by this ache in my heart, I asked, "Rama, can I speak honestly and openly with you?"

He smiled warmly and with a nod of his head approved. "Please realize, however," he said, "there may be some things I can't reply to this minute."

His words stuck in my mind as I asked, "Swuel and you just said that we would be feeling the same sexual needs on this plane that we had known on Earth. If we do have these desires, are we expected to ignore them for the full extent of the time that we are here? Why can't we share them, thereby satisfying our needs? Just today we heard that there are not evil or sinful acts and that One has given us free will. Why then is it wrong for us to participate in pleasurable affairs? Especially," I said with a desirous ache in my heart, mind, and body, "when you consider that it is our married past lovers who we will likely be uniting with. I personally wouldn't think that there would be any objections to our sharing love under those conditions."

"Believe me, Jim, you are not the first person who has asked me the very same question in previous sessions. I can only tell you now that your reasons for being here are more imperative than satisfying your own desires. They pale in true comparison." He paused a long time, and then added, "Sharing pleasures is not evil, but it is what might follow that concerns us. Becoming attached to someone during this restoration of your spirits could be dangerous. First and foremost, procuring this spiritual goal of enlightenment as well as aiding our honorable movement should be your exclusive aim. Secondly, following your transformation, we don't want anyone refusing to return to Earth because of strong romantic feelings. You see, there is a reasonable chance that you aren't going to be relocated near one another; you could be vastly different ages, different races, or even sexes. Those factors could create chaos for you students and us as well. Our cause is far too great to take any risks," he proclaimed excitedly. "We want to avoid your futile waste of time by searching for one another or having to deal with any of the other matters."

"What are we to do then?" I inquired with a troubled heart and craving in my mind and body.

"If this problem isn't resolved to your satisfaction in a few days, we'll ask Swuel to assist us."

"Okay," I said inwardly grimacing. "Except, what am I going to do in the mean time about my needs? I feel the strongest desire just to hold and kiss her. Satisfying my sexual desires isn't even necessary right now." Rama, only once had I experienced this vigorous of a desire, both to love and to be loved. How on Earth am I going to cope with this intense passion?" I couldn't move until this question was settled at least. I also wondered about the need for secrecy among these benevolent people. "Why," I asked myself, "if everything is supposedly open, would there be a need for any confidentiality? Why are our guides prohibited from discussing particular issues?"

Rama surprised me by placing his hand on mine. "Jim, you wouldn't be feeling this crushing passion if you hadn't experienced intense love in your prior life. Also, you've got to realize that you have just had love enhancement meditations and no one knows better than you what a difference that makes in one's emotions." Then with determination in his voice, he said, "Right now for the two of you, Jim, you've got to be stronger than your desires."

"Rama, every time I see her or feel her proximity in a given area I am overwhelmed by feelings of love! My need to love her is irresistible. It truly usurps my integrity." The idea of defying my feelings for this woman was compelling me to speak candidly to this practically unknown person.

Rama did the unexpected thing; he stood, stretched, and said, "I think it's time for dinner." I watched him as he walked boldly to the doorway and entered the restaurant-like area.

I reluctantly followed him, pausing only for a weary thought, *I surmise that Marza is saying or already has said very much the same things to Gail. We are both probably feeling and pondering the same anguishing thoughts. How are we ever going to survive these powerful feelings without mental, emotional, or physical gratification?* I felt forsaken because there wasn't any straightforward solution to this problem. With feelings of apprehension in my heart, I took those drastically difficult steps toward the dining room. Even though I ached to see her, wretched feelings of despair assailed me. I knew that I would have to deny all of my emphatic needs. Accomplishing that goal was going to be an enormous undertaking and I reflected, *How am I ever going to be able to face her and resist this terrible ache she arouses within me? Why are my feelings so utterly awesome? We have just met yet I feel like I cannot do without her for a single instant, let alone days or weeks!* I had to laugh to myself; here I was in a vastly different place and all I was thinking about was finding a method of achieving mental, physical, and most of all, emotional satisfaction! *What am I? A man or a mouse?* I quickly pondered.

"Here in Tesa," said Rama after I had taken my seat next to him, "all of our cuisine is vegetarian. Our vegetables are organically grown in the most stringent of conditions. The farmers take great pride in providing and preserving the highest nutrient value possible in their produce."

"I am a meat lover," I mildly protested, "and have never been into the vegetarian cuisine."

"Boy," he replied with a friendly grin, "sounds like you are a lover of everything." I smiled broadly even though my heart and body ached for Gail, who was sitting only a stone's throw away. "Well, my friend, you are in for a pleasant surprise then. If I hadn't already disclosed the fact that its totally vegetarian food that you will be eating, I bet that you couldn't have detected it."

"Do you have something against meat eaters?" I asked, wanting to gain knowledge of their viewpoints and traditions.

"We don't like having to kill for our meals. Vegetables produce thousands of seeds before being picked, but animals, eggs, and fish need to be alive to propagate." He was correct about these very special dishes. It was impossible to believe that the scallops I ate later were made from vegetables. I prided myself on my taste buds, especially for seafood. I was more than pleased to find that the flavor and texture were so exact.

"Remember," he said with gentle prompting, "nothing is evil unless of course you hurt yourself or someone else by it. If it bothers you to eat an animal that had to be slaughtered so that you could eat, and you do it nonetheless, then you are hurting yourself and that is immoral conduct."

No matter what I tried, Gail kept entering my mind. Once overhearing more by telepathy than physical hearing, "Empty your mind of him, dear. Otherwise you will find yourself engulfed by voracious desires that will become irresistible."

"Rama," I asked a minute after I had heard Marza's warning, "Swuel did inform me that we were lovers on Earth. Knowing this, I am surprised that you ever allowed us to sit near one another."

"Your sitting next to one another happened totally by accident. We got there a bit late and they were the only two seats available for us. As I've have already explained, this is a bizarre occurrence. To begin with, generally most of our students have absolutely no idea of the identity of the person sitting next to them. Until you have been here undergoing meditations for a few days, it is impossible for you or us spiritual guides to determine how strong an affiliation might be. We did see right away that the two of you were attracted to one another, but had no idea of the power of your affinity. If we had suspected this dominant of a bond between the two of you or knew of it, we would have immediately exchanged seats with another student and guide."

I then asked myself a big question, *Would I have liked that any better? Decidedly not*, I quickly admitted to myself. *Besides, we would have inevitably met*. To Rama, I said, "Since our feelings are so distinct, it probably would have been impossible to keep us apart. Even if we hadn't been sitting near one another, we would have eventually met and been faced with this same dilemma."

A few minutes later Gail and her guide left their table. And as they passed, Gail nodded to me, a shy smile curving her soft lips. With a suppressed grin of my own, I said aloud, "Goodnight, ladies."

She nodded again and simply replied, "Night."

A few minutes later, while having rice pudding, I said to Rama, "You can't possibly tell me this isn't made with real cream and custard!"

"Okay, then. I won't," he said with a chuckle. "It's really non-dairy soy milk and white salba."

After laughing, I said, "I've got to talk with the chefs here so that when I return to Earth I am able to also write a flavorsome vegetarian cookbook. Any chance of my getting some of the recipes here?

"Oh, yes," said Rama shortly.

"Humans have to know how good meatless dishes can really taste. Are there chefs here that I can talk to and learn some secrets about the foodstuffs and preparations?" A second after licking my lips I casually remarked, "I bet the heart attack rate would really take a nosedive if people cut out or at least diminished their meat intake."

"In your room you will find a book filled with recipes that you will be eating here in Tesa. There also are many vegetarian cookbooks available for you in the library that we passed through today." With hardly a breath, he answered the last point I had brought up, "Not only would heart ailments decrease, but also colon cancer as well. Most of the meats on your planet are rancid by the time that it reaches its intended victims. As if that wasn't bad enough, it's known that it takes the human body up to 24 hours to expel those carcinogenic wastes from the meat. In the meanwhile, the colon is being subjected to those unhealthy bacteria. The human's digestive systems were created for vegetarian foodstuff. Our small intestines are far too long for meat consumption."

"I've read all of the health books available in Braille, but never read anything like that," I told him with surprise.

"That shows you the power of the beef industry," he said with passionate feelings disclosing his frustration. "They have a tremendous voice in America especially. It's a proven fact, though, that carnivorous animals like the lion have a much shorter digestive system, therefore, they evacuate much faster. Combine that aspect with the fact that their meat is fresh killed and immediately devoured; they are not fatally subjected to these bacterium like humans."

"How 'bout a chef, is there one who I can talk with?"

"I'll introduce you to a few tomorrow, remind me." Minutes later we headed to the men's quarters where Rama showed me to my room. In my large, new domain I found a queen-sized bed, a dresser, a closet filled with men's clothing, a chair for meditation purposes, and a desk with a new computer. I also found another room that contained a well-stocked kitchen and dining area. "I can see that you have furnished these rooms for any needs that might arise," I told him after he had given me the tour. "There are enough provisions in the kitchen to last me weeks, and that's if I don't go out to eat some mornings or evenings. Those clothes are also my size. Are they mine or were they mistakenly left by a prior student?"

"All of these things are yours," he said, indicating everything in the apartment with a sweep of his hand. "It isn't necessary for you to use the kitchen; its only there if you so choose. The freezer is filled with vegetarian foodstuff. I'm sure you'll find everything to your liking. We even have a piano in the lounge downstairs where I know you'll enjoy spending some spare time. Our comrades Gary and Frank told me that you are quite a good musician. I'm sure there will be others here with you, so you guys should have a few good jamming sessions."

Unfortunately, I really don't have too good of an ear. I had learned and memorized music from Braille music books." With a short laugh, I said, "Now I'll have to learn print music so that I can learn some of the pieces that weren't available to me in Braille."

"No need," he told me with a winning smile. "Becoming more and more clear and free of your brainwashing will enable you to spiritually contact any musician or composer you wish. They will enter your whole being and, using your fingers, play their pieces perfectly. You need only to believe and play. Impossible rivers to cross previously will now have bridges. They have always been there for you, but you have been blinded by erroneous perceptions taught to you from birth."

"You mean I can play like Art Tatum, Andre Previn, George Sheering—"

"Not just play like them, but you are allowing them to be you. Now on a more serious note, not to make a pun, in this very dimension we are in right now there are more than 300 other humans in their own rooms. You are all in different densities of this same dimension; if you ever lose your way, you need only to focus on this room, and you will come back to this density again."

After he had left I studied the computer. I had wanted one for years, but had found the specialized software and hardware made for blind users was unaffordable. *Well, now*, I thought, running my hands fondly over the keyboard, *there is no valid reason not to put this equipment to use.* I took the manual downstairs into the living room, where I attempted to read for an hour. Half of that time was spent wishing that the manual that I was trying to read was available in Braille. My being blind and not reading print for the majority of my life made it a bit tedious. I really hadn't expected to find it an easy undertaking.

The piano and Rama's information about me being able to perform as the composer who would become me, were however too enticing for me to ignore for very long; I honestly felt grateful for any excuse to discontinue the monotonous manual reading. I found the piano in perfect tune and started to play jazz just like Art Tatum might. Five minutes later another man joined me, took a guitar off the wall where it was hanging, and began to jam with me. A half hour later there were four of us enjoying light jazz together. Along with me on the ivories, Bill strummed the guitar and sang like Ray Charles; Ralph, sounding like Jean Cooper, played drums; and Jeff played a fabulous flute and saxophone.

Our audience, coming in one by one, soon numbered more than 70. They cheerfully clapped and sang along with us. We jammed for almost three hours when one of the men who had been listening found a utility room. It contained washing machines, dryers, a sandwich dispenser, and a refrigerator filled with cold soda, beer, and other high calorie goodies. When he came back with his last armful, we quit and gathered around a large table where he and another guy had placed the scrumptious drinks and edibles. We soon were engrossed in light-hearted chatter and enjoyment of these treats.

Bill approached me, and switching a Diet cola to his left hand, shook mine and said, "Great playing, man. We've got to do it again—like soon!"

"Thanks, Bill. You sure can play that guitar beautifully and man what a voice you've got! Must have been doing it professionally."

"Only needed to focus on Ray—"

Before Bill could respond further, another man asked me, "Was that your wife who you were sitting next to? You couldn't have just met her today! Even a blind man could see that there was something special between you chaps."

I swallowed hard and answered him frankly. "I can only tell you now, that we were past lifetime lovers. Swuel and my spirit guide Rama told me that everything will be disclosed in short."

"How the heck did you ever get 'em to tell you that?" he grunted. Following a momentary pause, he said, "My guide wouldn't give me the right time of day if my life depended on it."

"What life you talkin' 'bout, man? If you were willing to give up this life, I'm sure that one of us would happily give you the time of day!" chimed in a tall black man.

"Well," I answered the other man without paying attention to the heckler, "I had already surmised as much, and Swuel and Rama willingly verified my suspicion."

Another man said, "Jim, you must really want to get it on with that beautiful chick! It looked to me like you were ready then and there—"

I felt uncomfortable with this conversation and didn't know how to reply. Thankfully, before I could answer, Ray interrupted and said, "None of your business, Jack. Can't you see that he's feeling a little uptight about this subject?"

Lou, who had been aloof until now, stood and said, "Men, we aren't supposed to be talking about these kinds of things. Remember, we're not to discuss personal matters or events." He turned to me. "Care for an evening stroll, Jim?" he asked, wanting to relieve me of this conversation. After eating this snack food, I've got to get out for a breath of air prior to hitting the sack."

"Oh, yes Thanks, Lou. I'd like to get out for a good long constitutional before I retire for the evening."

Lou stopped in his tracks, after we had walked for a mile or less, and said, "We've got a serious problem here, Jim and I want to help you solve it. As you've been told, you've been picked among many others to be a leader when you return to Earth. This job requires you to always be in command of your emotions. You can't permit yourself to become lustful, restless, angry, frustrated, or anything like that. Those negative emotions will hold you back and even drag you down faster than anything. You can't allow what others say to you or about you influence your command of self. Because of your blindness in your past life, you have a low self-image and are feeling slightly unfit. Our feelings can be deceiving and even deceitful, thus we mustn't act according to them alone. Emotional sense is physical and shouldn't come into play regarding spiritual matters. Whether here or on Earth, allowing cynical thoughts to enter your mind means defeat. You've got to clear your mind of all perverse thinking and never yield to it again.

'Focus only on your union with One, and be ye the Oneness of Him.'" His words were softly spoken and very poignant. "Also, as you told your students on Earth, 'be ye the light of the eternally burning Lovenergy.'"

While I recovered I wondered to myself how much he would and could tell me about these people and this territory. I faced him and confronted him with my innermost desire for knowledge. "I don't mean to pick your brain, Lou, but I have so many questions I'd like answers to."

He smiled warmly at me and said what I had expected him to say. "I, too, am restricted from explaining everything to you. Right now you are as vulnerable as a newborn and we are only trying to protect you. I was seeing and feeling your reactions to those men and had to stop it before you had gotten too involved." With a friendly slap on my shoulder, he continued, "That's why Swuel told us not to become too friendly and to avoid chatting with others."

The wind blew gently in my face as I smiled shrewdly at him. The air was so free of pollutants and filled with fragrances of grass and flowers, which seemed to have a tranquilizing effect on my distressed emotions. A ways off I heard a hoot owl calling its mournful cry. Like him, I wondered, *Who and what am I?* The sounds of the night's insects nearly drowned out a dog's distant bark, as I asked, "Lou, I have been looking for the perfect woman all of my life. Except for one woman who I dated for too short of a time, I've been alone. I can't explain this feeling I have for Gail, except that it is most extraordinary. Even though we have just met, I feel overwhelmed with love for her and I know that she feels the same about me, too. Something has always blocked my way with women; I think that it was their fear of dating a blind man."

"There isn't any need of you going on, pal," he said sensitively. "Your problem is very clear to me, and delving into it now can only be more exasperating for you. I can only tell you this," he said, pausing for a long time. "You've got to guard against falling too much in love with her. Over and over again we've seen the terrible pain that takes place when reunited couples have to separate from one another again. All of us here want to save you and Gail from having to go through that dramatic heartache. That's what is causing us to try and dissuade any allegiance between the two of you." In a softer voice, he added, "We've had a few who refused to assist us, of course. They moved onto their own very private paradise, but never fulfilled their calling."

"It's already too late, Lou. Besides," I asked, looking him squarely in the eye, "why do I have to do without her? Being able to share love now, even if it were only a temporary romance, would be better than nothing!"

"Oh, come on, Jim. We're both adults! You know that sharing love always induces greater and greater desires for physical gratification. In short, physical and emotional affairs lead to infatuation and often to separation of you from our cause. I can only warn you that the two of you may not ever meet each other in your next coming life. Once you reach Earth again, there is no telling your age, race, or where you might end up. Let's face it; your chances of uniting again are very dubious at best. We members of this team must always do our best for uniting self and humanity with the One."

Even though I had heard this before, his words hit me extremely hard. He was spelling it out for me and his bluntness was most telling. Right now, however, I was already too involved with Gail. The most worthwhile thing about my future life was the idea of being with her. I knew that our being together either here, Earth, or on some remote plane of consciousness was primary. "Why?" I asked, burning inwardly. Facing me, Lou raised his hands and sent green light. Deep inside my head I saw a greenish glow and immediately afterwards I felt appeased.

When he had concluded sending me the light, he revealed, "You have to realize that you may not even be the same gender, race, or age that you currently are now. You could even be from conflicting countries. We can't have you traveling the world searching for your lost love can we? Especially under those conditions." His eyes took on that familiar look as he gently reminded me. "You have been chosen for a specific reason and your duty is to this cause. You've only just met her again; don't allow it to develop any further. It is entirely up to you to stop it now," he said with determination and force written in his sympathetic eyes.

"Life is filled with risks," I disputed. "Sometimes we have to take chances, Lou, and this is a prime example. My heart is telling me to take this gamble rather than saying goodbye forever."

He smiled, vigorously shaking his head. "You're possibly thinking of only yourself, pal. Consider Gail's feelings in this matter. She may not want to be without your love when you return to Earth months from now. There is no telling where you might end up or under what circumstances you might be living. In all likelihood you will have to do without each other's love. It might then be more humane to you both if you had only resisted having an affair here." He then sighed, as if recalling a painful memory. "I urge you to put an end to it right now before it goes any further. It is up to you to stop it before it has become impossible. If you don't confine your enthusiasm now, well it might soon be too late! After all, you have only just met again; cease your fantasizing about what could be. Cool your heels," he said with conviction.

I respected his opinion, but still refused to contemplate this thought and contended, "Isn't it up to us to decide our own destiny? What if you had met your wife Winky here on this plane and realized that she had been a past life lover? You can't tell me that you wouldn't be feeling differently about it then?"

"Like me, you and Gail are here for specific purposes and it's not to find each other, renew your loving relationship, or to go home together in new younger bodies." Taking another path he said, "Correcting human's problems and solving Earth's defects should be your only ambition." He closed his eyes and said as if picturing his wife. "To answer your question, though, you don't know how much I love my lover and lifelong wife Winky. In a similar situation I would leave her. Unlike you and Gail, we've been together many times, too. She is alive right this minute, yet I refuse to search for her. I'd honestly like to one day find her again, but I am not going to consume valuable time and efforts by endlessly searching. I know personally how indispensable your new vocations are going to be. Earth will not survive on the path that she is on presently. Without our help she has no future. If you neglected this new occupation for the love of Gail, you may not have an Earth many years from now. It cannot endure this carnage for very long. You and I were recently on Earth and personally know how bad it is becoming. The demeanor of everyone there is degrading and most wearisome. Bombings, school shootings, and mass killings are unfortunately becoming commonplace events on Earth today. Terrorists in third world countries are beginning to develop nuclear weapons. I'm sure that like me, you know what that denotes. It puts every country in more peril than we've ever known before. We thought it was bad when we had the Cold War to contend with, well, pal, we haven't seen anything yet! Terrorists have just begun more deadly carnage on our prized Earth. Their butchery is only going to breed more slaughter, creating hell on Earth for everyone." Shaking his head from side to side, he added, "And I am not getting into the global warming issue with you."

Following another reflective moment, he said, "When I've gotten a little more free of these recent spiritual defects of mine, I will be entering one of these very volatile third world nations. We need to concentrate our efforts in these troubled areas if we hope to prolong life." He took a lingering breath and disclosed, "Even if I was blessed with finding my soul mate again, I wouldn't subject her to the peril that is going to be accompanying me into my next lifetime."

His words rang true in my heart, but because I was so mentally affixed on this subject I asked, "You mean to tell me that you wouldn't put up a fight for Winky?"

"Never have I purposefully searched for her, nor she for me. Each time that we did reunite, it happened totally by accident. Only during three of my seven lifetimes have I been fortunate enough to share a portion of my life with her. However, there were the other four entire lives when we were unable to be together. I had to live those lives without her. Although, thankfully, two of them ended prematurely. Because we were apart during my last lifetime, I have no idea where she is living now. I don't have any idea exactly what her circumstances are—marital status, sex, race or age. For that matter," he disclosed, "we have no idea yet what any of my next lifetime traits will be like. My searching for her, therefore, would only be a fruitless waste of time and energy. We members of the cause have no time to spare for futile dreams or dreamers. In truth, I am afraid for you. You are going to be ousted if you keep up with your futile dreams."

"Boy," I said, running my hand over my face while totally avoiding the last point that he had brought up. "Those years of separation must have been enormously difficult for you both. For my consideration, I've got to ask, were you aware of your bond during those years of isolation?"

"I can't lie to you," he replied openly, "we are both members of this cause and I did miss her horribly. Once you have obtained cosmic consciousness you are totally cognizant of all your many past lives among other things. Yes, we had full recollection of our romantic affiliations. During two of those separated pasts, I was fortunate enough to find alternate women who were very amiable and suitable mates," he said looking me squarely in the eye. "Searching for my lost love would have been aimless, and it would have deprived me of sharing my life with those two very harmonious women. As it turns out, one of them just happened to be another past lover of mine and we were grateful to be united again." Following another deep breath, he concluded with, "Even the darkest moments have shades of gray and even some light. If not, there wouldn't be anything to denote darkness."

"Or light," I added, more wisely than I knew." It seemed incredible to me that he could resist searching or fighting for his soul mate and I shook my head with incredulity. "Lou," I said, mortified with my selfish feelings. "You guys must be at a much, much higher level of consciousness. I honestly feel that this matter is out of my control." Persisting even further with my own heartfelt conviction, I asked, "You mean to tell me that if you had met her here, like I've uncovered Gail, that you wouldn't have struggled to love Winky on this plane?"

"Jim," he said, holding my upper arm tightly, "to begin with, the circumstances are very different between the relationship of you and Gail and me and my mate. My soul mate, Mary, known to you as Winky, and I are both long-term cosmically clear members of this crusade. You and Gail are fledgling spirits who have just reached this dimension and this level of virtue. To begin with, if Mary and I were where you two are now, both being apprentices, we probably would be feeling the same as the two of you are now feeling. However, being more aware now, we both would ignore our passions even though we would immediately recognize one another. Finding out that you had shared a prior life together isn't that uncommon and you shouldn't be putting all this much emphasis on it." He took an audible breath and continued, "I wasn't going to get into this now, but I've got to be frank with you. Being that Winky and I are at the same status, if we were fortunate enough to die on Earth at the same time and meet here, we would be secluded from the rest of you. Only then would we renew our union, and it would be located in a private area on another different plane of consciousness. Unfortunately, you and Gail are not spiritually competent enough. You might have been just moved to this level after all?"

"Then how do you explain our feelings? It's as if we had never been different people. Please understand, Lou, this is different. I am fully in love with Gail; it is as if we have never been apart from one another. We are one in heart, mind, and spirit. I don't have any tangible memory of her, but believe me we are a perfectly-matched duo. You have made legitimate points," I conceded, "yet this case is dissimilar in its amplitude of intensity." Pausing a second, I said, "I guess we could go on discussing this topic all night and not settle a thing. Rama had told me that if after another day or so of sessions with Swuel

I'm still feeling conflicts, that he and I will talk with Swuel and see if we can resolve this problem."

"Will you take a prescription from an old doctor of yours?"

"Sure, Dr. Hibard," I said, smiling as I remembered how I had loved and trusted that old doctor of mine. "I just hope that it isn't too bitter of a pill to swallow."

"Even if this prescription is bitter, I want you to take it in small, frequent dosages. I diagnose you with an overdose of Gail. What I mean by this is that you were once lovers, sat together here, and probably sent love to one another in that powerful meditation Swuel guided us through. You have been seeing each other too repeatedly and while in a more dominant state of passion due to the love enhancement meditation you developed. For now, just circulate, sit, meet, and chat with other men and women. Don't isolate yourselves so much from others." He cunningly smiled and added, "If this doesn't correct the disorder, please feel free to call on your doctor again. Do keep this in mind, especially if the symptoms should exacerbate."

His wisdom made sense of my problem and with hope and appreciation in my heart, I said, "Like Dr. Hibard, I love you too, Lou. Thank you for coming to me tonight. You helped me to get a better perspective of things." After hugging we parted ways and I walked toward a densely wooded area.

The sun had set and there were not one but two full moons above me. Yet they appeared only as silvery shadows in the intense light of One. In this clean and purified air it felt like I could just about touch them.

I loved nature and when a sighted kid, I had explored the woods—catching frogs in a pond, raising turtles, and enjoying all of life's treasures. Because I thankfully hadn't seen Earth's slow but definite decay, I was horrified to learn of her decline. Mentally, I had visualized her the way I had seen her as a kid. "I would love to return to my lovely Earth now and take part in her restoration," I thought optimistically. *There has to be a satisfactory solution to this dilemma with Gail and me!* I cried deep within my heart. *If Gail and I aren't to be together when we return, then I've got to forgo thought of a future with her.*

I've got to assist these people in obtaining their unselfish goals for Earth and humanity! I walked alone rejoicing in this plane's awesome beauty. Even during my 12 years of normal sight, Earth hadn't ever seemed this exuberantly sublime. I saw the perfection of One all about me. The vibrant colors exploded before my gaze. A bird sang out a rapturous song of love, harmony, and peace. With anguish in my heart, I reflected, *Things sure would be a lot less complicated if Gail and I hadn't met here. I would have been so thrilled with this whole aspect and motivated by everything that I am learning. I would have welcomed the challenge, which this movement symbolizes. Now, however, there is this overwhelming conflict and burden in my heart, mind, and body. Finding this long lost love of mine sure has put me into a tailspin. Unfortunately it is desensitizing me to everything except my longing desire,* I sadly realized. I waved my hand indicating the beautiful landscape all about me. *This all now wanes in comparison to that unobtainable goal of my finding personal fulfillment regarding my awaited love. Who was this creature in my other life and why do I have such a heartfelt need for her?* I moaned. *Can I or do I even want to try to abandon her for this deserving cause? This effort is worthy of my full attention and devotion. I've got to support it as best as possible*, I thought as I tried fluffing off this other, very human, me. Realizing this as truth at last, I peered into the pure heavens above me. "I can't be of any service if I'm dejected from this movement because of unrealistic emotional aspirations!"

I knew in the wholeness of self, which was enlightened with my closing reflection. *I am being tested. There is a lesson here; lovenergy is Universal and my neglecting to help to alleviate planetary destruction could jeopardize my ever being united with Gail again. Earth is deteriorating and . . .*

This other me who wanted to escape lifted off the ground and flew into the sky while asking aloud, "Is there any way that we can be together if we decide to forsake this cause? Why, if I am spirit, do I feel so much like a man? Why," I asked as I moved closer and closer toward the shimmering moons, "are there two conflicting parts of me going in totally different directions? This emotional part of me can only find fulfillment in the loving arms of this extraordinary woman. While the other spiritual part of me is excited about the prospects of learning more and devoting myself to helping my home planet. I guess," I said, slowing my ascent, "that's what being a human being is all about."

Turning in midair, I did a sort of dive and headed toward the ground. Moments later, seeing a stunning sculptured statue propped on a very high tree limb caused me to suddenly stop in my tracks so to speak. Changing my course of flight downward I flew directly to it and admired its elegant details. It was of a fetching young girl who in one hand held a globe that emanated a moon's silvery light and in the other, a sun that reflected the light of One. Her necklace was made of miniaturized planets and her silky looking hair was crowned with a lustrous rainbow. To the side of this fairy princess hung a plaque that mirrored the light of the moon and sun that she held. It read:

> "Whatever the circumstances may be,
> You created it One, and have the power,
> Spiritual wisdom, and righteousness,
> To make its outcome suitable to us.
> We are I am. Because I am, you are.
> Whatever, is my choice,
> For I am this One!"

I whispered these words as I sat beneath the same tree. "I am One and in charge of my life. Gail and I can select our own mode of living; the choice is ours to make. Damn," I swore under my breath, "who the hell am I to presume that Gail will agree to whatever I might choose for the two of us?" Picturing her communicative eyes, I tried to read what my imagination was writing in them. "I cannot decree her future and this really does deserve cautious consideration," I deliberated. "Telling her to leave with me could encourage her to immediately exit my life. Or," I painfully whispered, "cause my superiors to excommunicate us from this worthy crusade." Before these last words had fully escaped my lips I thought again of Rama's statement, 'If all of your questions are not answered very soon, Swuel and I will talk over things with you.' Smiling gently at myself, I advised myself, *You probably shouldn't be concerning yourself with this now. Especially since this thought about a separation is so petrifying!* Rephrasing Scarlet O'Hara's words, I announced aloud, "Let's wait and see what tomorrow brings. After all, tomorrow may provide a satisfactory resolution to this disheartening problem."

I was suddenly taken off guard by a rustling and snapping sound that came from a ways off behind me. I stood and cautiously walked toward the sound of branches being moved aside or perhaps stepped on. Right in front of me walked a stooped old man who was dressed in what looked to me like homespun clothing. With a wide mouth grin he placidly said, "Excuse me, sir, if I'm intruding; just out for an evening excursion before bed."

"Quite alright, sir. You are not inconveniencing me in the least. I had thought that I needed to be alone, but maybe you are an answer to my unasked prayer and can help me to revise my wrong thinking." Anxious to get everything into the open with an unbiased listener, I said, "It seems like I have flown way off course. Quite by accident, I've met an old girlfriend or mate of mine and gotten thrown for a loop!" Trying to keep it light and not expose my stressful emotions to him, I said with an exaggerated grimace, "Because all relationships are being discouraged, all I can think about now is escaping with her."

"Well, it's the old story of the green VW. If you are instructed not to think about it, well, you can't stop it from popping into your mind. If it helps, you aren't the only one wanting to flee. I've seen a half dozen people tonight all with the same objective. This is true of every class held here, too," he assured me.

"I bet!" I exclaimed. "It feels as if things have been happening too fast and far too drastically for anyone's comfort. One minute I'm alive on Earth, and the next I'm living in another dimension where what I had previously considered abnormal is commonplace and reality has an entirely different perspective; I have to wonder what is going to occur around the next corner."

"He made a slight correction in my thinking. There are only three dimensions: height, width, and length. But there are endless densities within them. Having lived here most of my life, I know quite a bit about Tesa and its surrounding areas. I am the supervisor of the landscaping team here and have seen a lot of activity over the past three 300 plus years that I've been resident on this plane."

His words hadn't sunken in about being alive for more than 300 years. Impetuously, I asked, "Could I impose on you for your guidance?" Turning slightly behind and to my left, I asked," Would you join me under my tree?" I pointed it out and the two of us walked to it and sat beneath the still gleaming statue. "First off," he told me, extending his hand, "my name is Wadsworth Watski, commonly called Wazzy."

"Pleased to meet you, Wazzy. I'm Jim," I said, taking his offered hand in friendship, "commonly known these days as Confused."

His eyes glittered brightly as he spoke and I had the distinct impression that he knew a lot more than what he was about to tell me. "Well, Confused'ous," he said with a chuckle at his own cleverness, "I remember you once saying, 'Man with his head in the clouds doesn't have his feet firmly planted on the ground.'" Following a loud laugh from the two of us, he said, "Not only have you gotten your head in the clouds, Jim, but your entire being. Please give yourself time to adjust to these abrupt changes." He placed his warm hand on mine and said, "It seems to me that you are being unfair to yourself, your mate, and to these righteous people. They want only to reverse Earth's rapid decline." He held his hand over mine and I could detect that he wanted to say something else, so I remained silent.

"I was born on the astral plane and moved up here when I was 11," he informed me. "It was three days after my father had died. It was my choice of where to live and being of age and spiritual development, I decided that this plane was for me and came here posthaste."

Not being able to hold my curiosity back anymore, I took advantage of a short pause in his narration and told him, "I incorrectly thought that people came to this plane or the astral after they had died—a sort of heaven if you will. If not, then, like me, they were transplants or mind travelers," I said, feeling quite baffled by his proclamation.

"True and yet untrue. Let me explain it another way. When a human gets a degree in college he/she may work immediately at a given job, which demands such degrees. Or on the other hand, they may choose to work in a menial job for years. Whenever he/she decides, they can choose to enter their vocation that they had been trained for. One has to earn their way here, but once they are spiritually worthy, he/she can go wherever they choose. Matter of fact, sharing the power of One, we can even create our own plane to reside. You can opt to return to Earth if that is what you want. Although, reinstating yourself in a human body could take years. Newborn babies don't have any way of guaranteeing race, creed, or gender. Still," he said, raising his hand, "why even choose Earth when you really can go anywhere in this endless universe?"

Sounding like an old broken record, I asked, "Who would ever want to go back to Earth when we could dwell right here in this purified area?" I said this with great conviction after having taken another look around. "It also seems that here or on any other plane we had selected, we would stay the same age as we are now. From what you have already told me and what I've heard, we could probably remain this age and in this blissful utopia for all of eternity." I smiled at him liking that thought and asked, "Using your vernacular, Wazzy, how does one earn his/her degree? What conditions conduct our lives? I mean, what governs the circumstances of our being here or on other planes?"

"First off," he said, reminding me of the truth, "just a second ago you said that you were thinking about escaping. Doesn't that mean that you want to return to that Earth that you just scorned? The simple answer to all of your questions is love. Like all light workers, you want to live on Earth so that you might play a bigger part in saving humanity. Also, you want to live with this unrecognized woman. I did just say that you could create your own utopia, but that's restricted only to those who have reached your evident spiritual status. In other words, I am informing you that you have already acquired your degree while on your planet. Realistically, you could now travel to any plane/density and live there, including one of your own specifications. Even though you are presently having a difficult time, remember that you are reaping your awards right now. Being chosen for this crusade is an honor and your being here didn't happen by accident. Life is a learning experience. Whether here or there, we exist to expand our spiritual Oneness with the universal mind of One. Feeling like just an apportionment of the flawlessness of One, we continuously strive to reach His supreme perfection. Procuring unification is everyone's definitive goal. While living on the physical plane of Earth in the best of circumstances, it may take some souls many millenniums to reach His revered state of consciousness. Even then, there isn't any guarantee that everyone will reach this optimal goal." He smiled kindly and replied to my last question. "Your consciousness is quite clear of defects."

Without pause, he continued, "Right now, however, you are being influenced by the indulgent human who has just been subjected to enormous changes. Your discovering an old lover only affects your troubled psyche that much more. Thus, you become more agitated with all of these extra stresses. As is true with all of our mates at this level of consciousness, you and Gail have most likely been unified more than once on Earth. That's why you have immediately recognized one another." Getting very earnest he said, "Whenever you return to Earth, know that you will not be in the body you are now. You will be a newborn of who knows what age, race, creed, or color."

"Are you telling me, Wazzy, that we are not forced to stay here? That if we mutually desire, we can freely move to another dimension or even create one for ourselves?"

"Density, not dimension. We are in the endless universe now and there is really only one dimension. It's universal—going upwards, downwards, any and everywhere for eternity. This dimension is One. The cells of One's body are densities and you can go to any one you desire. Lovenergy is the zero-point force field, or endless force, between these cells, and you can even reside there if you choose."

"Huh?"

"Sorry, this is a bit advanced for you. In brief, the zero-point energy is One, the energy force that holds everything together."

Putting that concept out of mind, I almost asked a question when he said with a wide-mouthed, toothy grin, "Go ahead and ask. I don't have any teeth left so I don't bite hard."

"A moment ago you told me that you've been here for 300 years. What if Gail and I do drop out of this cause and, after a period of time, get bored with one another. Can we get back into this crusade then?"

"Why not? If Earth is still existing, you will be welcome."

Changing the subject slightly, he asked, "Have you looked into a mirror yet?"

I said, "Well, Wazzy, as you probably already know, for a big part of my life I was totally blind so looking into a mirror is not something I would do. Even if I had, I probably wouldn't have recognized even my previous self. In any case, why are you asking? Do our appearances differ that much?"

With a knowing smile, he reported, "Naturally, I have no idea what you had formerly looked like, but now you are in perfect shape and have a masculine and very handsome appearance. No doubt your body is functioning better, and hormone balance has improved, et cetera."

His flattery didn't abate my need to know what I desired most. "So what do I do about my enhanced needs?" I bluntly asked, still wanting to learn the naked truth from him."

"You will learn very soon in full, but for now I'll give you one word, 'transference'. You have to learn how to transfer your sexual zest into spiritual expansion."

"Thank you, Wazzy," I said after a long period of contemplation, "I can see that there are many things that I have yet to learn here." I had been debating about his meaning of transference, although the word seemed to explain itself. It still held mystery in its effectiveness in converting two such opposing views: sexuality and heightened spiritual enlightenment.

Before standing, he said, "Our learning process is only complete when we have achieved unity with One. Reaching Clear and then the Cosmic State of Consciousness are our next two steps up. Nevertheless, there is still a higher state, although, when we've procured this unified field, we are not ourselves but one in the essence of our One. At that point your learning will be over and you will be a living conscious and functioning part of the perfection of One. However, this isn't achievable for us until we have unfettered all of our mental, physical, and spiritual imperfections. At this point you are unable to grasp the meaning of unity. We are One now, but until this reality of our Oneness is fully understood and accepted by us, we will remain outsiders."

After standing, he took my out stretched hand and held it a moment while declaring, "Jim, I know that you will not be leaving this plane until you have reached the zenith of your stay. On this astral plane we call it 'Clear'. There is a lot of work in your future and you are going to be well fortified by your teachers here. Believe me, you will be totally satisfied with your future on Earth and your participation in its reconditioning. Your unique talent will help to make your future more fulfilling for you and countless others. You wouldn't be here on this plane if you were a quitter, so don't limit your true potential by giving your reservation a second thought. Rejoice whole-heartedly in this very moment, time, place, and present situation for it is purposefully taking you to an expanding bridge. Once you have faced and successfully crossed it, you can expect a spiritual leap into empowerment."

Feeling better now, thanks to his sage council, I smiled genuinely into his wise eyes. I was excited that I would be playing a part in this wonderful cause, yet I was puzzled about how I might take part in such an endeavor; especially when you consider my state of instability. With true gratitude, I shook his hand warmly. After I had heard him say that we could create our own plane of consciousness, I hadn't been able to think of much but asking Gail if she would share a private place with me. However, that thought had dissipated thankfully. I asked, "In case I need more advice, where can I locate you?"

"Like I've told you, I'm the overseer for all of the real estate here. Before retiring at night, I survey the work for the next day's work crews. You will most likely bump into me again while I am about my nightly business. If you are in urgent need of me, just mentally call me, and like your spirit guide, I'll hear you and come immediately. Meanwhile, don't be afraid to express your feelings to your guide, that's why he has been provided to you."

"Wazzy," I said, feeling reassured by his friendly and sage advice. "You are far more than a landscape supervisor; you are also a great aid to troubled hearts and minds. Thank you so very much for all of your knowledgeable and prudent support." We separated then and walked in different directions. I took slow deliberate steps back toward the men's quarters while analyzing the word 'transference'. *It must equate to my mental energy*, I reckoned. "How could it feasibly pertain to my sexual and emotional desires? Wazzy told me that it is transmuting sexual appetite into spiritual enhancement. I have to disagree," I whispered under my breath. "I consider exchanging such contrasting entities to be impossible," I said, opening the door to the men's lodge. "How can mere mortals change carnal drive into moral behavior with the power of thought alone?" I wondered as I entered. Having experienced the powers of love, though, I revised my instantaneous impression and whispered, "It needn't be just thought. Add love to this former concept and you've given it the gusto that will transform most, if not all, addictions and obsessions."

Thankfully I found the living room and hallways empty of occupants. I really didn't want to face anyone else right now. I quickly headed to my room and stared at my reflection in the bathroom mirror. My reflection squinted back at a fairly handsome friend. *Why hadn't I run posthaste to the nearest mirror on my arrival?* I wondered. *After all, I hadn't seen myself for eons!* My dirty blond hair had become long, red hair; my child's face was now masculine and covered in a full rust-colored beard and mustache. It seemed that this person looking back at me was familiar, yet our resemblance had been modified. I questioned my mute companion in the looking glass, "I did have a beard and mustache, but I don't think that either they nor my hair had been this long or this color." Unlike my human body on Earth, this metaphysical one also had very pronounced muscles.

I reclined in my meditation chair after a long hot shower.

Mentally, I pictured myself again. *How could I be recognizing this stranger in the mirror?* Then, like a bolt of lightning, it hit me. *Of course! I've been visualizing myself for years and deliberately aging that image, too!* I smiled to myself with the realization of my doing a pretty good job of it, too. *Yet I am more muscular than I was in that other life. Also, I've got a lot more body hair. Like Swuel and Wazzy said, I guess that I am really another being, created by my own ideal self-image. Comforting to know, though, that my mental picture wasn't too far off mark."*

Relaxing, I decided to take Wazzy and Rama's wise advice to hold off on asking Gail to join me on our own plane. *Waiting another day or two won't hurt us, and may in the long run be most prudent.*

Breathing deeply, I blanked my mind and moved myself into my meditation garden and only seconds later was deep into the meditation state of mind. I then used "I am One" as my mantra, visualizing One's pure white light entering threw the top of my head. A minute later, and totally by surprise, I left my body. Once again I found myself immersed in the light of One and His knowledge was being imparted to me so fast that I found it difficult to assimilate all that I heard. I became conscious of these concepts as if I were actually thinking of them: *I am one in the truth of One. Our mind is my mind and His spirit mine, also. All of our thoughts, imaginations, sensations, needs, desires, pains, fears, worries, and joys are equally shared.* More powerful words came into mind. *Be ye then one with my mind, spirit, and power of will.* I bared myself wholly to Him and profoundly felt a unique Oneness of self. My body seemed to be exploding with the hugeness of His presence. I was the embodiment of One, and all of the universe's planets, stars, and moons were portions of my dominion. I was all there was to existence.

The Earth was a severe pain in a cell of my universal body, and the sensations of its painful past and excruciating future drilled through me. A fragile voice filled with distress swelled deep in my innards. "Help us, Jim, the Earth is dying!" I shivered with dread because that voice had belonged to my beloved Gail and her tortured words affected me with intolerable pain. An aching desire to negate all of the damage to Earth filled all of my extended Universal Self. I was the tangible One and by my denying Him and this cause by my selfish, sensual desires, I was actually turning my back on myself, Gail, and the totality of Earth's present and future inhabitants. I then witnessed the destruction of large cities; horrendous storms flooded America and washed structures like the Empire State building away. The Earth quaked and whole countries were swallowed up. The disasters were far more than mankind could handle. Crisis reigned and chaos took command of humanity.

The desire to aid all of creation was primary in my entire being when I returned again to my body meditating in the chair. "How could I be so blind?" I whispered aloud. "The value of this endeavor can only be measured by its success. It is virtuous and the true reason for my having survived that serious childhood disease. I had matured into a spiritual being for this very purpose," I said, suddenly realizing. Now, due to this meditation, I knew how important I was in fostering Earth's viable future. "If, as I've been told, I am to be a vital part of this future, then I must stop my selfish thinking and behavior. I will be faithful to the truth of One and serve His cause to the best of my ability," I vowed with sincerity seeping from the very essence of my soul.

The very next moment moved me to another dimension/plane/density on Earth. In it, I found some of my beloved Catholic family who had passed from the life we had shared. We were so close that for a period of time I was them— their thoughts mine and mine theirs. I was pleased to find their homes very much the same as they had been during my childhood. It was Sunday noon and I was there just in time for an Italian lunch with my grandparents, Aunt Rose and Aunt Ann, and two strangers I hadn't met. While waiting for Nana to bring our Stone soup, Aunty Ann said, "This is Heaven and I hope that you are only visiting us for a moment, Jamie." She then introduced the two strangers to me as my great grandparents. I only got to shake their hands before I was zapped into another density where I saw Buddha, Krishna, and some of their followers having a religious discussion. Only seconds again and I saw Moses focused on a burning bush. I was about to look around when I heard a powerful voice telling me to return to my body. For the briefest moment I thought that it was God speaking to Moses! Then this concept brought a smile to my lips as I realized that it had been Swuel's voice that I had heard.

Effortlessly, I moved back into my meditation chair and outside my window, I saw a new and better day rising in the arms of the morning sun. "Today I am going to personally experience the meaning of transference. Suppressing all of my human weaknesses, I am going to manifest emotional control and mental stability. I know that I am on the right track now and I will not allow a single misstep, nor will I dodge this honorable reality another moment," I promised the omnipresent mind of One. My aura had the same purity that I was feeling. Great happiness and joy filled every cell of my body. "I love you One and thank you for this permanence of will and spirit. With your sustaining blessing I shall not falter on this honorable path," I declared as I dressed.

Painfully remembering those feelings of oppressive apprehension the previous night, I paused for a momentary reflection before entering the dining room. While breathing in deeply of the substance of One and visualizing His pure light entering the top of my new metaphysical being, I detached myself from these illogical fears and forced myself to cross the threshold. My eyes fell on Gail sitting alone with a glass of juice resting on the table in front of her. My heart was throbbing irregularly, but because I was feeling secure in my conviction I gave myself permission to approach her and ask, "Is it alright if I join you for breakfast?"

She flushed slightly and replied, "I don't know if we can risk it, Jim. We might get too flustered."

"Nonsense, I am totally in control of my emotions," I imparted. "The question is, however, are you feeling confident enough?" I asked. Without giving her time to respond, I sat down across from her and after waiting for some response, said, "I've spent the entire night in meditation. I know now that everything is going to be copasetic between this cause and us. We've only to cross this bridge to greater and greater spiritual enlightenment."

Her voice came out in a whispered gasp, "Really? I wish that I felt as certain about it."

I gave her an assured smile and nodded my head affirmatively. "Our feelings for one another are not going to vanish, but One will help us to keep them in control. We can be in perfect harmony with the worthy goals of this crusade." I paused for a moment, allowing my words to reach the totality of who she was internally. She had to comprehend the urgency of this movement so that she could also override her emotional upheaval. "Today we are going to learn a method of gaining control over our emotions. We are all here for specific reasons and it's imperative that we follow through with this plan. We must not desist in supporting these people and their devoted efforts."

"Do you really think that it is possible for us mere mortals to control these overwhelming emotions?" she asked with a worried frown. "To be candid with you, Jim, I am feeling strong passions and they are nearly defeating any of my good intentions. Right this minute I am not at all sure that I can suppress my desires all that much longer. What you've just told me sounds nice and neat, but aren't you maybe being exceptionally idealistic?"

Seeing her reasoning, I said, "Realistically, Gail, we are the only ones to be or not to be in control of our futures." I looked deep into her troubled eyes and offered, "I'm sorry my love, I guess that I am a bit overwhelmed with what I've learned during the night. Would it be easier for you if I move elsewhere?"

"Oh, no. Please," she said, reaching out to hold me back. "I only wanted some assurance from you."

"Yes, it is possible for us to master these enormous passions, Gail," I answered, hoping to reassure her with my certainty. "We are, after all, the people and creators of every condition in which we find ourselves involved."

Her cheeks became more flushed as she said, "Like I've told you previously, Jim, that's awfully nice and neat. For me right now, though, it is impossible for this poor, pathetic human to accomplish. Please tell me how I can arrest these powerful emotions?" She moved uneasily in her chair and I wanted to take her hand in mine and gently alleviate her fear. I withheld my eagerness to please her in that way because I was so concerned that it would only heighten our mutual emotions further. Right now, I felt myself in control and I wanted it to remain that way for the two of us. Knowing that the road ahead was invisible and wanting to avoid any chance of mishap meant that I had to preserve our passion. A little thing like holding her hand could disturb the serenity I was now feeling and I knew that I had to avoid it. I understood her emotional state, having been there myself only the previous night.

"You said, 'for us humans'. What you have to know is that you are not just a human, especially at this moment. We are all equal parts of the wholeness of One. As a part of the sea of the Universal One, He is us and we Him. He has given all of us free will and we can be either a quiet member of His sea, your own little ripple, or a giant title wave if that's what you choose. In any case, like I told you, today we will learn the secret of transforming our emotional and sexual drives into spiritual enhancement. Again, I firmly proclaimed, "Know that you are one with the love and understanding of One. We are His mirrors of universal perfection. These overwhelming sensations that you are experiencing are those of the One. His profound love is now a strong part of you. Release those that you cannot handle and allow Him/Her/It, I cleverly added, to remove them."

With disbelief showing in her voice, she asked, "How is it that today you possess such self-assurance when only yesterday you were shaken to the quick like I am currently feeling?" With only enough time to take a breath, she asked, "Where on Earth did you gain this assurance and your knowledge of what we will be learning today?"

"Not on Earth, that's for sure," I said with a laugh. "I met a man last night who gave me inside info."

"And I assume, like our mentors, you're not privileged to disclose anything." she said with her familiar Mona Lisa smile crinkling her lips.

Oh, how that smile filled my heart with joy! Captivated by her aptitude I unintentionally digressed and averted the subject. "I am impressed with your intelligence, Gail. Were you a teacher in your just concluded life?"

Her smile immediately changed into a grimace. Her lips parted and she irresolutely answered, "I have no idea who or what I was in my former life."

"That is impossible," I proclaimed impulsively. "You have to remember something about your preceding existence."

Gail shook her head and said, "I cannot recall anything of my past; it's totally a blank slate. This seems to be my very first experience of life."

"How can that be? Like me, you know that we had intimately known one another in a prior life. Although," I confided, "I have no explicit recollection of it I'm reasonably sure that we knew one another in this last life. I doubt that our feelings could be this dominant otherwise."

"I can't deny that the sense of knowing you is very strong. Nevertheless, I have no memory of a past life with you or with anyone else for that matter. It's as if I hadn't ever formerly existed."

Even though I was feeling baffled by what she had told me, I spoke my thoughts aloud. "From what I learned last night I know that if you had been born on this plane you would have some kind of memory of a past life. So along with my earnest feelings about you, I am persuaded that you did live on Earth and that we had known each other. Furthermore, I was told that both you and I were lovers back on Earth. What had happened to your past life memories is beyond me right now. I do know that we will soon learn of our pasts during a meditation and I guess that we both will have to wait for that day of reckoning."

Her smile returned and her discerning eyes inflamed my heartache a bit more. With a genuine look of relief, she replied, "That's comforting to know. Regardless, here I am and here I'll stay for an undetermined period of time." I felt myself relishing some time alone with her while desires of escaping from this glorious land once again flickered in my head. This time, however, I managed to remove it from my thought before my craving desire could vex my intentions to aid these people in whatever way I could.

We giggled and compatibly talked right through our whole breakfast. Moments before I left her, Gail asked me with an inquisitive lilt in her voice, "I had asked you how you had learned so much about this place and everything concerning it?"

"There is an old man by the name of Wazzy who works here. I met him last night and he apprised me of many of the things that I had been puzzling over. Because of our encounter and a whole night of meditation, I feel like a new and highly-inspired person."

"Marza and I spoke about this plane and this movement which we will be assisting. Until now, however, I didn't feel surer of myself and/or my reason for being here, but you've helped me there," she assured me with an appreciative twinkle in her eye.

Taking her warm hand in mine, I said, "Thank you for your delightful company during a delicious breakfast. See you later in class."

I jogged for two miles and followed one path to its very end. At that point, I sat on a large rock overlooking a pond with a few swimming ducks idly paddling past me. I noticed that I was feeling like a million dollars. The air was so fresh, clean, and cool that even after a vigorous run like I had just finished, I didn't feel exhausted. At home, my caring brother allowed me to hold his elbow while jogging. Running two miles with him would make me feel hot and quite exhausted. Remembering that time in my past caused me to think about my parents. *I hope and pray that they aren't taking my death too hard.* "No," I said aloud, a breath later. "Rama had told me that another member of our cause had replaced me in my old body! How he would recognize anybody who I had known, was beyond me. *How will he communicate with my loving family?* I wondered. *For a very long time he wouldn't be able to identify anyone, so how could he really accomplish a meaningful conversation with any of them? Will my family accept him? Will they notice any differences in my behavior or personality?* My next thought shot through me and I moaned slightly as I voiced it, "How would he survive in a blind man's body without first knowing Braille and cane travel?" Then I thought of my best childhood friend Lance. "I bet that he is replacing me! He did learn Braille and watched me use my cane hundreds of times before his early death." With a shake of my head, I spoke to the universal mind of One. "There is an awful lot of things yet that I'm going to have to learn before I am prepared to return to my endangered planet. Please help me One, to learn the necessary tools that will enable me to perform best for this mission ahead of me. "

Following a minute of meditation, I focused on the small lake at my feet. The pond was exceptionally clean which gave me the desire to do some swimming. I stripped down and did a shallow dive into the cool, refreshing pool. The water felt delectable and I swam to the opposite side and stood upright. At this end the water swirled around my waste. Two precocious ducks slowly approached me and stopped just short of reach. I slowly extended my hands toward them, not wanting to scare them off. Despite my caution they quickly moved away. I turned my hands so that my palms faced them and sent their quickly retreating forms pink light. I was somewhat surprised by the instantaneous results. They turned and swam toward me halting when they had reached me. Then, gently floating, they paused one, on either side of me, while I gently fondled them lovingly. "Thank you, One, for your Universal love. I find it wherever I go and whatever I might be doing. Life is more than perfect here in Your paradise."

I then did what most people would consider ludicrous. I bent down and gathered these wild ducks up in my arms. I wanted to feel even more love from and for them. Hugging them both, I brought their heads right up to my cheeks and whispered, "I love you wonderful creatures of One. You are the very thought and lovenergy of His pure land of Tesa and the entirety of the universe!" Love for and from these creatures poured into my whole being and pulsated through me like warm, passionate waves. After kissing them tenderly again, I put them back into the water and walked on shore. A large, flat boulder stood directly in my path and I used it for the very reason it was there. It felt so good as I lay down on it in the warm brilliant sunshine and light of One. I only had a second alone when, with my eyes barely shut, I perceived a scrambling noise. Turning my head in the direction of the pond, I opened my eyes and was startled to see five or six ducks coming out of the water and waddling clumsily toward me. I laughed loudly as they surrounded me on all sides. "So you want more love, huh?" I opened my arms and started sending pink light to them. The next thing I knew was that every duck in the pond had gotten on the same rock where I was laying. All of them had their heads touching my body and the two that I had first touched and held had even climbed onto my chest and rested their heads against my face.

Less than two minutes later, I heard a snapping sound on my right and saw Rama standing among the trees. "Excuse me, Jim," he said, grinning from ear to ear, "it's almost time for class. I've been observing you for sometime now. I didn't want to interrupt your discourse with these critters, but you do have to ready yourself for class."

"Sorry, but I've got my arms full right now." I caressed the ducks on my chest.

He stepped forward and all but the two ducks in my arms fluttered off in alarm. I then realized that I was naked and swiftly swung my legs uncomfortably away from his view. "Excuse me," I said with my back toward him. "Go to Tesa and I'll join you in seconds when I'm decent again."

"You bet," he said, rapidly rising into the air.

"Well, guys," I said to the ducks still in my arms and the others who were cautiously approaching me again, "you've got to excuse me. Tomorrow, or maybe even a little later today perhaps, I'll be back again." I promised them and myself as well. Walking to the pond's edge I warily lowered them to the water. "Bye for now, guys," I called to all of them. I began to step away when every duck faced me and let out a chorus of quacks in farewell.

Chapter 4

Transference

Minutes later I sat heavily in my seat, painfully noticing Gail's absence. "Lovie, where are you?" I whispered under my breath. "Why," I questioned, "am I disturbed about your not sitting next to me right now? Only an hour or so ago I was totally in control of my emotions. Now?"

Rama, sitting on my left, bent closer and said, "Remember what you had experienced only minutes ago with those ducks," he reminded me. "At the same moment you shared love with them you were expanding your own perceptions. That is why you are feeling so enraptured now; not that I have to inform you, of all people."

Before I had a chance to reply to Rama, Swuel stepped before the microphone and inquired, "I am sure that all of you have questions and impressions from last night and today that you would like to share with all of us. Well," he said after waiting a minute in dead silence, "don't all of you answer at once. Come on now, it was your first night with us and you've got to have things on your mind?" Although I wanted to tell everyone about my two experiences, those of my meditation and ducks, I had remained silent not wanting to seem egotistical. "Since none of you are willing to share those stories with us, I guess that I'm going to have to call on you myself." He waited a second. "Okay, Bill, you tell us about it," he said, pointing at the guitar player who sat a few seats to my right.

"Me and a couple guys," Bill started, after getting to his feet, "jammed out last night. I've been playing the guitar for years and I thought I was pretty good, too. Last night I really played exceptionally well. I played cords that had been impossible for me to play in the past. Even my ear was better then usual. My question is," he said after a quick look around the room, "do we have greater abilities here? Greater that is, than what we had on Earth, I mean? If so, will these abilities vanish again?"

"Yes and no," Swuel obscurely answered. "You aren't really any better, it's only that you are becoming more clear. You will find all of your faculties and skills improving as you become more and more clear of your brainwashing. Your own perceptions of yourself have held you back from reaching your optimal goals. Your worst enemy has been your erroneous impressions of your potential. As long as your faith doesn't become diluted by your old beliefs, you will be more competent in everything you do here as well as on Earth when you return."

Swuel's eyes looked directly into mine as I sat still and silent in my chair. After waiting another minute, I reluctantly stood and spoke. "As you guys know, I played the piano like a pro last night. It was like being a great jazz musician. I don't have an ear either, but what I did was to turn over my body to some of the greatest jazz musicians. For hours I played, felt, and even thought like them. I felt like I was inside them instead of their being in me." Because I didn't want to seem a showoff, I made my explanation of my experience with the ducks even shorter.

After I had completed my stories, Swuel said, "Your being here is a learning experience for all of us. You learn in three ways: One, by your teachers, Two, by individual experiences, and Three, by hearing testimonies from others," he said, raising his fingers as he counted. "We will be calling on you not only for your own benefit, but also for the good of the whole. In other words, don't be afraid or feel at all uneasy about relaying your personal experiences." Feeling that his statement was aimed at me, I nodded in acquiescence.

"Sir," said a little man in the front row, "I've never been one to talk with strangers. Last night I was one of the men listening to some great jazz and I found myself chatting congenially and feeling really confident in myself. Just yesterday I was a timid man, shy about talking with one person let alone before hundreds as I am doing right now. I have to wonder what could account for such a radical difference in my behavior?"

"None of you, Dennis, are the same person you were 24 hours ago," Swuel began. "Since being here, all of you have had enfites detached from your brains. These inhibitors diminish your effectiveness in whatever you might be attempting. In simple terms, they prevent you from reaching your full potential. You become conditioned by these wrong perceptions of yourselves." With a quick look around the room, he continued. "You can only progress as far as your psyche allows. Expand your mental horizons and every goal will be reached exactly as you desire."

After he had addressed another few questions and comments, he told us to relax. "One of the most effective ways of rectifying your backward thinking is by learning while in the state of meditation. Your subconscious minds function, adapting to new philosophies, much more rapidly when in a relaxed state. When your brain waves are moving at a slower pace you also have greater control over all of your faculties, and that is why we will be using meditation so often here. You are all familiar with your special place of meditation and in a minute I will ask you to feel yourself drifting off into that peaceful place." He slowly walked up and down the center aisle and, looking each of us in the face, either nodded or shook his head. I pondered about the reason for it. He went back onto the stage and moved behind the podium where he said, "I can see that most of you are ready to undergo this life changing process. Though there are a handful of you who are still feeling uncertain about our cause and the part you play in it. For those of you who are feeling a bit reserved, this next meditation should dissolve your qualms and strengthen your convictions. Before I get started, I want to tell you that you are going to be repeatedly hearing phrases over and over again. This is because we are reinforcing these teachings, arduously trying to transcend your numerous lifetimes' worth of brainwashing and degenerative conditioning. You've been hearing these outright lies on many levels of your mind for many lifetimes now. So as you might conceive, it's going to take us time to remove them and that's the reason for all of this repetition."

We complied by relaxing and, with our eyes closed and our bodies slumped and free of tension, Swuel guided us into another meditation. "I want you to visualize a perfect Earth," he said after he had counted us down into a deep state of detached attention. "Everything you see there is filled with absolutely beautiful color. See the oceans gleaming with differing shades of blue? As you can see, there are no waste materials or pollutants along the shoreline or adrift in the ocean. The creatures of the sea are strong and healthy, just as our Universal One had created them. Even the cities are clean and without litter. The Earth's rivers, streams, and lakes shine with the purity of this plane where we now reside. The trees, flowers, and grass show with the purity and brightness that hasn't been seen on Earth for decades. The blue of the sky is free of smoke and smog. Visualize the ozone layer full and without holes. Picture cheerful children playing and their smiling parents happily observing them. This is your planet! Its perfection is due to our joint success of corrective measures, which our crusade has made possible. Your loving care and perseverance has brought about these changes. Also, due to your work with Earth's inhabitance, world peace, harmony, and love prevail everywhere. As a result of this united effort, everyone is doing what he or she can to help their neighbor. There is no greed, hunger, neglect, or personal strife anywhere on your planet. More than anything you desire to maintain this level of purity and tranquility on Earth forever. Feel the love and pride in your heart for the alterations that have taken place because of your efforts. You are feeling good about your well-defined goals being achieved. Of course, it has taken you many years of love and devotion to achieve this essential objective, but your efforts show in Earth's perfection. Feel all the joy in your heart as you look at Earth's utter perfection." His narration stopped and I remained relaxed as huge waves of love, joy, and pride washed over me. "Now, with faith and belief in yourself, mentally say the following: 'Thank you, One, for your instruction of the ways and means of achieving these worthy aims.'" He repeated the phrase three more times and following a short interval of silence, he instructed, "Feel a perfect unity with the Earth and One. You have brought about enormous transformations and you are to be congratulated. Feel your own pride grow as you observe the perfection of your accomplishments on Earth." Pausing a longer period of time so that we could feel and think righteous about ourselves and our part in procuring and achieving our goals, he said, "Now that you've gotten an absolute faultless world, using your power of will, mentally say, 'I am going to give this project my utmost priority.'"

Following another short break, he instructed, "I want you to transmit loving pink light to all of Earth's creatures of the land and sea, and don't forget her vegetation." He remained silent for a few minutes while we complied. I felt love flooding my senses, mind, heart, and spirit. Breaking this tumult of feelings, which were making me more and more ecstatic, he said, "The love being returned to you is the perfect unconditional love of One, via all of His life forces. Whenever you transmit love to another, the Universal One in it will reciprocate. Because One indeed is the very essence of everything, loving another element of His creation is really loving the Universal One Himself. Therefore, as you generate and project love, His perfect love is returned to you hundreds of times over again." I was sensing spasms of love and pleasure as it quaked through my entire body. My stomach contracted in pleasures that were similar, I imagined, to what a woman feels when having a myriad of orgasms. "Now transfer those sensations you are experiencing into creative energy. Know that you can transfer this force, better known to you as sexual drive, into empowering powers of will. Learn to use it as the tool it was intended for other than procreation. It is a valuable tool of transformation, use it during tough periods in your life."

Swuel counted us out again and without a word left us alone to contemplate what he had taught us. The room remained almost silent. Like me, everyone was reflecting about his or her personal innovations and sensations coming from the meditation just concluded. For me, the Earth during it had been just as perfect as Swuel had described it. All of life had seemed completely natural and, yet abnormally beautiful and exceedingly healthy. Regrettably this parallel ended right there. The Earth that we knew today was very much different, having been defiled by pollution. I had only one desire now and that was to consummate this one supreme goal—saving my home planet.

A minute later, I was surprised to see Swuel go to the back door and appear again with Nick on his heels. That man who had been so mad at Swuel only the day before was now smiling warmly. "Please take a seat, Nick," Swuel said, indicating the chair next to me. "You have been privately instructed and only missed a few of our group meditations. On-the-other-hand, in your absence you did miss out on meaningful comradeship with your peers. It is vital to your progress that you don't miss any other sessions with us."

Walking stiffly as a robot might, Nick took the vacant chair next to me. I found myself involuntarily wishing that it were Gail who was sitting next to me instead. Without looking me in the eye, he vaguely said, "Hi," and continued looking straight ahead with a conspicuously robotic smile on his face.

Looking at us from behind the podium, Swuel smiled and nodded his head approvingly. "I hear in your thoughts your decisiveness in regard to this obtainable purpose. Your minds will indeed achieve this change. Your believing attitude is most essential to your achieving this goal." He smiled again as he looked us over. "It is gratifying to me and to your spirit guides that you are becoming more solid members of this crusade. With your help, achieving Earth's survival is closer at hand."

His smiling eyes altered slightly as he changed the subject. "Former people of the light like Christ, Buddha, and countless others have taught us that we are all One. The ancient writers were not the only people One spoke to; He/She writes today that we are the creators of our lives; that we create all the situations that occur. All humans are in different acts and scenes of their individually-created screenplays. Deluded thinking determines the outcome of one's performance, likely corrupting it at the roots. Unlike other humans who blunder their way through the melodrama of life due to inaccurate teachings, you will soon be experiencing the flawlessness of One. Being that you and the Universal Mind are becoming one with the wholeness of existence itself, you are capable of writing your melodramas to your own specifications. Every human is of course able to do the same, but because of their contaminated thinking brought about by inaccurate authorities, few recognize this fact. Instead, they act as only puppets, allowing circumstances, incorrect concepts, and/or others to manipulate them and their lives." He paused for a rather long time while staring deep into Nick's eyes. I couldn't help but steal a look myself. A callous, indifferent stare now met my eyes and I unwillingly recoiled.

Following a negligible shake of his head and an unrevealed smile of recognition, Swuel said, "To help you in your conviction of these new truths which you are hearing, we are going to guide you into another meditation. We want you to bring into your hearts, minds, and spirits the total truth of a new concept for some of you—that of our being one with the One. There really is no separation; you are the reality and the totality of One. Since He is everything, you are universal." He paused, allowing his words to be understood. Then in a softer tone of voice, he said, "Please close your eyes and make yourselves comfortable. Bring your minds into that quiet peacefully secluded place of meditation." He became silent while we resumed our relaxed state of mind. "Now feeling yourself totally composed, visualize yourself lying on a beach. Feel the sunshine, listen to the cries of sea gulls flying above you, hear the ocean's waves, and smell the fresh salt-scented air." I saw myself lying on a perfectly clean beach with an ocean as pure as the one I had seen during the previous meditation. However, because I had used all of my senses as Swuel had instructed, this one was a bit more vivid for me.

"One lives within all of us," he said in convincing undertones. "You, being a part of the thought of One, have His powers. Believe that fully and you will exhibit the power of One." For purposes of clarity, Swuel rephrased his words slightly and said, "You are One and you possess His powers. You can make this true by totally accepting our words as truth and believing in its actuality. By belief, we mean coming from your trinity of mind/One heart/your beingness and soul/One consciousness. Unveil your innermost identity and expose the reality of your Oneness with One." He paused while we executed our feelings of unity to the best of our individual abilities.

Taking a deep breath, he continued, "I am now going to guide you into a specific meditation that will greatly enhance your feeling of unity." After another minute, he said, "Now imagine yourself becoming smaller and smaller on the beach. Notice that the grains of sand are getting larger and larger beneath you. They are now the size of pebbles growing into small stones, which quickly become rocks. Feel and see them increasing in size, as you shrink. Each grain of pink sand has expanded into the size of large boulders. Visualize yourself lying on top of one very large stone. You are still getting smaller. See that rock you are lying upon expand into a towering mountain. See yourself sitting on a single atom of that growing mountain. Now you are shrinking more, moving into the center of that enlarging atom. See yourself standing on the neutron and see the protons surrounding you and the electrons spinning in invisible rings all around you. With conviction coming from your heart, mentally repeat after me, 'I am the center of every moving atom, even those in stones. I am the force that is lovenergy/lifenergy/Onenergy. Everything within existence is my creation, the wholeness that is I am.' Now feel yourselves becoming even smaller. You pass through molecules and subatomic particles. You are now the zero-point energy field, the One force that is everything, and holds everything together. Repeat, 'I am the center of the universe. Everything that is present, even the vacuum of space, is because I am. I am a part of every atom and have mental, physical, and spiritual control of their existences. I am the essence of every atom throughout the universe. I am One, creating all that I need and desire. I am capable of making my universe perfect, orderly, and pure. Earth's purification is my responsibility; I can and will correct her malignancy. Earth's safety and enhancement is my allegiance to myself and my brothers and sisters in this movement. Also, to all of mankind, and to the Universal One of our expanding awareness of self.'"

Swuel remained quiet for several minutes then had us repeat the phrases over again. After we had repeated the last one, he said, "Now suddenly notice yourself growing bigger. You are on top of that atom and still swelling, getting larger and larger. The mountain is shrinking below you as you expand even more. It is only the size of a boulder once again and getting smaller. Now you are standing on a stony beach and getting bigger all the time. The pink sand is only dust fragments beneath you as you expand further and further. See yourself growing taller, reaching skyward. The Earth is the size of a large pink ball. You are still increasing in size and soon extending into space. Soon you contain the entire universe within you; the suns, stars, planets, and galaxies are all contained within your boundlessness. You, the universal mind of One, are lovenergy: all there is to existence. Again, I want you to say with total conviction, 'I am all of existence. I am the universal mind of One. I possess His power of will within my mind and spirit. I am the universal mind and, as such, govern everything and have total control over all that I desire. My physical, mental, and spiritual desires are being transformed into viable energy, which will change Earth to what it had been when, I, One divine lovenergy, had created it. It's total restoration is only a breath away from where I am at this moment.'"

Having paused again, he said, "Now I want you to feel a stinging in your pinky toe; it is Earth with all of its impurities piercing your Oneness. Mentally caress it lovingly while repeating every one of these phrases three times after me, 'I will heal you Earth,'" he said, giving us plenty of time to repeat it three times. "'I will begin to create a strong, healthy Earth as soon as I return. I want most of all to restore and purify it to its original level of perfection. Being the power of One, I will have the ability of achieving all that I want and all that Earth needs so badly. I will love and care for it until it is totally well again. I will not rest until this goal for Earth has been attained.'"

We were counted out of our deep meditation. Afterwards, he told us, "Whenever you are feeling stress use this meditation to transfer that negative energy into positive power." He walked up and down the center aisle looking each of us in the eye. "I can see that all of you are now equally suited," he told us with a broad grin. "Despite this obvious fact, we want you to restrain from talking to anyone during the rest of the day. Meditate, walk, swim, play music, fly, read, or look through the archives of Tesa. Our only request is that you take part in these activities unaccompanied by your peers," said Swuel with a knowledgeable smile. "Go anywhere and do anything you like, but do it alone. Also, we ask that you abstain from food intake, preferring you to fast until tomorrow morning. The remaining parts of today and tonight are yours to do as you wish, use this free time wisely. Lastly, we require you to limit your flying to this plane only, we don't want you getting lost in this endlessly expanding universe."

As soon as he had gotten off of the stage, I knew that we were free for the rest of the day, and flew with a new inner feeling of unrestrictive joy toward the duck pond. I was feeling acutely unified with One and all of His creation.

Right now I was truly one with the universal spirit of One and with all of His existence. The inhabitants of the duck pond not only remembered me, but also clamored over one another trying to get to me first. We communed on a different level. We swam together, flew into the sky, we played tag, dove for fish, and had a tug of war with every fish I caught. We exchanged love of each other, life, and our own perceptions of freedom.

Following that winsome frolic, I meditated on the rock, which I had previously occupied. When I exited from a complicated meditation I found my companions lying closely at hand. They were completely quiet and motionless, as if they didn't want to disturb me from my meditation. Silently, I stroked them and thought over what I had witnessed during the meditation. *Love is your first assignment*, a voice had told me. Rather than being an external voice it seemed to come from my inner being, but I couldn't tell if it was my mind, heart, or spirit talking to me. With a shiver of gratitude I realized before whispering my thoughts aloud, "No doubt I am wholly portraying my Oneness. *You are One; the always present lovenergy*, that inner voice informed me. Then I heard or rather sensed, *Loving the positive things of life are easy, but our universal lovenergy is unconditional. Opposites like wealth and poverty, cleanliness and filth, love and hate, sharing and greed, neglect and , anger and compassion, or frustration and serenity—to name a few—are equal pieces of the perfection of love. In short, lovenergy is the curative force for all negative emotions and attitudes.* The voice of my inner One continued, *Always be optimistic, not complacent or impatient with yourself or others. Even when things seem to be going wrong, remain positive. Never fail to see the purity in every situation; even problems occur for distinctive reasons. Beyond every defeat is an advantage, every hardship a win, every poison a medicine.* Those words were said while I, being in a deep meditative state, had flown over various countries of Earth. While my other body still rested on the stone at Tesa, I was told by this inner voice, *There will be wars until all the people of every religion and country realize there unconditional Oneness. There is only one race, the human race. Your work will not be completed until your world becomes one nation founded in lovenergy and unified in the name and reality of our Oneness.*

Your spirit, I was told overlooking a battle in Africa, *will exist over and over again in different bodies. You will assume new bodies whenever needed. This will enable you to continue your necessary work with us until all of our collective goals are achieved. Our goals being a healthy Earth and a world of peace for all mankind.*

After I had witnessed this upheaval, I was taken over a future Earth. I saw friendliness and peace prevailing everywhere. In what had been Communist China, I witnessed Americans sharing work and capitalism equally with their Asian brothers. There was no inequality or harmful behavior. The planet showed its pristine purity in everything I observed. The air, sky, water, and land were as pure as I had first seen in my flight over the astral plane. *This is our new world that we will create. Until then, only financial chaos, inequality, war poverty, and greed will prevail*, my inner voice told me.

I then saw a horrible scene; the Earth was burned almost beyond recognition and practically void of life. I saw only one or two ailing trees per mile, a few weeds, no grass, nor birds to be seen anywhere. America was dwarfed in comparison to the past. New York, Florida, and California were gone. The coastlines were greatly diminished north to south and east to west, and a writhing ocean made living near it impractical. South America and Canada were gigantic ice glaciers, which crept south and north respectably. The horrible spectacle caused me to cringe. In my meditation I cried out with deep seated feelings of heartfelt terror, "My One, I will not permit this to occur! I only pray that my colleagues and I are capable of preventing these catastrophes! Fill me with your knowledge and wisdom. Teach me the necessary steps that I must take to prevent this terrible calamity from transpiring on my planet! Provide me with the learning tools so that I can avert this carnage from taking place!"

For a brief moment I found myself resting on my stone surrounded by my silent and very still creatures. I only had time to quickly review my meditation and then was drawn down into another deep state of unconsciousness. Mentally I was taken into Tesa where I was suddenly faced with shelves and shelves of books stacked from floor to ceiling. I quickly scanned a few titles: *Earth's Salvation, An Old and New World, Its Destiny, Life As It Must Become,* and *Earth's Ensuing Sons and Daughters.* Other books with words like, ozone, peace, oceans, needs, human enhancement, and purity, shown in the titles of books on other shelves also marked with golden stars. "How could I ever possibly read all of these books?" I ruminated with a heavy heart.

"Although corrective knowledge is being taught to you now, individual study is also essential for fulfillment of your enrichment of mind and acquisition of your goals. You will not be alone on Earth; there will be others who will assist you in gaining further comprehension and wisdom. We have many people who are currently involved in Earth's restoration. This class that you are participating in has many others who are mentally equipped with different bits of knowledge in various corrective areas. The Earth will have a better chance of survival with new wisdom and insight and everyone's cooperation in this necessary cause. It is advisable for you to learn as much as possible so that you will be better prepared for what lies ahead," said a stranger who had mysteriously appeared.

I perused the extensive variety of books over his shoulder as he NOW explained, "I am Hue, keeper of scripture." This slim, distinctive-appearing man had shoulder length hair as white as snow. His eyes held me captive in their depths of wisdom and his smile was warm and welcoming. "I will assist you in your search of accurate information and spiritual enlightenment. Feel free to call on me day or night for help," he said in a rich baritone voice.

I whispered in awe of his graciousness, "Thank you, Hue, for your generous offer of assistance." Then, impetuously, I asked, "Where do I start?" Waving at the endless shelves of books, I added, "We could fill hundreds of libraries in America with these."

"I would suggest that you get started in the beginning of course," he said with a laugh and a gesture toward the extreme left side of the huge room that seemed to go on continuously for miles. "Here," he said when we had gotten to the desired shelf. Handing me a large, hard-covered book, he pleasantly said, "This is easy reading and for a novice like you, it's a good place to commence."

I only had time to look at its title and was then transferred back to my meditating body. Its title was *Earth's Beginning and Future*. Picking my head off the rock where I had been meditating, I realized, in shock, that a copy of the book was mysteriously lying on my chest. "Now how did that happen?" I asked aloud with bewilderment in my heart and showing in my high-pitched voice. "No time like the present," I said, staring down at its cover. I was anxious to get started and didn't want to squander any time debating on how this book found its way onto my meditating chest.

Without any further prompting, Rama's voice answered this puzzling question for me, "Simple, Jim, you bilocated."

Memory of a priest friend reading to me about Saint Pio brought a smile to my lips. In that particular story I had learned how this saint had been seen in two places simultaneously. I shook my head in disbelief and said, "Me? In two places at once?"

Looking down now at the book, I read:

> The Abundance Of Existence Within One Has Neither Beginning Nor End. Therefore We've Got To Enable His Creation To Exist within One's US (Universal Spirits)." This caption was below a colorful picture of Earth—sparkling lakes shone with the lovenergy of One, and humans glowed with their unification. Opening the book, I read further. "In the beginning there was only potentiality and His Universal Lovenergy/Lifenergy/Onenergy. He/she desired to share abundant love and to experience existence in other aspects/dimensions/ apportionments outside of His universal soul self. So He imagined existence in endless forms. Until then there was only One, and nothing existed outside of His absolute Oneness.
>
> In time—although time is only an endless moment like an eternally long train made up of an infinite number of cars, each one decorated differently, but the same never-ending train—on a planet of a large Supernova, a wide variety of life forms proliferated. Human-like beings multiplied their own kind, each generation evolving. However, due to its high levels of carbon dioxide, this sphere failed and its inhabitants were lost except for a handful of Noah-like space travelers.
>
> Conscious that they were creators of their own destiny, they soon founded another planet they called Earth, which means "home" in their native language. In time, and in the enormity of space, these beings propagated on other suitable planets. Earth became a term widely used to denote home on whatever planet these beings inhabited. When one of these Earths failed, in the continuous light of One, there were always others available to reside on, and they always found suitable planets.

I was really getting into this and wanted to learn all that was possible. So I carefully scrutinized a few more pages.

> Human beings have inhabited the current Earth for 930,461,041 years. Its present inhabitants evolving as well as existing for the longest period of time—nearly 400 centuries. Unless the current residents learn to change their venomous ways, however, life on the planet Earth will expire for the third and last time. Unlike prior eras, Humans would then cease to exist in the Milky way, although human-like beings in other planes of consciousness would still exist. Earth's two previous periods of nonexistence were each 30

million years in length. Two other planets that have provided the necessary conditions for the evolution of mankind in the Milky Way are no longer available because of caustic pollution. As in former cycles of life, the Industrial Age has been destructive to the natural resources and environment of all three planets. As of this writing in 1989, the future expectancy of the Earth's sun is less than three million years. Its carbon dioxide level is rapidly increasing as it slowly defuses. Even if we were able to ward off destruction of our sun, the life forces on planet Earth face permanent extinction. The prevalent affects of her already beginning failures, due to human neglect, are the worldwide floods, droughts, deterioration of the ozone level, global warming, earthquakes, erupting volcanoes, radical weather changes, and worsening storm conditions; all of which will increase in severity and frequency as time transpires.

With feelings of panic in my heart, I was only able to read a few more words:

The irrevocable signs of her steep decline will be a shift of her axes. This last catastrophe will cause worldwide paroxysms and deaths. Billions of humans will be starving and in their desperate attempts of survival, they will become like mad animals. An irreversible end to all remaining life forms will soon follow. Therefore, if we fail to expand Earth's lifetime expectancy, this very well could be her final curtain.

I closed the book greatly, agitated with this bleak prophecy. "Please One, give me the knowledge needed to prevent this permanent destruction of my magnificent Earth." Tapping the cover of the book on my lap, I rephrased and repeated my prayer to One who was burning in my soul. "Please give me an unquenchable desire to learn all of the necessary steps that I need to take in order to assist in the eradication of these grim problems that face all of us homo sapiens and other living creatures in this part of the universe. If I am supposed to write, help me to remove all barriers that might block my way of being successfully published. Help me to have my revealed beliefs, truths, and teachings accepted by anxiously-seeking people everywhere."

The flame was ignited and I blazed with determination. Opening the book again, I read until the light of day failed. I had to finish the last few pages in the light of the nearly empty dining room. I drank three glasses of water for my fasting mealtime and then returned to the library for more reading material.

"Jim," said Hue, meeting me by a bookrack. "I know that your next vocation on Earth has been partially disclosed. Nevertheless, it is a little premature for you to be searching through all of these books," he said, tapping a large pile of them that I had set aside. "If it is indirect and general information you are looking for, I can better assist you. That book that I had given you earlier this morning is an unbiased known history, an introduction to our enterprising cause and a future prognosis of Earth. There are several others I'd like you to now consider reading. They are follow-ups and will give you a more distinctive view. When the mystery of your future vocations have been entirely revealed, I can better aid you in procuring the precise books that you will need in your studies dealing with those given subjects."

"I've got to learn all of this if I hope to achieve my paramount goal," I said, tapping the books that I had chosen. "Earth's survival is going to depend on us, and I've got to have all of the required tools necessary to make rescuing it feasible!" Indicating the endless shelves of books filling this stadium-sized library, I strongly pronounced, "One has given me a burning desire to read and learn everything possible."

"Excuse me," he said with wisdom written in his eyes, "But you don't need to study them all. In fact, that task would be monumental if not utterly impossible. Maybe if you were to be here for 300 years, but we need workers not just thinkers. Your friend Lou, who has been assisting us for numerous lifetimes, hasn't read a tenth of these books. He will also tell you how impractical that thinking is. When you accurately learn what your next occupation is going to entail, you explore that given area of specialization. It is only a matter of time until this unique aptitude of yours will be disclosed to you and your teachers. For now, I strongly encourage you to resist overwhelming your mind with the insurmountable goal of reading all of these books. Even if it were possible, by the time you got them read, there would be thousands more written. Like the light of One, universal knowledge is continual, extending forward and back through eternity. Until you become unified, cosmic consciousness will not be yours. When you do become one with the Universal One, you will know everything; the entire universe shall all be you. It is already, but you are not enlightened enough to realize this fact. Your spiritual enrichment hasn't yet blossomed adequately for a total realization of this truth."

"What do you mean?" I asked with a shrug of my shoulders. "Sorry but I don't understand your reasoning. I've got to learn everything so that I can better—"

"Excuse me, didn't mean to interrupt you. Like all of the other students who have been with us, you were chosen for a specific reason. Only when you are aware of your unique ability, do you go searching for that precise reading material. It's admirable for you to desire to more quickly reach your goal, but this one I am afraid is illogical. Learning everything is utterly impossible," he said while reaching for a weathered old volume. "Here, read this one next. It will inform you of some necessary vocations most essential in the reformation process. It will also give you knowledge to refer to in years and lifetimes to come. Not until your special expertise are imparted to your masters and you, will you be of much help?"

"As you undoubtedly already know, Hue," I interrupted, "I have developed a foolproof method of creating love and my masters here are leading me to write a book about it. I know that it will enable me to teach it to the world when I return to my next body."

"I think there is another necessary step for you to study beforehand. Undoubtedly, like most of us, you've got to polish up on your grammar, spelling, and home up on your writing skills before you try writing a book." He smiled benevolently.

"Okay then, let's take that for granted."

"At this point, then, English books will be a better place for you to start right now." I could tell that he wanted to say something else and waited patiently. Following a pause, he added, "Like all of your colleagues, you will be soon exploring many of your past lives. We all will see a pattern and on that data, determine your next human vocation."

I immediately recognized his wisdom and internally concurred. So without another word, I gratefully took another old book that he was holding out to me. Then with a bashful smile, admitted, "I guess I've over reacted a bit, huh?"

"Believe me," he said with a rewarding smile, "You're not alone there. Don't feel out of place. I must have seen at least 60 other newcomers today who have all responded the same way, and it is always the same with our new novice pupils."

I smiled, relieved that I wasn't appearing so ridiculous. "Misery likes company," I admitted to him with a laugh. "Thank you, Hue, for all of your patience with me and the others. We all really appreciate your help in this critical matter," I told him. "To be frank, when I got that book from you earlier, I wasn't at all sure that I remembered how to read print. I guess that it is like riding a bike; it's something that you really don't ever forget how to do." I tapped the new book fondly and asked, "By the way, Hue, how did I get that other book from here to where I was meditating? When I exited my meditation, I found it mysteriously resting on my chest."

Excited with this revelation, Hue startled me further with his ability of understanding.

"No doubt you bilocated. I would bet that while in a relaxed state you had a very strong desire for learning materials, so you procured your goal by coming here." Speeding up his speech some, he said, "This is evidence of another important area of competence in you. If this is truly your potential, when you resume life on Earth in the future, it will also be tremendously helpful to our cause." He took another weathered book off a shelf and turned to the index. "Yes, here it is," he said, like an excited child might on Christmas morning. "Page ninety, Chapter Eleven. 'The Miraculous Two'. This chapter will give you ideas about what could be done to help our movement by a person endowed with this rare talent. After you've read this chapter, I'd spend some time seeing if you can achieve that feat again." He raised his hand as if warning me, and said, "You won't have the same degree of urgency, and so I wouldn't get upset with myself if I were you. Most likely it was a one-time occurrence."

Despite his wariness about my ability to achieve it again, I left the library feeling jubilant and very optimistic about my ability to assist these people. It appeared that I would be of great service to this honorable cause, although, only time would disclose if I was really capable of bilocating at will. I was more than thrilled with my prospect of success and left with exuberant feelings.

I spent half the night in meditation and half in reading. In fact, the rising sun took me quite by surprise. I had lost all notion of time; hours had glided by like only minutes. I quickly undressed for a shower and prepared myself for another enlightening day of revelations. Somehow I felt expectant, as if something momentous was going to be communicated to me. I had failed in my attempts of bilocating, but still felt an inner assurance and peace about achieving it soon. Reading Chapter Eleven had made it very clear that once accomplished, doing it by power of will took only practice. So needless to say, I was feeling quite smug about my accomplishing it again. Though I realized that doing it by random was a whole lot more uncomplicated than doing it intentionally. "Soon," I told myself trying to bolster enthusiasm and positive feelings, "I will be able to do it any time I desire."

The air outside felt exceptionally cool and refreshing on my still damp body. The day was so clear that the sun overhead seemed to be shooting rays at me. I could actually see individual sunbeams radiating. "Thank you, One, for another wonderful day," I prayed, walking toward the dining room. "My only desire is to make Earth's environment this beautiful and perfect. Please give me the ability, One, to improve living conditions on my planet. If it is your desire that I be in two different places at the same time, then let it be so. I want only to serve you in whatever capacity is most essential."

You are my desire, I heard deep within my metaphysical body. *By serving yourself you serve this significant crusade and the divinity of One."*

I sat down and started drinking the coffee that had been placed in front of me after I had chosen my table for two. Gail wasn't there yet and I was hoping that she would soon join me. After spotting me sitting alone, Nick walked to my table and said, "Hope you, don't mind if I have breakfast with you, Jim?"

My heart sank. "Of course not, Nick. Make yourself comfortable," I said, pushing out the only other chair with my foot.

He smiled, although grimaced would be a more apt description of it. "Been enjoying this new communist world that you're now involved in?" he impudently asked me. "Our lives are no longer our own; we are under their command now."

His words seemed so very unrealistic that I laughed aloud. "Oh, come on, Nick. You can't believe that baloney? Where is your spirituality and sense of loyalty? We are engaged in the perfect world right now. With our support and vigorous efforts, our Earth will soon be as flawless as this plane. Our leaders here are dedicated to this worthy cause, as we have to be, too. I hope you—"

"I sure as hell do mean it and, unlike you puppets, I don't have to do anything I don't want to do!" he said, rubbing his hands over his black, heavily bearded face. He was a short, heavyset man with wide shoulders and a disheveled appearance that made him look like an alien in paradise. "I guess that I am the only person around here that hasn't been brainwashed and who sees the parallel," he stated proudly, as if we were blind, unknowing viewers of this picture of the real world he was drawing us. "I lived in communist China and know what it is like being under constant surveillance."

"Are you referring to our being under the eyes of our mentors?" I asked feeling perplexed and uncomfortable with his comments.

"Yep," he said with disgust evident in his voice. "It seems that we have no choice of our own around here. We've got to perform according to their programming or we are shoved into nowhere's-ville! And they," he said with his voice rising, " declare us brainwashed! Ha, it's they who are doing the brainwashing!" I shifted, ill at ease, in my chair. I wanted to leave, yet I didn't want to appear rude. Being that he had been in Communist China, he was understandably seeing things from a different perspective than I ever could. In my heart I felt that I must make allowances for him and so I kept silent. Following a short pause, he irritably said, "They are the same here as in China. You have to act, think, and feel the way they decree. If you have your own ideas and they aren't comparable, you are in serious trouble."

"Nick!" I protested strongly. "We are here for specific reasons. Our whole selves have to be involved fully in this humane cause. It will not be accomplished unless we can give it our undivided attention."

"Bullshit!" he yelled. "There's nothing wrong with Earth! They want us to believe that and needed us thinking and acting in one accord. They won't tolerate dissension between us and especially between them and us. When they have gotten us clear, our brains unfit to defy them, they will fill our minds with their contrived crap and we won't be able to fight their distinctive programming. It's time for us to band together and denounce their heinous violation of our rights. Otherwise it's going to be too late for us to do anything!" Without a moments reflection, he said, "You talk about their righteousness, well, just look at what they are doing to you and that beautiful girl. Why, you guys are meant for one another and look at what they are doing to the two of you?"

His words hit me right between the eyes and without thinking I bitterly responded, "What do you know about it? Who's doing what to her?"

"Well, I guess that I've got your interest now, huh?" he grunted triumphantly.

"Nick," I objected, "you weren't even there with us!"

"No, I wasn't there every moment, but that isn't saying that I'm not privy to something," he said. "After all, I was there when Swuel spoke to my guide, Wayne, and your guide as well as that girl's."

I reacted impulsively, saying, "Well out with it then!"

After a repugnant laugh, he said, "I overheard Swuel telling your respective guides that they were to do their best to keep the two of you apart. He said, and I quote him, 'They both are very important to our crusade, and we must deter an affair between them.'"

I wasn't about to turn my back on this honorable society because this man said something derisive. I knew my own mind and felt that this cause was essential for Earth's survival. I wasn't going to allow this person with perverted scruples to keep me from reaching a harmonious goal for us all. I had seen with my own eyes, the necessity of correcting human perceptions of life on Earth. Without all of us desperately fighting against things like hatred and pollution, it couldn't survive. Neglect was the most powerful tool of destruction against our planet. Every human played a significant part in its ruin and each of us crusaders needed to work for its preservation. I wasn't going to turn my back on her or the members of this praiseworthy cause. Looking Nick straight in the eyes, I coolly said, "Please stop your ridicule of these blessed people and leave me alone. Knowing what is right, and what is best for humanity I can't forsake—"

"Bullshit on your forsake," he bellowed. All eyes turned toward us as he said, "Gail is your long lost lover and how can you even conceive of turning your back on her! She's so glamorously sexy; you can't deny your mutually shared desires for very long. Face it, neither of you can exist without the other."

Mentally, I summoned Rama and said to Nick, "I've heard enough. Now please vacate the premises or at least go to another table. I will not have anymore talk of resistance here at my table," I firmly commanded.

Nick's next few words struck hard at me. "But she's sick and needs—"

"What do you mean," I asked him with his mouth still agape after Rama had appeared at my side.

"That's enough Jim and Nick," he said forcefully. "You are supposed to be like little children in this new world; instead, you are acting like enemies in the old one. Don't you realize that you are upsetting yourselves and your peers?"

"Gail. I only need to know if she's all right? Nick said that she—"

"Jim," Rama said consolingly, "she'll be fine in less than an hour at most." His comforting words didn't quell my desire to learn what was wrong.

In alarm, I stood and stepped closer to him. "Then she really is sick?"

"Its only emotional problems," he said reassuringly. "This often happens with women you know. We see it all the time, especially in the beginning. Look around you, there are at least a dozen women down with the same disorder today."

"It's their doing," said Nick, pointing a finger at Rama. "They have upset her with their forced separation—" At that moment Nick became very stiff and unable to articulate further. His guide Wayne appeared, took Nick's arm, and showed him clumsily out of the building.

"We thought that his attitude had changed enough that he could be included with the rest of you. I can see now that we were wrong in letting him mix with others," repented Rama. "We will continue working on reducing his anger. We will also try to fortify his ability to accept our word as the truth. He's needed in our movement. Nevertheless, we will exclude him from this class if he doesn't show improvement fast."

An hour later, Swuel stood in front of the 300 of us in deep contemplation. He was analyzing Nick who was sitting next to me and anxiously fidgeting with his hands. After coming to some conclusion regarding him, he spoke as if Nick wasn't currently on his mind. "As I have said before, meditation is the greatest method of reaching the subconscious. It is your conscious minds that pass data to this intuitive portion where it is stored and then when needed, forwarded to your consciousness where decisions are made. That's why conveying correct information to that inner knowing becomes so imperative. You will notice yourself after every meditation growing mentally wiser, more discerning, and more spiritually aware. I'm also sure that because of this unfolding of your enlightened self, you will be soon aware of your expanding vocabularies. In fact, a few of you may have already sensed some mental expansion. Because you are going to be moving into and out of past lives and having your brainwashing dissolved, your emotions, sense of being, and mental competence will all be undergoing beneficial altercations. You are to realize, as often as possible, that all of your experiences are past illusions. Be grateful for the lessons you will be gaining from any hardships you might have to face."

He quickly looked at Nick and then at Wayne; not seeing what he wanted, he shook his head. "Therefore," he said with a smile that brightened his countenance, which I noticed was aimed at Nick, "we will often be repeating phrases and be using the technique of meditation to escalate your evolution." He took a few steps away and circled around the microphone, then settled behind it again. "Now I want all of you to totally relax, close your eyes, and move yourself into that familiar place of comfort."

Nick, sitting on my right, swore angrily under his breath, "Oh shit, not more of this programming again?"

"I'm very sorry, Nick," said Swuel, "but we aren't going to accept this behavior from you any longer. We will not tolerate these interruptions," said Swuel, walking to the stairs and briskly descending. Taking a few more steps toward Nick, he said, "I guess we were mistaken about your readiness to return. You are obviously more psychologically demoralized by your incarceration in China than we had judged. It's apparent that you are unable to be with your comrades here or any other areas in Tesa." Shaking his head no, he said, "We cannot trust that you won't corrupt indecisive members of this group. So I am afraid that we are going to have to stop you from associating with anyone here."

"Man," said Nick, jumping to his feet and sweeping his arm and a pointed finger across the room, "do I feel sorry for you guys!" He roared belligerently. "You are becoming their brainwashed puppets and—" Swuel discharged blazing indigo light into Nick who suddenly became mute.

"We will have no more of this, Nick," said Swuel with restrained anger in his voice.

Nick's spirit guide stood and took him by the elbow. "Come with me, Nick," he said, directing him toward the back of the room, through the doorway and quickly out of view.

Swuel mounted the stairs and said, "I'm sorry for his display of wrath." He shook his head reproachfully and said, "We should have known after his behavior this morning that he wasn't ready. It was more aspiration than reality I guess. We did want him to be a member of this particular group. However, despite his deprogramming, his deep-seated resentment is overpowering our best efforts. He was a freelance reporter in communist China and was imprisoned for his insurrection and outright rebellion against the controlling forces. Unfortunately, it appears that he hasn't yet responded to his love enhancement and deprogramming. Although to be honest, we've only been using it for a tiny bit of time. However, if he continues to be this disruptive, it will affect all of you and we can't allow that to occur. He would have been extremely vital if he hadn't suffered and been influenced by the conditions he had to live in for so many years." With a sigh of disappointment, he said, "We have realized that none of you have his aptitudes and, therefore, we're in need of him. Besides journalism, he has done extensive research in the field of alternative sources of power. With him in our circle of friends, he would have been a great asset to our cause." He closed his eyes and sadly said, "So far, though, we've failed in our attempts to correct his unacceptable deportment."

I wondered why Nick was insisting on displaying his indignation. *Could he really have been that demoralized in China?* I asked myself. *Rather than be irritated by his behavior, I've got to feel sorry for him,* I rationalized. *What, though, if he is right and we are all being used?* Seeing the consequence of his perversion, I denied myself the right to speculate any further. I corrected my childish opinion and thought to myself, *This cause is not corrupt as he would like us to think, nor as he himself believes.* Mentally tapping my chest, I thought, *This Doubting Thomas in me is filled with so many uncertainties and that's even after what I've been experiencing lately! It is virtuous and deserves our honest and foremost efforts,* I asserted.

"Excuse me for interrupting, sir," called a man whose aura shown with the same clarity of Lou's, "there really isn't any reason for discontinuing his study with us. I'm sure we all can tolerate his temporary ridicule and outspokenness. I personally know that when he has received enough lovenergy and corrective meditations, that his conduct will improve sufficiently."

"That's considerate of you, Renny. We also feel that the power of love's purest energy will correct his demeanor. Nevertheless, I am afraid Nick isn't quite ready to collaborate with us in this class. Perhaps in a few more days he will be adequately removed from this distortion so that he is more harmonious. Until then, however, we are not going to permit him to attend these classes nor to mingle with any of you." He cleared his throat and half-heartedly added, "As you know, Ren, there are several densities here and two classes will be ending within a short period of time." Then he quickly added, "so there will be others starting soon when and if he is ready."

Clearing his throat again, Swuel said, "Now let's resume our meditative position." He paused while we relaxed. "I am going to count you down from number ten to one. Every descending number will take you lower and lower into a deeper and deeper state of relaxation and mind control. When I reach one, you will be in total control of your blessed sense of Oneness. Your brain wave activity will be greatly decreased and you will have greater powers of concentration. At that point everything you tell yourself or I tell you will have a much greater effect on both your conscious and your subconscious minds. When you've done it often enough, you will perceive things differently. It will alleviate conflicts which are challenging you right now." During the count down I noticed myself becoming more and more oblivious to thought and senses. I was intent only on his words and the relaxation that was washing over me.

Having reached one, he said, "Now you are at a deeper level of consciousness. Your brainwaves have slowed and you are gaining greater command of yourselves. You alone rule your mind and body. No one can negatively control, influence, or upset your tranquility. Relax and recognize this utter dominion over yourself. Your subconscious is now easily reached and under your authority."

Following a few seconds of silence, he continued, "Each of us are the creators of our own living conditions. Our sole reason for living is to obtain our desired goal, that of obtaining full awareness of the Oneness we already are. The only reason for us to exist lifetime after lifetime is to learn from our errors and use those experiences to grow spiritually. Eventually, as long as the Earth still exists, a majority of us will attain enough realization so that we are once again united with the universal mind of One.

We are actors in the great screenplay of life. How a person plays one scene in their life determines the outcome of their future. When you make an error in judgment or commit a karmic crime, you pay the price." He shook his head as if dismissing an impression and said, "This next concept is important, but very difficult to comprehend. Be assured, though, that I will do my very best to clarify it for you. If any of you need further explanation, I will be available to you after this session."

He stepped away from the podium and bent to his toes, then stretched tall. Moving back to the microphone again, he told us, "Naturally One can't commit an evil act, but the person He inhibits can even be a murderer." He elucidated this point with, "A gun isn't the enemy in war, but the soldier holding it could be. All good or immoral acts receive their proper justification. This implementation of restitution is known as Karma. The real consequence of human blunders is a loss of spiritual heights previously gained. This deprivation brings these beings to a lower rank in their current lives. Also, if bad enough, it negatively affects their future. Conversely, when humans have done good things for others and themselves, they receive good karma. Because we are bypassing your karmic status here, we are circumventing orthodox restoration. This bridges a cosmic law and requires us to breakdown all of your past lifetime enfites so that you can progress to the next level. All of you, including Nick," he said with a slight hoarseness choking his words, "have conducted yourselves admirably during your just concluded lives. That's why, my friends, you've earned your positions here on this higher plane of consciousness. Our job now is to prepare you for your rebirth on Earth where you will still be under the same karmic law. If in your next existence you don't live up to this law and thus create bad karma, it will negatively affect you. Now you know the reason why we need to break down your brainwashing and dissolve your enfites.

We need you passionately and solidly aiding our cause. During your stay here or back on Earth, you cannot be influenced by any opposing conflicts. They will only prevent optimum accomplishments and we must prevent that from occurring. At this stage of your enlightenment, any odious barriers will restrict your capacity to accept our word as truth. We can't have anyone doubting our methods of changing your old, adulterated beliefs; for what we say is genuine truth."

Following a brief pause for a few mouthfuls of water, he said, "Your reformation will be accomplished by daily meditation and positive affirmations among other things. Your whole sense of being mind, body, and spirit are undergoing immeasurable changes. Using meditation, we more easily reach your subconscious and will be more swiftly helping you to adopt an enriched philosophy that will bring about further enrichment. Simultaneously, we will be dissolving your implanted enfites due to those learning inaccuracies taught to you by your parents and promoted by religious institutions."

Swuel was silent for an interlude allowing us to digest his teaching. After it, he said, "Since I've talked to you for those few minutes, your brainwaves have raised some and I want you to relax more and allow yourselves to move back into that state of total control. Now," he told us a minute later, "with a feeling of optimism in your minds and sincerity in your hearts, the center of your emotions, mentally repeat each of these favorable affirmations three times. He gave us plenty of time after each one to repeat them as requested. "I am because I am, you are because I am, we are because there is only the One, who is, I am. I love you spirit of One, I am becoming spiritually aware of you and myself, I love myself better every day, I love life, I love people of all kinds, I am spiritually maturing, my life is under my control, I am the creator of my life, I love myself and will accomplish all of my goals, I am always in control of my emotions, only I have control over my life, I have great important aims that I will always procure, I am going to accomplish great things in my new life, I am becoming a new and better self, I am totally aware of my new vital spirit and soon to be new vocation, I am going to lead people onto the right path and, along with others of our crusade, improve the living conditions on Earth. There is no duality; for you and I are One, not two, and because you are, I am."

He paused a longer period of time after the last positive affirmation. My mind stayed still and not a thought entered. Moments later I found myself aboard a strange looking vehicle and racing across space. Albeit, I was fully alert, I somehow saw and felt It touch down on a tiny planet. Two human-like beings approached the ship and loudly yelled so that I would hear them. "It's been a long time, thanks for visiting us again, John, Bill, Jose, Renzo, or whoever you are portraying in this life! Fear not, for you are to be united," said the female.

Swuel's next words brought me swiftly back to my chair. "Remain relaxed," He had changed his position. From the front of the room, he said, "We are going to do another love fortifying exercise to improve your feelings of love. Visualize yourself standing naked on a pink beach. Using all of your senses, hear the sound of the surf crashing ashore, watch the curling waves approaching you, hear the cries of seagulls and observe them as they fly overhead, notice the regal palm trees on your right, and smell the fresh salt laden air." After a short pause allowing us to follow his instructions while using all of our senses, which I knew would enhance our memory, he said, "Now feel the sun's warm light on your naked bodies. The reflected pink light on the beach is soaking into your skin. Feel the color pink of the sand also being absorbed by your feet." Pausing briefly, he said, "Feel love's energy extending upwards from the pink beach as it penetrates through your feet and saturates every cell of your enlightened body. This love energy is made even more stimulating by the presence of the Universal One who is represented by the color pink. The sand and everything within perception was this same divine One. It is increasing your sensations of love that much more intensely. Feel your whole body vibrating on a higher plane of consciousness." My body felt as if it had received a painless electric shock. It shook with an inner vibration stronger than I had felt before, except, of course, when I had been in the presence of One Himself/Herself/Itself. However, this exquisite perception emanated from me—the true/One source of lovenergy. Yet I knew that it was far more than the me who I had known for all of my life. His pink light was authentic and true to my mind, heart, spirit, and new metaphysical being. Inhaling deeply, I brought this virtuous love into every cell, rejoicing with the feelings that more forcefully coursed through me. I was receiving pure love from myself, a pulsating universal energy that was more than just I. It was divine and every cell of my body celebrated in authentic pink light of this reality.

Minutes later, Swuel spoke in a strong contented voice, "Now that you have personally created this pure love of One for yourselves, know that you can just as easily procure His perfection of spirit. You are the essence of One and His love is your manifestation. You are in truth the embodiment of One. His love is yours, His perfection of spirit is yours, and His universal power, wisdom, and knowledge is also your own," he said, pausing for a long time. "Like a drop of water in the ocean is every bit the ocean, you are the Universal One. The sea's waves are your thoughts and actions; some are but tiny ripples and others huge title waves. Regardless, they are the sea, each created, reaping, and exhibiting their own powers of self-realization." He paused again while we contemplated his insights.

"Now please visualize a pink ball of light traveling over the sea toward you. It is 50 feet in diameter and moving closer. See it getting larger and larger as it approaches you." After a second of silence, he said, "Now visualize it descending and smothering you in pure love. The pink cloud of love from One surrounds you, extending beyond your line of sight. It expands the horizons of the concept of love for you. You are One and as such, you are universal love. Breathing in, you are inhaling the purity of One. Exhale, and you are adding your own love to His perfection, expanding this bubble of light even further. It extends for light-years, encompassing the entire universe and penetrating every atom in eternal existence."

Again he stopped talking so that we could reflect on his words. "Visualize two seagulls flying overhead and send them love. Watch them as they fly in circles around your head. From your exchanging love with them, notice your own sensations of love being enhanced even more. While your One is receiving more love within you, it is loving the Oneness in others more and thus it is an ever-spiraling expansion of love within the wholeness of One. It's an endless cycle of love compounding itself endlessly. Only by giving more love can we receive more. Love intensifies your awareness of love, and you will observe after a week or two that you are feeling happier, more loving, more optimistic, more caring, and more in love with yourself, others, and life in general. This effect will hold true even when you are back as a resident of Earth. Our major goal for you is to have the ability to constantly project love to others. In return, you will be loved perpetually by One and, believe me, there is no better union than that!"

Swuel walked to the stage at the back of the room and, by the sound of his footsteps, I believe that he walked its width and back again. He was looking us over for some reason, I reckoned, but he gave us no indication of what it was he was seeking. Resuming his place in the middle of the stage and after a slight delay, he continued, "Now I want you to create a bubble of pink light of your own. Increase your field of love until it encompasses the ocean and all of its inhabitants." During another short pause I noticed a thrilling sensation. It was like millions of little sparks of love being returned to me. These expanding waves of love became more and more intense as I sent the creatures of the sea more love. The Universal One's purest love washed over me and cleansed every objectionable offense of my life, and I became the embodiment of love itself. "Feel the love of all those creatures bouncing back to you. Allow it to flourish in your heart," he said, confirming my impression. Swuel was once again quiet as I exposed more of myself to the living animal and plant organisms of the sea. Without decisively creating it, I suddenly visualized new gulls flying into my bubble of love. They became titillating to watch—flying in silly showoff circles which became smaller and smaller. After awhile they were at the point of almost colliding into one another, in my imagined scene, or was it imagined? I actually was there witnessing and taking part in this presentation. In fact, I was designer, actor, playwright, and producer all in one. This self-created world of my imagination seemed to become a brighter and more loving place because of my awareness of it. I was one with my planet and all of its inhabitants. Animals, humans and plants were united with me in this perfect light of divine harmony. Their pleasures were mine, their feelings mine, and even my eternal hopes for Earth's recovery a mutual desire. In this instant I was Unified, being an embodiment of One and all of His creation.

My sensation of being on that beach during that meditation was overwhelmingly powerful. However, there wasn't any way of my confirming or disproving the sensation of my bilocation, but I felt certain of it occurring.

Rama tapped my shoulder and I suddenly tuned into Swuel's voice instructing, "Bring yourself back to this reality still projecting your love." As he counted us out of the meditation, I noticed that the room was becoming dynamic with heart-rending emotions. All of us were feeling the effects of our love projection. Sending it, then receiving it from others present in the room, we naturally produced even more. It amassed and we dispersed more passion. It became an endless burning circle of escalating love. Subsequently Swuel said, "I am certain that all of you are experiencing the power and purity of the love of One. Remember, it is your love, too. Without your active part in the creation of it you would be feeling nothing. You are what you believe you are: loving, hateful, rich, poor, happy, depressed, accomplished, or defeated—and all exist because of your beliefs. This goes for every perception of self that you might possess, conscious and subconscious.

On the other hand, if you perceive something that discomforts you, there is no rule that you have to accept it. I choose to love myself so I can then love my neighbor as myself. If you are feeling ill at ease, view it differently and refuse to allow it to negatively effect you."

My emotions were so heightened that it was difficult to contain myself. I was feeling extremely energized and needed somehow to suppress or vent my mounting vigor. "My friends," he said with an understanding smile, "we are aware of your jubilant feelings and will give you a half hour break so that you can examine your impressions of this experience of love. Participate in any activity you like. You have plenty of time to take a stretch, go for a short walk, visit with the person sitting next to you, and even do some vigorous exercise if you are so inclined. Let me first give you a word of warning, though; please keep your emotions under rigid control. Because of their elevated conditions right now, you will be more susceptible to overwhelming desires of love and sexual gratification. Please be on guard against your emotional and lustful desires."

Swuel was right. As soon as I had turned to leave, my eyes fell upon a young plain-looking girl and I immediately fell in love with her. Blinking her Bambi-like eyes at me, I could see adoration written in them as well. *Help me One,* I silently prayed as warning bells went off in my head. *Please don't let me see Gail while I am in this state of mind, I won't be able to oppose these powerful emotions.*

"Rama, can I leave Tesa for a few minutes?" He only had time to nod once and I escaped through the roof. I flew into a sky filling with rain clouds and for a few minutes I was part of them. I, along with every drop of water they contained, was the perfection of One. Everything about me was there because I had created them, including my body that hovered far above the reality of blindness. The fear of seeing Gail was gone in my newly released spirit. I was love itself and all of existence was a part of my Oneness.

Not expecting anything, I asked, "Please, One, talk to me." I listened silently for a moment.

A thought came promptly to mind, "I am you and you me, so if you want to hear my words, you have to imagine them. My thoughts are yours."

I smiled joyfully and said, "That's right, we are One! Thanks for being me!"

"Thanks for being me, for you are bringing me into existence," One replied in my mind's imagination.

I heard Rama's voice like a single spark in an endlessly consuming fire, "Jim, come back now."

I once again became the spirit in my body, which was sitting in the chair at Tesa. I then heard Swuel's next teaching. "You are not alone. Every one of you is sensing intensified feelings of self-esteem and enhanced sensations of love. Also, a few more of your mental blocks have been broken down, allowing more of the light of One to reach your subconscious more clearly. Remember, too, that you were loved by perhaps millions of creatures of the sea. The release of love from the 300 of us in this room has also elevated your realization of love. As you know, whenever you produce and transmit love to others, you are naturally magnifying the responses from the One within the object of your attention as well as yourself. Loving the One in others is loving the One in yourself as well."

Nick's spirit guide walked up the center isle to speak with Swuel and I whispered, "Rama, what is going to happen to Nick? Will he be able to join us again?"

"He is receiving fervent reprogramming and will most likely be with us soon."

"Oh, I'm glad to hear that," I said with genuine feelings of gratitude. I felt that this crusade was critical to Earth's survival and I was glad that there would be another person serving this commendable cause.

"Excuse me," said Swuel, "I am going to dismiss you for an undetermined period of time. "Please use this time constructively and allow yourselves to exchange love with nature. We will call you back when matters are taken care of."

"You know," Rama said, scolding me with his eyes, "you almost left Tesa. Be more careful."

At the doorway, I extended my hand to Rama and apologized. I had no idea that I was exiting, Rama. Thanks for catching me in time." After saying goodbye to him, I walked alone into the nearby woods. Everything I saw, heard, and felt excited me with its intensifying beauty and wholesomeness. All of the trees, insects, and birds held me spellbound by their display of beauty and harmony. I walked on a wide path, deep into the woods, studying every tree, bush, and flower I passed. I stopped next to a weeping willow whose abundantly flourishing branches hung to the ground. Suddenly a small bird of unknown variety jumped from it and landed on my shoulder. Its tiny bill opened and she greeted me with an unbelievably beautiful song. I leaned my head toward her and whispered, "Who are you and what are you doing tempting me in this paradise?" She replied with a peck to my cheek and then flew off. My laughter poured out of me as never before and I fell to the ground in happiness, joy, and love of life and nature.

After recovering from my glee, I walked deeper into the woods. I felt so thoroughly happy that I began to sing. Soon my song became an unrecognizable chant. Despite the fact of being foreign, the words had a subliminal significance. I stopped in my tracks and deliberated. *These words I sing are foreign, yet I fully grasp their meaning. What is the source of this unknown language and why do I understand it?" I wondered aloud. Within the deep recesses of my mind came these interpreted words of the chant I had been singing. I am, because I am an infinite part of the unity of One. A part of One, which knows all and believes in what I know for truth, doesn't distort perfection, nor does perfection the truth. I am because I am. I am a creative mind that creates beingness, a state of being which creates existence. I am a healer chosen by One. Healing is my vocation because I am. Existence is, because I am.* The next three words were repeated in a different language, ten times over—*believe and heal.* There were many other verses revolving through my brain as I sang with a freedom never before experienced. Those last words repeated over and over again in my consciousness. "Believe and heal," I sang joyously. With a deep breath, I yelled, "I am a healer." And I brought that reality into my heart.

Reaching out, I dubiously snapped off a tiny branch of an old oak tree. Desiring enough power of belief that I could restore it once again. I held that little twig and pressed it against the broken area for a few minutes. I failed to accomplish a thing other than becoming frustrated and feeling like a fool. After another minute of trying to mend it, I crumpled to the ground in perplexity. "You charlatan," I admonished myself, "some healer you make!"

With a whirl of wind and a bending of the grass, Rama was at my side scolding me unmercifully. "Here you are just getting started on right thinking and you degrade yourself this way. One actually spoke to you only moments ago and now you are mocking His words. This kind of thinking is only going to decrease your abilities, forfeiting your training and spiritual advancement."

"But, Rama," I objected, "I believed in my heart that I was capable of mending that branch. In fact, Rama, it seemed to me that I was somehow informed by an external force of my ability to heal."

"Need I inform you that I was at your side? I am fully aware of what came from your very own mouth and mind. It came from an inner source and, being that it was One who doesn't lie, you are censuring His very words."

"Tell me then, Rama, did I misinterpret His words? Was my translation so flagrantly inaccurate?"

He reposed next to me on the ground and placed his hand on mine. "Now," he began as if he were talking to a child, "you are sadly mistaken. What makes you think that it wasn't a precise translation? That voice was your One enlightened spirit speaking directly to your mind. If you want to be correct in your perceptions, you are not to judge your inner words but to take them literally. How else is the universal Mind of One going to communicate with you? You were singing and He chose to use your voice to convey that message; most often He will use your intuition."

"The words to that song that came out of my mouth were from One? I was only echoing them then?"

"Our spirit always had a voice, but it couldn't be heard because of our mental blocks and mind chatter. Because more of those barriers were broken down today—"

In my eagerness to learn more, I was intrusive and apologized for my poor etiquette. "Sorry for the interruption, Rama, but what do you mean by, 'Your spirit always had a voice?' I didn't think anybody's spirit talked to them. Although," I said after a fleeting thought, "weeks ago, before I died, I was having spirits talk to me and patients via my larynx. Also, I clearly remember people talking about people speaking in tongues, but I wasn't sure that it was legit."

He smiled at me and I vividly noticed love in his shimmering eyes. "My son, you've got to slow down. You are always in a hurry to get things done and to learn more." His next words were said slowly and with embellishment displayed by his cheerful countenance and a heartfelt smile, which showed in his voice, "All in good turn, my boy. The mouthpiece of your internal spirit as well as those external, or so they seem, are spirits you might allow to speak to you. In other words, spirits can talk to you through your own voice, tongue, and lips as you so aptly demonstrated today."

As an afterthought, he said, "They also can confer internally with your cognitive mind. Moments ago you spoke in an ancient primordial language and your mind translated your spirit's foreign words so that you might comprehend what you were being taught." He nodded his head as if permitting himself to answer the second question. "Now to your other inquiry; in very rare cases those believers were speaking in the tongues of angels, man, guides, and the universal language of One. However, because of corrupt teachers and inaccurate instruction, some were only babbling nonsensical gibberish."

For a moment I wondered if the language coming out of me was real. Reading my thoughts, he answered, "I told you that the languages that you spoke a minute ago were genuine. They were ones that you had spoken during past lives." Rama shook his head and his voice raised as he said, "Don't you ever denounce or question your spiritual communications, Jim, and it's the utterance of One who you are now. Your spirit happens to be the bridge between you and the One who you haven't totally accepted yet. You are One and until you realize this, you will only be an outsider, an incomplete bridge. The wholeness of One Being universal happens to be everything, even your doubting mind is His." He looked at the branch I still held and said, "Don't allow this temporary setback to create feelings of failure in you."

"Rama," I sadly declared, showing him the pathetic twig, "we cannot argue that I failed to heal this broken branch and I was told that I was a healer!" At this point I was still feeling disappointed and disillusioned about my abilities. "I held that twig there, expecting and believing in my heart that it would grow back together again. I failed to accomplish a thing other than making myself feel absurdly foolhardy!"

I saw a smile in his eyes and felt camaraderie move between us. His hand pressed against my shoulder as he leveraged himself to his feet. "My boy, you have already moved further than you realize. Because of your exemplary goal to help us it seems to you that you aren't progressing fast enough. You were chosen."

Unable to remove this personal failure from my mind, I asked as I stood next to him, "Rama, why was I so wrong? What caused me to so utterly blunder like this?"

"Simple, Jim," he aptly said. "You still doubt your ability. Immediately before you snapped that branch off, you worried about failing, which paradoxically caused your fears to come true. You didn't believe in your heart that you desired enough belief to heal it, and that's tantamount to subconsciously admitting that you already didn't possess that ability. Like your perfect beingness in One, your mind has to be pure and without fear or doubt. If there is any negativity such as uncertainty or distrust, procuring your goals will be completely impossible. In that perspective," he said with a friendly smile, "no matter how honorable they might be, your aspirations are doomed to fail. Feeling assured and having an optimistic mind should be your ultimate goal for now. Besides," he told me, looking upward as if searching for assistance, "rarely are students informed of their future vocation at this early stage. Believe only that you are performing as you've been instructed. When you can do it without any doubts, you will see the rewards of your undertaking. Once you have become clear of all mental blocks you will be a whole being in the light of One and able to achieve every desire in your heart."

We turned and walked together as if led by invisible guides. It was like we were following directed instructions. I followed my internal guide in the direction that we were to travel. Every footstep was placed in exactly the proper position as we moved toward an undetermined place. Rama purposely hung back, allowing me to take the lead. I became interested in where my spirit was taking us, for I followed an inner director and had no idea where we might be headed. The air was cool and refreshing on my skin. Even after climbing a towering hill, I was still comfortably cool and energetic. Reaching its summit, we then encountered a deep cliff-like precipice which overlooked Tesa. The scene below us took my breath away and filled me with awe and immense joy. The panorama revealed this enormous building bathed in brilliant sunlight. It looked from this height like a smiling face. Its eyes were glittering, large, crystal covered apertures in the two topmost corners that reflected shimmering rainbows of color. Its nose and mouth were made of those beautiful, three-dimensional, stained glass windows created from precious jewels. "Rama," I said with heartfelt emotion showing my ecstasy, "I can't fathom ever seeing such magnificence! After being blind for so many years, I thank One every minute for granting me sight. Spectacles like this gladden my whole mind, heart, body, and spirit." Lifting my arms high, I thanked One again for allowing me to see this exceptional splendor. "Oh my One!" I cried incredulously, "Those windows look as if they're really alive."

"I am very happy with your progress, Jim. Do you know that you allowed your spirit to direct us here? You followed its guidance without a bit of hesitation. You didn't allow yourself to feel threatened by not being totally in control of your actions," he proudly proclaimed.

"Thank you, Rama, for always being here for me," I said, feeling distinguished by his acknowledgment. I suddenly stepped back, bewildered by a staggering spectacle. A young woman holding a star in one hand and the moon in the other catapulted from Tesa and quickly rose in the air toward me. Even though I knew she was only an image from a stained-glass window, she startled me just the same. She hovered about eight feet higher from where I stood. Without reckoning, I drifted in the air to meet her. She was a colorful replica of the sculptured girl that I had seen high in the treetop. Without warning, she retreated as quickly and as suddenly as she had appeared. I settled on the ground next to Rama and stared deeply into his knowledgeable eyes. Feeling somewhat disturbed by her sudden disappearance, I asked, "What did I do wrong now, Rama? Why did she recoil from me like that? I only wanted to look into her beautiful eyes?"

"You didn't do anything wrong," he said reassuringly. "It's only that it is a reflection, or maybe better said, a result of your animated imagination."

"You mean to tell me that I made it all up?" I looked down at Tesa to see where the girl had gone. To my unreserved surprise, this structure no longer resembled a smiling face. The girl was back to only being an insignificant image in a colorful window.

"You are beginning to see the effects of your training, Jim. Your mental blocks and barriers to the perfection of your Oneness with One are being broken down. There is nothing to be disturbed about. As you've been told, we are the creators of our own lives. That includes everything that occurs in them, too. You merely wanted to see her closer, and your subconscious brought her into your vicinity. Then you flew up to see her before she vanished again. By your subliminal act, flying up to see her before she disappeared, she only did as you had unknowingly commanded."

I felt real shaky now. What I was now learning meant that my future outcome was going to be a lot different than I had ever contemplated. Up to now I had thought that I would be ruled by the same physical principles by which I had previously lived. Suddenly those ironclad constraints were becoming flexible. "Do you mean that I can manifest all of my desires just through the power of will?" I asked with incredulity displayed in my passionate voice?"

Rama nodded affirmatively and surprised me further by saying, "You have always had that option. Ignorance is the culprit here," he announced.

"You mean that on this plane I can always have things as I desire, right?" I asked, feeling still shaky about this revelation and yearning for more clarification.

"There are no restrictions neither here nor on Earth," he confided." "It's the brainwashing story again. You were told by your parents that if you stepped into a lake that you would sink. Equally, collectively you were taught that walls are solid and therefore couldn't ever be walked through. We are a living part of One and as such, have the birthright to create our lives to our own specifications. The only obstruction between you and this reality is a deficiency of belief. Increase your sense of unity with One and you will have all things as you desire."

My growing faith in the truths that Rama was sharing with me began to crumble my old beliefs. However, there were questions I still needed to resolve. "Why then are Gail and I prohibited from being together?" Quickly removing myself from that painful area of contemplation I asked, "Why did our loving forbearers lie to us?"

Rama smiled cunningly and replied, "You know the answer to your first question that you tried to slip past me. To answer your second question in one word—conditioning. It was primitive mankind who was deceived. He stood on a rock and said that it was solid and couldn't be penetrated. They put their hands into a brook to drink, thinking that if they could submerge their hands then water was liquid and therefore was unable to support them. To fortify this impression, they slipped on a stepping-stone and fell into the brook, confirming their misconception. These delusions were passed on to their offspring and maintained to present time." Raising his hand so that I would heed his next words wasn't nearly enough to prepare me for what he said next. "You didn't have to remain blind after your optic nerves were destroyed. With the correct power of belief you could have regenerated them, created new nerves, and seen through your eyes without them even functioning." My heart and mind told me that this exciting philosophy was the one that I was going to adopt. "That's right," said Rama, reading my thought. "Belief is the power of reality. Believe without doubt and make it real. Mankind is One whether you realize it here or elsewhere."

I was really excited now and needed to know more. Pursuing this topic further, I asked, "How, Rama, do we attain the necessary magnitude of belief? Jesus walked on water, but how do we mortals become that sure of anything? I fly through walls here, are you telling me that I will be able to do it on Earth just as easily?"

"With infallible belief, everything is possible," he told me with conviction in his voice. "You gain this ability by degrees of intensity. A, by exchanging doubt with faith and B, by removal of brainwashed illusions." He smiled warmly at me with his red beard shining in the radiant sunlight. "Simply put, we have to have undying faith in ourselves and revise all erroneous perceptions. This last barrier is the most difficult to overcome. There are a few of your peers who haven't yet been able to fly and many who can't move through walls. All of you have no idea of what you are going to be doing when you've returned to Earth." Again he held up his hand, stopping me from asking questions. "To complicate things further, you are going to be replacing a human being with a family that already has their own conceptions of reality, which we know are close to a hundred percent inaccurate. If you keep yourself faithful in what you learn here and don't allow anyone's teaching to corrupt your wisdom, everything you desire will be possible for you."

"Why are diverse vocations being shown to me, Rama? How am I to know my true calling?"

"Simply put, maybe all of them are, Jim," he said with honesty written in his eyes. "No doubt you will be gifted with many attributes in future existences."

"Simple, huh?" I said shaking my head. "Sure, Rama, why don't you tell me to put out a candle in another room or to stop the rain from falling?"

"That's minor stuff, I'm telling you to walk on water," he said with a laugh. "It may seem like an impossible task right now, but that is why you are here," he said reflectively. "I wish, as you do, that we could discuss this further, but Swuel is about to call us back. In a few minutes you are going to have more of your mental blocks removed. Every successive meditation will put more cracks into the wall of misconceptions your brainwashing has created. You will notice a striking improvement in your abilities, thinking, and over-all functioning after every meditation. Just as long as you sustain your faith, your mastery will follow you to Earth and you should have nearly all of the abilities that you are developing here. The only problem that might crop up deals with memory loss, but more on that later."

We stood in total silence while some of Rama's enlightening words rewound through my head. I had just completed my analysis of them and heard and/ or felt Swuel's wish for us to return.

Rama and I smiled at each other and then relocated into Tesa. I merely visualized my chair and metaphysically repositioned myself into it. "Much better isn't it?" Rama asked as we sank into our respective seats. "No need of flying down to Tesa and then having to purposefully sail through her walls and try finding your chair."

All in one fell swoop, after I had transferred, I became aware that Swuel was standing tall and proper a few feet back from the podium, that an obese woman on my left was still chewing the remains of a meal, and the man four seats to my right still smelled of tobacco. The realization of Rama's words about truth and illusion regarding my earthly blindness came into my mind. I wanted to think about this important concept, but I somehow knew that the smoker wanted to say something to me. I smiled and nodded affirmatively at him. With a shrug of his shoulders, he confessed, "Still haven't felt the compulsion to give up my smoking."

I wondered to myself what had caused my sudden awareness of these miscellaneous details. Filing it away for later examination, I smiled at the man and said, "I was an avid pipe smoker, but since leaving home I haven't felt any desire to pick up that dirty and harmful habit again. I have no idea even if pipes and tobacco are available here. I hate to admit it, but you are talking to a man who couldn't tolerate his pipe not being continuously lit. For most of my life, from the minute I awoke in the morning until bedtime, the moment it went out I relit it again. I only stopped for absolute essentials like eating and sleeping and, believe me, an ashtray was only inches away."

The room became quiet as Swuel stepped before the podium. "Forgive me, but I was reading your minds and overhearing your comments to one another. I do this from time to time so that I have an idea where you are and what we must examine next." After stepping off of the stage, he walked the length of the room and slowly climbed the four steps back. With a wise look in his eyes, and a friendly smile, he started, "Throughout the ages, all humans have debated about things like grace, evil, heaven, hell, and reincarnation. Each culture professing that their philosophy is the Word. I am here to inform you that in the perfection of one's Universal One there aren't any such things as good, evil, heaven, or hell." He stepped off of the stage and walked to a man, handing him a dagger. He then made a face at him and said, "Man, you're so ugly, you should do us all a favor and kill yourself immediately! The man's face got bright red and he got to his feet and the knife rose in the air threateningly. Swuel stopped him with two words, "That's hell!" He took the dagger with his right hand and with left tapped the man's shoulder. "Thanks, Colonel Frank, for your quick and apt reaction," he said with a brave smile.

The contrite killer was now crying profoundly and moaned, "Swuel, please forgive my embarrassing act!" With a shake of his head, he said, "You took an awfully risky chance, I nearly murdered you!"

Turning to us, once he had taken his place behind the microphone, Swuel valiantly said, "Genuine feelings of feeling sorry are good models of heaven," he directed at the still flushed colonel as well as the remainder of the room. He shifted his feet slightly and continued. "Right and wrong are controlling dogmas of religion. The enlightenment of One is righteousness."

Defining heaven further for you here, heaven is reaching the supremacy of One and becoming a functioning part of His universal mind. Hell is being ceaselessly trapped in non-existence. Reincarnation is the spirit's equalizer. Striving to obtain the proper learning tools, which will bring non-condemned spirits into the light of One, all of these seeking spirits are born into new bodies in diverse situations. This enables them to experience life in all facets, allowing them to learn needed lessons."

He paused as he walked to the front of the room, and then stopped and peered directly into Nick's dazed eyes. Because of his mute behavior, I hadn't even noticed him sitting to my right and one row back. "Are you with me so far, Nick?" Swuel asked with hands on hips.

"Ye ye yes, sir, I'm completely aware of what you are saying," he stammered, having given up the attempt of getting to his feet.

Swuel turned and slowly returned to the podium. He grimaced ever so slightly and started again. "Living a perfect life is impossible for humans unless, of course they, are unfettered by traditional beliefs. Feelings of guilt, fear, worry, dread, and separation, among other things, create defeat for every living being. I've told you that the purpose of life is learning via experiences, thus, our spirits of One create adverse situations for growth. This next concept is going to be rather difficult for you to comprehend and accept, nevertheless, it is true and time for you to learn." Swuel stopped talking and scrutinized our faces for a few moments. He strongly said, "Religious societies are the creators of the concept of evil. Originators of these establishments created it to teach morality to the common people thousands of years ago. It was effective then, but that era has long past. To begin with, One is infallible and couldn't ever produce something as imperfect as evil. But as humanity evolved, people in charge needed to create purposes for doing right and correction for doing wrong, thus they created the concepts of good and evil. Man, who accepted their righteousness or condemnation, lived accordingly."

He stopped and walked promptly to the row where I was sitting and candidly asked the man who I had spoken with earlier, "Not to single you out, Larry, but I have to ask; in truth, do you expect to continue harming yourself and others by your smoking and not have to pay for it in some way? Off the subject, but avoiding serious disease if you had stayed on Earth is realistically another problem that we won't get into today." He paused a second to let us know that he was getting back onto the subject and said, "We all know that in truth it pales in comparison to the spiritual disregard you're paying to the perfection of One. You are a beautiful replica and very precious because you are the Universal One itself. You are One having a human experience!" He looked at all of us and declared, "All of us are as vital as every person you might threaten with your misdeeds. Therefore, it is expected that each of us preserves and maintains our lives and those of all our acquaintances to the best of our ability."

Larry, who had been questioned accordingly, grumbled incoherently and shifted uncomfortably in his chair.

Swuel immediately stepped away and said, "For learning purposes only, in a smokers current or next lifetime he might create cancer or decide to come back a chronic asthmatic." Dozens of hands concurrently rose and, being a pipe smoker for so many years, I felt the pang of his words and my hand was one of them. "Excuse me," said Swuel, motioning with his hand to lower our raised arms, "but I am going to preempt. All of your questions will be answered I assure you. I, too, felt the way you are now. I have to be honest with you," he explained, followed by a deep breath, "even though I knew that smoking was harmful, I still persevered until I was enlightened." Getting back to what he was telling us, he said, "For that reason, when judging your past life, you and your masters may give yourself a lower ranking in your subsequent life. Our spirits cannot grow in the truth of One when you are killing yourself or harming others with abusive behaviors. Good karma reduces punishment from your transgressions." His words were ringing true in my ears as well as, I'm sure, of those around me. It was rational that we couldn't get away with harming ourselves and others. "Humans very often penalize themselves harder than their spirit guides would for their misbehavior," he told us. "Only by correcting improper conduct do you remove your self-imposed karmic chastisement." Pausing for a few he walked back and forth on the stage. Turning to us again, he said, "When at a lower level of consciousness and spiritual development, we are ignorant to the harm that we are doing to our spirits. Therefore, in our next lifetime we tend to be more lenient on ourselves. Although to be candid, poverty stricken souls only know poverty and often create similar living conditions. Regardless, when we become spiritually enlightened, we will be aware of any behavioral inconsistencies and delete them from our lives. Now that you are aware of your errors, we are sure that you will want to modify any misbehavior. Don't fear suffering withdrawal symptoms, for they will not occur."

During the next meditation that we are going to guide you through, everything will become crystal clear." He smiled shrewdly with his eyes focused on Nick. Getting no negative response from him, he continued, "This next meditation is going to take you places you have no memory of right now. You will be guided to a spiritual level where some of your prominent past lives will be revealed. We have had several students who experienced more than ten lighthearted lifetimes during this session. Others experience only one or two pasts, but they are very intense and dramatic, thus taking longer. Often they show past life's crises that will aid you in removing grueling barriers and enfites. Still, others have many short bits of their lives portrayed to them. No matter what yours might be like, know that you will be learning necessary lessons from them. During this meditation you will be reliving actual portions of those lives again."

The large room became as quiet as a small closet in an uninhibited house. All of us were anxious to learn more about our past lives and to hear what our teacher had to say about them. "I say 'experience' because you will not only see, hear, or feel yourself in another life, but will be literally taking part and reliving that past life—you being them and them being you. At first it is going to be like watching a television, pausing only a few seconds on each channel while you see scenes from your different lives pass quickly before your eyes. As you go deeper, you will be reliving larger segments that could be extremely arousing. Living through them will correct difficulties that have to be alleviated right then and there. Your enfites will diminish and some will even be entirely dissolved throughout this powerful meditation. During it, some of your past life situations will feel as if they are taking you longer periods of time, especially if they are difficult moments. As you already know, egos and time are illusions created by mankind. Our ego systems were not created within us, we developed them shortly after birth and fed them throughout our lives. The past, present, and future all exist in this moment. By beholding and taking part in your previous lives, you will be reliving and absolving that deluded person who you were in that past life. Like I said," he said seriously, "in some cases you will even be removing enfites implanted during that life. As a result, don't be too shocked if you suddenly are much more intuitive or clairvoyant when you awaken afterwards." Taking a sip of water he observed Nick's appearance over the edge of his glass. Not getting any opposition from him, he continued, "Being scarcely aware of this other spirit within that life you are reliving, you will be viewing these lives in a subliminal sense. However, with a full awareness of the moment, you will be reliving those periods by actually being those people you had been in your past life and you will hardly be aware of the spirit you within them." Following another brief pause, he said, "We are limiting this meditation to two hours. However, to you who are encountering these episodes, adversities, and horrors, it could seem even like years. Have no fear, no harm can occur. You have already lived these lives and are only re-experiencing them again. There must be critical lessons in them that you need to master. Therefore you will be encountering those particular events and lives again. There are good experiences you need to examine, so on a happier note, some of these experiences will be joyous and you will want to stay in them longer." "

Having concluded with those words, he walked from the front of the huge room to the rear and slowly back again. "I am still feeling some of you in trepidation." He raised his hands and said, "To give you more confidence I am going to send you aqua light. This will calm down any apprehensive sensations you feel at this moment." His hands literally became light green in color as he projected aqua light. It had a profound calming effect on me and by the relaxed look in others, I could tell that they were also feeling more at ease.

"Now," he started with a smile creasing his lips, "close your eyes and feel yourself immediately drifting into that familiar place of comfort." After a momentary pause, he continued, "I am going to count you down into a lower level of consciousness. When I reach one you will be totally relaxed and stress free. Every descending number will take you deeper into that place of happy reflection and mental tranquility. Now take a very deep belly breath and let it out very slowly. As your breath leaves your lungs, feel yourself becoming more and more relaxed and unified with the Universal One."

When he had reached number one, he said, "Now you are totally relaxed and have greater control of yourself—a glorified self. Your brain waves are much slower and giving you more power over your subconscious as well as conscious mind. You, and only you, have control of your life; no one else can have that power over you. Everything that occurs during your life is because you have given it that authority. If you are a smoker, obese, or slothful, only you have the power of change. Ridding yourselves of those injurious habits will make you feel accomplished. Anything that gives you discomfort is harmful to your emotional, mental, and spiritual tranquility. If you are feeling depressed at any time and can't seem to get out of it, remember that only you can allow yourself to feel that way. All you have to do is say to yourself 'I don't want to feel this terrible depression' and feel instantly happier. There is only one person who can make you unhappy, hateful, overweight, or suffering from some kind of addiction, and that person is you. We are who we believe we are and the truth can't be anymore simple than that can it?"

After another fleeting pause, he said, "I am going to take you much deeper. Your brain waves are going to slow down even further giving you more and more control over your conscious minds. This portion of the meditation is going to give you REM, rapid eye movement sleep, which will be the same as a deep sleep. Nevertheless, you will remain fully awake and cognizant of every action that you witness and word that I say. This measure of the meditation will bring you into a trance-like state which will allow you to visit your past lives." He paused shortly and then said, "When you get sufficiently deep, you will lose control of your will power as you do when you're asleep. Now I want you to imagine yourselves standing in front of a waist high wall on the edge of a towering cliff overhanging the sea. In your left hand you are holding three golf ball-size pieces of rose quartz. Pick one of these crystals up with your right hand and extend your arm outward over the water. Release it and follow it as it falls down and feel yourself going deeper and deeper with it. See it now as it moves closer to the sea. Notice yourself drifting further away and mentally follow it downwards." Allowing us time to refocus at a deeper level of responsiveness he whispered as if miles away, "Watch it now as it splashes into the water and follow it as it sinks slowly beneath the surface. Feel yourself drifting deeper and deeper into that unknown, but previously experienced, territory of your past lives. There, the pink quartz has hit bottom. Now pick up another and hold it aloft. As you release it feel yourself falling down beside it. You are moving down deeper, deeper, and deeper into the areas of your past lives. See that second crystal splash into the sea and slowly sink. Follow it down until it reaches the bottom where it comes to rest next to the first one. You are much deeper now than you have ever been before. You might begin to see odd bits of your past. Now pick up the third and last piece of crystal and release it and yourself from all restraints. Follow it down toward the gently curling waves of the ocean. There, it has broken through created veils blocking your pasts. It has touched bottom and is laying right next to the other two." He was silent for a few seconds while we caught up with him and then he soothingly commanded, "As my voice fades into the distance you are moving into a former life. Don't restrain yourselves in any fashion; just let yourselves flow with the changing tides of time."

Swuel's voice vanished and I was now seeing pictures and scenes of obscure places and people flashing instantly before my eyes. I seemed to be a living functioning part of it all. I was not only the reflection before my eyes, but the actual object in the mirror of my memories. Even though my appearance was at times totally different, I recognized myself in them, for I was reliving those moments. In the first of my pasts I witnessed my newlywed parents having intercourse. I innocently overlooked their lovemaking and anxiously waited for my moment of entry into existence. I personally observed my birth as dad's sperm and mom's egg united. For me, the spirit in that just-created fetus was like watching a beautiful painting come to life. At first there was nothing, then a spark of light, which intensified, and brilliant colors then were splashed over the canvas. Rising and setting suns then inflamed these colors into cellular forms and I blossomed inside my mother. I heard her as she whispered to my dad, "James, you have just given me the best wedding present that I could have gotten today. I know that I am now pregnant!" she said with conviction.

In the next scene, I was a Caucasian boy of 10 who was pelting a black boy with stones.

Then, in a flash, I was a sickly baby in my loving mother's arms. My mother was crying and was in great emotional pain because of my sickness. The sorrow my mother felt was agonizing for me to perceive. Because of an intimate affinity between us, I seemed to also be a living part of her psyche, yet it was different. Personally, I felt her misery, but physically we were two distinct beings. I positively knew that I was the ailing baby who ached so to reduce her pain.

The channel of time switched again and I was a patient father watching his beloved daughter riding her new two-wheel bicycle. Reaching the end of our long driveway, I called to her to turn around and come back to me. She made a broad turn that took her into the road, but finally got the bike turned and was headed in my direction. All was taken from me within only agonizing seconds; a speeding car took away my voice and my little girl! I truly was that father and intimately felt his grieving torment as he ineffectually raced to save his daughter. I realized that I was the spirit within this mourning father as well as being him in all actuality. Nevertheless, I was somehow aware of being a spirit and not his body. With agony in our shared heart, he painfully screeched, "My baby!" and ran as fast as possible toward the road.

Then, in another flash, I was a different person. I was a man being chased down a dark, endless path. I felt the fear and anguish of that man being pursued because I was him. I also was tremendously famished for food and wanted to stop and eat the loaf of bread that I cradled in my arms like a baby. I knew if I stopped that I'd be caught and killed. The three men chasing me were close to capturing me when a huge bear stepped onto the path just behind my quickly retreating body. The three pursuing men I saw had stopped and I was free and felt the joy flowing through my body. I ran on for a few more feet, stopped, and ravenously tore at the bread wrappings. My mouth had just closed over the heel of it when I heard something rapidly moving toward me. Turning, I saw that immense bear and knew that he was on the hunt for food, which could be me as well as the loaf of bread I was trying to preserve for myself. Swearing under my breath, I once again turned and ran for my life. My body was weak from a lack of food and water; it felt as if I were about to pass out. Then MIRACULOUSLY to my left I saw a tall fence and directly in front of my left shoulder I saw a shining gate. With my last bit of strength I vaulted toward it. To my horror, however, I found that I had come to a fastened gate, which blocked my reaching safety. I could hear the angry creature in quest of sustenance slowly approaching. With fear and great distress in me, I screamed and hammered at the ungiving obstacle between protection and me. My breath then departed my lips in a sigh of pleasure for my eyes beheld a beautiful woman coming to my rescue. In some remote part of my brain I seemed to recognize her countenance and demeanor. Even though I had never seen her before, I felt a tremendous love for her that was overwhelming my sensibility. All of my attention was on her as she played with the lock so lingeringly slow that I thought for a moment that she'd never get it open in time. Finally when it swung open, I jumped through it and helped her replace the lock before the bear could overcome us. Because of my extreme fatigue and weakness due to the chase and my starvation, I had to support myself against the gate. Before breaking off a piece of bread for her, I rotated my head slightly so that I could look her in the eyes while asking my cherished companion, "Why were you tantalizing fate that way?" To my chagrin and horror, I then noticed hundreds of starving people gathering around us. "That's why," I unfairly accused while pointing a bony finger at the people collecting behind her.

"No," she cried, "I had no idea—" Before she could utter another word, the famished people were upon us and grabbing at the loaf of bread that I still held tightly in my hands. Seeing that I wasn't intending to release it, they jumped on top of me and fiercely beat me with their fists. Right before I lost consciousness, I remembered, in revulsion, my having beaten a man over a loaf of bread in another past life. "I forgive you," I moaned aloud, thinking of my past self, the pretty woman I had just wrongly accused, and the people atop me. *Please forgive me*, I mentally asked again while visualizing the man who I had battled over a loaf of bread, the black boy who I had stolen two fishes from, and the me who I felt were parts of a universal me who is eternally a part of us all.

The channel of my mental TV changed again and I found myself lying on a fur-covered floor of a wigwam. My hand was caressing a woman's soft stomach and my lips suckled her breast. Looking up and into her eyes I recognized a past life lover. There was a strong feeling of familiarity that stimulated memories of my past. I whispered desiring words in a foreign language, which I oddly comprehended. "I adore you, Soft Feather." That other part of this man, the me who dwelled in his spirit, thought, "How is it that I know her name or this language I'm speaking? How do I know her so intimately?" I knew in my heart that she was a long lost mate of mine. "These sensations are genuine," I recognized. "I truly feel emotional love and sexual yearning for this divine creature." I put my face into her soft, wet pelt and partook of her essence—gratefully partaking of the flow of the universal love that we shared. I was that Indian, yet very much an independent spirit within him. A powerful insight filled me and I realized the truth, "We are all One living in bodies of human beings during different periods of time."

The next shift of awareness found me aboard an ancient schooner during a raging storm and all about me was mayhem. Our sails were only shreds of canvas clinging to badly battered masts. The ocean's angry waves crashed on deck with one purpose to their wickedness, to destroy everyone and everything that resisted their supremacy. I found myself tied to a mast while being swamped and almost drowned by every crashing wave. The rope, which was my only support in this fragile life, was fraying. My good buddy who I loved with my whole heart was tied to the mast in front of me. Seeing my dilemma, I noticed him foolishly untying his lifeline. "Hang on pal! I know that you gave me the better rope and I'll be with you in a jiffy!" he yelled in a foreign language.

"No," I screamed in reply, "don't you dare!"

He persisted and continued to struggle with the swollen knots holding him to the mast. I was about to scream 'No' again when he accomplished his task and rapidly moved toward me with the rope dangling from his hand. Reaching me, he twisted the rope around us both and I held it while he attempted to tie it fast. Before this could be achieved, however, I was horrified by another gigantic wave crashing over us. Sight of him being swept overboard caused me to rip at my rope, which was still strong enough to hold me fast. Completing my task, I ran toward the stern where my friend had vanished from sight. Another gigantic wave crashed aboard and the mast that we would have been fastened to snapped with a loud report. It swung toward me and was carried into the savage sea with me. *God help me, I've got to live so that I can join my loving niece,* I thought while submerged far below the surface of the ocean. My held breath failed me and I temporarily lost consciousness. Something nudged me hard in the stomach and awoke me just as I began to inhale seawater. I started to gag on it and noticed three dolphins swimming rapidly around me. Again I felt a driving force, this time on my right side. I saw a fourth Dolphin who, along with his buddies, was intentionally pushing me toward the surface of the angry sea. Reaching it, one of them drove hard once more into my stomach forcing me to vomit seawater and inhale reviving air. With a friendly wave of his tail, he joined his team swiftly moving ahead of me. Looking after him, an inner voice muttered words in a strange language. These unrecognized words quieted us both, me the swimming man I had known for 31 years and this inner me who just seemed to have blossomed. Intuitively this sailor who I was portraying somehow understood these strange words without even a thought. "Thank you divine creatures of the Universal One!" it said prayerfully. My niece's face then appeared in my mind and I immediately noticed that she appeared extremely feeble. With a burning desire to comfort her, I reached out and held her in imaginary arms.

The still seething sea exposed a bobbing mast on the next wave ahead of me. As swiftly as I could muster, I swam toward it. Before I was able to reach it, however, another wave crashed upon me. By the time I had managed to reach the surface again my only means of survival was nowhere to be seen. Despite that fact I struggled onward. I was soon feeling weary from the conflicts of breathing, swimming, staying afloat in frigid water, and having to bear an intolerable fear of death that nearly paralyzed me. Thoughts of giving up struck relentlessly at my heart and mind. I desperately wanted to catch up with that runaway mast and just managed to resist the desire to quit. Giving up to the bone chilling water and fatigue was so tempting! "No," I cried bitterly. "I have to live for my beloved niece! Besides, that mast is only over the next wave," I told myself, trying to bolster courage and strength. "My loving niece depends on me; I've got to save myself so that I can enjoy a long life with her." Reality reached my numb mind with a startling insight; I love her! Not just as a niece, but as a devoted mate! I have to live so that we are united again! My life will be unfulfilled if I fail to join her. She is the reason I am alive right now, and I struggled on with some of my strength renewed.

Cresting on the third wave, I saw it directly in front of me. It was only feet away, but on the side of the next rising wave. "If only I were God!" I cried aloud. Hearing a voice here surprised me beyond words. It said, "One." Thrashing out with my last bit of strength moved me piteously closer. I plunged steeply downwards on this wave and immediately fought my way toward my desired goal. It went over the top and my hopes sank as it vanished from sight. My head dropped below the water; death was only a breath away, and I took it. Seawater filled my lungs and everything soon grew blurry. "Is this all there is to dying?" I asked providence. I suddenly heard that mysterious inner voice and it said, "You needed to correct your karma and your endurance has proven you worthy—now fight, for your life will be majestic!" As if understanding those mystical words, my dolphins joined me again and worked together in an effort to rescue me. One of them drove hard into my abdomen again forcing the water from my lungs while another one wedged himself between my legs and hastily swam upward. Simultaneously, another swam between my arms that involuntarily wrapped around him. As I reached the writhing surface, another dolphin powerfully drove the water from my lungs again. Together they propelled me toward that bobbing mast. In only seconds my rescuers had brought me to it and didn't move from my side until I had successfully pulled myself onto it. Turning, I threw them kisses and yelled, "God bless you." Then, within me, I sensed these words, *No, it's One, our unifying selves who unites and blesses us all, including them.* Dutifully, that inner voice screamed after them, "May the light and love of One grace you eternally!"

With a quick toss of heads and in a chorus they sang out, "Love, the bonding light." My feeble mind had grasped the meaning of their singsong voices despite the fact that they were so alien and unintelligible to me. "Like those dolphin voices," I thought to myself, "I will never understand why this new inner voice has so powerfully come into my life. I hope it will stay around!"

My past mind shifted, realizing his enormous love for his niece, and he wisely declared, "Now that I have admitted my honest feelings, I know that we have to get married." Another thought hit him and he questioned, "Although I honestly don't know how she would feel about a betrothal. He scratched his head and pondered, *Can I possibly hope that she will approve of this wild idea and me?*

I, or rather he, looked up as the wave crested and then the mast crashed downwards into the bowels of hell. He heard a groan of pain coming from the other end of the beam and was enormously thrilled to see his feared-dead buddy. His body was partially covered beneath sails and he had splotches of blood on head and face. He was also hanging onto this transformed stave of life. It had once moments ago, yet whole lifetimes past, been means of propulsion in the lives which we had called normal. Because of particular circumstances seeming to be out of our control, we found ourselves adrift in the sea of life grasping to a shredding leaf blown in a tornado-like storm. Fragmented bits of the canvas sail mysteriously rose on invisible ropes out of the water and blocked all vision.

The obscure hands of time shifted again without premonition. Light became dark, turmoil transmuted to inactivity, and frenzy was suddenly inertia. Blinking my eyes with disbelief, I opened them again and found that I was indeed entombed in total blackness. All about me was mysteriously ominous and still. Not even a breath of air stirred this death-like destitute world of blackness. The air was so foul with the smells of human waste and death, which made me wonder if I were maybe experiencing death itself. *Am I in my own coffin?* I wondered. Then to my horror, a remote *me* vaguely realized that I was resident in the body of another past life man who was stinking of these repugnant odors. That inner knowledge of me in him was an unknown feeling of another presence. In a grave voice speaking a foreign tongue, he said, "Am I going crazy now God?"

I was able to understand him and I replied in the Latino-sounding language. My voice was like a spirit echoing thoughts in his confused mind, "We are One my brother." Within only seconds, I was experiencing this new living me more fully and my spirit self an obscure voice/awareness.

This human me was blindly walking as if on eggs. He put his arms out to either side and on the left, and I felt cold, rough stone. Being solely him by now, I strained my eyes trying to see if there was anything before him. However, only an impenetrable empty sea of blackness lay ahead. He crept onward over rough flooring and around boulders that he ran up against. In hopes that he would find something in the direction that he was moving, he labored onward. After a long period of time he debated about just sitting down and waiting for whatever was going to befall him. In truth, even in that distant past life, I wasn't one to just give up. Instead he blindly pressed onward with my inaudible prompting. All was still, silent and dead-like. "Am I destined to wander this hell alone eternally?" He asked through a dust-incrusted mouth. "God," moaned the man who I was now, "I call upon you with plaguing sensations of destitution deep in my heart—please help me out of this quandary!" Regardless of the predicament that he found himself immersed in, a sudden feeling of optimism ensued which replaced those feelings of forlorn desolation. It seemed as if he should see or hear something any minute. Therefore, with promising feelings in his mind and heart he crept onward.

An hour passed in comparable manner and only a tiny glimmer of ebbing hope kept him from turning and retreating. That shimmer of hope, I realized, was me. I was the spark of spirit in that forsaken man. "Blind," he sobbed aloud in his native tongue. "I am a blind man trying to find my way back to some familiar pattern of civilization." Again this man who I was now, got that urge to quit and to just lie down and expire. "No," I yelled, "you've got to struggle on." With strong motivation, this new living me said, "I will discover what I desire most."

Squeezing between the crumbled wall and a huge fallen stone, he next encountered a solid mound of broken rock that was 10 feet in height. At the top it seemed a trifle bit lighter and he immediately felt joy. Climbing over this mountain of fragmented stone would be his next objective. Because of the light, hopefulness raced through him. That light seemed as though it was miles away and it didn't help to enlighten this barrier confronting him now. It was light nevertheless, and he felt grateful for this discovery. Later we learned that the gap at the top of this obstruction was also his only means of survival, the fresh air coming in through it had been the only thing that had prevented him from being overpowered by seeping gas into this mine shaft.

Me, a small entity in him, inwardly wondered, *Where am I and how did we end up here?* Our shared mind suddenly opened and the knowledge of all preceding events suddenly flooded into my awareness. "He is a coal miner in Peru who got trapped in a cave days ago. Thanks to providence he is about to be free now," I thought as excitement raced through his blood. Sweat poured from his forehead as I relived the recent catastrophe. He was working on his own about 10 feet from the rest of the crew, when there came a coal-miner's nightmarish sound.

"It's a cave-in men!" old Sam had screamed.

He flattened himself to the floor and before he could protect his head he was knocked unconscious. When he woke some unknown time later, he noticed soreness and blood dripping from a head wound. All was pitch black. After trying to move his legs behind him, he found that they were pinned below piles of heavy rocks. "Sam, this has separated us. Are you and the guys still alive?" he yelled, hoping that his words wouldn't cause a further cave-in. After some dislodged pebbles crumpled to the floor he said, "I hope that they aren't buried beneath piles of stone. If so, then please, Father, let them be dead," he prayed. Bringing his attention back to himself, he sadly noticed that his right leg hurt terribly and he prayed that it wasn't broken. Feeling in front of him, he thankfully noticed no fallen rock blocking him in. Leaning back, he could feel bits and pieces of stone covering his upper legs from his buttocks right down to his knees. Inches below his knees, however, he sadly found that his legs were totally covered in layers of various-sized pieces of rock. Extricating his legs was the next and major concern. Despite the pain in his head and the oozing blood, the immediate soreness of twisting around quickly surpassed his other pains. Notwithstanding, he relentlessly tore at the rocks holding him fast. "Every stone I am able to remove," he moaned aloud, "brings me closer and closer to freedom and to the arms of my beloved Vanessa." He had to tell himself this whenever feelings of frustration arose.

Pain was soon making him cry out with every attempt of moving his body. His fingers were soon bleeding and nails all but torn off. Thankfully his head wound had stopped bleeding, but the pain in his leg was ceaseless. Against all of the odds facing him he struggled further. He spent days working furiously at getting himself released from this cold-hearted tomb. He would work for as many hours as possible, stopping only when he passed out from fatigue or pain. Waking again, he'd take up where he had left off formerly. At various times he yelled out for help, always failing to get any response to his supplications. The only sounds that reached his ears were the occasional bits and pieces of stone falling noisily into the stock stillness about him. The wall of stone behind him had cut him off from the rest of the work crew, and it was doubtful that anyone else had survived. He wouldn't allow himself to think about what lay ahead of him. The fact that he was in absolute blackness was all the evidence he needed to know what fate had in store for him, although neither he nor I reflected on that grim thought. Giving up was out of the question, no matter what! He was fortunate enough to be alive and for that reason he must battle the threat of death or any gloomy suggestion of failure.

He was entrapped in a perpetual vacuum, which was void of light, sound, and all external life forces. His innermost emotion of love was his only saving grace and He had to live for Vanessa! He knew in his heart that if he managed to extract his legs and reach her, that they would have an extraordinary future ahead of them. "We had only been married for two seasons," he thought. "Yet I feel an eternal affinity that can't be defined in terms of time." It seemed to them that they had always been united, each of them knowing more about one another than could be gleaned in only one lifetime.

By the second or third day he found himself nearly consumed with an endlessly persistent thirst. His lips and tongue were severely split open because of a lack of fluid. He got so desperate that he wished that he could engineer a method of saving his own urine so that he could partake of those precious drops of fluid. He couldn't fathom being so urgently in need that he actually cried with tearless agony whenever those priceless drops of liquid were wasted! "How long can I last without water?" he asked, visualizing the morning sun rising in his Vanessa's loving eyes. The pain of his fractured leg and the lack of water were soon forgotten. With enormous feelings of woebegone sorrow at his spiritual depravity he caught himself praying for a permanent release. Facing death was easier than suffering this living hell that he was now experiencing.

Finally, he freed his surmised, broken leg from a huge stone that was pinning it so tightly that he hadn't been able to move it a fraction of an inch. His skin was totally numb from the knee down, and he feared that the deadweight of that rock had totally disrupted the blood flow and that it had caused cellular damage. This would mean that he couldn't ever walk on it and that repulsive feeling briefly paralyzed his heart and mind. Minutes later, when he first moved it, he discovered how wrong he had been. The leg was violently broken and piercing pain tore at the still very alive and sensitive skin. Nevertheless, this fierce pain struck even harder at his dehydrated and unnourished mind, causing him to black out again.

In a dream, his naked bride faced him standing on a beach and taunted, "Why are you imprisoning yourself like this? Come and get me," she said after turning her back and running away. He tried his best to catch her and suddenly awoke to the veracity of the black cell he found himself imprisoned in. When he awoke to this still too prevalent reality, he arched back ignoring the harsh pain that tore at his innards, lower back, and broken leg. Feeling his other leg he shrank even deeper into depression, it was still rigidly layered in a massive pile of broken stone! Unlike his other leg, however, he could move it ever so slightly which gave him high hopes of it not being badly damaged. "I will never get this leg free in time, though; I'll die soon unless I can get something to drink!" With a short moment of thought, I asked One, "What is the meaning of that dream? Is he really free and this predicament he finds himself in now only an illusion? Is his dream of chasing after Vanessa the genuine article?"

He cried out very loudly from the depths of his heart, "Please God release me, even if it means my death!"

Deep within him came my voice of a spirit, which he called later his God. "In the power and light of our Universal One, I release you with abundant love."

His most consuming fear then came true. A very loud cracking sound echoed through the quiet and he recoiled with consternation. "How can I ever escape this eternal prison of hell?" he cried out as more debris showered him. "Oh, power of life and death either release my bonds of imprisonment or release my spirit from this incarceration!" he cried out in desperation. As if in reaction to our dire petitions, still another exacerbating resounding crash pierced the stillness. The Earth seemed to be quaking under and all about him. More stones and dust fell and covered him from head to toe. He lay quiet, sure that his entreaty for death would be granted this time.

He fell into a stupor and dreamt that he was flying over an unheard of place called Tesa. How he ever knew its name was beyond him. A beautiful and familiar woman rose to meet him; she was holding a moon in one hand and a star in the other. Her lips parted and she whispered, "You have always had the indisputable power of obtaining all of your wishes. Believe and be free!" Having delivered her vital message of will to him, she once again resumed her place as a gorgeous woman in a stained glass window in that temple-like structure. For years he wondered, *Where have I heard of that place, and what was my Vanessa doing in a stained-glass window?* His existence had abruptly become an unsolvable riddle. For some strange reason he was feeling like more than just one man. In that fleeting scene, he had floated into a sky that shown with an unusual light, yet it was oddly familiar just as that building had been.

When he returned to his imprisoned body, he willed himself free.

He was ready to accept his own death when his consciousness seemed to drift off again for a second. A man with a little red beard said, "No, you can't die yet; finish this life, Jim."

"I am Jose, not Jim," he said aloud. Those words had been spoken in English and he was Peruvian. Sadly he found that he was still captive in his body and a black coffin of stone and dust covered him. Deep in his heart, he knew that we were adjoined and asked this other part of him, "Who are you, and why are you in me?"

The words, "I am a future you," came softly into his whole being. Then a moment later, "You are the Universal One and have created your wish. Now be ye free!" I demanded.

He stretched his nearly dead body in the black tomb he found himself still embodied in. Until those last words had been decreed, he was prepared to expire. "No," he denounced loudly, "I am not going to die, I am going to be free and right now, too!" He bent backwards one more time and cheerfully discovered that the large boulders pinning his leg had been shifted just enough during that last tremor and he soon was free. Using a large slab of stone that had collapsed to the ground only inches from his head, he struggled to his feet and shook the small rocks and dust off of himself. As he placed his bad leg on the ground, paralyzing pain raced through his entire body and he instantly crumpled over. That pain actually brought dry tears to his eyes. Lying there, he wondered how he was going to make it out of this hellhole without two strong legs.

That other internal him, who he still tried to distinguish, asserted through his own larynx, "Your entire body is healed in the light of One's love energy." Like before, that mysterious voice had said those words in perfect English.

What was even more surprising was that he comprehended every word spoken and somehow sensed their inner meanings. Without a bit of fear or hesitation, Jose stood and put his full weight on that previously fractured leg.

He painlessly walked straight forward in the direction of the mine opening. He wished for a greater understanding of this inner voice that had so suddenly come alive in him. He then took notice of his hands; they had stopped hurting. Obviously a miracle had occurred; his leg was healed and his hands didn't even have a scratch on them. He felt his head and not even a small bump was to be found, nor the scar or any of the dried blood that he knew had been there only days before. "I am totally healed," he cried aloud with wet tears dripping from his eyes. "Even my driving thirst has been quenched! I will live and strive to increase my understanding of you, God. Then he timidly amended, "One." Tapping his chest, he said, "You are my savior, I would have died if not for you, One!"

I laughed and said, "We are the same beings. All of us are united by the authority of One. You are now witnessing me, a future you. Now feel our lovenergy of One, and allow yourself to be free of your old beliefs."

Communicating with an inner voice was preposterous to him and he laughed and said, "Sure, I'm God/One and all I do all day is go around causing cave-ins and healing my wounds. Now get me out of here!" he demanded with a bit of frustration.

"Now you're catching on," came that laughing inner voice. "Would you have me doing everything for you, One? Now struggle forth in faith and get yourself free."

Neither of us spoke again and only two or three hundred feet further he had hopefully come to the last collapsed remnants of the coal mine cave-in. He grinned with the mystery of that other remote me shimmering in an aloof part of his mind. "Who are you?" he asked me in his native tongue. From where he stood it looked like there was a brighter gap of light at the top of this hopefully last barrier. It was awfully restrictive, but the possibility of escaping stirred him into action.

Not expecting an answer to his last question, he excitedly climbed upwards. His heart fluttered excitedly when he, over the tops of large pieces of tightly-packed stone, clearly saw a large, sunshine-filled opening. In a hurry, he squeezed into the narrow opening. At times he found himself having to cram harder between shards of boulders and partially collapsed walls. He felt deep in the core of his ravenous heart that this had been all dug out by hand. He was here on this spot because of the diligent work of his friends and colleagues. Within only 10 minutes of scrambling over giant pieces of the collapsed mine shaft, he emerged into brilliant sunlight and saw what looked like a large bunch of men packing tools away.

To his right and around a piece of stone, he saw his beloved Vanessa. Tears were streaming from her eyes and when she saw him she shrieked with ecstasy, "Jose, you've risen!"

"You are the only reason I survived this ordeal," he told her outright.

After smiling up into his eyes, following vivacious kisses, they embraced wantonly and she languorously said, "I felt deep in my heart that you were in need of me and raced here. I was waiting to hear word of you only minutes after the cataclysm. I have been here praying, fasting, and sending you love around the clock. It's now five days and I haven't even stepped foot away from this area except to relieve myself. I knew that we would be united again, and I wasn't going to abandon my post until I held you in my arms again— and alive, too." Ruefully, she softly told him, "The smell of death was becoming more and more powerful, and many of these men were giving up. I told them that I wasn't leaving—and here you are only minutes later!"

She was evidently overwhelmed with emotions, never had she spoke so much and so rapidly. Only by covering her mouth with his own did he stop her onslaught of words. Smiling into her radiant blue eyes afterwards, he painfully asked, "Has anyone else escaped?" He wondered about the other 11 men who had been with him. "Did any of them get out before me?"

Far off, I heard a man's voice commanding, "You are now returning to this reality. Enter your bodies in Tesa right now." I abruptly became aware of a seat beneath me and was unable to learn the fate of my co-workers in the mine collapse.

Oh my One, I thought to myself. *I really was in those other people's lives. Yet I was not completely them. There was still a flicker of me who was an outside element of their reality. Oh, how I wish that I could remember what had happened to each of them. It would be especially nice to know what had happened to that miner and his wife! Did that sailor ever make it to shore?* Curiosity haunted my romantic spirit and smiling at these heart-warming memories, I acknowledged, *I wish in that I could have remained in each of their lives longer, I'd like to know what happens.*

"Remain still and inactive. Don't even allow external thoughts to enter your minds. I know that you have many questions and we will get to all of them in a few minutes. First though, in silence with your eyes closed I want you to recall as much of those past lives that you have just witnessed. Like with dreams, you will remember them better if you don't allow your minds to become flooded with other thoughts." Swuel was totally silent for a long time. I recollected many of my past lives and the tremendous amounts of love, fear, anger, futility, the dire needs, and so much more. The thought that struck me the hardest was how much suffering we endure during our lives and I am now learning that none of it is necessary! "We create it all through bad karma and the need of deleting it via good karma in future lives allows us to live." Having an innate realization that I had always had a dearly loved person present in all of my lives thrilled and warmed my heart exceedingly. In fact, it transcended all the pain and frustrations, making them trivial in comparison.

"Now," Swuel said, following minutes of silence, "I am going to bring you back to this present place and time." He then counted us out of the meditation.

When I had reached the alert state again, I became aware of a man crying bitterly. Swuel said, "Excuse me a moment." He stepped off the stage and moved quickly to the side of a grieving man. "Now quiet down, Hank, and tell us all about it."

"I loved my father in a past life," he began with a cracking sound in his voice, "and I did everything he told me to do. Why did he have to take advantage of me and abuse me like that? I would have done anything except—" His words were broken off by another outburst of tears.

"Now release all of that pain, Hank," said Swuel sympathetically. "That was in a former existence. Let it go now and don't allow it to affect you here.

It's another, entirely different life that you now have and there's nothing to fear in this one. Let it pass and be totally free of your anxiety of that forgone existence. You must forgive your father and forget it, for it is over." Turning to us, he said in a louder voice, "Be in harmony with the present and let go of your pasts. You are light workers now and mustn't allow past moments of darkness affect you negatively."

"Why did you have to bring me back there?" asked Hank. "Didn't you realize—"

Swuel spoke with sincerity showing in every word. "I'm sure you saw what a bad person you were in a prior life."

"You shunned a person who really loved and needed you," said Hank's spirit guide, "and your deportment caused her years of anguish."

"In your following life, it was necessary for you to endure pain to grow spiritually moral. You had destroyed a loved one with your neglect and in your succeeding life a beloved person hurt you. Because of that injury, and your rising above it, you have become a more spiritually enlightened person. Now that you are passing that bridge into eternal peace and love, release it and forget that it had ever taken place. Abide as the free-loving and forgiving man that you had been for many past lives. You created that very existence so that you could grow again and you have accomplished all that you desired. Your attendance on this plane testifies to your spiritual enlightenment."

I saw Hank's lips part and a smile crept out. "Thank you, Masters," he whispered gratefully, looking at Swuel and his guide. "Thanks to your guidance, I have now forgiven my past self who wrongly treated her and my father who hurt me. I will not allow it to harm my learning here or my future work on Earth."

Swuel took his position behind the podium again and said, "We have just witnessed a child's brutal pain. Forgiveness and forgetfulness are essential to our inner peace and harmony. If we were to retain our anger and hatred of a person, we would be only wounding ourselves. Thankfully it is of a past life and we really can't do anything about the person we may have been in the past. We only have the people we are right now to abide with. We are the creators of our life, living according to our own choosing. Therefore, it is imperative that we expand our true comprehension of existence. Love and forgiveness are fundamental. Knowing what functions they play in our prevailing lives is essential to our spiritual growth." Smiling generously and nodding his head toward a grinning Hank, he said, "Let's not be bashful; we want to hear from the rest of you. I know that all of you are bursting to tell your stories and have them interpreted for you," he said in a teasing manner.

A very short and heavyset man stood and asked, "How do we know that what we had just experienced weren't merely dreams but actual incarnations?"

"Well, you could just take our word for it," replied Swuel with a broad grin. After we had stopped chuckling, he continued, "Then again I know that you'd like to personally know the truth, so I will share it with you now. For one thing," he commenced, "during the past two hours you've experienced actual moments of many of your past lives. While perceiving those events, you weathered through every obstacle that broached your path. You survived every catastrophe and are here now despite what had occurred. One or more of you even experienced death, birth, and another life. The true reality of past lives is that they can only be relived while in another plane of consciousness. When you dream you're only falling asleep and not reliving experiences. I bet that all of you remember everything that had occurred during that long period of time.

"I am going to try making it a bit more easy for some of you; there is still some apprehension here. I had to guide you down into a different plane of consciousness. For a moment you were passing through the dream stage. Remember those fleeting experiences? They were where dreams are created. Generally, only people who can move themselves into a trance or who are catatonic by their own power of will can leave this state of being and enter that different consciousness. You spent all of two hours in those past lives of yours, actually reliving the events as they occurred. No matter how fascinating or involving dreams might be, they only last seconds. You live in them as present selves, witnessing what was taking place. You were separate thinking beings within that person and only occasionally were you able to communicate with them. As you moved deeper into that other dimension, you were taken more fully into the living movies of your past lives. If I hadn't brought you out of it, you could have remained in one life or another; reliving it minute by minute for only One knows how long. It's even possible that you would be consciously absent for the remainder of your life." He held up a finger and added, "Autistic people are most often reliving past lives. Being mentally present in their current existences is a struggle most autistic people don't allow to fully take place."

All of us gasped at the profundity of that idea. I couldn't conceive of myself having to live a minute longer in some of those horrifying past lives that I had encountered. The awesome idea that someone would prefer staying in them was incredible

A moment later a rather cute girl stood and said, "In this meditation I saw my autistic son who had died a year ago; where do they or anyone go when they die?"

"Evie, some dead autistic spirits are awaiting rebirth like normal people, however, most are immediately brought to higher planes of consciousness."

Another person stood not allowing Swuel to elaborate further. He said, "It may seem odd to you and to my peers, but I would like to research different levels of consciousness. With this in mind, will you be teaching us how to achieve trance-like states of consciousness? How many others are there?"

"It may be a little difficult for you to understand right now, Dr. Brian, but as your mental blocks are broken down through similar exercises, it is the law of cause and effect that everything you desire will be achieved. You will be restricted only to the extent you deem appropriate."

A voice came from the back of the room and asked, "What was the necessity of that particular lesson?"

Swuel smiled to himself and replied, "As I told you before we entered into it, this meditation was designed to erase enfites and spiritual damages due to past errors. I am also sure that all of you received substantial spiritual strengths because of them. Taking a deep breath, he disclosed, "Your past lives are also powerful learning tools for your instructors. Because of them we now know you a whole lot better."

My heart leapt for joy on hearing Gail's voice. She asked, with a troubled heart, "In my last life I was born to a drug and alcohol abusive mother. Due to her neglect and addictions, I died shortly before my third birthday." I remembered Gail telling me that she had no memories of a past life and this apparently was the reason for it. "What would be the purpose of my experiencing it again?" she shyly asked.

"Well my dear, Gail," he began, "it would depend on a prior existence. By any chance did you also relive it?" he asked knowingly.

"Yes," she said sadly. "I was a deaf-blind black woman who committed suicide after her Caucasian lover left her."

Clobbered by this revolution, I involuntarily jumped to my feet gasping, "No, it can't be true! Can it possibly be you, my most beloved, Claire?" Finally because of the improbability that it could be true, turning my back to Swuel, in the deaf sign language I asked, "Is that you, Lovie?"

"My One!" she screamed, just as bewildered as I was feeling. "Jim, it's not feasible that you are the same man?" she signed as well as verbalized. It all fits, though. You did tell me yesterday that you were a blind man in your just completed life. Only moments ago I learned that in my prior life, I mean the one before being that poor child," she said, fluttered by these startling events, "I mean . . . oh—" She broke off for an instant and quickly said, "I learned that Claire's teacher and my lover was named Jim. He was also totally blind! It was you wasn't it!"

"I am the same. It was me, Lovie," I returned out loud and in the same sign fashion. We then simultaneously started moving toward one another, disregarding our spirit guides who were endeavoring to hold us back.

"No," said Swuel abruptly, "this has to stop this instant! Now both of you take your respective places and no more exhibitions of this sort. You are all to be in command of yourselves!"

My heart was on fire with excitement and gargantuan sensations of love. "No wonder we have these strong feelings of love for one another!" The woman I had devoutly loved and had been denied on Earth was with me again. Rather than doing what I most wanted, I instead chose to protect my family from their imagined disgrace of my marrying a black woman, and had caused her to commit suicide. Because of it I had caused endless years of sorrow and severe loneliness for myself. *Thanks to the grace of One we have been fortunate enough to be reunited at this exact moment*, I reveled to myself. *This will give us another chance at celebrating the love that we had been forced to forfeit.* I knew in my heart that I had to have her now, but how we would accomplish this task was beyond me. *How could Swuel or anyone possibly comprehend the urgency and desire of our deprived hearts?* I wondered as I walked slowly to my chair. *That's why we have loved each other since our first meeting here!* I realized as I sank heavily into my unyielding seat.

Chapter 5

Eternal Soul Mates

With a far off look in his eyes, Swuel stood in total silence for several minutes. Then stirring out of his meditative stupor, he said, "Claire . . . I mean Gail and Jim, your spirit guides and I were just conversing. We concur about wanting you to remain here after this session." After another short moment he resumed and what he had to say next surprised me to no end. "Friends, we are witnesses to an exceedingly unusual occurrence, two soul mates finding each other by accident on this plane, although accidents don't really happen; One creates every incident in our lives for given purposes. In any case, this is an especially rare occasion being that they found each other on this plane, in this very center, and at this very moment! It is far more reasonable for them to find one another on Earth. Although they simultaneously die, Claire as a young child in her following life and Jim in the same life in which they had shared. However, no matter how you might look at it, it's significantly improbable that they would rediscover each other here in Tesa! Especially when you consider the improbability of their dying approximately at the same time, plus their gaining equal spiritual levels allowing them to be here with us now."

He sipped his water again and continued. "Soul mates are lovers who find and live together for one or more lifetimes. These two individuals are extraordinarily strong lovers. When we closely examine both of their pasts, I'm sure that we will find them always together. Even if they happened to be the same gender in a past life, I'm sure they were lovers. Whether their past life affiliations were as best friends, husband and wife, or parent and child, we will find them together. Dying approximately at the same time, they often returned to Earth at similar times."

Straightaway on arrival, they sat together here and became reacquainted lovers. Without any prior knowledge, they are truly reunited, heart, mind, and spirit!" With an effervescent smile he surprised me by saying, "You both are to be congratulated. You are very lucky people to have once again rediscovered each other." He smiled to everyone in the room and said, "Friends, Jim and Gail could not recognize one another because they both had been blind when lovers." He raised his hand and said "Couple that with Gail living another entirely different life afterwards and, well, you can see the conflicts there."

I had to wonder how lucky we actually were. My Claire, who was now Gail, was still isolated from me and I longed to have her in my arms. From where I sat it didn't appear that we would ever again be united. Yet in my heart, I knew that we had to be mated again otherwise neither of us would find contentment in this present life. Nor fulfillment in any future lives.

After a slight pause, he continued, "Okay, now let's get on with your questions and comments dealing with the meditation just concluded."

My mind being preoccupied with the finding of my long lost love made it impossible for me to concentrate on the other goings-on in the room. *Claire, my loving Claire,* I mentally soliloquized. *I am overjoyed at finding you once again! Gail, imagine you being my Claire all the time? No wonder I was so powerfully attracted to you. How could I have ever been willing to give you up in that just past life of mine, Claire? Where was my mind and most of all, where was my heart? Swuel was right,* I joyously thought, *we are soul mates!* There was always someone special in all of my past lives, I vividly recalled from the meditation just completed. *I was that ailing baby in your arms. Also, you were soul mate to me, the miner in Brazil.* I then visualized the sailors tied to the masts. *I loved that other man, I realized.* Then again there was something on the periphery of my mind about a niece who I also adored. *I've got to see if I can get myself back into that lifetime,* I deliberated. *Then I would know if my soul mate was my sailing friend or my niece.* In the background I was partly cognizant of people talking and the voice of Swuel replying to their questions. My mind, nevertheless, was almost completely absorbed in the thought of Claire and I being lovers once again. *Lovie,* I mentally yearned, *I want so badly to be with you after today's teaching and to be able to love you physically again! They've got to permit us to get married or at least give us a few hours alone every day. I've got to have you as a part of my life; otherwise I will not be able to survive these tormenting desires for very long!* I visualized her head resting on my shoulder with her long, red hair draped over my naked chest. "Oh my One, please help me."

Suddenly I was jolted back to reality with Swuel's last few broken words. "Tomorrow morning. Please be in front of Tesa at precisely 8:00."

I was still partially in a stupor when people started leaving. "Wait here, Jim," said Rama walking toward Swuel.

I was startled further by the man who had been sitting on my right, walking to my side and saying, "Larry, that's the name. Luck with you an' that sexy dame."

I half-wittedly replied, "No sweat man, it's as good as done."

He then removed a pack of cigarettes from his breast pocket, showed them to me, and crushed them in his large hand. "Died from emphysema in a past life and added asthma problems to my kid in the last. Guess it's 'bout time I give 'em up, huh?"

"Good luck, Larry," I replied, extending my hand to him after getting to my feet. Afterwards I stood uncomfortably, shifting my weight from one foot to the other. I was impatient and wanted to locate my beloved woman. Having to stand here waiting for One knows what, was getting me edgy. Even in my past life as a blind man I wasn't one to just sit around do nothing. I was waiting to be joined by Swuel and Rama, hoping that Marza and Gail would soon follow.

Within only minutes they were at my side and my past life lover Claire and I stared passionately into each other's enraptured eyes. Since neither of us had been sighted in those just completed lives, we were seeing each other for the very first time. The passion I saw on her dazzling face caused a familiar reaction; my body coveted her. My arms began to rise as I reveled with sensations of an overwhelming yearning for an endless embrace.

Swuel spoke joyfully to the two of us. "As I said before, it is phenomenal that this event has transpired. When it comes down to it, there is only one way to handle it." He looked us both in the eye as Gail and I stood with our hands barely touching. When he said his next words, we concurrently fell into each other's arms: "We've got to let you eternal soul mates get married!"

I became electrified with the feel of Gail's body pressed against mine. Her voluptuous lips on mine nearly caused my knees to collapse. Only by some miracle was I able to contain my enthusiasm. After giving us some free time, Swuel continued, "We are inordinately privileged to be taking part in this uncommon occasion," he announced to us with pride in his voice. As Gail and I kissed and embraced each other with joyous feelings of deliverance he called to Rama and Marza. When they had reached his side, he said looking us in the eyes, "From the beginning we were in the same accord. We felt that the two of you were soul mates. Now we know that not only are you mates, but eternal soul mates! We had to be sure of that fact, though, and that is why we held this past life meditation a few days earlier than usual. We have seen total strangers meet here and fall madly in love at first sight. Also, we have had many past life lovers rediscover each other here, but this time we have eternal soul mates being reunited!" With some hesitation showing in his demeanor, he said, "So, we had to be cautious despite our strong impressions concerned in this matter."

"Rama, is that why you asked me to just wait a few days? You told me, if things weren't resolved in a few days that we would speak with Swuel. In any case," I said with fervent relief, "are you telling us now that Gail and I will be soon together again? Can it be here on this plane?" I asked with hope in my heart.

"Jim," said Swuel preempting Rama, "we knew that everything would be unveiled during today's meditation session. If, in fact, our suspicions were correct and you were eternal soul mates, ceaselessly having each other every single lifetime, we knew that it would be disclosed to the three of us. Now that that fact has been clearly revealed, there is only one recourse. You, being unfamiliar with the meaning of eternal soul mates, have to understand that it isn't a simple matter. If you were unable to be united you would be totally disconcerted with life and our movement. As a result, you would function only minimally, if at all. Not only are you soul mates, but eternally united. As so, you are especially attuned to one another's thoughts and emotions. Immediately after you are married, you will find that your aptitudes will become greatly enhanced. Your true potential will blossom shortly after your marriage and the two of you will become one exceedingly powerful unit! You will ascertain the truth of spiritual stimulus once you have become one. For that reason, the two of you must be married tomorrow morning at—"

"Eight a.m. right?" I cut in. "I had heard you telling everyone to be present here at that hour. I had no idea though that it was for our marriage!" I told him with an exceedingly large smile. I was extremely thrilled with the prospect of marrying Gail, especially since it was less than a day away! Because of my heartfelt feelings of enchantment with this whole notion, my next words stunned me. "Aren't you presuming an awful lot by just marrying us off like this? Sure, this woman and I have been lifetime lovers; no one is denying that. However, we haven't been together for many years. How do you or we, for that matter, know if we still feel the same way about each other? Don't we have any say around here? You had kept us apart until now and only a day later uniting us in marriage!"

I was proud of Gail's unhurried completion of my thought. "Jim and I have loved each other in the past, Swuel. Nevertheless, we are both different people now. Jim hasn't known me, this girl named Gail, nor had he been with Claire for years. I've lived a little bit of another entirely different life. In any case, the emotional association that we had shared has dissolved because of years of separation and my other life. Jim had to daily suffer with the pain of his loss. Also, the fact that I had committed suicide because he had righteously refused to live with me, a woman of another race."

I only had time to give Gail a shake of my head, indicating that I wasn't harboring any anger toward her. Marza, who until this juncture had been silent, spoke up. "Not to break your trust, Gail, but I've got to speak the whole truth. Since you and Jim first met on this plane, I've seen, heard, and felt your strong attraction toward one another. Rama and I have frequently discussed your reciprocal feelings for each other. Even though you have lived another life and Jim has been without you, soul mates vigilantly perpetuate their affinity even if they aren't physically united. Because you both need to hear this, I am going to attempt paraphrasing what Swuel had told you." She smiled and said, "We know from experience that you two need to be adjoined. If not, he also told you, your lives will not be rewarding to either of you and you will miss out on immense spiritual growth and potency." Smiling kindly at us, she said, "During your stay here, and especially when returning to Earth, you will need all the extra powers that being united will give you."

"Heck," said Rama wisely, "you might have even left us."

Swuel nodded his head toward Marza in approving recognition of her input. Then with another nod at Rama, he said, "You're right, they could have gone to another density, or plane of consciousness." Looking at us, he gave condolences to Gail and me. "I'm sorry for presuming that you'd want to immediately become espoused. I only thought of all the pain that the two of you went through years ago. We just presumed you would want to make up for those lost years by finally getting married. I am truly feeling excited for you and want only to please you both. Gail, Marza was with you throughout the meditation and had seen your mutually shared sentiments during those intervals when you relived your experiences with Jim. She had told me that there couldn't have been a closer bond between the two of you. Rama told me that, for the sake of his Grandmother's health, Jim had begrudgingly given you up. Rama had seen and heard that entire showdown with Jim and his family. His Grandmother was close to having a fatal heart attack and Jim did the honorable thing. He promised his grandmother that he wouldn't cause the family to break up because of his romantic feelings for you."

Standing next to Gail, I felt tremendous amounts of love pouring out of her. Tears were now running down her cheeks and I spontaneously leaned forward and kissed them away. Because of our close proximity and my escalating desires, my body became excited and exceptionally warm. I began to perspire and felt that I had to do something to remove myself from this enormous challenge of will. Coming to my rescue, Swuel said, "In no way have we wanted to push or force this issue. Knowing the fervor of love that eternal soul mates share, our sole intention was to fulfill your needs. We want you to be totally satisfied and content as well as competent with your lives here and on Earth when you return."

With my heart racing, I asked, "You mean to tell us that we won't have to do without one another here or especially on Earth? That we will be love partners always together?" My head was spinning with excitement and surprise with this encouraging revelation. Gail squeezed my hand and we turned and faced each other with feelings of joy.

Swuel looked shyly into my eyes and replied, "Seeing how the two of you have been constantly renewing your relationship, it only stands to reason that you will once again be united when you return to Earth. You share an eternal union that customarily incapacitates ordinary obstacles. Your reunion may not be immediate after returning to Earth, but I assure you that you will eventually find and be together. In truth, it depends greatly on the age and locations of your new human bodies. Right now we cannot tell if you are going to be children, adolescents, or young adults, so there could be some delay concerning when you will be reunited."

Not saying another word about our meeting on Earth, he continued, "As an eternal team, I know that you will be enormously helpful to our cause. For that reason, we want you married here. When you are ready to be reinstated on Earth, we will do our best to get you into bodies that will match in age, location, and race. This will enable you to have a faster reunion."

Facing Swuel head on, I said, "If we are to be married in the morning, the two of us must be alone tonight so that we can rejuvenate misplaced emotions."

Gail said, so demurely that I had all I could do not to gather her up in my arms and smother her in kisses, "We will be married in the morning. First, though, Swuel, we need some time alone and without any chaperones conflicting with what we have to rediscover about one another."

Our three masters communicated in their unique way and then our requests were addressed. "I'm sorry, my dear," Swuel replied to her frankly, "but you will have to have some surveillance. Rama and Marza will be passively watching you. They will help in case your passions become overwhelming. We will give you the whole night to discuss old emotions. We agree that rejuvenating your emotional feelings about each other is crucial. We've got to do everything possible to strengthen your relationship. Do remember, though, that this is holy ground you are on. So please," he said with some embarrassment, "please refrain from intimate sexual activities."

"You have our solemn oath on that, Swuel," I vowed sincerely.

"You and Gail are going to be a tremendous team," said Swuel. "To secure your rapid evolution, we will be taking extra time and including special training." For a minute he conferred privately with our spirit guides. Afterwards he spoke to us in a consolatory voice. "You are going to receive private instruction away from your peers and we ask that you not break the fact of your special developmental curriculum to anyone. We can't have any jealousy among our students." Unaccustomed to the feelings and words that he was about to say, he paused and shifted his weight from side to side. He shrugged his shoulders, cleared his throat, and said, "Also, there is a minor inconvenience that we have to ask of you both. You'll have to sleep apart tonight. We've got to preserve your virginity, honoring One at all cost. You are both virgins right now in these metaphysical bodies. It is likely that you will become overwhelmed if you sleep together. We can't allow you to take that risk. Unrighteous acts will cause a rift in your spiritual maturation and we don't want anything disrupting your favorable futures," he said somberly.

"Marza and I will show you to your new quarters," said Rama a minute later. "We have had a few reunited couples visit us in the past and have special living arrangements for you. Once you become husband and wife, it will remain your lodging for as long as you are with us. Right now there are people preparing your home for our arrival. I've been assured that it will be ready by the time we get there. For that reason, however, we will walk rather than fly to your new abode. This will also give you an opportunity to see the colorful setting in which you will be living."

"May the light and love of One follow your pure and virtuous paths," said Swuel.

Without saying another word, Gail and I walked hand-in-hand following behind Rama and Marza. We passed the men's quarters and proceeded down a curving, steep, dirt road behind it. Within only a few minutes we were in an area that I hadn't yet seen. There were tall, stately trees draped with colorful and sweet smelling honeysuckle vines and large open meadows beyond them. Another five minutes of walking brought us to an exquisite view. Gail and I squeezed each other's hands with feelings of excitement and enormous joy that filled our hearts and minds. Our eyes were dazzled by a sparkling crystal clear lake with green lily pads whose white flowers glistened in the brilliant purity of the light of One. Two graceful snow-white swans glided majestically toward a wooded area on the left end. Three gray babies followed closely behind. Set back and to the right of the lake was an old-fashioned barn with a huge red and white painted silo attached to it. In front of it was an adjoining stable and three horses frolicked joyfully. In the foreground was a large Victorian mansion reposing on a gentle slope to the far right of the lake. Like a mother hen watching over her chicks, it overlooked the lake and all of the striking scenery before her.

"Well, folks," said Rama with a broad smile, "how do you like your new home?"

"Oh my One, all of this is really ours?" cried my gratified companion.

"Ra-Rama, Marza," I stammered excitedly, "this is our own little paradise? I thought that we were just stopping along the way to give those workers more time!"

"I can't believe that this majestic home is ours! How did we ever get so fortunate?" Gail asked jubilantly.

"The horses," I asked, feeling perplexed by all of this luxury, "are they also ours?"

With a pleased smile gracing her pleasant face, Marza replied, "I hope you can ride?"

Smiling even more, Rama said, "Everything you see here is yours."

"You mean to tell us that we will be the only people here?" I asked, sweeping my hand from side to side with a feeling of incredulity in my heart.

Rama smiled and said, "Except for a few maintenance workers who will be here early mornings."

Marza smiled warmly at the two of us who were overwhelmed with feelings of joy. "Remember that Rama and I are always available for you. If a problem should arise don't hesitate to call upon us. Following your marriage we will not be overseeing your activities; you will be left alone except during classes or if you contact us for a specific reason."

After saying our farewells, Gail and I walked up a dirt path toward our superb utopia. The horses shied a little as we approached them. Stopping in my tracks I said to Gail, "Send them pink light, Lovie."

"Oh, Jim," she said, raising her hands toward the timid horses, "I get chills whenever you call me Lovie."

We hugged each other then sent our horses pink light. I was still in awe of everything I beheld. I had never, in my wildest dreams, fancied that this kind of grandeur could ever be my abode. And yet here I was and with the most ever desired woman of my life. This majestic setting was my home. Less than a minute later I proudly proclaimed, "See! It works all the time!" With their tails swishing in the air, three not so shy horses trotted to our sides and touched us lovingly.

"You better not send me your magical pink light tonight," she teased. "I might not be able to control my infatuation. Oh, Jim," she said, sounding like a little girl might. A second later, and with a clap of hands, she said, "look how friendly they are now!" She giggled blissfully as one of them snorted and nuzzled her neck.

"As you can see, they're no longer afraid of us," I said, envying that lucky horse that had gotten to kiss her. How I wished that I could hold her and allow myself to express my heartfelt feelings. Pragmatically, though, I was genuinely worried about my ability to handle the profound love that was mounting into a crescendo within me. What made it even more exasperating was that these feelings were getting stronger and more demanding. Sure, I did want to feel genuine love for Gail, but at this rate, I was getting panicky about my ability of withstanding my intensely growing desires.

It was as if my Claire and I had never been apart, having been separated by death and years of detachment. Yet I knew that this was different; I was also falling in love with another woman. *Although,* I admitted to myself, *she is my same eternal soul mate.* I knew and dearly loved my memories of Claire; nevertheless, right now it feels as if she were another person, diverse from my newfound love. "Perhaps," I thought, "this is only an illusion due to the fact that I am now visibly beholding Gail."

Another shocking question raced through my mind. *If I had had sight and had noticed our racial differences right off, would I have acted more professionally and not gotten sexually involved?* Without hesitation, I nodded my head yes. *It sure would have helped me to avoid problems and would have also kept her alive.*

Then I wondered, Being *that she was my eternal soul mate, would that have made my falling in love impossible to deny*? I did realize that I had been able to leave her that lamentable night, though I knew deep within my heart that it would have been impossible for me to remain apart forever. *If only she had lived, I surely would have gone back to her again,* I sadly acknowledged to myself.

The obsession that I was now feeling for Gail was a renewed passion that

I had felt for my beloved Claire. Yet in reality I knew that it was separate and distinctive because these were two separate individuals.

Gail's next pleading whisper detoured my thought and reduced my mounting desire, "Oh how I wish we could ride them."

"Your wish is my command, Missy," I mimicked in a poor interpretation of a western cowboy. Taking her hand in mine, we ran toward the stable. "Let's go and see if there are some riding supplies in that shed," I said. We entered the barn and inside we found all kinds of farming equipment, some of which I immediately recognized and others I had never seen before. On the side of the barn we found a door that led into the stable. There, we located all of the riding accessories we needed.

What we experienced next I wouldn't have ever believed possible elsewhere. Gail and I piled the implements for riding outside the barn doors. Every time we exited our ponies greeted us warmly and with great excitement as if they rationally understood what we were intending. After we had gotten the riding gear for two horses piled outside, we tried to decide which ones we would ride. "Jim," said Gail pointing to the speckled mare who had snuggled her, "can I please ride that one?"

"Sure thing, missy," I said, glad to grant any of her wishes. "You got 'er."

Laughing, she ran to her mount. I joined her with a saddle blanket and a gem garnished saddle and placed them on the back of Gail's horse. Before I could bend down to fasten the girth straps of the saddle, another horse pushed the first one out of the way and stood in place of her. We started to laugh when it was performed again. Gail and I laughed for several minutes as one horse after the other got pushed away and was replaced by another.

"There's only one way to settle this," I said with a thunderous laugh, "we'll have to saddle all three of them." As if understanding my words, they settled down and waited for each to be saddled in turn.

For a few hours we rode through some of the most beautiful country that you could find. Because of the purity of this plane and its immaculate landscape, every blade of grass was as colorful and healthy as it possibly could have been. The panorama was breathtaking and not a drop of litter or pollution could be seen. Hills threw shadows onto neighboring hills and vibrant colors burst out of the sunlit areas. Streams and lakes appeared to be mirrors, clearly reflecting perfect images of whatever was close at hand. Pausing on one hillside we stared down at ourselves mirrored in a lake far below us. Looking down at our reflections, I saw joy and great ecstasy written on our faces and in our eyes. I desired this woman so much and found it hard not to demand that we get off of our mounts and lay down in the soft, green grass. Suddenly the horse that was loose started to charge at us as if he were going to try and knock us down. He swerved just in time to prevent a calamitous collision. It was almost as if he had read my mind and wanted to make us get to the ground!

I had found that in order to keep the devout horses appeased that it was necessary for me to dismount one and get onto another every mile or less that we had traveled. It seemed odd to me that these horses were only content when they were being ridden and that the one that wasn't being used would make a nuisance of himself. If tied to a saddle horn of another, horse he would just refuse to move or charge ahead. Or worst yet, he would swerve in one direction or another. If he were unconstrained he would run circles around us, stop dead in its tracks, or try anything to get our attention. "What are we going to do with them, Jim?" Asked Gail sitting firmly on her mare and looking like she had been born in a saddle, yet neither of us had ever ridden to our knowledge. "I have never seen animals behave like this," she said with disbelief. "It seems like they love us so much that they feel unhappy unless they are serving our needs by being ridden. I think that the one who isn't aiding us is actually jealous of the others."

We dismounted and stood still as the three horses came face to face with us. Their noses were literally within inches of our own. "Look, Jim," said Gail with a little titter, "it's like they understand us and want to listen to what we have to say to them."

I raised my finger in front of the two that I had been riding and scolded them like little children. Remarkably they behaved themselves until we got nearly home.

We stopped at the lake near our home on the way back to give the horses a drink and to also relax for a few minutes. Feeling slightly strained from this unusual exercise, we both collapsed heavily to the ground with groans of relief. The air was sweet with the fragrance of close growing honeysuckle. "I love that smell," said Gail as we sprawled beneath vine-covered trees.

"Lovie," I said taking her hand in mine, "we've got to talk. It seems to me that you have been a little inhibited. You've been so quiet, are you perhaps feeling afraid about marrying me?"

"Oh, no, Jim, don't ever think that! It's just a little shyness owing to the fact that Claire wasn't ever able to vocalize her thoughts or feelings. Also, because I had lived for such a short time following, well, I just never developed communication skills as that little scared child."

"Is that what is making you seem so bashful, Lovie?" I asked with concern. Even though we were soul mates and I was feeling enormous love for this woman, we really didn't know one another very well. Unlike her, I regrettably didn't have total recall of my past lives. Therefore, I was feeling unsure of this beautiful creature that I was going to be marrying in the morning. *Who was she*, I wondered silently. *What does or doesn't she like*? These facts, among millions of other bits, were a mystery to me and I wondered if I would know them before our marriage. Although, it was as if we were being married on Earth, only knowing so much about each other. Even after being together for many years, couples still discover things about their mate. With an internal grin I realized that we had known each other for eternity and you would think that I'd know her thoroughly by now. I laughed to myself with the realization of her being my eternal soul mate. *You can't get anymore never-ending than that*, I thought. Nevertheless, I didn't know her in this life now, nor have much memory of her in our many pasts.

With a far off look in her eyes, she hesitantly asked, "How do I say this without hurting you?"

"Just say it," I told her, "you can't hold back anything now. You've got to voice all of your feelings whether they be uneasy or appreciative."

"How 'bout you? Don't you also have to voice your feelings, pro or con?"

She paused for a long time then weakly started, "Jim . . . Jim," she began again, "I really don't know how I feel about us getting married tomorrow morning."

I nodded my head in agreement. "I know, Lovie. I, too, am feeling a little reserved about their abrupt decision about marrying us off like this. How can they make this kind of request, especially with them not even discussing it with us firsthand?"

"They evidently know eternal soul mates. So, we have to presume that everything will work out for the best," she wisely advised. "Like you said, though, we really don't know each other all that well. It's been years for you, and I have even been another person since Claire. After our last meditation I have total recall of that person called Claire, but I'm sorry to say that emotionally speaking, she is dead. Even though you've been without her, you at least have some of those passions remaining."

"Sorry to admit," I divulged, "but Claire is only a very fond memory for me. I have little arousing ties with her now. All the same, I am finding myself growing more and more fond of you, Gail, a new, yet old, lover."

Because of her alluding to that child she had told us about in class, I was intrigued and asked, "Who was that other person and what kind of things did she think or feel?"

Without a bit of uncertainty, she honestly replied to my question, "I learned during that meditation that she was Gail, a very sad and frightened child. Her mother was an uncaring alcoholic who abused and neglected her unmercifully. Gail always desired to be like other little girls, living in a home filled with love," she sadly replied. "I always tried to help Mommy get better. Whenever she drank she became nasty and hit me until she passed out or I stopped crying. The week before my fourth birthday she was away until after I had gone to bed. She came in with some man and started screaming because I had forgotten to put the milk back into the refrigerator. I tried to get out of my bedroom window, to sit on the roof where I often went when she was in this mood. Just as my foot touched the shingles outside, she grabbed at me, knocking me to the ground. My skull was fractured and neck broken. Thankfully, I died on the spot." Tears streamed from her eyes and I gathered her up in my arms.

Wanting desperately to console this Gail and that poor neglected child she had been during that past life, I fondly patted her arm and made silly little noises. I commiserated and tears rolled down my cheeks with her earnest grief. "My poor Gail," I said with heartfelt remorse. "I am affected so much when I hear stories that negatively impact innocent children. When I return to Earth I've got to write a book telling everyone about the pink light and its powerful effects on love. The world's citizens have to learn how easy it is to create this blissful sensation for themselves. Using this technique will bring contentment into the lives of every love-deprived human. There will not be neglect, hatred, divorce, or any disharmony. Even the most hardened criminals will become caring and loving people. Everything stems from our heart consciousness. People have to learn how to expand lovenergy into the nucleus of every cell of their own bodies. As a result, this emotional boosting will positively stimulate their lives and those of their loved ones. Then love will enlighten their minds,

hearts, bodies, and spirit. It will thereby correct all of the defects of mankind."
Warming to the subject, I said, "Until humanity learns how to create love for
themselves via this method, discord will reign on Earth and humanity will
destroy all they find objectionable."

"Hooey," she reveled, "that's a mouthful!" Then, clearing her throat, she
said, "Unconditional love is what the world's people all need. How, though,
do we get heartfelt love to all of mankind? No matter how good it might be,
how do we send it to everyone? Getting others to practice and advance this
technique once we've taught them is hard enough. Getting it to needy people
everywhere is going to be a huge undertaking."

"My dear, we are all One. Once they have found out how grand it feels
and how easy it is to use they will be joyfully practicing it willingly. Everyone
who experiences it will make it a daily activity. Starting their mornings with
a 15-minute love projection will transform their own feelings and eventually
those of the entire world around them. Protesting against the evils of society
doesn't work. However, transforming ourselves with lovenergy does. For love
enhancement, what better way to start every day?"

Thinking of our situation again, I changed the subject and said, "It is
surprising that they want, and even expect, us to get married suddenly
like this. Although, Swuel did tell us that our effectiveness would be vastly
improved and I am sure that this is their main objective for all of us. Making
us as strong and powerful for this cause is there ultimate duty to humanity
and our One." With a smile more to myself than her, I said, "I feel tremendous
love for you right now. If I were to start kissing you as I want and need,
well, let me tell you that our passions soon would become uncontrollable,
especially for me!"

With a sigh of regret, she said, "I was another person and I am afraid to
tell you that I am disconnected from Claire's emotions." With an after thought,
she asked, "Besides, what makes you think that I wouldn't be turned on
just as fiercely?" she asked, raising her hand to stop me from responding.
"The truth is that women's sex drives are every bit as demanding as men.
The difference is wanting you to feel masculine; we women give you men the
illusion that you are the aggressors. Regardless," she said with a diabolic
smile, "I am not Clair. I am another person now and have fallen in love with
you afresh. I would melt in your arms if you were to start kissing me. I need to
experience those incredible sensations that your kisses would evoke, but for
now we've got to deny ourselves. Like you, I've got to remain in control of my
passion. Releasing myself for even a moment will cause me to yearn too much
to restrain myself. I just can't endure craving you more than I am right now."

My primary goal now was to love her in whatever capacity I could. At this
precise moment it seemed that it meant my having to restrain my zeal. Feeling
her distress about her childhood and knowing that our marriage arrangement
was putting more tension on her, I suggested, "Maybe we should call off our
wedding plans for a little while?"

"No, no!" she cried, getting to her feet in alarm. I stood, gently enfolded
her in my aching arms while trying my best to soothe her frazzled nerves. "Oh,
Jim," she whispered, "I love you and can't imagine my life without you being a
part of it. You have always been present in my many lives and I can't conceive

living without you another day. I've got to have you and the sooner the better!"

Being near to where we had been reposing, I pushed gently downward and we sprawled on the soft sweet smelling grass. "Only the second before, you told me that you didn't emotionally feel anything. Now you allege to love me and to be unable to do without me. Inform me please, Lovie. Tell me which is it?" I abruptly asked her.

"Oh, One," she whimpered, "I am so confused that I don't know what I am saying or feeling. It's these conflicting sensations in me: the old Claire who was so hurt and whose love had been denied, a child whose life was always so vulnerable, and this new me who knows you from every life, but who is so unsure of herself right this moment. Couple those discording conflictions with our eternal affairs and the completely new me who I am living this second who would be at a loss if I were to lose you again. Oh, Jim—"

My pressed lips stopped her discord. Like her, I was on a cruise and having similar feelings, although in comparison, I was only in a dinghy. Regardless, I asserted, "You've got to be sure of your feelings before the morning arrives. Who are you right now and what do you really want?" Without saying another word I began to kiss her sweet delicate lips and neck. The feel of her naked skin drove me further. My hand found the top button of her blouse, which I intentionally unfastened. My tongue found the cleavage between her breasts and my craving increased proportionately. Her response was as urgent as my own. Her legs opened and welcomed my full weight upon her. The feel of her body beneath mine compelled me to give into my desires for a more satisfying sensation. Fortunately, rationality quickly awoke the necessary force that enabled me to stop before it went any further. I knew that I couldn't yield to this temptation and after pressing myself hard against her and moving ever so slightly I got to my knees. With devastating desires I moaned aloud, "Oh, Lovie, as much as we crave, we can't indulge in this passion we are both caught up in!" Her hand found and caressed my swollen member while I knelt at her side and continued kissing her. Unable to restrain my zeal much longer, I had to compellingly pull away from this source of temptation. I was fully engorged with yearning. "Please wait here, my love," I said, needing to find a release for this insistent drive. I got to my feet and began running as hard and fast as I could.

The three horses that evidently thought this was a new game joined me, and boy what pranksters they were! While I ran as fast as I could, two of them ran double circles around me as if I were standing still. Another one of them who had been following me suddenly circled and dove into my path. He landed flat on his belly, only feet in front of me, and with horses on either side, I was boxed in! The only recourse I had was to put out my hands as if I were sleepwalking and do a quick somersault over the top of him. After landing on my feet, I turned and charged full speed at him. I was amazed with his agility. He not only got up and out of my way, but also lunged at me from behind. As he caught up with me, I swerved and put my arms around his neck as he came abreast. I held on tightly as that horse carried me back toward an anxious Gail.

By the time we reached her she was standing anxiously with her hands clenched in prayer fashion. "Oh my One, Jim," she said, running to my side as I slapped my friend affectionately on his flanks. "You could have been killed out there!"

I only laughed and hugged her.

After a few more kisses, I said, "As long as we are standing, let's head back to the homestead, Missy." We were only a few minutes away so instead of riding I put my arm around her and we started walking back.

"Do you know that you could have gotten killed or crippled by those ludicrous antics you and those crazy horses pulled?" she asked with a worried frown creasing her forehead.

"Hey," I said in fun, "I thought you'd appreciate my gymnastic abilities."

"Oh, you did some gymnastics? I'm sorry, I must have missed them."

After laughing, we made the horses comfortable in the stable and retired to our mansion. From its large front porch, Gail pointed into the sky and asked, "Have you ever seen a more beautiful sunset?"

"No I haven't, Lovie," I replied with certainty.

"Just look at those colors, they're absolutely radiant! They are vibrant with every color imaginable." She was right; I saw shades of yellow melting into purple with fiery rust-colored edges and blue fusing with pink and orange to become a distinguished color of its own.

"That splendor is our wedding gift from One," she whispered, out of breath by its spectacular luster and significance. "I asked Him for a sign and this has to be it! "Never," she murmured with awe displayed in her shimmering eyes and on her wide-open lipped smile "Never have I seen such beauty," she moaned. We stood there spellbound by its glory for several minutes.

"Sorry, my love," I said, feeling opposed to missing this radiant display, "but we've got to go indoors and talk." I felt a decisive need to learn all I could about this ravishing creature that was going to be my wife in the morning. I knew that we couldn't put off getting reacquainted again. "Please," I beseeched, "let's get inside and do some serious chatting and rediscovering of emotional links. We can't really afford to procrastinate any longer!"

I began to guide her to a nearby couch in the living room, but was halted by her plea, "Can't we please first examine our new home?"

I reluctantly relinquished my hold and said, "Sure thing, Lovie. Where would you like to commence your tour?"

"Right here," she said, walking over to a large mural on the wall overhanging an ancient marble-mantled fireplace. I scarcely noticed the huge living room filled with antique furniture or the splendid mantelpiece. My eyes were fastened on Gail who was staring into the eyes of a gorgeous woman holding a sallow appearing child. I seemed to recognize the woman. *Maybe she's someone famous?* I speculated. Then it hit me. *No, she's from one of my past lives*, I thought after racking my brain in an attempt to place her.

"Jim," said Gail after a tentative minute of scrutiny. "That woman is me from three lifetimes ago. The baby she is holding is you and you're very sick," she finished, affirming my waking memory.

"My One, you're right!" I replied, astonished with how our minds were working in unison. "In that last meditation Swuel guided us in, I remember your loving arms holding me and your beautiful face looking down at me. Thinking about it now, I remember feeling especially secure and dependent on your heartfelt love." I wondered about my next sensation, but knowing it to be true I said, "It is unusual for a baby to feel this, but I was passionately in love with you as well. That feeling is almost as potent now as it was during that life," I admitted to her and myself.

Following a short moment of reflection regarding my just completed statement, she said, "Yes, you were so sick that all I could do for you was to love and comfort you as much as possible. I poured my love out to you every waking minute. When you died, being heartbroken over my loss, I only lived another four months. We know now that we were eternal soul mates and that explains why we felt so much love for one another. I still have to wonder, though, how did that portrait get here?"

"I presume our spiritual guides saw us together during that meditation," I surmised. "I do have to wonder, though, how they came about acquiring this particular painting so quickly? Especially when you consider the facsimile. It's as if they somehow duplicated what we had seen during that meditation and, in only 90 minutes or so, get it reproduced!"

"Could we have been here in this very house following another one of our past lifetimes? If so, during that time, you wouldn't have been a baby so how did they acquire this perfect likeness of you?" She echoed my thoughts as we examined the picture. "I am totally unfamiliar with this plane, yet have a slight feeling of familiarity about this house," she said. "Having total recall of all of our past lives together, you'd think that I would recollect our presence in this most memorable setting. I remember perfectly every one of our pasts, but have no reliable memory of ever visiting this realm with you, anyone else, or even alone for that matter."

"Funny, I was just wondering about the very same thing," I told her. I thought of the reactions of the horses and paused in both my movement and thoughts. "Gail . . ." I said with a probing tone in my voice.

"What is it, Jim?" she asked after waiting a few seconds for me to finish my statement. She had a puzzled far-off look in her usually communicative eyes and I was unable to read anything obvious in them this time around.

"I just had a curious thought. I have wondered about the over-friendliness of the horses for some time now. Do you suppose it's really because they remember us?" I suggested.

"Oh my One," she said, covering her mouth with her hand. "Do you think that it's really feasible that we were here once before? Why don't I remember any of it, yet have this persistent nagging feeling of recognition about this house?"

"If we've really been here with those horses, my only question is how could they have lived so long? We are talking about prior lives and I know that horses can't possibly live that long! But how else can you explain this phenomenal occurrence? What's even more perplexing when you think about it," I said, with a probing laugh, "is that neither you nor I were horseback riders in our just past life. Yet for some unexplainable reason, we both felt right at home and rode as if we were born in the saddle. During the meditation, when I was reliving my pasts, I hadn't visited a moment remotely connected with horses."

"Well, Jim, we were good riders in a prior life." Then she called out, "Marza can you and Rama enlighten us about these matters?"

She had scarcely completed her question when our spirit guides appeared at our sides.

"We've been nearby and know what you have to ask." Marza looked into Rama's eyes and, deciding to complete her thought, said, "It's simply because the separation of past, present, and future time in the endless continuum of space doesn't exist. One moment is the same as another. We've learned that not every area one might exist in follows the same law of three dimensions: height, width, and length. On the contrary, infinite densities of time have to be added to that concept. Division of time is only an illusion, a figment of humanities imagination. Humans needed frames in which to store events and, therefore, created the deception of time."

She smiled at us and startled us further by saying, "To answer your prior question, you might have been here only a few densities past, especially since all of them occur at the same moment! That's why the horses recognize you and why you are such good riders."

"Remember," said Rama, "densities exist in the same three dimensions. Also, We have artists who can move from one of those densities into another."

"To be completely honest," Marza said with a light-hearted laugh, "this zone where we are now is even in a different density from when at Tesa. It is only used for enlightenment of members of our cause. This particular plane where you reside now, is for soul mates needing to be absolved and unified. To expand on what Marza said about time being an undeviating perpetual moment, we know that it's not the least bit separated." He scratched his head while thinking. "Densities are like an eggplant parmesan casserole, layers upon layers of cheese, sauce, and eggplant. There are many other soul mates living right here where we are now. In fact, as complex as this might seem to you, you are here only because there are other densities within what we call the law of dimension. If there were only a 3D dimension, well, we would never fit! The very space that we are occupying now also has more than 5,000 soul mates present. They are living simultaneously in houses like this one."

"In very simple terms, Jim and Gail, all of us are infinite with One existing universally on this and every plane of consciousness," Marza told us.

"Remember, there is only One. We are the beings of His imagination. "I've got rather advanced truths, but by your questions, we feel it is the time for this to be disclosed. You have both previously been here, or in another density, on this plane of consciousness," Rama revealed. "We followed and you took us into this particular density, so we knew that this version of this homestead was your own during a past existence."

"You mean that our horses actually do remember us!" I asked joyously.

"But why don't I have any real memory of this magnificence," Gail asked with mystery showing in her eyes. "Because during your cleansing your earthly memories are your consciousness and it doesn't exist anymore. Unfortunately your subconscious, metaphysical memory, is rarely heard in your next Earth life."

"During your reincarnation passage, all of your falsehoods have to be erased."

After a minute of quiet, Rama said, "In truth, the human race back on Earth is tarnished by teachers who teach false doctrine and perpetuate wrong concepts. Thus, feelings of iniquity are created in you while young. Wrong conceptions keep you guys prisoners of feelings of immorality and retard necessary spiritual growth."

"Perfection can only create perfection. One couldn't create deficiency," Marza said.

"We know how ideally perfect our blessed One is, so how could He create less than perfect?" asked Rama.

"Can we ever hope to help all of humanity?" I asked, thinking of the love enhancement book I hoped to write.

"Concurrently," said Rama, "there are many different tiers of human-like beings on our Earth. Like it or not, though, there is only the one called human and it is they who are destroying our planet. The others all need a healthy Earth so that they can keep on surviving. Four of them are still in their primitive phases, and that's why the members in this movement have to stop this carnage. Our crusade is presently too few in number to absolutely correct this bedlam, however, we are helping to slow the deadly evolution some. I can't imagine what would happen if we had to assist other groups of beings there who might be sabotaging her as well."

"To answer your unasked question," replied Marza, "yes, if we can get enough of mankind reading your book and, most importantly, practicing your method of creating love, emotional healing will be possible for everyone."

"I can't conceive of more than one layer of existence on our home planet!" Said Gail with surprise. She cleared her throat and quickly added, "Not that I am doubting you of course."

"But why haven't we heard from scientists, philosophers, or psychics about their existences?" I asked, picking up Gail's hanging thread.

Rama and Marza were smiling as he explained. "Einstein's theory of relativity is only correct if viewed from a limiting 3D perspective. Although he appraised the feasibility of other dimensions simultaneously coexisting on our planet, he was never able to scientifically validate his theory. Although he spent years of trying, he failed to appreciate the ability to materialize in them by augmentation of self."

"He did write about zero-point energy, gravity or the source energy as he called it. We know it as One and He is lovenergy, the force of existence. If you use a microscope and study your finger, you will first see cells. Below the cells are molecules, still deeper atoms, and then subatomic particles. Then still deeper nothingness: Einstein called zero-point energy. However, that nothingness is One, the force that is gravity, and sustains everything within existence."

"That zero force is space, or rather the vacuum of space. Looking into outer space is like looking into your finger with that powerful microscope. Looking into space or your finger is similar in appearance. Both are constructed of atoms or spheres respectively. One is the substance and the space is zero-point energy."

"Jim and Gail," said Marza, "this is eternity; this very minute you are existing in is the moment of forever. That is why you need only expand your spirits into other realities and you are there. You will know the entirety and accuracy of this on Earth when your brainwashing has been removed and all of your enfites dissolved. For now, just relax and don't concern yourself so much with every infinitesimal detail. Like we've told you, not until you are attuned cosmically will you totally comprehend the meaning of omnipresence. In brief, know that as units of One, we are infinite beings." She smiled into our eyes and I drew a deep breath, beginning to understand the significance of what we were learning. "Right now," she told us, "it's time for you to firm up your emotional alliance, and you should be devoting all of your efforts to achieving that end."

Wanting to make a point or to fill in what Marza had said, Rama added, "You guys will reach Clear while with us and your reckoning will be fulfilled."

"Ra-ma!" said Marza, faking exasperation. "We've got to let these kids alone! This does bring up a vital point, though, and I want to briefly touch on it while you are recalling past memories. An essential goal for you while here is to remember everything that takes place. You've got to implant all you are learning into your subconscious. Memorizing what happens here is imperative so that when you return to Earth in new bodies, you can access it and be more dynamic members of our crusade."

"Good point. Thank you, Marza."

Gail asked, "If we'd been here before, why couldn't you identify us as soul mates?"

"Simply because you have different bodies every lifetime and your souls are not visible."

Wanting to learn more, I asked, "You mean to tell me that you can't identify our spirits while in these prevailing metaphysical bodies?"

"Isn't that what I just said?" she asked with a chuckle. "Your present bodies are your own personal envisage. By our observation of your many lives during that meditation, we were able to compare each of your past lives and determine if they parallel one another. You might say that we got to see the real you through your deceptive shields. All of us build an artificial mask, portraying only what we want others to see or what we perceive ourselves to be. The cloak of your body hides your spiritual identity. Because our spirits are One whether or not we might accept Him, they are all identical. As well as being a part of you during that meditation, I was also a segment of Gail and Rama's mind and him of mine, while Swuel was a component of us all. Nevertheless, only between lives did we get to see your soul, and that's as it moves from one body to another," she revealed.

"Like Marza told you, we saw your spirits moving between new bodies and we witnessed your infinite affiliation. Thus, we knew that you needed to be united again," said Rama.

"To take a step back, the moment you inhabit your upcoming bodies your spiritual identity will no longer be discernible. In short, that's why we will need you to keep in touch with us when you return to Earth. Because of your eternal union we also need to unify you here and on Earth as promptly as we can. We will not have foreknowledge of whose spirit you will be supplanting. We don't use just newly created fetuses, as is generally the condition. Customarily reincarnates only get to inhabit whatever fetus might be generating at the exact moment that they might be passing, first come first serve. Although, there is a condition: souls have to be pure so that they are able to enter that just fertilized egg."

"Like we said, we hope to find you same age adolescent or young adult bodies. Normally we have no idea of whom you will be replacing. As usual, we'll have to wait to learn about availability and that is generally only minutes previous to a soul dying."

"If this is the moment and everything exists here and now, why can't you previously identify our future body's age, location, or sex?" I asked feeling more confused than ever. Moment by moment I was realizing that there was a huge amount of things that I would be learning in the near future.

"We can't because everything is conditional on your procuring Clear. After that, you will be prepared so that you can replace an earthbound body."

"Now, do understand; because of your powerful affiliation, reaching Clear will be even faster once you are married."

Except for the meaningless sound of a ticking of a grandfather's clock, all about us was silent and unmoving. The absurdness of its purpose in life made it undeniably clear that there were far more urgent matters to attend to in one's life. We had to live in the moment and with our own power of will, move into the next forever presence of One—an ever changing now. "Because of your powerful association, reaching Clear should be moderately fast," echoed Marza again. Right now, there's no telling how quickly this will take place."

"Prepare yourselves for a roller coaster ride of a lifetime," said Rama, pretending to hold onto a steering wheel or some kind of safeguard.

"If on these planes we are only replicas of what we imagine ourselves to be, why then are there so many people of contrasting ages? Why are there old people and why aren't any of us children?" Asked Gail, still trying to assemble all of the pieces of this complex puzzle.

"Like Swuel told you, we are as we picture ourselves. No one is forced nor are they prohibited from creating their own lives as they desire. Some even visualize themselves as older beings. They are only doing as their own minds conceive. If they prefer, while on another plane of thought, they can stay forever youthful. There are no controlling prerequisites whatsoever. Enabling your powers of belief and will is all you need to do to create your lives exactly as you decree, and that's true for earthlings, too."

After this new revelation, I urgently asked, "Please answer this, Rama: because time is undeviating, does this mean that our loved ones will still be alive when we return home?"

"Jim," said Marza cautiously, "you are now venturing too far out on a shaky limb.

"You are not to give anyone in your old family recognition if you did happen to run across someone. Even if in the remoteness of chance you were to be reincarnated to a past life family member or neighbor, you couldn't acknowledge your association with them. Doing so would create chaos and believe me, you want to avoid everything that could negatively influence your future or our cause," warned Rama sternly.

"Okay then," I replied. "Will you please explain it all to us? Our recognizing one another on this plane of consciousness right now is a unique situation, but what prohibits every earthly human from recognizing past life friends and family members when again reincarnated?"

Rama was silent for a period of time and then, as if in a trance, said, "I've been instructed to give you more information about your family, Jim. First realize that it is impossible for you to learn everything in one night! You are amazingly correct in your analysis of this, so to enlighten you further, I will touch on it briefly. First, your parents and siblings will be alive. Also, past life memories are deleted in rebirth. At a later time, Jim, we will expound on all of these points."

"For now, though," said Marza, "put all of this aside and focus all of your attention on regaining your heartfelt connections."

"There is one more item we need to explain now," said Marza, looking Rama in the eye. "In your case, Gail," she pointed to that large mural, "that baby as you know was Jim. What you don't know is that he was also Kevin O'Connor in his prior life. During that life your greatest love was killed by a jealous suitor while Kevin attended a family wedding in Athens. That murderer raped you immediately afterwards and you were impregnated by him. Jim is Kevin's incarnate. If you had known that or if Jim had a memory of his former existence as your beloved, things would have been even more chaotic for both of you."

Rama quickly added, "It's not an enigma for a baby to be born to a parent who they had molested in a previous life. With that sort of awareness, can you imagine the tribulations that would be created in that newborn baby's mind? Anguishing fears and worries of retribution would haunt them all of their life."

Marza's words had naturally possessed more of an effect on Gail then on me, for I had no memory of Kevin. "Back up please, Marza," she moaned with tears eclipsing the light in her eyes. "Are you telling me that Kevin and Jim shared the same spirit in different lifetimes?" Confirming Gail's question with only an affirmative nod, Marza allowed Gail to intuitively respond, "Maybe that's why I loved my baby so fervently. That would also explain Jim's inner feelings toward me. He told me just minutes ago that as an infant he had felt enormous love for me, and this explains it all."

"Because One is all there is, and eternal soul mates are especially chosen, they always manage to unite," imparted Rama. "Jim, in your just concluded life you had shared an extraordinarily powerful love with two people who shared the same spirit: Claire and one of your best childhood friends Terry who died young. As you can see, every soul is connected to another. In each of your distinguished loves your spirit was united with your eternal soul mate. The odds of this occurring here are overwhelming us all! This should prove to you both that you cannot be kept apart; you've got to be united!"

Shameless tears of joy ran down my cheeks. I wasn't only getting my lovely Claire back now, but my best buddy who I had loved and lost when less than 10! "Oh my One," I cried aloud, "Lovie, you were also my very best friend!" I reveled to myself with the realization of how nicely these loose ends were fitting together. This new revelation rang true and appropriate in my heart. Because I had loved all three of them so furtively, it stood to reason that my best friend, Claire, and Gail were incarnates—perpetually united with me. It did, however, blow my mind that Terry, Claire, and now Gail were all the same spirit.

"Evidently we both needed to learn the meaning of love, Jim, and that's why you had my spirit with you twice before me!" Gail said intuitively. "I can't believe, though, that you are the same being who I had previously loved as Kevin, my baby Timothy, Terry, and now you, Jim!" she whispered in awe. She suddenly got a distant look in her eyes, "Oh Jim, but when did you lose your sight?" she asked from the perspective of my buddy Terry.

"Slipping into my prior 12 year old body, I replied, "Only two years after you left me, pal." Looking her in the eyes, I still saw my friend in their depths of compassion. "But I've got good news; even though I was blind, I heard that builders were destroying our woods and I managed to save our treasure box! After hearing a plow in the woods the very next day, I went in search of our fort. It was gone, but using Lookout Rock as a landmark, I was able to find the box right where we had buried it. Terry, I hadn't been there since losing my sight two whole years before! Months after I recovered it, I buried it in another secret place. I had to preserve that part of our past! It was vital and losing it would be unbearable." Smiling into her eyes with genuine feelings of joy and love, I said, "Gail, I can't wait until we have the opportunity to retrieve it and rediscover those treasures together again! We've got to plan on savoring those memories when we return to Earth!"

"I can't wait either, Jim! Remember our arrowheads and how 'bout that cement ice sickle we broke off of the bridge, we called it a stalactite! I'd love to visit that old neighborhood with you again. If One is willing, we may even be able to visit other places from various past lives! Imagine our once again revisiting that mine, you know the one where the cave-in happened?"

"Rama and I saw the two of you sharing thousands of lifetimes and I know that there were many more, " Marza said.

"You guys are supposed to get married tomorrow morning and we're not standing around all night while you play the 'remember this' game!" said a joking Rama.

"You've got more important things to accomplish than just trying to capture memories and emotions of all of those past lives. For now, I'd just see if you could stimulate your passions as Jim and Claire/Gail," said Marza wisely.

"Swuel, Marza, and I examined your affiliations and jointly concur that you have shared an eternal union. I bring this up again because you have no idea how rarely this occurs. In some capacity you have always managed to share life and a love for life and each other. Right now in reality, we have no direct knowledge of the number of lifetimes that you have shared," said Rama with a confidence-building smile. "In one life we even saw you as cliff dwellers. So you could have been together for millions of lives." With a resourceful smile, he shocked me further, "We even know of one couple that spanned a 33,000,000 year, worldwide extinction of all life forms! They experienced life genesis, being present as last humans alive in one and first primates to walk upright some 33,000,000 years later."

"They are now members of the Cosmic Consciousness Center, a group of masters who are living on Earth and aiding members of our cause. You will visit them as part of your wedding ceremony," said Marza.

These riveting facts staggered me. I again found myself wishing that I could just meditate about what it must be like to see the death and birth of mankind. Although, in my heart I felt that Gail and I had shared many of our lives together, I had never surmised that it could be anywhere near that number.

It does make sense, I thought to myself, *that a newborn baby has all of their former memories erased prior to birth. It would unavoidably be damaging to their mental security if not done. It does unfortunately prevent us from more quickly procuring spiritual enlightenment. Nonetheless, who's to say that a newborn wasn't a lot better off not knowing if it had been controlled by evil in a prior life. It indeed has both favorable and objectionable purposes. I couldn't have ever left Claire if I knew that she had also been Terry or any other past life lover. One only knows what that would have done to my family.* Interrupting my own insight I said aloud, "If people had a memory of their past wrongs, it could feasibly stop criminal conduct or at least diminish it a great deal."

"Like animals, early humans did have mental retention passed on from one generation to the next. However, like you presumed, Jim, it was soon found to be degenerating, so our spiritual leaders thought it better for them to be purged. The primary reason for terminating them was the gender dilemma. Our leaders found that transformation of gender often caused disorientation of psyche or self-identification instability. If a given person has total recall and is born the opposite sex in their next life, they would more often become sexual deviates. This inadvertently caused procreation problems. Therefore, it was decided by the universal masters to abolish regeneration of instinctive memory."

"Is this 'disorientation' the origin of homosexuality?" I asked with an aspiration of gaining greater insight.

"Questions this direct and studious deserve to be answered," said Marza flatteringly. "To more fully enlighten you and to answer your amazingly comprehensive hypothesis, though, there are four distinctive contributing determinants to homosexuality. In short, they are cultural, environmental or parental genesis, memory of prior gender, and genetic deformity. When it comes down to it, there is no good or evil, right or wrong behavior, we are One and all free to live as we elect."

I was really getting involved with this discussion and was about to probe further when Gail touched my shoulder and said, "Thank you, Marza and Rama, for coming and answering our perplexing questions. Although we may have been here previously, neither of us have reliable recollections of this resort. Your detailed responses have supplied answers for our most baffling questions."

"Lovie, we've only gotten started!" I teased.

Rama nodded at me and said, "Jim, we will expand on these topics another time. In the meanwhile remember," he explained to Gail and me, "that the two of us are monitoring your progress tonight. Please," he emphasized, "don't think that we are snooping into your private affairs. We have already noticed how you handled yourselves, and we are proud of you for not giving into those dominant temptations." Without another word said, they wiggled their noses and vanished.

With a winning laugh at their nose wiggling like in the TV show Bewitched, I took Gail's arm and guided her to that large antique couch where I had intended to talk with her before she requested the tour. "Now let's take some time to get reacquainted. We cannot postpone it any longer," I said, after kissing her passionately. We momentarily sat in silence while the majestically swinging pendulum of an exquisitely carved grandfather's clock was the only audible sound heard. "Part of me," I began, "wants only to sit here with you and absorb this moment of us being together. The other pragmatic me, says to talk, so talk it is." I put my arm around her slim shoulders and moved her head to my shoulder. "Do you remember how much I loved you back then? You, the Claire who I couldn't have in my life. And now I find Terry, my best buddy who I lost so long ago. Lastly, can you possibly comprehend how much I adore you? I mean the you who you are right now and the you who is my eternal soul mate?"

"Wait just a minute," she said, moving abruptly sideways to face me. "You could have had me, but you refused to love me just because I was a black woman!"

"Oh my love," I asserted, "if only I had known what I know now! Having no prior past life memories, I lived on another lower plane of consciousness. At that time I wasn't strong enough to oppose my family ties. Although, if it hadn't been for my grandmother's—"

"Why, oh why, couldn't you have loved me enough?" she asked, pulling further away from me.

"Please, Lovie, hear me out. I really loved you who you were and our racial difference did not affect my feelings in the least. If it hadn't been for my grandmother's heart problem, we would have been together. Regardless of how my parents felt about it, I would have been with you in some capacity. Alone, my dad's threats of disinheriting me and not ever acknowledging me as his son wouldn't have caused me to leave you." Tears dripped from her eyes and I drew her head to my aching shoulder again. "Lovie," I said kissing her tears away, "interracial marriages were viewed as immoral during those dark ages of the 60's. If I only had the boldness, or maybe being more fair to myself, if I had been selfish enough, the outcome would have been uniquely grand." I moved somewhat closer and pressed my lips firmly against hers. "Oh, Lovie," I whispered between fervent kisses, "I wish all that could have been different. I would have enjoyed my life so much more. Without your participation, Claire, my life was only an empty shell and totally void of meaning, pleasure, and purpose."

After another few kisses, Gail erotically said, "You have no concept of how much love you forfeited. I loved you more than life itself! In the new life that you had made accessible to me via Braille as a deaf-blind mute, I had every reason to want to live. However, after losing you, all of my will to live escaped me. Reading and writing Braille lost their enchantment to me; the entire thrill of communications had evaporated and I felt really alone again. I was feeling so empty that the thought of prolonging my existence was intolerable."

"I do know what I had lost," I replied in earnest. "And that's why it hurt me so horribly. Excuse me, Lovie, but I am going to speak frankly, but please don't take it to heart," I said with another inflamed kiss. My next words poured from my mind and from my heart. "You chose the easy method of escape. I had to live daily with the painful realization that I had lost you and unintentionally caused your death. For the rest of my years on Earth I had to endure my enormous loss and tremendous guilt. In the beginning I had become an alcoholic, given up my job, and nearly gave up on life itself. I was feeling so desperate that first night after learning that you had kept our racial differences a secret, that I even ruminated about committing suicide as you actually did only hours later. Now wouldn't it have been ironic if I had followed through?"

Her eyes regained some of the luster they had lost as she suggested, "Maybe we would have come here sooner?"

"No. We both would have needed to experience other more difficult lives. In that case, our meeting might have been delayed longer." I kissed her hard and said, "Claire, I mean Gail, I also needed to grow more from my experiences of discovering, developing, and then teaching my love enhancing technique on Earth. Gaining good karma is what allowed me to come here. Clearly, until this moment, neither of us could have come to this plane. Its a good thing, we might have missed one another otherwise."

"Jim," she postulated, moving right back to where we had been previously. "I couldn't live with myself thinking that I had caused you to hate me because of our racial differences. Oh my One, if my treacherous secret had caused you to commit suicide to . . ." her voice failed her momentarily. Changing the subject, she went on. "I truly couldn't live without your fulfilling love." Painful emotions and memories had been awakened in her and following more agonizing tears she continued. "You came to say goodbye, and I tried desperately to force you to make love to me. You righteously refused my enticement and because I felt that I wasn't going to have you in my life, I called an end to the threat of a forlorn existence WITHOUT you."

Her words stung my heart with excruciating pain as I realized again that I had caused the woman I had loved so overwhelmingly to kill herself. Naturally she was feeling rejected and having feelings of abandonment. I caused to feel inadequate by denying what she needed so desperately. "My poor Claire," I groaned with a catch in my throat. "If only we had talked that night! I have to believe that you would have understood the predicament that I was in. I really had no choice; my decision meant the loss of you or the death of my Grandmother. I was literally torn up inside. I was losing what I treasured most, our equally shared passion, but I loved my family, especially Nana, and just had to preserve her life for as long as possible. If only you had been willing to talk with me," I repeated. "I think that it could have saved your life." Taking a deep breath, I imparted, "Gail, if only I had known your intent; I would have done anything conceivable to save you. I would have made love to you as you desired instead of leaving. Nonetheless, I knew that I couldn't have left you the following morning, and it was impossible for me to preserve both your and Nana's lives. Dad wouldn't have ever allowed me back and Nana . . ."

"I know now that we couldn't have abided with the guilt of your grandmother's death. It would have driven us apart. At that moment, though, I knew only that I was losing you. I just couldn't live with that; as I saw it, suicide was my only option."

Reality of her truth struck home, although, I did feel a need to decree, "I am sure of the immeasurable depth of my adoration. I would have stayed and loved you for the remainder of my life if I had known what you intended to do. More than ever," I said with an audible moan of remorse, "I wish that I had known we were soul mates!" I was opening my heart to her and wanted to spill out everything. Without allowing her to reply, I said, "Lovie, what I have to disclose now is not meant to hurt you further, but only to explain my devotion and adoration. If only you had lived, I would have eventually joined you again. I know now that it would have only been a short matter of time. I really couldn't have remained away from you forever." I kissed her again and opened my heart even more. "Nana only lived for two short years after that appalling episode. I know that if I hadn't joined you beforehand, I would have united with you after her passing," I told her honestly. "In retrospect, though, I doubt that I would have been able to last a month apart from you. I loved you far more than I had thought possible. I'm sure that I would have been sneaking into your home a few times a week at least! Sharing our mental, emotional, and physical bonds would have been a necessity that I couldn't have ignored."

With tears now pouring out of her eyes, she whimpered, "I couldn't have forced your hand like that or let you destroy your family allegiance, and I didn't even know everything back then."

"Oh, Lovie—"

"Jim, the truth was that I truly loved you and thought that you found me detestable because I had hidden our ethnic differences. February 14, when you gave me that engagement ring, I knew that you were going to inform your parents of our engagement and since they knew I was black . . . That very night you came and said goodbye to me, and I had to say goodbye to life. Though, I have no idea what Claire would have done if she had known the real cause of your leaving her." Following a sorrowful sigh then a diabolical smile, she said, "I did fantasize about your stealing into my house, but I just couldn't request it. As I saw it, I had no recourse . . ." Gail's beautiful body shook with heartache and tears ran from her eyes. I enfolded her into a compassionate embrace and held her tightly in my aching arms. My right hand stroked her red hair and my lips fused with hers. For a moment I was with her on Earth and loving my beloved Claire again.

Awhile later, with feelings of regret, I said, "I know it's necessary to release all of our grief. Nevertheless, let's consider our future, which is full of love. Our future lives can and will be all of the things we want them to be. It's up to us to produce them as we desire. Like Swuel, Rama, and Marza told us, we are the creators of our lives. What we thoroughly believe in and want the most will become a rewarding reality for us. I want, need, and desire you to be my wife here and now as well as in our future."

"Oh yes, Jim!"

"I don't want to keep on rehashing the painful 'If only'," I told her seriously. "As of this moment, those days of the past are gone and finished. We've got to release that pain and joyously advance into our future together."

"Jim, can we really dismiss our misdeeds from our past life?" she whispered.

"Like you, Lovie, I am a novice at all this. Swuel told you that you wore off the last of your negative karma in your just-concluded life. As I told you, after your death I did give up. I tried to drown my sorrow in alcohol and stayed depressed for years. Only when my money ran out was I forced to correct my wretched behavior."

I could tell that she wanted to interrupt, but, not given the opportunity, she remained still and heeded my words. "With a new awakening of spiritual awareness, I became determined that I'd use every adversity that came my way as a bridge to right thinking. I soon knew that every dilemma was a crossroad to a new chapter in my human life. I knew that if I chose the correct path and conducted my life properly, I'd learn a vital lesson from every tribulation that might occur."

"You shouldn't have ever run out of money; I made sure of that before ending my life!" Even if you never worked another day and had continued drinking like a fish, there was enough."

"Well, my dear," I said, debating whether or not I should disclose her sister's atrocious stunt. "I never got a penny," I said, deciding that the whole truth was best. "Rena contested your last will and because of my guilt, I didn't dispute her claims of your insanity."

She jumped to her feet and decreed in a screech-like voice, "Oh my One, I can't believe that my sister did that to you! After all, she was already a multimillionaire and the million I left to you was only a drop in the bucket!"

"We never again even muttered a single word to one another. She didn't even acknowledge me at your funeral." Pulling her downwards, I said, "Gail, I wouldn't have discovered the power of the pink light or have grown spiritually. Honestly, I probably wouldn't have met you here on this plane if I had gotten hold of your funds. Can you imagine that tragedy! See," I said after lightly tapping her arm, "every good and/or unfortunate mishap does occur for a reason or purpose. Nothing happens by accident. We have objective reasons for every situation that we create during our lives."

"Still it would have only been a tiny icing on her cake!"

"Gail," I said, kissing her hard, "let it go; it's hurting you spiritually. Besides, like I told you, I thank One that she did it. "Having to go back to work helped me to recover my self-respect."

"I had visualized you opening your own business with the money that I had left you. I fantasized about how happy and successful my money would make you," she told me wistfully. Without even taking a breath, she asked, "How 'bout my tenet and friend Ruth? Did Rena take away or prevent her from inheriting my house, too?"

Helping her back into my arms, I said, "No, I would have done all I could to prevent that from happening. Because I had inadvertently caused your death, I felt myself unworthy of your gift and guilt kept me from claiming it. Even when Ruth offered me your old apartment rent-free, I refused. Living with memories of you would have been intolerable." Gail was crying and I paused to kiss away her tears. I repeated, "My memories of us were too powerful; I just couldn't bear living where you and I had been so happy!" I kissed her and then said, "Now let it all go my lovely Gail. We can't permit it to hurt us further."

My kisses were becoming more passionate and after a few more she said, "I can't believe that you overindulged in alcohol like that. I'm sorry for inadvertently causing it to occur. Jim, I am also sorry for the way my sister treated you," she said, pushing herself slightly away trying to get me cooled down. "I'm sure you recognize the truth that it wasn't my intent. I had thought that by leaving my money to you, it would enable you to devote more time and energy into encouraging and aiding other disabled people like you had done for me. Also, I thought for sure that you would use it to become a success in your esteemed work." Then with a slight giggle in her voice, she warmed my heart by saying, "You were a great teacher for Claire, Jim, and here you are being my teacher again. Matter of fact," she said with a refreshing smile, "as either a doctor or psychic, I remember you always being a great instructor to me and others in most of our shared pasts."

"You have only one thing to regret," I told her candidly, "not permitting yourself to live." With a lustful breath, I questioned, "Me a doctor or psychic?" Feeling my desires growing, I backed off a bit this time. "How is it that you remember past life experiences so vividly? I only have vague memories of a tiny portion of my pasts and I'm talking of the pasts that I visited only a few hours ago, too."

"Don't ask me," she said with closed eyes.

"Oh my One, but you are beautiful," I said after a long period of wordless admiration. "Were you this glamorous in all of your prior lives?"

With a playful smile, she replied, "I couldn't have been this gorgeous in any of my former lives."

We laughed together and years of pain disappeared in seconds. It now seemed to me that I was once again with that woman who I had loved with all of my heart, mind, and body. We clung tightly to one another in fear of losing what seemed to be so elusive.

"Gail," I cowardly began, "have all of your feelings of fear, anxiety, apprehension, and worry dissipated?"

Observing dismay in my eyes, she said, "Jim, I have gotten over my fear and doubt. Those disturbing memories of Claire's dismal death and pain are too brutal and distinct to be omitted from my memory right now. Despite them, I am feeling a whole lot better about us." She smiled and added, "My emotional feelings have virtually returned. Although, it might only be that I am falling in love with you—my eternal soul mate."

"Oh, Lovie," I moaned. "I am feeling the same way about you." Following another long, silent moment of kissing, I asked with interest, "How detailed are your memories, Gail?"

"Before that past life meditation, I had no memories of any of our pasts. Probably because it removed more of my mental blocks, all of my previous lives have become too vivid for my liking. In fact, since the meditation I've been having what might be called flashbacks. In them I get a particular vision, thought, and I actually relive those moments of our past. When you told me about our treasure box just a few minutes ago, I actually saw us hunting for arrowheads and other treasures. Then when you told me how much you loved Terry, I witnessed him on his deathbed telling you to enjoy life and live it up for him, too. If I think about an incident, I can remember everything that occurred in their proper sequence of events. In a way, it's almost as if I were still in that meditation reliving these incidences again."

I sat upright, finding it incredible that she had absolute recollection of all of her previous lives and could experience them so significantly. "Whew," I exclaimed with envy, "I really would enjoy connecting to my pasts like that! Boy do I wish I had—"

"No you don't, Jim," she said, interrupting me. "It's often too harrowing to experience again. I relive those good and painful episodes in full detail. This afternoon, for example, your words, 'I love you, Lovie,' evoked a painful memory of Claire's preparing herself for death. For a while I became her and truly felt her grief of losing you and the life she was beginning to enjoy again. Her heartbreak was mine and I truly relived that anguishing episode all over again!"

Shaking my head violently, I hugged her hard. Through tightly closed teeth, I said, "Oh, my beloved, I didn't think of that. It has to be really tough reliving some of those anguishing pasts! Having to re-experience them over and over again like that must cause you enormous anxiety."

"Oh, Jim," she said with a wearisome gasp, "hold me tighter and promise me that you will never ever let me go again."

I drew her closer and more sympathetically kissed her lips. This woman was an innocent and unknown part of my conscious and subconscious mind. The sensations she kindled in my heart made me feel like a newlywed. "Please, Gail," I said, kissing her tears away, "know that I won't ever let you pass out of my life again! You and I are earnestly adjoined for eternity. Know that we will be united tomorrow morning, although, in truth we are forever adjoined." I sealed my next words with a feverish kiss. "Inform me whenever you're having those episodes. We can perhaps dilute the stress of them to some degree by working together."

"There are so many prized ones, too, and they make the pain tolerable; some even change pain to joy. Losing myself in them," she said dreamily, "is almost too enticing." With a vivacious smile, she said, "I am so delighted that I once again have your love. I know now that my life would never be complete again without you as a part of it."

Beaming into her glowing eyes, I said, "Despite the fact that I don't have total recall like you, Lovie, my feelings are identical to yours. Without your presence, my life would be a vacuum. You know something," I announced after another interval of wanton kissing, "even if I hadn't been madly in love with you as my rare flower Claire, I'd be totally captivated and in love with you as the person that you are right now."

"Well, Jim," she said pragmatically, "I think that is because we are eternal soul mates. It's unlikely that our passion would be this powerful if that hadn't been the case. I remember you and I being together in all sorts of circumstances. Even though you don't have direct memory of us as I do, you are indisputably feeling connected again."

"How far back do your memories go?" I asked with interest.

After a long pause for reminiscing, she said, "All the way to the birth of mindfulness," she decreed with some surprise in her voice. "There were supreme human-like beings who were inhabiting Earth when we reached the point of memory retention in our evolution. We soon were to discover that they were using us helpless females to satisfy their extravagant sexual appetites." Pausing with her eyes closed as if focusing on an inner scene, she robotically stated, "Their greed was repaid by total destruction of their highly-developed race." She briefly faltered again, watching that internal film. After a minute, she continued, "Although, because of their excessive sexual behavior, our evolution was greatly sped up by enlightened offspring. In my next existence I was a great-grandchild of the past inhuman me. She was a race above where I had been in the prior life and slightly below the extra terrestrial beings who were next to inhabit Earth."

I wanted to learn more about those other human-like beings, but my curiosity of our own not-so-distant past prompted me to ask, "Any events in our past lives stand out?"

"The most reveling in my mind was when," she paused and then reported with a confident smile, illustrating her joy at uncovering the episode, "you were a fisherman and I was your dependent niece. Some gypsies had killed my parents and you were my only family and took me in. My name was Tina and I was age thirteen. Your name was Peter and you were twenty-three years old." She paused again, I imagine to summon her recollections; I remained quiet wanting to hear it all. "Yes," she replied anxiously, "it was after your fishing boat had gone down during a storm—"

I waited for a second, but she didn't continue so I prompted, "What are you talking about, Lovie?"

"Sorry," she said, secluded by tender memories, "I was trying to pinpoint the moment I realized my love for you. I am just recounting my fondest memory of a past life. Anyway, your boat went down in a horrible storm and you were missing. Two of your men came back half-drowned and had no idea what had happened to you. Both you and Brian, your best friend and mate, were feared dead by everyone except me. I knew that you would come back to me. I waited for two whole weeks, barely eating or drinking. Then you both were brought in by a foreign crew that had spotted you far out to sea."

I remembered wanting to relive a portion of that life immediately after the meditation so that I could discover what had happened. I was eager for her to finish so that I could make my own comments about it. Finding it curious that this particular lifetime was so prominent for both of us, I waited eagerly for her to conclude.

Her eyes became misty and she moved into a trance-like state. "I see you right now getting off of that foreign ship . . . our eyes link and I can see that we both feel the same way about each other. You are now off the ship and I am falling into your arms and smothering you with kisses. Brian and other bystanders are extracting me from around your neck . . ." She paused for a longer period of time while she evidently viewed different scenes. She then moved out of that meditative state and described what she had seen during that interval of silence. "I was sick for days afterwards and you never left my side. After I had recovered, we talked seriously and you admitted to me that you were in love with me as I was with you. You said, and I quote you, 'My dear Tina, people are cruel and their tongues will wag about us if we are betrothed.' With romantic logic taking control of me, I asked, 'Would not it be better if we were espoused rather than remain as secret lovers?' You agreed with my deduction, and thus we were married only a few weeks later. Our neighbors did talk about us, but we were extremely happy and so much in love. We just didn't permit their cruel gossip to disturb our equally shared love and ecstasy."

The passion I saw in her eyes and on her exhilarated face compelled me to hug her hard. "I also remember reliving a part of that past life during the meditation this afternoon," I said, continuing on to tell her about the dolphins who saved my life. "In the meditation, as I fell into the sea, I remember thinking that I had to live for my niece. Until now, though, I didn't know why it was so imperative. Thanks to your wonderful memory and your telling me this story now, I realize that it was because of my measureless love for you that I had to live. When time allows I've got to ask Marza or Rama why this specific memory has so much significance to us both."

"Simple, Jim. During our past lives we had always conducted our behavior as demanded by our churches. In this reunion, though, we disregarded the dictates of the time and married against traditions. There isn't any reason for calling on Marza and Rama again now, is there?" With a cunning smile, she said, "Recapturing our befuddled passions should be our major concern. I'd especially like to perceive those sensations of love that I experienced as Claire. Although, I do fancy these growing feelings between us now."

"You mean that you can't remember our feelings of great love?" I asked with a little misgiving.

"Of course I remember, it's only the passions of the past that have been somewhat diminished. It's like when you burn your hand; you can certainly remember doing it months or even years later, however, you can't really experience the painful burning sensation again."

I realized how accurate she was in her analysis and showed her with a lavish kiss, which caused unruly desires to return with a vengeance. "You know, my love," I said, trying to diminish my lustful longings, "things have now reversed and you are now being the teacher."

Following a snicker from her, I said, "Gail, I have all of the love for you that I had thought was gone. Deep within my heart it feels as if I have my adorable Claire right here in my arms. You know, our having to use sign language didn't make that much difference. Oh boy, but do I desire to make up for those years without you! If only . . ."

With apprehension in her voice, she said, "Like I told you before, I am falling in love with you again. However, it's also the Jim who you are now as well as my eternal soul mate who I am loving. Is it me? This Gail," she asked, tapping herself on the chest, "who you are in love with or is it a memory of a forfeited love?"

"Of course it's you, Lovie," I said, brushing her red hair back from her eyes. "Even though I have full memory of the emotions I felt for Claire, I am loving you anew. Naturally I can't exclude the love I had for her, she was my first meaningful lover. We are eternal soul mates and that makes you and Claire spiritually indistinguishable." I relished aloud. "I am so graced by having you, my precious lover, in my life once more! I can't wait until we reach eternity and can exist in the forever of the always-present moment."

"Eternity is now and we can live in this moment of eternity."

After we had played the "remember when" game for another hour or so, we became aware of our passion becoming more ardent with our stimulating memories. "Lovie," I said, breathing a little more rapidly, "I think we better go out for an evening's stroll."

"Yes, Jim," she said, promptly getting to her feet. "I think we better do something else, otherwise it is going to be too late. Personally speaking, I know that I am ready to explode with my emotions so heightened. Talking about our past experiences coupled with our kissing and expressing our feelings has stimulated me almost to the point of no return. Besides rekindling those nostalgic sentiments, I am also falling enormously in love with the you who I have before me now." Moving her hand over her eyes and murmuring a great sigh, she said, "Combining these new and old sensations is nearly overwhelming my ability to cope with expanding desires."

The air as well as our slight separation during our walk outdoors was restoring and within minutes we were once again able to reflect on our past and future lives without becoming overly aroused. "Jim," said Gail, cross-examining our plans for marriage, "we aren't rushing this too hastily are we?"

"Well, Lovie," I began with a savory look into her shining eyes, "I know that I have made a valid choice in the matter. I love, need, and want you more than anything else in my life. You've got to speak for yourself though; how are you feeling about us being wed in the morning?"

"I know that we are meant for one another," she said reassuringly. Then, with the next breath, she said, "I feel concerned . . ." and her voice fell off into space.

I stopped dead in my tracks and bluntly asked, "What is worrying you, Gail?"

"It's just that it is so sudden. One minute we are only acquaintances and the next we are companions who can't turn back. We do share the same passion, but because you don't share my memories of all of our pasts, I have this uneasiness about your honest sincerity. I have total knowledge of our past lives and know that we have never been apart. To you, though, this is virtually a new romance. Can you possibly love me with the same authenticity I am feeling toward you?"

"Gail," I emphatically declared, "my mind is made up. I am yours for life, like it or not!"

"Jim, what if—"

"If nothing," I proclaimed, bending and kissing her firmly on the mouth. "If you keep this up you will have to marry me holy ground or no holy ground!" I stopped walking and turned to face her head on. "Gail, before I even got to see more of our past life associations, I was thinking of leaving this plane with you. Wazzy, that man I told you about, advised me to wait. He said that you might not be willing to leave this plane with me. He told me that I was presuming too much and might be unfair to you if I forced you to depart your training and the goals of this cause. I'm so glad now that I had met him and listened to his wise counsel. We've now gotten the endorsement from everyone here. We've been virtually told that we wouldn't endure separately. So, no more of your doubting."

We approached our house and as we stepped onto the porch, two full moons with pink loving light encircling them simultaneously touched our minds, hearts, and souls with a feeling of euphoria. "Look," she said pointing to them, "it's a sign from One."

"Oh, Jim, you actually debated about leaving with me?" she said a breath later. "That desire had also occurred to me, but like you, I was warned that you might not be willing to turn your back on this deserving cause."

Silently I wondered if Wazzy and Marza had acted alone or if Swuel had orchestrated it all? The brilliant silvery moons shone to our left and Gail managed again to dreamily speak before I could voice this thought. "It seems like we could grab those moons and hold them in our hands. Earth's moon never appeared so close, full, or luminous as that," she said, pointing upwards.

"You're right," I replied, mesmerized by their proximity and majestic supremacy of the night's sky. I clasped Gail's shoulders and pulled her hard against my aching body. "Like you said, it is a sign from One. We have made the appropriate decisions and we are to get married in the morning. Also, we aren't to retreat to our own orb one day, but are meant to stay here for now."

"Yes, we have made the correct decisions haven't we," she answered, laying her head on my shoulder. We stood there spellbound and incapable of movement for several minutes. Then, still wordlessly, I bent and pressed my lips hard against her receptive and supple lips. My tongue separated them and I rejoiced with the blending of our oral essences.

Without a word, I guided her indoors and upstairs to a bedroom. I again kissed her lips, opening them slightly with the tip of my tongue. "Oh, Jim," she gasped afterwards with a shiver, "you used to always kiss Claire that way." With a hard press of her body against mine, she said, "Except that last night when you kissed me goodbye with just a brush of your lips!" With a realized quiver of recognition, she said, "Oh, how I had wanted to hold onto you that night and not permit you to walk out of my life. I felt unworthy and therefore failed to kiss or arrest you by forcing my desires on you. When you justly resisted my sexual entreaties that night, I surrendered to my predetermined plan of escape. You know," she said, her breath coming out in forceful gasps, "I am feeling those old emotions again. I am really Claire at this moment except, unlike her, I am white and can hear and see you. Oh, Jim, you enlightened my life as Claire by showing me Braille items, which enabled me to communicate without those two essential senses. Previous to your bringing communications into my life again, I had considered suicide when the doctors removed the tumors and I lost my sight and hearing." She quickly changed the subject and said, "I want so now to abandon myself to lovemaking. I want to wrap my legs about you like I had wanted to do that night. Oh, how I desire to hold you here, now, and never allow you to leave me again!"

Her intoxicating disclosure thrilled me beyond words. The one woman who I had loved more than anyone was finally fully returning to my aching heart. I had to arrest my growing needs before I caused a crisis to befall us. It was up to me to stop this tremendous craving and I had to do it now or else! "You're the one with a perfect memory," I said teasingly in an attempt to take our thoughts off of that very last time that I had kissed Claire and the urgency of our mutually growing desires. "Have I ever kissed you that way during past lives?"

Pinpointing recollections, she delayed her response for a second then answered, "Yes you have always kissed me that way. Kiss me again and I will show you what I used to do as your wife Vanessa in our past life in Brazil."

I did as she proposed and low and behold she bit my tongue. "Ouch," I loudly chided. "You mean to tell me that I tolerated that abuse? With a laugh, I said, "I always kissed you that way, huh? At least you can say that I am consistent," I chuckled. "See you in the morning, bright eyes."

"Why did you call me bright eyes?" she asked with a wrinkled brow and a grab of my hand.

I smiled to myself not having a specific reason. "I guess it's that for the first time I am acknowledging your intuitive, sparkling eyes. Why do you ask?"

"In another former life, as your Viking wife, you didn't call me by my given name, instead you always called me bright eyes." Preoccupied with another thought, she gazed up at me with an expression of love and desire that all but dissolved my will power. "Please sleep with me tonight?" she beseeched. "I can't abide with the idea of us being apart another minute."

"I share your desires, Gail," I said solemnly. "However, I couldn't survive the night keeping pure if we slept together. We can't," I entreated. "Neither of us would get a wink of sleep. I'd be tossing and turning all night having to restrain my compelling desires." Without moving or saying another word I instructed her, "Please say goodnight, Gail."

"Goodnight, Gail," she obediently replied with a giggle. It was all I could do to close the door behind me. I started to step away when she called to me again. "Jim," she implored, "can't we please sleep together? I promise to keep my distance. We can even put pillows between us if you like."

"I'm sorry, Lovie," I answered, stepping through the doorway. "I would like nothing more. I will be close, only downstairs from you. I know my body, as I'm sure you do. No matter how determined I am now, there is no denying my driving need. My mind and heart are far too much in love with you for me to withstand the pressure from physical demands. It's especially risky now that I have a normal body. My driving need might have more power over me now that I have a functioning pituitary gland. Unlike my earthly self, my body is producing all of the hormones it needs. I just don't know and we can't risk it!" I said with finality in my voice, mind, and heart. If she had been able to see my betraying member, she would have seen how much my body yearned for her.

"You're right, Jim," she sadly agreed. "Please, though, give me just one more passionate goodnight kiss."

Without a bit of caution inhibiting me, I moved to Gail's side of the bed. Picking her up in my aching arms, I briskly covered her mouth, face, and neck with lustful kisses. "Oh, Gail," I hoarsely groaned. "I want you so desperately! There! Can you possibly know how much I desire to satisfy our craving?" I said, sniffing a pure exciting smell of nature in the red hair that framed her gorgeous face.

"No, no," she panting almost as hard as I was. "Your righteous thinking and behavior are commendable. You're totally correct; we must persevere." She turned her face from my aggressive kissing.

I was in trouble and I knew it. That moment of freedom had essentially overwhelmed my pragmatic power of will. I nearly doubled in pain, but by some miracle I didn't give way to my driving need. With throbbing deliberation, I firmly rejected my long-awaited desires and struggled upright again.

I threw her a kiss from the doorway and without giving my actions thought, I soon found myself saddling one of the horses for a midnight chase with the moons. The land lay at rest, silence prevailed, and spirit of man and beast of man became tranquil. We rode hard and swift to where I had no idea or care. The moon's and the light of One made everything around us distinct but ghostly. Eventually we climbed a rugged ridge and paused on its crest. Reposed below us slumbered a lavish city with its lights barely distinguishable in the light of One and the brilliance of the full two moons.

Aloud, I mused while scratching my sturdy stallion's ear. "Strange thing seeing a metropolis like that here. Any reason you took us here?" It was so vast that it looked essentially like a major city in America.

"How long have I been here? Only two full days?" I asked myself with disbelief. "Oh my One! It isn't possible that so much has transpired in only days; it feels more like weeks! It's impractical for me to think that I could ever have full knowledge of all of the occurrences hereabouts," I said to my trusty mount. "Even after being here for a month I couldn't expect to know just the small chunk of landscape where we reside, let alone this whole realm! Especially," I murmured with a grin, "since this, too, may only be an illusion, another entirely different division from Tesa or where our home is located!" I scratched his ear again and asked, "Have you taken me into another separate density? I'm glad that it isn't one where horses ride people!" I said with a laugh—accompanied by a whinny from him, as if he was laughing at my joke.

I surveyed the city below me and to my still panting horse, I asked, "Are you up to a close-up? It's an awful steep decline and very deteriorated, too," I told him. "Without a detectable bit of prodding from me, he snorted once and cautiously commenced a slow and deliberate descent. Dirt and small stones broke loose and cascaded downward beneath his feet. Our progress down that very sheer bluff was slow, tedious, and disquieting. In a perverted way, I also found it exciting, though, I soon found myself wishing that we hadn't undertaken this foolhardy notion.

I was about ready to climb down and give him some assistance down an excessively steep precipice when my trusty mount suddenly grunted. The ledge under his front legs suddenly gave way and we were being forcefully thrown forward. At the same precise moment he did a bizarre thing; with a great push of his hind legs, he hurled us into unobstructed space and we fell swiftly downwards. He landed hard on his feet at least 25 to 30 feet below. On impact, his legs crumbled beneath him and he let out a ghastly shriek. Still attempting to protect me, he responsively rolled slowly to his right side, giving me time to extract my leg before his unwieldy weight had pinned me beneath him. He lay still; the rising and falling of his side as he breathed was his only sign of life. I stood and quickly surveyed the scene. We were balanced on a ten-foot island ridge; deep ditches surrounded us except for a narrow path on the other side. I noticed that if my poor horse had failed to leap to this promontory and hadn't rolled to his right side, that we would have tumbled to our deaths at least another 60 or more feet below. The ground that we had been descending was now totally void of soil. It left a twenty-foot gap between where we were now roosting and the area that we had been traversing. "If you had failed to leap into space at that precise minute, we wouldn't be alive now," I told him thankfully.

I laughed to myself with my next realization. "I'm already dead, but I do have to wonder if this temporary metaphysical body of mine can die, too? Why not?" I concluded. "I am having very ordinary human sensations in this metaphysical body of mine. Other than lustful desires, I've done nothing wrong except this." I pointed down at my friends crumpled body. "Time now for me to rectify this wrongful act."

I quickly bent and examined my unconscious steed. Discerning that he had four fractured legs with bone sticking through his skin on two of them, left me stupefied and grieving for him in this perilous condition. Closing my eyes and folding my hands, I did the only thing possible; I prayed with all of my mind, heart, and spirit. "Dear One, I ask you in the name of decency to give me the power to heal this virtuous creature. You are him as well as you are me and you are perfect, therefore, he is completely whole." I imagined him trotting, tail held high and no bones in sight. I laid my hands on his muzzle and with the power of the Oneness I was part of, I decreed, "I restore you to full health by the true power of One." I immediately sensed him stirring and then felt a warm moist tongue lick my arm. He abruptly stood with me hanging onto his neck. Getting my feet on the ground again, I gratefully put my arms around him and squeezed him hard. With joy in my heart, I said, "Thank you One for the ability to heal this noble creature." I hugged my horse again and lamented, "Oh, friend, how irresponsible I was to attempt such a fool-hearted thing. Especially when you consider that all that was necessary was a desire. How about getting out of here the easy way?" I asked him. Holding my hand against his shoulder, I concentrated on floating and we gently rose into the air as if raised by invisible helium-filled balloons.

"See you another time," I said over my shoulder as we trotted away from that city that I never would get an opportunity to examine. Our ride home was appreciatively uneventful and we made good time. I kept reproving myself for my absent-mindedness pertaining to power of will. "We could have just flown down there, pal, if only I had remembered. If it weren't for your prudence, I may have driven us to our deaths, old friend," I said, affectionately patting my sire's neck. "You would think that retaining knowledge of this power would have prevailed. Particularly when confronted by a crisis," I said, chastising myself.

Then with that revelation entering my mind again, I said, "I am already dead!" With a choked laugh caught in my throat, I asked aloud, "Is it possible for me to die here? Am I and my horse celestial or are we really alive on this plane?"

Rama's voice whispered, "You are the concept and your Father One, the conceiver. You are the eternal light and sound of every living or inert entity. The universal light that radiates within you is the same energy force that emanates in One and His entire omnipresent self. As Him, you are the ocean of life itself, not just the separate drop of water that you've considered yourself to be. Even though it has many living organisms existing in it, each drop is a part of you and all are made manifest by means of your creative imagination almighty One."

I looked into the sky and thanked Rama with my heart, while trying hard to believe that I was everything that could be created. "I am the actuality of

Buddha, Christ consciousness, and every other realized master who roamed the Earth. I am the Oneness of the stars and these shining moons. I am vegetation—every blade of grass, leaf, tree, and life giving weed. I breathe the oxygen they produce. I am every grain of sand or dirt, drop of water, and every ray of light that is the eternal LovEnergy/LifEnergy/OnEnergy of the Oneness of 'I am'." Within my mind, the night sky opened and I saw that all was connected as the molecules, atoms, and subatomic particles that zero energy held together in the might of One. I was the lovenergy and the pink light that activated every atom as well as the force that held them together. From my indistinct body, for I was all of existence, came an interlacing labyrinth of colored lights. Every concept of creation had its own unique vibration that was illustrated by these dazzling colors. I was the pure pink light of lovenergy and this entire splendor was an extension of my supremacy. "I need only to recall who I am, reminding myself as often as possible of this truth. Inevitably the validity of my powers and of my identity will sink into my mind and become full awareness of the reality of my Universal Oneness."

"Thank you, friend," I said, unsaddling my trusty steed. I gave him a good drink and an extra portion of oats.

Entering the house again, I felt that lustful desire rousing deep in my body. "I am surely alive; this body of mine is feeling just like it did on Earth." I smiled to myself recalling my lovemaking adventures with Claire. "Oh my, Gail," I rejoiced, looking upward to her room. "Thanks to providence I've gotten my rare flower back again. Plus all of my past soul mates and you my new incredible lover," I exulted.

I showered and retired at 3:30 a.m. I thought about my upcoming marriage. *What will the wedding ceremony be like?* I pondered. *Do they have a unique ritual for eternal soul mates or is it like any other marriage observance?* Then, thinking of Gail, I whispered, "I am sure of the stability of our commitment to one another. Uniting with the woman I love and joining on Earth in the future will absolutely be the greatest conclusion imaginable." I visualized her in bed and fell asleep while transmitting lovenergy to her reposing body.

It seemed as if I had only crawled into bed when a muted tapping on my bedroom door awoke me. "Jim," summoned Gail softly. "Rise and shine." She waited only seconds and before I was able to even get my eyes focusing, she serenely opened the door. "Come on you sleepyhead," she reproved. "It's already 6:30. You'd think that you were up all night or something," she scolded after getting no response.

"Come over here you gorgeous creature," I said, still feeling a bit groggy. "You can't henpeck me until after we've been hitched."

"Whose chauvinistic rule is that?" she asked with a disapproving scowl and her hands placed firmly on hips.

"That's rule number eleven thousand of the manual on proper marital rights of husbands," I said after she had given me a warm reviving kiss.

She looked down at me with a loving smile; her brown communicative eyes had a crackling glimmer that was, I'm sure, inspired by her enthusiastic spirit. "Wait until you see the manual on the rights of wives; it blows yours out of the water!" she said with an exaggerated glare. With a warm smile, she said, "I've got coffee brewing and biscuits baking. Now get into the shower and join me at the table and I mean pronto!"

An hour later, Gail and I left our cozy home and were immediately greeted by our friendly horses. After we had given them the attention they had come for, they joyfully pranced off. With our hands clasped tightly and our arms swinging, we walked toward Tesa. Within a minute we were flabbergasted by the spectacle that greeted us there. There weren't just the three hundred odd people that we had expected to attend our wedding, but thousands. Bells pealed throughout the land and could be heard for miles away. *I had heard them*, I thought to myself as soon as we had rounded the corner near the back of the men's lodging. *Is that when they had started, or is that the cross line between two densities?* I wondered. Nothing else had differentiated the crossing point. *So this dividing line is totally imperceptible.* I found it exciting to think that moving from one density to another was only a simple matter of desire, faith, and purpose. We were getting married and wanted to be in the Tesa density. As a result, we easily materialized there. I wondered if having all of our heart's desires gratified was only a matter of cause and effect, wishing and believing, and, thus, attaining our own creation only the response to our beliefs and vivid imaginations.

"Oh, Jim," cried Gail excitedly with her hands clapping together, "are all these people and all of this celebration to commemorate our eternal union?"

"No, Lovie," I replied, teasing as I came out of my contemplation. "They are only here to attend our wedding."

She half slapped and pushed my shoulder. "What am I going to do with you?" she asked just as Swuel turned and advanced to greet us.

"I pray that you got adequately balanced last night," he said mechanically." You must be absolutely harmonious, mind, body, and spirit for this regal occasion. For that reason we will also be assisting you to intensify your union of spirit. According to Rama and Marza your deportment last night was commendable. I knew that you could be trusted and we are grateful that you lived up to our expectations."

We assured him of our readiness, both of us feeling euphoric. My heart was racing with the thrill of our marriage. This woman was considerably more than I had ever envisioned. She kept squeezing my hand whenever Swuel introduced us to another guest and I palpitated with stimulated passion every time.

"Sir Harold Klemp," Swuel called to a tall and very distinguished looking gentleman. "I'd like you to meet Jim and Gail, our soon to be eternal soul mates," he said, introducing us. Turning to us, he said, "I'd like you both to welcome our Mahunta (esteemed leader) on this domain."

Taking my hand, this distinguished man said, "Pleased to make your acquaintances. Jim, we've met before, but then I was doing a little roll playing. I was helping you new students, aiding this grand cause, and introduced myself to you as Wazzy."

Shocked by this staggering disclosure, I scarcely managed to quell the shriek that swelled in my throat. We simply greeted one another with a shake of hands. "We are very pleased and honored that you could attend the renewal of our eternal union," I told him.

Before replying, Gail looked at me for confirmation and asked, "Are you the elderly man who met my soon-to-be husband in the woods the other day?"

"Jim and Gail," he uttered, following an affirming nod, "I am once again anxious to witness this majestic ceremony. In fact," he conceded, "everyone on this plane is looking forward to the supernatural transition that will be taking place here today. We are privileged to be witnessing your reunion."

Before Gail or I could press him for greater details or even ask him for an explanation of what he had meant by 'supernatural transition', Swuel was introducing us to another person. "Gail and Jim," he said, "this is Angel, your spiritual counselor. I have assigned her with enhancing your inner most feelings toward one another even more than they are presently. Angel is also going to take you into the chapel for experiencing the House of Love, your revelation, and edification rituals. They will prelude your marriage."

Before either of us could respond, Angel said, "I am aware that you both have had concerns about emotional deficiencies." Looking Gail in the eye, she said, "This is especially common in soul mates that have had to relinquish a relationship and endure another existence alone. No matter how short it might be, it does cause controversies. We've had eternal soul mates who were unable to renew their relationship until very late in life. They always felt pangs of longing, but had to wait until the right moment for their reunion. When it did finally come, it didn't take them long to recapture their feelings of Oneness. However, if one or more had to endure another different life it was more challenging." She looked Swuel in the eyes then back at us and proudly declared, "However, since you are here and will be undergoing a mystifying ritual, you will experience an immediate expansion of your emotional feelings. Minutes from now you will have an exceedingly electrifying sensation that will awaken any of your still dormant feelings. You will become unified heart, mind, spirit, and body in the truth of the love light of One." After a momentary pause, she closed with, "Please come with me to our chapel."

The three of us walked around Tesa to a tiny room located on the far right side of its main door. It took a few seconds for my eyes to adjust to the dimness of the interior. Once they had adjusted, I became fascinated with the paintings and many sculptured art pieces that filled this chapel-like section of Tesa. I saw a woman with a baby in one hand and a glass of pink liquid in the other. She was presenting the pink-filled drinking glass and baby to a man. This man who stood across from her held out a glass of the same pink substance and in the other hand he contained a coconut-like seed, both of which he held out to her. In another painting a man and woman floated in a pink speckled sea and all around them swam dolphins and whales that shown with lovenergy. I saw love and understanding written in their warm-hearted eyes and wished that I could be swimming with them. Another canvas depicted two spheres of glittering white light. They were surrounded by pink light and lightning streaks of the same color radiated from and toward each other. In a third illustration, male and female bodies were enclosed within the outline of One who was a brilliantly glowing light. The next took my breath away. Gail also noticed it and gasped intensely. "Look at that, Jim!" It was a face of a minuscule man within the form of a tiny woman who was within the outline of a man just a fraction larger who was within yet another larger woman, and this pattern continued on until the large mural was permeated with them. There were no details other than the exquisitely painted facial features; the bodies were only slight outlines. Each diagram of a being showed a smiling face that seemed to touch the observer with enormous love and contentment. The outermost being had no face but displayed the light of One. "Jim, they are all of us from different lifetimes!" said Gail breathlessly.

The inescapable faces of truth gazed back at me. I recognized a few of them such as the miner in Brazil and his voluptuous wife Vanessa as well as the mother and her sickly child. What affected me the most was the face of a beautiful black woman who I knew immediately had to be my Claire. She stared at me with sadness written in her unseeing eyes and the passion captured in them forced me to ask, "Why, oh why, were you black?"

"Because we, you, and I and the Oneness of love created me that color," answered Gail sagely.

Although I knew that her words were honest and that I needed to focus on their meaning, too many things were happening in that instant for me to delve into her wise insight. Regrettably, I was forced to put it off for the time being. I had somewhat of a reserved feeling about the rest of the people in the painting. I could only remember seeing a few of them during that life-changing meditation, yet I realized that most of them were intimate to me.

Looking at the smiling black woman, she asked, "Was I really that beautiful?"

I smiled at the glaring evidence of her beauty smiling back at me. "Even though I never saw you, Hun, I'm sure that you were that gorgeous," I told her.

"Just as I was then and am now, I am yours forever. Like this shows," she said, pointing out the men inside the women and women within the men, "we are in fact part and whole of each other as we have been since the beginning of time," she whispered with inner knowledge.

"That's because we are all One," said Angel. Without warning, the room began to glow with pink light. From every corner, bend, and crevice came soft pink beams of light that permeated the chapel and us. I was transported to a higher plane of consciousness. Angel's voice seemed to emerge from a remote region of my subconscious. "You are being immersed into the Universal Consciousness of the house of love. Allow your celestial bodies, hearts, minds, and spirits to follow unrestricted by your awareness. Make your minds totally blank and immerse yourselves in my words. Feel yourselves growing feathery and lighter in weight as you are ushered into the universe of One and His eternal love."

The hands of time moved awkwardly through the continuum of space. I first moved into my pasts, some of the lives I beheld were duplications of the last all-inspiring meditation that Swuel had led us through. Others, especially those created for preparation of an enhanced sensation of love, were contemporary and even revolutionary. Minutes later Gail and I explored new and very distinct universes. Gail was always at my side and I grew more and more in love with her. We traveled to remote stars and exchanged love with human and alien beings. We seemed to be a part of everything as it became a portion of our awareness. Being a part of One we were universal, becoming everything that we observed and all of it segments of our own being. For the first time in my long existence, and I didn't know until now how long, I suddenly had total recall. I possessed absolute knowledge of everything that had ever existed. Anything that had transpired in my own personal life or that of the universe became a vivid part of my understanding.

My all-knowing mind expanded and I was suddenly the Big Boom and the many universes were created in the wholeness of who I was—One's unconditional lovenergy. I was zero-point energy itself. In short, I realized that One is the very force of imagination. Lovenergy is the creative force that binds this divine energy of existence together. Every cell of our body, and the tiniest molecules that compose them, is the very perfect One. For the very first time I totally understood that I existed because I solely was the very Oneness of the One. "We are the souls of the One," I whispered to Gail.

"Yes, and our bodies His divine being," she whispered in reply.

Next we partook of Earth's creation and dinosaur age. Earth's axes shifted: north and south becoming east and west. The landscape was torn apart by earthquakes. These events preceded an Ice Age that seemed to last for a millennium. Finally, vegetation, bacteria, mammals, and medieval mankind made their timely appearances after ages of torpid developments. In a flash, the cycle began over again. These visions were not only images witnessed in a dream-like trance, but also an inner recollection as if Gail and I were participating in the creation of those events. Later I realized that One and I were not two, but one, and that I shared these various evolutions and this reality in the wholeness of self-awareness.

In the reality of One, Gail then spoke in an odd sounding voice. "You are the sun, Father, and I am the earth, Mother. All that we conceive is existence—our divine seeds. Jim," she continued in that peculiar voice, "we are One, the source energy that you call lovenergy, and that's all to creation; there is no more. For there is only One, I am."

I swelled with thoughts of love, desire, and care. I seemed to be confused with only one fact: her/his identification. At that precise moment I couldn't remember who this mate of mine really was. I knew only that this soul had been my lover throughout existence. "Yes, it is Gail who currently possesses the spirit of my eternal soul mate." I realized a second later with a smile.

Again the whole universe unfolded before me and for another brief moment I attained cosmic consciousness. A pink rose blossomed in my mind and galaxies filled with stars and planets flowered before me. I was the connecting light of all that I witnessed and all was the perfection of lovenergy.

"You are now transferring to the Cosmic Consciousness Center," Angel told us. "There, you will gain the blessings of people who are realized components of One." Smiling into our beaming faces, she said, "Travel in the reality of your everlasting love and harmony."

Without another word we sped off into space passing planets and stars during our flight. In only seconds we moved through the atmosphere of a globe that I immediately recognized as Earth. Without a moment's delay we found ourselves sitting in a large room with seven enlightened people whose auras exhibited their Oneness and perfection of spirit. Their eyes held an intriguing inner light, as if possessing eternal knowledge. A man acknowledged us with a nod of his bald head and in a near whisper, he said, "Our eternal soul mates have come before us for the ritual of edification." Smiling into our eyes, he said, "I am Rajah and we are pleased to have you with us on this momentous occasion. It's always moving to behold the reunion of eternal soul mates. We know that this union will enable you to deliver enormous powers toward our goals for humanity. We know, too, that phenomenon will occur whenever you desire it to transpire. What would seem like impossible tasks for others, you will instantaneously achieve."

Standing, another man said, "I am Owl from the Inca Indians. You are present in our favor and we honor your alliance here in the Cosmic Consciousness Center. Envy, covetousness, and adultery are deadly evils and must be avoided. Wisdom and impartial judgment must always guide your steps to eternal bliss."

The next speaker was a plain ordinary woman with a radiant smile. Like the others preceding her she said only a few words. "I am Syena. Believe in unification, for you are wholeness of One. Nevertheless, do share time and allow each other freedom to spend time alone." Then she cleverly added, "All One. Remember, you're equally sharing time with yourselves and the One. Therefore, even when separate, it is a perpetual conscious affirmation of your Oneness."

Another man said, "You have already received my first gift, which is love. My second gift is love, my third gift to you both is love and the last is eternal love. Keep it always secure in your hearts."

"I am Gandhi and I have only one gift and it is a selfish one, too: fidelity," confessed an elderly man. "Be inventive and innovative throughout your future lives together. Create ways to please each other and be ye eternally faithful."

"I am Krishna," another man told us. "Each of us is one with the Universal One and very soon you are going to be made into one unified couple. Know one another thoroughly so that your days together may be fruitful and fulfilling for you both. May your eternal Oneness be perpetual from day one until day Oneness," he said with a sly smile. "The day approaches when all will again be One; all beings, life forces, and even presumable nonexistent matter will be a perfect unit of our complete wholeness of One."

I wanted to ask him if he was the renowned Krishna, but Rajah, the first man who had introduced us, now stood and spoke profound words. "Today both of you have momentarily touched Clear and even briefly became cosmically aware. I am confident that as new children of the light you will try at all times to keep yourselves free of impurities. We, the people before you, are unclouded individuals. In our cases, though, we are eternally clear beings and, as you can see, our lives are not over yet. In fact, our lives are now eternal," he laughed and the rest of them joined in on the joke. On reaching this level, you will also live forever as a cosmic extension of One. When you return to Earth shortly, you are going to be humans again and confronted by challenges. You are being equipped with two infallible weapons: unity and power of will. Use them astutely and all hardships will become harmonious, what is difficult or impossible will become easy and feasible. At this stage of your progress, it's unrealistic for you to expect to stay clear for much longer. Utilize your power of belief daily, bringing the reality of the light of One into yourself. Doing thusly, you will inevitably achieve all of your aims in life. Including, at the completion of them, Eternal Clear. We then look forward to your joining us; we know that you will become a valued segment of the

Cosmic Consciousness Center." With a genuinely pleased smile, he stated, "You will learn shortly that there are no restrictions or requirements forced upon you. You have free choice on whether you join us, establish your own plane, live on Earth as humans or in another density, or eternally explore and wander the endless expanse of your created universes. As equal parts of the Universal Being, you are free to exist however you choose. Because of the validity and perfection of your wholeness, be ye truth, light, sound, and love in the unconditional entirety of One."

"We now give you our edification blessing," said a tall slim man who hadn't spoken to us previously. All seven masters rose and turned their hands toward us. With the white light of One entering our bodies, we heard them say as if light years away, yet a vital part of us, "May the pure enlightenment of One guide you on His righteous path of love, pleasure, goodness, joy, happiness, and fulfillment of all heartfelt aspirations. Keep the light of One with you as you make headway on Earth, restoring her to health again. May your paths remain clear, peaceful, and unified in the light and lovenergy of One throughout your eternal marriage."

Gail and I made a prompt departure and a straightaway arrival in Tesa's chapel. "I can see by your joyful countenances," said Angel, looking deeply into our eyes, "that your journey was fruitful."

Glancing into Gail's eyes, I was astounded and almost unnerved by the love, serenity, and devotion expressed in them. "Jim, am I looking like you? I mean you seem so full of love and joy?" she asked with her Mona Lisa smile about ready to break free of all restraints.

"I wasn't aware until now that you could easily read those emotions on my face," I replied honestly. "To answer your question, though, you do appear as I feel, passionately in love and profoundly at peace."

I moved toward Gail to give her a kiss, but Angel stopped me by stepping between us. "Stop," she abruptly ordered. "We have learned from similar experiences in the past that we cannot permit your bodies to touch in the least. Following this powerful exchange that you two have just undergone, it is often impossible to separate eternal soul mates if they exchange even a slight touch. Once you have been reunited by a kiss or even a touch of hands, you are literally coupled," she told us. We've got to preserve you for your true reunion, which follows very shortly. Gail and I sat frozen and eagerly staring into each other's radiating eyes. The longing in my heart was virtually impossible for me to contain. I desired this woman more than ever and here I was being forced to suppress my most zealous feelings. All I wanted right now was to hold and kiss her. Angel's warning actually paralyzed me, strangling any attempts of movement. "I empathize with you," she said with a grimace. "I personally know how long you've had to wait for this reunion here. I have just witnessed your past life alliances and know that only once before did you have to do without one another for a longer period of time."

She looked down and softly said, "As your counselor, I am obligated to inform you that you have to be prepared for an upcoming separation," she apprised us. "It takes place when you return to Earth at unknown locations and in new bodies. Being eternal mates, though, this time will seem longer than it really is going to be."

Her words lashed hard at my heart and I burst out. "Swuel said that we would be united again on Earth!"

"Yes, but there isn't any way of our knowing the exact date of your reunion," she said in earnest.

Gail started to cry and despite my own heartache, wanting to console her, I extended my hand toward her. Before I could touch her, however, I was persuaded to stop by Angel's crucial "No Jim, please constrain yourself!"

"I'm alright," said Gail, regaining her composure a minute later. "It's just that insufferable idea of our separation that compelled my temporary instability. I love you so thoroughly now that I don't know how I can exist a single day without you, let alone longer!"

"Remember that your emotional sensations are greatly intensified by the powerful love enhancement exercises you've just experienced," Angel replied positively." Following a momentary period of observation, she said, "Because of this negativity, you have lost your transitory Clear. Have no fear, we will immediately remedy your disharmony with the Universal One."

Getting to her feet, she confidently said, "Come with me and we will be sure to get you Clear again. Please don't touch. Even an accidental brush of hands will cause an internal fusing and only One knows what that might do to the rest of our ceremonial plans." We cautiously followed her to a small room beside the chapel. This chamber contained only a few chairs, two small tables, and many shelves of books. Angel perused the titles while we, one on each side of her, examined them. She found one identified simply as *Soul Mates*. "Yes," she said lightheartedly. Resting the book on a table in front of her Angel impetuously turned to the index. Her finger moved rapidly down the page and stopped at Chapter 11. I read the title. "Meeting Place." I smiled because of the frequency of the lucky number 11 showing up so often. It appeared as if she had forgotten our crisis and us, as she quickly rifled through the pages. "Here it is," she pronounced as carefree as could be. My heartache subsided and our auras grew brighter as she started. "Ah, this means . . . No. Let me read it to you without any interpretations. 'While present on this plane, eternal soul mates should meditate regularly. Their goal should be to disclose their future meeting time and place on Earth. If this should fail to reveal necessary data, then they should predesignate a time and place for their meeting.' In all likelihood," she told us, "you will learn during your meditations when and where you will unite on your planet. The thing I stress most is that you have a follow-up date just in case circumstances should be unfavorable for your first rendezvous."

Smiling broadly, Gail said, "Oh my One, how simple that makes it!"

"That will eliminate our deep-seeded worries," I said, looking into Gail's twinkling eyes. I looked into Angel's comprehensive eyes. "It is imperative that we are together and this does give us the assurance we both desire. Our future happiness and purpose as well as effectiveness will be greatly enhanced now." Scratching my head absentmindedly, I said, "Now let's pray that it will be soon after we've become humans again."

"Your Clear is showing again," announced Angel with a warm grin. "It's time for us to retreat from this sanctuary and return to the ceremony about to get underway. First," she emphasized, "make sure that neither of you touch or rub against the other."

As we neared the door of the chapel, the sun shown through a stained glass window and its colors fell to the floor in fragments. Just as we began to glimpse it, a large egg that was in the middle of the window seemed to split open and reveal its hidden secret. Our slow movement toward the door and the shading of the sunlight caused by our slow tempo, formed the image of a couple that resembled our present appearances drifting directly toward us. The intensity of love that poured from them mirrored my own passion and greatly added to my heartfelt sensations. I was suddenly vibrating from head to toe and my heart also seemed to be racing with this lustrous spectacle. Adding that to my enthusiasm and relish for the quickly approaching wedding caused me to pant slightly. "Gail is the same woman who I had desired to marry so long ago," I joyfully realized. "Here I am on another formerly unknown plane and I am finally getting the opportunity to share my life with the same woman who meant everything to me. Never would I have expected this dazzling of an outcome!" My arms ached to reach and gather Gail into an unending embrace. Instead, we were forced to walk awkwardly apart.

"We were created to be united like this," said Gail, pointing to the image of the mirrored couple drifting before us. "From the very source of existence we were born a part of the endless circle of One, the Universal One! Everything that is, I am, and you are too."

The throng of people assembled began to applaud as soon as we had vacated the chapel. Gail was glowing more than ever and I was even more vibrant from the sight of her. *How can I ever satisfy my enormous love and desire for her?* I wondered as we approached the huge swarm of enthusiastic people gathered to celebrate our wedding ceremony.

Swuel advanced with Rama and Marza following respectively behind him. When he had come abreast of us he said, "You're looking real jubilant. Are they fortified enough and familiarized with the following exercises, Angel?" he asked.

"They are as strong as two unattached individuals might be. I have left the explication of this ritual for you to explain, Master," she answered with a slight curtsy.

With a scowl of endurance on his face, he followed with, "We are going to test your fortitude and devotion to one another and our cause. Rama," he said, half calling and partly commanding, "take Jim to his tree and please take Gail to hers as well, Marza." We were each guided away and, within a few feet, stopped in front of two living crosses. On either side of the center trunks were thick branches with leaves growing out of each end. The growing mainstay of the crosses reached at least 30 feet in height. Their tops were full of large green leaves, which fluttered willowy in a faint breeze. I painfully noticed ropes tied to the lower branches and instinctively knew their purpose. "We are going to hang both of you on these crosses," explained Swuel, confirming my suspicion. "You are not to use your power of levitation to assist you; elude your pain. You will be suspended there for an adequate duration of time to test your fortitude."

Marza suspended Gail and Rama suspended me while other men fastened the ropes to our wrists. Only then did they release us. Pain crept sluggishly into my shoulders. Moments stretched into minutes and the ordeal I was feeling grew into genuine pain. Gail allowed a repressed moan to escape her lips and the reality of her being in pain increased my own fierce sensation of pain. "Gail," I called as brightly as I could muster under these circumstances, "feel my arms around you, Lovie; they are supporting your weight and alleviating your pain." Miracles of miracles, my own pain subsided as I imagined my arms propping her up.

"Oh my, Jim," she said with a sigh of relief. "I am sensing your arms about me and they are elevating my weight and spirit. Thank you so much for your devotion and undying love. I couldn't have handled it much longer otherwise." Directly, Rama and Marza ascended into the air and we were delivered from our weighty bondage.

"You have achieved our approval in this examination of your marital fortitude, stamina, and allegiance," replied Swuel proudly.

He now guided us to a raised platform; with Rama and Marza on our heels, he rapidly ascended the steps to the top. When we had joined him, Swuel said in confidence, "Because of your sharing your powerful love enhancing method with us, Jim, in just one minute you both are going to have almost 2,800 loving people sending you energizing pink light. Along with the love you have already received through Angel's mediation, you will be launched into an even higher plane of spiritual awareness. Don't worry about the unknown; your fears would only hamper your progression. Relax in the now." With Gail and I on either side of him, he guided us to the middle of the stage. "In a second we will ask you to join hands and at that point you will once again experience true intercourse, the perfection of your Oneness of each other and One." As our hands met, he, Rama, Marza, and all of the people assembled raised their hands and sent us pink light.

Chapter 6
True Intercourse

With the touch of hands, we molded and became lovenergy—the wholeness of One. The unconditional lovenergy of One poured in and through us. The reality of duality was gone and we experienced our Oneness. Our united spirit floated in the macrocosm of the universal wholeness of One. We, this new concept of self, passed hundreds of stars and sojourned past thousands of planets. Some of them resembled Earth so closely that I wanted to stop and examine them for life forces. However, not having any control of this voyage we only fleetingly observed their similarities and allowed ourselves to be freely transported to wherever our destiny was taking us. We were immensely enraptured, feeling ourselves as an intimate component of the omnipresent One. With bona fide feelings in our entire being we knew that everything that existed was an apportionment of our divine Oneness. We were One and our reality being Him, was universal. "Now that's true intercourse," I thought with a broad grin. "There is only One, and the existence of His being Lovenergy was perfectly divine!"

A moment later we landed on one planet that was so identical to Earth that I expected to see humans walking and driving cars. Its absolute purity of nature was its only true disclosure of the remoteness of my impression. Standing atop a tall ledge, we were then joined by three other pure white beings. Swuel spoke via one of them saying, "Through, and in the loving power of One, I rejoin these two eternal soul mates into one spiritual unit."

Created in the perfection of truth and love, Gail and I became one. Our two bodies merged together, becoming twice as large and purely radiant in the integrating power and light of One. For the first time in my life I sensed another person's state of mind and emotion. We were truly one in mind, heart, body, and spirit. I knew that she perceived my libido, joy, love, and my desire for a perpetual life with her. With a true sense of union, I also comprehended her corresponding sentiments. I instinctively knew that she was feeling, as I was, a perfect fusion and alliance of two spirits in one being. I knew at that moment why we hadn't been allowed to touch moments previously; it would have welded us prematurely. Orgasms of pleasure ignited our feelings much more powerfully than sexual bliss. They swept through us in gigantic waves that propelled us into other expanded proportions. We were being united with each other and One and nothing could equal that joy and pleasure of being! We were part and yet all of each other and the light, sound, power, and love of One. Being One, we were an extension of His divine spirit—equally sharing His purity of heart and almighty power. Our life was His and His ours. We knew everything and had total power of all His creation. The beautiful flutes of One played our wedding song. We had expanded throughout the universe, becoming one with everything that existed. We were multi-dimensional, both creator and the created energy of all that subsisted on all planets and in all planes of consciousness.

Suddenly we were in the light and presence of One. His Oneness of spirit touched us in a special way and it was if He had put His loving arms about us. Time had no tangible medium; we were the eternal moment whose existence was universal and continuous. Like a great flowing river, knowledge of all time cascaded through our combined presence of self. Our true intercourse with One and our eternal Oneness with each other soon expired and we regrettably separated from this absolute perfection of Oneness.

We then reappeared on the platform at Tesa. We were two individuals again, but I still felt a part of this unity of self. Just as I knew that I was a segment of her reality, she was part of mine. With a puzzled look in his eyes, Swuel quickly came over to us and asked, "Everything alright?"

"Yes, of course," I said jubilantly. "Why do you ask?"

"It's just that your last excursion was not on the agenda," he answered with a notable worried look in his eye. "The three of us had to search for you and force you here again."

I looked at Gail and was captivated by the angelic twinkle seen in her eyes. She appeared purely innocent, yet you could see that she was swallowing the canary. "Gail?" I inquired with a question mark emphasizing her name.

"I only wanted One to witness our sacred union," she virtuously replied.

"That should reveal your true potency to yourself," said Marza and Rama concurrently.

"True," verified Swuel. "Like all of you, your mind only has to do some catch up work with your given spiritual abilities. Through your fulfilled desire, my children, you actually became the reality of the One!"

Gail was even more aglow with Swuel's endorsement. "You mean to tell me that all I had to do was to desire being there with One?" she asked with true mystification shining in her perceptive eyes. Before she was able to continue, the subject people from the audience started coming up the stairs toward us. "Why are these people coming up here?" she asked curiously.

"They are the inhabitants of this plane who are coming to pay homage to the both of you. You're not only rejoined mates," said Swuel, "but eternal soul mates. You were sanctioned before all of them by the light and power of One. "While your spirits were being reunited and witnessing all of the creation of One, your bodies were here displaying your eternal union. You actually became different people, all of us seeing the persons who you had replaced during many of your foregoing lives." Because I had thought that we hadn't remained in our bodies during our journey, I yearned to question Swuel further concerning this divulgence. In the power of our unity, I wondered if perhaps we had experienced a different form of bilocation. However, like my desires for Gail, I knew in my heart that the answers to these questions would have to wait.

A dark-skinned man walked to our sides and stopped in front of us. "I am Reeby, a Bahamian from the island of Great Exuma," he said. "As a small child, I had found this good luck charm on a beach. It is my treasure from Earth and I wish to give it to you. It is a sea-bean, which had traveled by ocean currents for thousands of miles. Keep it in your hearts always and luck and love shall accompany you forever." He handed me a palm-sized, heart-shaped bean. Its smooth, hard shell was well polished and it gave me a feeling of jubilation—more from the meaning of the heartfelt gift than its own powers.

I handed it to Gail. She warmed our hearts with a gracious smile, and then imparted, "Reeby, in a past life Jim had brought one of these treasures to me as his niece and eternal soul mate! He had been sailing off of the coast of Africa and when stopping there for water and food supplies, he saw this unusual-shaped nut growing on a tree and picked it specifically for me. Being the romantic person that he is, he waited until Valentine's Day to present it to me."

"Then I'm sure that you had great love, joy, and luck in that past life of yours," said the Bahamian with a broad grin.

Our bobbing heads confirmed his declaration.

Next came am Indian woman whose long, black, braided hair fell almost to her heels. "I am Twisted Hair, a Shawnee American Indian," she proclaimed proudly. "I have brought you an ancient arrowhead from my tribe." I held it with reverence, remembering how my best friend Terry and I had searched so diligently for them in my youth.

I smiled at her appreciatively and said, "How could I ever repay such a generous gift? In my most recent past childhood, and two prior existences ago for my lovely wife, we had searched endlessly for treasures like this."

Then, with exalted feelings, I passed it on to Gail. "Oh Twisted Hair, how dearly Jim and I searched and treasured our arrowheads. In fact, after years of daily searching, we had found only two that were genuine. Most of what we found only roughly resembled arrowheads, but to us they were the legit article and we enjoyed them enormously."

"When we return to Earth again," I anxiously imparted, "my bride and I will add this to our treasure box. Once again we will share our childhood treasures and remember you and your generosity."

Smiling into our eyes and grinning faces, she said, "Hearing that the two of you had scouted and valued them warms my heart so much more. Thank you."

"I am William of the United Kingdom," said a tall and distinguished looking gentleman who took the place of our Indian friend. "I am giving to you a picture of my beloved London. Visit there when you return to Earth," he instructed. He handed Gail a tiny hand-painted oil painting and we instantly saw its rare magnificence. It was only four by seven inches, but clearly showed the Buckingham Palace in great detail and color. A golden carriage drawn by white horses stood to one side; minuscule, gaily-dressed people approached it while a throng of bystanders observed them.

"Oh my One!" said Gail, staring at the precious work of art which she held delicately in her hands. "Like all of these gifts, this is too elegant! Please, friends," she said beseechingly while holding the gifts out to our guests, "we can't accept these incredible presents. Please," she implored, "we want all of you to keep these spectacular memorials for yourselves. We can then appreciate your generosity even more."

"If you keep them," I said, backing my wife up, "we will be enjoying them even more because all of you, rather than just the two of us, will be treasuring them."

Smiling into our eyes appreciatively, William said, "These gifts will be returned to us when you depart Tesa. Although we collectively wish that you could take all of them back to Earth with you. In the mean time, I would love you to savor this replica of my cherished city. For more than six decades I have enjoyed it and now it is yours to derive pleasures from. Then it will be mine until you eternal soul mates borrow it from me again," he said with a winning smile.

Next came a man in what looked to me like Arabian garb. He said softly, "I am Shahid and I give you a replica of an Egyptian pyramid made from jade. I made it myself when I was on Earth." It was green and glistened brightly in the light of One.

"My eternal soul mate and I were Egyptian slaves and we partook in the construction of the Great Pyramid of Khufu," Gail revealed to all of us. "My mate was killed when I refused to give sexual favors to a sentry. Besides getting my husband killed, my resistance to that man enslaved me for the remainder of my life. I was laid to rest only miles from that great pyramid. I instructed our children to place one of their dad's, my eternal soul mate's, bones at my side." I was feeling disconcerted about her relating this private story to everyone within hearing distance. I also found myself coveting Gail's total recall. Since returning back to this platform, I had lost my temporary cosmic consciousness, and was again regrettably in the dark to all of our past life affiliations. I was absolutely unable to recollect any of our history other than those memories that I had viewed during the meditation led by Swuel.

We received more than 1,000 relished gifts collected from our home planet. These colorful people dressed in their native costumes had favored us with their most cherished chattels. Gail and I were thrilled with them and their obvious generosity, yet we were, grateful that they would be receiving them back again.

After the gifts were given and delightfully accepted, the leader of Tesa advanced and addressed all of us that were gathered there. "My renowned eternal soul mates," he commenced, "on this prodigious occasion I, as well as everyone here, am pleased to be attending and celebrating your reunion. Every person needs to locate their mate and glorify in the Oneness of the boundless love of One. Being able to play a part in your reunion is an honor and celebrating this grand occasion with you has been rewarding for all of us. As you have so aptly demonstrated today, the glory of your blending spirits has been sublime to all of us beholding it. We are expecting even greater things from you as time progresses." His next announcement was said with great dignity and flourish of hands. "I am enjoying imagining the whole universe being at peace, in love, fulfilled, and gratified to the magnitude you both have attained today. That is why you and your teachers are here. One day you, along with your many colleagues, will procure worldwide peace and harmony for all beings on all planes of consciousness to enjoy. Then, all future earthlings will be extolling your reunion as we are doing today. Go in peace, love, and fulfillment of dreams for all mankind," he said with a slight bow to his people and to us.

A huge barbecue was then started and we ate and conversed with all of our guests until the setting sun sent everyone home.

A more private party followed next, which lasted well into the night. Only our fellow students and their guides attended this reception. Ray was acting DJ and played records, tapes, and CDs with songs from the '30s to contemporary rock. My lovely bride was a dear with everyone. She didn't seem to tire from dancing with every requesting man there. At one point, though, I had to be frank with them, asking, "Please, guys, I'd like to have my new bride in my arms, too."

At precisely one minute before midnight, Swuel walked to the podium and said, "It has been an exciting day, but I'm sure it has also been exhausting for everyone, especially our eternal soul mates. I am also sure that they are very anxious to be alone on their wedding night," he said with a cunning smile and a diabolical twinkle in his eyes. "Lastly, in their honor we will refrain from holding classes tomorrow. This means that we will need to double our efforts the following day, but I am sure that all of you will welcome a day of rest and recreation. Our only request is that you limit your activities to this plane. Don't try being like our newlyweds and explore more of the universe."

After extending our goodbyes to our guests, Rama and Marza accompanied us outdoors. "The people of Tesa are very hard-working people and treasure their lives here enormously," said Marza. "Tomorrow is another workday for them and that's why they left us at sundown."

"You mean that these people here depend on their working income?" Gail asked, acting a bit flustered. "I was under the impression that all inhabitants at this juncture were metaphysical beings and that they didn't need to work for their survival."

"Working is an option. What they are doing is providing services for us and for one another. If they choose to work, their rewards are felt spiritually. No one is forced to live on this plane or any other. The inhabitants of this plane opt to live in the lifestyle characteristic to that of Americans. One has given everyone of us the right to live as we elect. People here on Earth or any other plane have free selection on how they create their living conditions. If not hampered by wrong concepts, we can determine our own futures and by using our powers of imagination and will, we can live exactly as we desire. From prior lives we know what we need to learn in any given life and thus create the tools to achieve that goal."

"Each of us are One and, when desired, we can choose to live by serving one another as parts of our unified One-self." As you know, Jim, there are huge cities here as well and the majority of the populace of this plane choose to live in them rather than to live in rural areas," said Rama, finishing Marza's startling disclosure.

"Yes," I replied as we walked toward our home. "I saw a vast city last night. Like my wife, I wondered who these people were and I wondered why that huge city was here. Now thanks to your explanations, Rama and Marza, all is very clear."

"Not to all of us it isn't! You did what last night?" questioned Gail, before Rama or Marza could make another comment. "What were you doing outside last night and why hadn't you told me that you were going?"

"Oh," I said, feeling slightly embarrassed because I had neglected to inform her. "I just went out for a midnight race with the moons. I was feeling vulnerable and afraid that if I remained in the house longer with you that my power of will would give way."

"Why, though, didn't you tell me?" she asked like a little girl might. "I would have fancied a moonlight ride with you."

"I'm sorry, Lovie," I conceded, "but not until I got downstairs from your bedroom did I decide that I needed to get outdoors. It was essential that I cool off my lustful desires and I realized that a fast horseback ride might do just the thing. Doing it, I discovered that One had given me a power of healing. My poor horse had broken his legs and with a gift from One, I restored him to normal health again!" Then I thoroughly explained the occurrences to my bride who was most likely the only one in the dark.

"Oh, Jim," cried Gail enviously. "You have exposed your talented gift!" You are a healer as you have been in many past lives. I have to wonder then if I am going to be psychic in my next life as I had been during many of my own pasts lives with you."

Marza looked into my eyes with an enlightened glance and nodded her head ever so slightly. "The only correction that I would make to your tale and to Gail's recognition of your power is that One, wanting to experience life via you, gave you the freedom to create your own life and you always had this power of healing. The fact is that He/you had a need for it and you used the gift that was already His/yours."

With a diabolical laugh, Rama said, "I guess that you won't need to cool off tonight! Matter of fact, I doubt that you'll have to worry about doing that again as long as you remain with us."

"I think I feel a headache coming," said Gail with a toothy smirk. "I just don't think that I am going to be up to anything except sleep tonight."

With a mischievous laugh of my own, I said, "Well, Lovie, my new wife, it's a good thing then that I am a healer! You as a psychic should feel that your headache is vanishing right now!"

Reaching our homestead, Marza said a curious thing. "When you visited the Cosmic Consciousness Center earlier today, you were actually on Earth. Those people of the center are there monitoring everything that occurs on Earth 24-7. Just for your own knowledge and feelings of security, we want you to know that they assist anyone in the cause who calls on them for help. It's only a matter of desiring to be with them and moving into a trance. We will be teaching you this technique in the very near future."

"The two of us were on Earth?" we said, echoing one another.

"Yes, you were," decreed Rama. "The leader of that distinguished group is the reincarnated Siddhartha Gautama, better known as Buddha—the enlightened one. In the life he is presently in, Rajah's current human age is 357 years. When you recommence your lives on earth," related Rama, "know that you'll be authorized to occasionally visit with him and his collaborators for guidance or solving needs." The idea that Gail and I had personally spoken to Buddha blew my mind. I was about to ask Rama a question when I noticed that we had paused at our pathway. All but one thought passed quickly from my mind. *At last I am going to be able to make love to my wife!* I inwardly rejoiced.

With a winning smile that sparkled in the light of One, Rama said, "From now on we will no longer be observing you. However, you need only to mentally or physically call out our names if we can help."

Goodbyes were said quickly and Rama handed me the other sack of gifts. Marza said, just before retreating, "As Swuel told everyone, tomorrow is a free day. Also, since the next day is Sunday you will have the day to yourselves. Beginning on Monday, Rama and I are going to be coming here to give you private tutoring. Our arrival time is precisely 1:00 p.m. and there isn't any set time for termination of lessons. Really, it's up to you how long we stay. Only if we fall behind will we intensify the length and depth of your instructions."

Smiling mischievously into our eyes, Rama said, "Have a restful weekend, you're going to need your endurance. Monday afternoon we will be here and will be very busy."

"Gail, I want to make love with you beside our lake" I said, directly following their departure. Please come with me right now," I implored with compulsion displayed in my voice and demeanor. The bags were placed on the ground right where we stood. I was mindful of their contents, but my need was too urgent to be waylaid another moment. We reached the crystal clear lake in only two minutes and laid down on the luxurious, dew-dampened grass along side it. The midnight moons shone down upon the pageant that was taking place beneath their wide-open cavernous eyes, their mouths agape in awareness of the intensity of our passions. The fragrant honeysuckle-suffused air encircled us, bathing us in its enhancing perfume.

At last my savage appetite was going to be satisfied. Yet for her sake and my own desire to prolong my own pleasure, I preserved our lovemaking as long as possible. My mouth and tongue found its refuge and gratification in her mouth, neck and breasts. Straightaway, I became swollen in desire and maleness. Wanting to extend time to its fullest, I quickly carried her into the cool lake where my stimulated body became manageable.

"Oh, Jim," she protested as I took her deeper, "it's awfully cold!" She quickly acclimated to its coolness, though, as we vigorously swam and played. Her exquisite body was so slim that she glided effortlessly and swiftly through the water like a dolphin might. In fact, as fast and powerful as I was in the water, keeping up with her was grueling.

Then finally I cut her off and after dunking us both under water, I grabbed her ankles and pulled her to shore. Immediately carrying her to a soft mossy bank, we resumed our lovemaking. Our cool, wet bodies reveled with sensations of pleasure as we titillated each other with loving touches and warm kisses. Her moist skin was succulent and I lingered while nursing at her firm ample breasts. Rubbing my tongue on the tiny bumps on her breast, I asked, "As my eternal soul mate, especially since you were Claire in our last union, you should know what these tiny bumps are—" Before she could reply, I said, "This is Braille for 'suck here'." Our joyous laughter echoed over and over again. It was almost like hearing all the angels and spirit guides laughing right along with us. Our bodies were created for one another. We both instinctively knew what the other wanted and needed. In a now shadowed memory of my Claire, I seemed to recall that we had also shared this same foreknowledge. *It must be another trait of soul mates*, I briefly thought. Neither of us hesitated in producing the sensations that we each desired. "Oh my wife," I moaned aloud, "Claire was never this good!"

"That's because she didn't have total recall of our pasts as I now have. I can easily summon all of my recollections regarding your fervent yearnings and my own responses and longing. You are not making love to only me, but also to Claire and all of the other people that I've been in my past lives. I am making love with you and all of the you's of your countless pasts."

Our bodies joyfully united and worlds and suns were born in the big bang of our incredible pleasures. "I love, need, and want you for all eternity, my beautiful wife," I sincerely said, following our lovemaking. "I am so enormously pleased with our reunion. Who would ever conceive that making love could be this profoundly beautiful? I want to lay here on this spot with you forever and love you for all eternity," I said.

"Eternity is the present," she whispered as she reached for my spent member. "Forever is this minute that we are experiencing right now. You and I are the existence of this moment in the totality of infinity. We've been told over and over again that we are One, ergo we are the very presence of now, which is the reality of eternity."

"There is only one thing wrong with what you intellectually said, Lovie," I teased.

"And what pray tell is that," she asked curiously.

"It should have been me saying it! I love that concept of now and eternity being the present moment. That's why we've got to enjoy this very second to the utmost," I said, rekindling our lovemaking. The second time wasn't as urgent and, therefore, more meticulously exercised, giving us even greater thrills of ecstasy.

"Oh my, you're so good to me!" Gail moaned as I strove to satisfy our mutually-shared fantasies. You claim not to have memories of your past and yet you knew what I needed just now."

"Lovie," I said, "I am only satisfying my own desires and love for you."

A half hour after refreshing ourselves in the lake, I turned to her, preceding our return home, and said, "Gail, you're the greatest person I've ever known. I am so thankful to One for bringing us together once again! We have been growing in the truth for many lifetimes now. Since arriving here, though, we will be more emphatic in manifesting our powers of will. Our belief systems will be getting more and more fervent in the coming days and weeks and our abilities will be expanding. Already our brainwashing is being eliminated as well as the enfites caused by wrong concepts. Your previous declaration about us being the moment is a perfect testimony of your rapid evolution of spirit!"

Smiling shyly at me, I read gratitude written in her sparkling brown eyes. "Thank you for your accolade. I pray that our lives stay as content and rewarding as they are right now," she said sincerely.

"Beeeeeep," I said, mimicking a buzzer on a game show. "You're wrong!" Your brainwashing is showing again," I said with a snicker of reproof. "Only minutes ago you said that we have this moment and you were right. We've created this very moment for our incredible reunion. Know in your heart that we have all of eternity to explore our personal creation of love in this very eternal moment. There is no longer need for praying, wishing, or daydreams; believe and hence create reality."

We both laughed and afterwards she said, "When will I realize that the requirements for routine wishing are gone forever? I profess to be spiritually endowed; still I make absurd statements like that one! I've got to remember that it only takes the power of belief to procure all of our goals."

"Don't be so critical of yourself. We are only novices at this novel realization and it is going to take a little time before we don't think, feel, or say erroneous things. Every time we make pessimistic statements or downgrade ourselves, we do deplete spiritual heights already gained," I told her with a warm embrace. "That is why we need to dissolve our enfites; it is a necessary step in the correction of our inaccurate and limiting judgment of self and what we are learning."

"Sorry, Jim," she said as we stepped onto the porch of our house. "You are absolutely correct. I've got to alter my way of reasoning and my belief system—and forever, too!"

"Not alter, Lovie," I replied, "but like all of us, you've got to bolster your confidence and positive comprehension. Also, and this is critical, we collectively have to totally delete enfites. We've been wrongly conditioned for so many lifetimes. It is going to take time before we have overridden those old fallacies. Just look at where we were yesterday and only One knows where we will be tomorrow!"

After showering, we lay in bed and talked over the day's events. "Gail," I said with my arm around her, "what an eminent day we've experienced. It will remain prominent in our memories for many lives to come."

"Unless we choose to make this next life on Earth our last."

"That's true and I would enjoy living with you on our own plane. Like Lou, though, we might also elect to return to Earth again and again. After all, our work with this cause won't be finished until our planet has been cleared of human debauchery. Then, the necessity of our living and working on Earth will be complete and eternity is ours to make of it as we desire." Thinking of an exception, I honestly said, "Right now I want only too celebrate life with you. I'm sure my feeling will change some, but right now I don't even want to contemplate unification with One! I want the rest of eternity to love you and reflect on our memories of this day."

Turning to her side, she put her head on my shoulder and her arm across my chest. "Who's Lou?" she asked sleepily.

"He is the man I was talking with yesterday," I answered. "When I was a young boy he was my family physician and friend. You were there that first day when he informed me that he had been Dr. Hibard in a prior life, forty plus years hence. In his desire to aid this crusade, even though he is spiritually unified, he told me that he freely chooses to live as a human over and over again."

With a yawn, she said, "He was that man with the bright aura. Come to think of it, I wonder why he wasn't present at our wedding, hope he's okay?"

"I also puzzled over that," I told her. "That's enough chatter; sleep is what we both need now." We kissed once more and in only seconds we were fast asleep.

Time lost its identity to us; it was an unintelligible moment in the days and weeks that swiftly expired without reckoning. Every minute of every day was filled to capacity with love, learning, and stimulating experiences. We worked daily on a one-to-one basis with Rama and Marza. Different mental blocks were being disintegrated with every meditation. Because enfites are the results of inappropriate teaching and personal interpretations of them, we daily visited past lives that showed these errors, which helped to alleviate wrong concepts.

To my astonishment, I frequently found myself a healer in a past life that I was visiting during the meditation. One day after such a session, I asked Rama, "Why does it seem that I've lived so many different lives, yet so similar? 'This moment is eternity' you told us', but how long is that? Every life seems so long while living, yet reliving them here they seem so short."

"I can see mental advancements progressing from one life to another," said Gail. "I imagine that there will be more spectacular intellectual, medical, and spiritual revolutions in the future."

"Only if we can change mankind's destructive ways," I said.

"The Universal One is boundless. Time is never changing; it is all one continuous moment. It is an eternal bridge taking us from one moment, minute, hour, day, year, or life to another. Like the people in those cars on a bridge, we do have different experiences, but it is still this one eternal bridge."

"One is eternal and will continue after the cars have all stopped and the bridges crumbled."

"Humanity is an apportionment of One, however, only as you have seen a tiny component. One is eternal because He is lovenergy which is eternal and never-ending."

"In today's just concluded meditation, I found myself a homeopathic doctor. As such, I gave restorative remedies made from flowers to my patients and virtually all of them were healed. Infrequently, I gave constitutional remedies and some patients were even healed of debilitating diseases."

"I also find myself being a healer. More often, though," said Gail, "like in today's meditation, I seem to be frequently giving people advice or being clairvoyant for their benefits. Why are all of these similar occupations being revealed to us through our meditations?" she asked with a mystified look in her eyes.

Rama and Marza looked each other intensely in the eye and Rama slowly responded, "We've already discussed your future callings, but now, to be more explicit, we will get into advanced information regarding them."

"As you've learned, we are all a part of One," said Marza. "Each of us equal portions of His sea of creation. As such, His seed, our very souls, dwell in us and simultaneously exist in Him. We each share equal portions of one another and this makes each of us our brother's keeper. For we are but mirror images of one another and One."

"Jim and Gail," said Rama, looking at each of us in turn, "this is the reality of One. We are one in the perfection of His lovenergy. Humans need only to realize their righteousness. However, because of doubts and fears due to obstinate church teachers who teach deceitfully, mankind has been enormously retarded. Humans are taught to believe themselves separate beings. They were taught about original sin and to believe themselves evil right from the moment of conception. Consequently, they are told that they are unworthy to have any part of God in them. That He is a supreme being who sits in judgment far above them. This is absolute nonsense and worst yet the people in charge know it! It is a money-making business. The more they imprison their parishioners with these inaccuracies, the more money they make! We are One who is Lovenergy, not ignorance or hatenergy!"

"Yes," all four of us chimed in together.

"Over and over again we souls are born into human bodies. The purpose is to learn the tools that will enable us to realize our divine Oneness," said Marza. "Strangely enough, we are fighting an unnecessary battle trying to make ourselves worthy. Humanity needs only to realize that their very souls are already One. Their bodies might be defiled, but their souls are divine."

Marza didn't allow me time to contemplate this powerful issue. Instead, she metaphorically drags me kicking and screaming from it by informing us, "We've known your unique aptitudes for some time now. Knowing that it was essential that you discover these truths for yourselves, we've been patiently waiting for you to attain this conviction. Jim, you already showed us your ability to heal that night with your horse. In your next lifetime it is likely you will be a gifted doctor. Attaining even more healing ability by expanding your powers of belief is your duty to humanity."

"The soul, S-O-U-L Rama cleverly spelled, reason for life is to realize our Oneness."

"Gail," said Marza, "your being endowed with the ability of reliving your past lifetimes and those of others always enhance powerful psychic abilities. Combine that with your wise teaching; you will bring others into the light of their Oneness."

"Why make all of this your exclusive secrets though?" asked Gail, after they failed to say more.

Wanting to get back to Rama's teaching first, I raised my hand and asked, "Why then are there so many of us, and why is it necessary for you enlightened people to hold other classes? I mean, if we are all one and there aren't any variations of time?"

"One's imagination is fathomless," said Marza. "He is conception and His concept is mankind. Man's soul reason for living is to realize his Oneness."

"I thought that I had explained it simply enough," said Rama with a little mocked frustration. "Basically it's because mankind hasn't yet realized their Oneness." He took another deep breath and went on. "Every released soul doesn't pass off of their path at the same place. Though they all do come to a place like Tesa when the body they're in dies. They are all taught accurate truths and return afterwards to Earth in newly-fertilized eggs."

"Their past life karma determines their next life status."

Immediately I spoke, "Why aren't those truths they've been taught changing them into One?"

"Despite their Oneness at birth, their past life memories are deleted." Rama answered. "Couple that with the fact that they are quickly corrupted by self-serving teachers and you have confusion."

"Sorry for interrupting you, Rama," said Marza, "but you left out one important detail."

"Well, please teach us, Marza," he said with a laugh at his intended humor.

"It's only that we cannot take precedence over any karma that a soul may have obtained in its just concluded life."

"Thanks, Marza, for your correction," Rama said with another laugh. Gail and I joined in with him this time.

"Only the soul who created that karma in the past will be able to diminish their corrupt karma. The worst karmic defiled beings can uplift themselves with sufficient moral living, services to others and righteous thinking and behavior." Immoral karma will negatively affect future existences."

"Your," Rama began, reverting back to the discussion we had been having, "exceptional karma and gifts coupled with your marriage have brought you into an exalted state of consciousness and faithfulness to one another and this movement. As you have been seeing, this pattern has held true in most of your pasts. You always worked together as doctor/healer and telepathic psychic. It wouldn't have done you much good if we had disclosed this beforehand, you had to come to the conclusion of it being your next calling."

Smiling at me, Marza said, "Jim, in your just concluded past you were becoming the psychic. As you already know, in your preceding life you were a homeopathic doctor." Looking Gail straight in the eye, she said, "As Claire, you had a medical aptitude. Despite your loss of sight and deafness, you had the intelligence, ambition, desire, and wealth to realize all of your goals. Using Braille books after you lost your sight, medical school was very feasible again for you. It was your desire as well as your calling."

Not wanting either of us to feel guilt because of past life deeds, Rama looked us fervently in the eyes and said, "There's no need for debating about what could have been. The point is that the world is an open oyster and you are to take advantage of all of your training here. You are both here with us now for very specific reasons and you have just discovered your calling."

Preceding your life as Claire," Marza informed my ravishing wife, "you were a fantastic medium and thousands of people called on you for assistance. You taught them valuable lessons by channeling their deceased and people became followers of your wisdom."

"Is it only an illusion or is it fact that our vocations interchange every passing lifetime?"

"From what we have been observing in your pasts, it appears that both of you have equal aptitudes in these fields," said Marza. "Thus, your roles did interchange between these two occupations, which prevented monotony."

"Because you both do have distinct innate intellect in these two specific areas, you do favor them over other professions," said Rama. "In only one life were your stations identical, both of you being psychics. You created that experience for yourselves because it produced rivalry and you wanted to test your Oneness. Passing that test with flying colors, it consequently was the only lifetime that it occurred."

My enfites were getting broken down and I was having past life recollections while fully awake. Memory of that life suddenly flooded my mind and I vividly recalled the competitive contention that it had created between us. In fact, it had been so consuming that for a short period of time we had even contemplated divorce. Thankfully we realized our Oneness and corrected our jealous behavior.

Waking one day on a bright Sunday morning a few weeks later, Gail asked me, "I wonder if there are any kind of religious services held in Tesa's chapel? If so," she said with an enthusiastic smile and clap of hands, "I'd really enjoy my husband accompanying me there."

"My darling wife," I pronounced, "if it's a church service you want, you've only to believe that there is one being held today."

"Yes," she said affirmatively, "we are going to attend mass together. It's a 10:00 a.m. service, too," she emphasized with another clap of her hands.

Two hours later we sat in the chapel along with Swuel, Angel, Rama, Marza, a dozen members of our group, and 80 or 90 natives of this plane. Hymns were playing on an invisible organ as Angel walked to the front of the room. With a broad smile, she announced, "As you assuredly know, our newlyweds have telepathically summoned us here. So," she said a second later, "without further adieu, let me present Gail and Jim to you." And she promptly resumed her seat.

In shock, Gail whispered in my ear, "What will we do now?"

"We serve them and One, Lovie," I replied, getting to my feet and giving her hand a tug.

"How do we know what to say or do?" she asked nervously. "I don't want to say or do something that is going to be inappropriate."

"I have no idea, Lovie," I honestly admitted, "but I believe in myself and you. Furthermore," I substantiated, "we just give One our burdens, believing that they are lifted and just allow our eternal One in us to do as He directs us to do." Still holding her hand and not yielding to her reluctance, I led her to a makeshift altar. It was a small square table with a candle and Bible-like book atop it. I sensed unconventional feelings, which assailed me as soon as we moved behind the altar. Gail opened the book resting on it and we both, anticipating nothing, entered into a soul-consciousness that neither of us remembered experiencing before. Gail randomly read a passage from the book, "The infinite mind of One has our pains, worries, and fears at bay. One doesn't want any of His children to suffer." I was utterly astonished when Gail then closed the book and attested, "There is a woman born to this plane who has just been informed by her doctor that she has cancer on her left breast. Please come forward for healing."

A middle-aged woman slowly stood and glided forward. As her skirt touched the table, I raised my hands and transmitted healing indigo blue light to her. It poured from One who was a distinct part of me. I simply said, "Your cancer is cured through the intervention of our One. Go in peace and love my child." With a smile of gratitude, she curtseyed and resumed her chair. Instinctively, she felt for the lump. Not finding it, she screamed joyously, "It's gone! Only minutes ago it was very detectable and now it's not here!"

Gail surprised me again as she spoke to another woman. "Rose, your children miss you and visit your grave weekly. They are pleased, though, that you are in heaven and don't have to go through those emphysema episodes anymore. Your son Jeff got a new best friend weeks ago and that boy's dad recently passed away. Your husband met the boy's mother and the two of them are falling in love." After a moments view, Gail added, "Your daughter Jacky," she said with a giggle," is right now riding her rocking horse with your slipper on her lap."

"Is she still sucking her thumb?" asked a tall, pleasant-looking member of our group in training.

Gail smiled and replied, "She is sucking it right this second. Her dad . .

." she paused for only a second, then said, "Bruce is disturbed about it. He's tried everything to correct this habit, but nothing has halted her compulsive thumb sucking. In fact, since your death seven weeks ago, Rose, she sucks it even more. She has even gotten a callus on it where her little front teeth rubbed it raw."

Less than three hours later, 15 people had been healed of their emotional, physical, and psychological infirmities. Another 22 individuals had received psychic readings from Gail and everyone attending was totally satisfied.

Our service ended with a prayer from Swuel who we had asked to join us behind the altar. "One," he started, "we have all witnessed your powers through these two resourceful individuals and we thank you for bestowing your powers in them. They are prime examples of your fulfilling power of belief and their eternal union." Turning his attention to all of us, he said, "To all of those who believe, shall come their heart's desires. Feel yourselves worthy, have unyielding faith, and know that ye shall reap your just awards."

After everyone who had attended had thanked us lavishly and shaken our hands, Swuel stepped between Gail and me and put his arms over our shoulders. He proudly paraded us outdoors while saying, "I am astounded by your mystic abilities. When Angel had suggested your leadership of this service earlier this morning, I felt skeptical of your advancement. I hope I am exonerated by you both," he said apologetically. "It's just so uncommon, especially since you've been here for only weeks. I should have known that once you were united you would display extra powers like you did today. I can't wait to see your future services!"

"No offense taken Swuel," I told him.

"Until we moved behind that table," explained my wife, "neither Jim nor I had any idea of what was going to take place this morning. We thought that we were just attending a regular weekly service."

He graciously smiled at us and said, "We knew that following your unification that your powers would be magnified. In truth, though, none of us had any idea to what degree this would hold true." With a shake of his head, he said, "When Rama and Marza told me that they were positive that both of you were prepared after discovering your prevailing vocations, I still felt dubious about your capacity of holding this service."

"Swuel, as we went behind the alter I was transported into a trance-like state as I'm sure Gail experienced. Is there a more fitting term for it? Can we use that technique for learning and problem solving when we return home?"

With a broad grin, he answered, "What you really accomplished was to subconsciously enter the Cosmic Consciousness Center. Very often our workers, writers, musicians, and other people, when intensely concentrating, subliminally go there for problem solving. So, naturally you can consciously use that method for solving your own difficult tribulations or those of others. Generally," he said with a clearing of his throat, "a person uses a trance state to achieve a goal or to metaphysically move to a particular plane, place, or time. In the causal plane you can relive or explore your pasts." He smiled at us and explained, "You will be learning how to move your mind into a trance so that you can mentally travel here, the causal plane, or Cosmic Consciousness Center. It will be a useful tool for you to learn. Your instructors will be teaching you this skill and informing you of its many purposes."

Rama approached us and announced, "We have beheld a remarkable exchange of mind and spirit power. As a result of your presentations at this wonderful service, Swuel, Angel, Marza, and I want you to hold a weekly service here for us all. We are also going to be working even closer and more extensively with you two innovative spirits. Your next lesson will be learning about the application and operation of the trance states of mind. I was tuned into you when the topic surfaced between you and Swuel. You and Gail have already illustrated your ability of using this medium. So what we will be teaching you next is how to use this technique to its fullest extent. Expect us two hours earlier tomorrow."

"As you can imagine," I said, looking both men in the eye, "I am thrilled with this aspect and most anxious to learn how to use it effectively. Having more time with you and Marza will be most exciting and enlightening, Rama."

Thirty minutes after arriving home, we went horseback riding and made love in our favorite location. This time, however, she created a sex-driven maniac out of me. You would think by my behavior that I was a sex-deprived person instead of a satisfied honeymooner! Gail again protested as I carried her nude into the cool lake. After I had released her from my arms, she made an unanticipated turn and began to swim rapidly toward the opposite shore. I lunged after her as she passed by, but failed to even get a finger on her toe. She swiftly swam to the opposite bank and called to me, "If you're going to want some loving this afternoon, you are going to have to catch me first." I saw her doing a disappearing act behind some trees in a widely wooded area and started off in pursuit. As my feet touched firm ground, I heard a distant, "Over here," and I charged in that changed direction. My naked body soon became scratched from head to toe from the branches that I anxiously shoved my way through. From an entirely different direction I heard her say, "I guess you're not desiring any pleasures today." I blindly lunged in that new direction of her voice. I chased innocuous shadows for a half-hour without getting more than a glimpse of her. Finally, not hearing her enticing words for some time, I retraced my way back toward the lake. I reached the lake's edge soaking wet with perspiration, a wounded ego, a multitude of scratches, and feeling beside myself with lust. There, floating compliantly on her back was Gail!

I plunged into the lake and embraced her as if I were afraid that she would escape me again. "Oh there you are," she said as innocently as you please. "I was just wondering where?"

Squandering no time or energy on goading explanations, I energetically swam for the opposite shore with her in-tow. On reaching it, I eagerly released all of my pent up stress and passion.

"You know," I told her that night after completing an exceptionally flavorful meal, "that you created a nymphomaniac out of me this afternoon?"

"Jim, your brainwashing sure did show itself today," she replied with glee in her eyes. "After all, you only needed to believe and to use your powers to locate me. A few times I floated only inches above you."

"You know," I acknowledged, following an outburst of laughter, "you're right! It astonishes me how susceptible we are to our old conditioning. I wonder how long it's going to take us to rid ourselves of our wrong thinking? We've been so deluded with those poor modes of thought and incorrect actions that

I'm becoming weary! I've got to be on guard all of the time now. Otherwise, like today, it just sneaks in on me unaware." Pausing an instant, I asserted, "I've got to pray to One for reminders of who I am. I've got to realize what I am thinking, saying, and doing before I react."

"That's true of all of us, earthbound and free." Without pausing, she added, "Rather than 'conditioning', don't you mean 'brainwashing'? Or doesn't that apply to you?" she needled me unmercifully.

We laughed together and I found myself loving this woman more than ever before. "Yes," I said thoughtfully, "we've only to think, act, and react as One instead of always reacting to others and other conditions. I was actually hurting myself, feeling great frustration and even anger! You know, Lovie, like I said before, it seems as if you are now the teacher and that I am becoming more infatuated with you every day."

"You better love me more, like it or lump it, you're stuck with me now!"

"Well, there is that cute little blond—" I replied with a diabolical smile.

"Never mind that shit! As far as other women go you better be like Claire—blind, deaf, and dumb," she sternly reproved.

Again the days and weeks passed like lightning. Rama and Marza spent four to six hours every day with us exploring new and exciting avenues of perception and besides that, we spent hours in the library studying and our spirits grew with an expanding awareness of reality. Our comprehension of our own aptitude increased as our mastery of this spirit life unfolded like the petals of a brilliant red rose. We went to the causal plane periodically to dislodge past life enfites or weaken brainwashing.

More and more often we were updated on the happenings of Earth. One afternoon at 2:00 p.m., we found ourselves watching a film of the inhabitants of New York City. It confronted the adversities of mankind on other humans. A proven AIDS infected man purposefully raped countless women, a pedophile maliciously accosted young boys, an addictive mother harmed her newborn by inexcusable neglect, suspected terrorists crashed planes filled with people into the Twin Towers, and two wars quickly followed.

"Oh my One, if they only knew the truth about love and our given powers of will, they would instantly reform!" said Gail with unfeigned empathy.

"The truth of your powers of will in the hands of a terrorist would be hazardous and criminally exploited. In the untrained commoner's hand, it wouldn't be properly utilized," proclaimed Rama sagely.

"How then," asked Gail with a valid interest, "are the conditions of people corrected, and the woes of their victims abolished?"

Before either of our instructors were able to reply, I answered, "Well, Lovie, that's where you and I along with the rest of our comrades come into the picture."

Frowning, she asked, "What difference can only a handful of ethical beings make against billions of depraved and immoral humans?"

"You don't have faith in the powers of love my book will bring to the world?" I asked with famed disappointment.

"Of course I do, but getting it to enough people is going to be a problem."

"My dear, Gail," said Marza placing a hand on her shoulder. "At your first healing service, less than 100 people attended. There were more than 200 people at your following service, and that number has been nearly doubling every week. I expect," she valued, "to find more than 1500 people gathered for your next one. The number of people attending will keep increasing with every service you hold and we are talking about a few million people available here in Tesa. We do expect followers in other densities to somehow learn of you and start joining us."

Rama continued with the same realm of thought, "When you rejoin each other on Earth, you can establish yourselves in the spirit world. With unerring discipline, web sites, motivating lectures, healing and perceptive readings, you will influence millions to the same extent that you are doing here at Tesa. Teach the world how to love unconditionally and all circumstances will improve."

"Love is the secret," I said with conviction. "If we can teach enough humans how to create it in their lives, there won't be any discord, bickering, divorce, cruelty, war, arguments, or any of what we saw there." I pointed at the now blank screen before us. "I will record an mp3 love enhancement meditation and offer it on my lovenergy web site when I return to Earth in my next human body. After that I will write a book about love and might very well decide to write about my experiences here if that is permissible?"

Rama shook his head. "I don't know. We will have to discuss that with Swuel and the distinguished members of the Cosmic Consciousness Center."

"Your training has consisted of several levels," Marza pointed out. "Power of belief, spiritual enhancement, willpower reinforcement, usage of energy forces, and, most momentous, clear deportment of self and powers. You have almost achieved Clear. Soon you shall both be returning to Earth." She walked between us and placed a hand on our shoulders. "With these tools," she replied, while pushing downward for emphasis, "you will possess and recreate the human race to the moral specifications One desires for all of His children! The future," she said, after a minute of silence, "and pasts, are present in this moment of existence. Open your veils of deception and see the light of truth and your futures."

The wall before us faded and became obscure. In its place we viewed the inside of an enormous cathedral filled with thousands of cheering followers. In different bodies, Gail and I stood behind an altar with our arms spread wide open in a gesture of embracing love. Pink light coursed out of us and flowed over them in a blanket of love that everyone felt. The passion returned to us was almost more than we could withstand and our projected love became even stronger because of this recycling love. I witnessed throngs of those believers being healed by a future me. An even more attractive Gail was a mediator between Earth and the world of spirits. Besides personal readings, she foretold of ensuing global happenings such as terrorist plans and acts of nature.

The wall again reclaimed its place and Marza said, "Believe in what you just witnessed. Neither Rama nor I had any idea what you would encounter. There is no deception, for you uncovered it yourselves. That is your future and you've only to believe and thus allow what will take place in your futures."

"Oh my One," resounded Gail, short of breath, "it all seems like a grandiose illusion. Nothing that significant could really occur in our next life!"

"Your brain washing is showing again, Lovie. Also," and I looked at Marza and Rama for confirmation, "you've lost some spiritual tiles on reentry."

A crinkle burrowed her lips as a wrinkle furrowed her brow. "I've only to believe," she dutifully replied after a prolonged descending whistle.

I kissed her full mouth longingly and said, "You got it; just believe wholeheartedly."

Following a few minutes of silence, Rama said, "When you return to Earth, you will both have to remember not to demonstrate your powers posthaste. It is necessary to mask your true character for a period of months and perhaps even years." He looked over at Marza and asked, "Why don't you tell them one of your experiences as a returnee?" He looked reflectively into her eyes and said, "You know the one that I am alluding to don't you?"

She grimaced ever so slightly, then, resigning her reservation, told us a rousing tale.

I replaced a 16 year old girl who was killed in an auto accident. Her father who had been harassing and molesting her daily had been fighting with her when the collision took place. She died on the spot, but with me replacing her exiting spirit I made a quick recovery. Five days later, dad showed up in the hospital alone. He held his fist to my nose, which had been broken, and threatened to bust it all over again if I betrayed him. I guaranteed him that I'd remain silent. A moment later he scowled at me in his hungry way and said, "Daddy's got something good for his little princess," and he began to lower his pants. Having been his little princess for only days I did the natural thing, I screamed as loudly as I could. He drew back a clenched fist and was about to hit me when we heard running footfalls in the hallway. "Just wait till you get home. You'll pay for this, missy!" he said with vengeance exhibited in his voice and on his glowering face. "Damn it all,' he replied while struggling with his pants. "I can't beat you now anyway. They'd guess something is—"

Three nurses burst into my room and asked what had happened. I remained hushed while he explained. "Jennifer was asleep when I got here and I tickled her feet like I always do. This time I guess with all of the shock of the accident, pains, and comings and goings of strangers in her room, she woke up screaming."

I took advantage of the company being present and said, "Sorry, Daddy, but I'm so tired. Can you possibly come back another time when I am feeling better?"

"Well," he started, as the nurses slowly began to file out, "I'll have to see how things go at the office tomorrow."

"Jen, this door should remain open at all times," said one of the retreating nurses from the doorway. "Please inform your company of that fact," she said, looking suspiciously at the cruel man who was my new father.

I told her that I would remember, and then looked into his glaring eyes. The anger I saw there made this new me cringe with fear. "I better," he warned me, "not hear anything about our private lives," he said, stressing the word 'private'. "Remember, Missy," he declared, holding up his index finger and waving it in my face, "you still live under my roof. If you still intend to go to that nursing school, well, you'll have to keep mum about our personal affairs."

Marza took a deep breath then continued.

Oh how I had wanted to use my powers then and there on that man! Instead, I turned to prevailing powers. Just after he had left I asked for the head nurse and a social worker. When they arrived, I disclosed everything to them with enormous feelings of relief for my future and the real Jenny who I was secretly replacing.

The next day following that horrendous episode, my mother started another. This one was even more ghastly because she denied her own daughter's word and supported that insufferable man. "Your daddy loves you, Jen," she said with unconvincing tears flowing. "How could you accuse him of such terrible behavior and have him arrested for it?"

"Mommy," I began feebly, "he began molesting me when I was only five and raped me three to five times every week! For more than eleven years I had to live that nightmare every single day of my panic stricken life!" Now I was in tears, too, but unlike her tears, mine were genuine and driven by fear.

Even though I had been that poor child for hardly a week, because of my being in it and very much a part of her life for seven weeks prior to her death, I did share the sincere anguish of Jennifer."

"My mother jumped to her feet and said, "Oh my God, I can't believe these filthy lies coming out of your mouth! You horrible lying fiend! I will not permit you to go on telling these lies about your loving father like this. You stop it this instant, hear me?"

My doctor, unable to find other reasons of keeping me hospitalized, released me five days later. My best friend Joyce picked me up at the front door and I began another adventure into this troublesome life. "What are you going to do?" she asked with a concerned frown. "Your dad is there right now awaiting your return. I rode by there on the way here and saw him on the front porch drinking and waiting to ambush you!"

"I only want to finish school, Joyce. In a few weeks he will be tried and found guilty. Mom? I guess I'll just have to put up with her ridicule until the end of this year when I complete high school. Nursing school won't be any problem since I'm intending to live near the university and work in a local hospital to pay my own way, if mom should opt not to help me."

My nice and neat plans made a brief detour. "Never mind dropping me off here, Joyce," I told her, having seen Dad's vicious expression from the safety of the car. "It is going to be better for me if you drop me off a half block past the house. Please," I implored as she pulled to the side of the road, "leave me here and don't look back. Just take off real quick, okay?"

"Are you sure?" she asked, glancing back at the house with worry. "Might be better for you if—"

"Leave right away," I said, getting out of the car. "Thanks again for the lift. As you know, I really couldn't ask Mom, and even though he asked, I refused to allow him to drive me home!"

Silently, I asked One to protect this innocent girl and me.

"Well, missy, 'bout time you're home!" said this drunken man who called himself a father. "You got something good for your loving daddy?" he asked while flagrantly scrutinizing me over the porch railing.

Without replying or allowing his scandalous behavior and smug stare to affect me, I quickly mounted the stairs to the front door. I stopped suddenly hearing a mournful cry from Jenny's beloved dog. "You let him go!" I yelled, before turning to face him.

Turning on my heels, I recoiled when I saw dad's exposed genitals. Even more so, when I saw Jenny's cherished dog contorted in pain. This ugly man had Rally's ear twisted tightly in his hand. "If you're not here in front of me on your knees within 10 seconds, I'll rip his ear right out of his skull!" he threatened. With a little whimper, Rally cried again, and my heart—"

"No, no!" Gail cried, breaking the thrilling adventure we were all caught up in. I reached out, but before I was able to gather her into my arms, she said, "I'm sorry for my outburst. I guess that the name of your dog, along with that horrible spectacle, was more than I could take. In a past life, I had also had a dog with the same name. My aggressively jealous husband who claimed that I loved Rally more than him, killed my puppy with his bare hands!" More tears ran profusely from my wife's tightly clenched eyes.

Being at last able to gather her into my arms, I sincerely whispered, "Oh, my poor baby." I kissed her tear-dampened cheeks and stroked her hair lovingly. My aching heart went out to her with my words, "Forgive and forget, Lovie." I only wanted her laughing and enjoying life to the fullest. I wished that we could have been alone so I could have more uncompromisingly removed her mind from these painful memories. When she had gotten herself settled again, I spoke up with surprising information of my own. "You talk about synchronicity, boy do I have one for you!" With a question of probability in my own mind, I said, "I had also had a dog named Rally! My beloved pooch was a guide dog. Drastic circumstances took him from me." Even though it had been many years, my next words of explanation came hard. "He was killed saving my life. Cutting us off, a speeding car illegally made a turn and drove immediately in front of us. A responsive Rally threw a hard body block on me, knocking me backward over the curb." Seeing panic in Gail's eyes, I quickly added, "Because of his fast action, I only got a tiny bruise." Noticing some uneasiness still in my wife's eyes, I gave her a reassuring smile and a heartfelt kiss.

"If we are finished with the digressions," Rama said, "we should allow Marza to complete her tale."

Gail anxiously said, "Oh, yes, please do tell us what transpired."

With a warm smile, Marza continued.

"I only wished that his dangling cigarette would fall where it would really burn him." She paused, allowing us time to recover from our laughter and then resumed after a laugh of her own. "Needless to say, it had its desired effect. In severe pain, he jumped up releasing Rally and hollered something about my having bewitching powers. From that time until he was imprisoned five months later, he didn't even so much as show his face around me. I finished high school and even completed nursing school while he sat in jail spreading exaggerations about his daughter the witch who had set him on fire and who had gotten him incarcerated for 25 years."

We hadn't yet ceased our laughter when I said, "As you have so aptly taught us, life is never a written script with which we all must comply. We are spectators of a game of life in which we are participants. How we perform a given duty, is a determinant of future and greater responsibility and burdens. There also are no fluke chances. Everything that occurs in life is another crossroad, meant as a learning tool for a given purpose." I smiled at my need of speaking these thoughts aloud. "I'm sorry," I apologized to Rama, Marza, and Gail for my rambling. "However," I said, still trying to explain my behavior, "I am attempting to fit all of the random pieces into their proper sequence.

"Our each having a favorite dog named Rally—an accident? Unlikely!" After a momentary period of deliberation, I asked with interest, "Is it possible, Marza, for you to give us an approximation of the date of that occurrence?"

"Let me see," she said, resting her chin on her open hand. "Jennifer was born in 1900 and was 16 when this event took place," she said a minute later.

"Okay," I replied. "We're talking about 1916 then. Gail, can you recollect the date of your Rally's death in that past life of yours?"

"I am going to have to count the years aloud so you can help me," she said. "I was born into that life in 1894 and was 21 when my poor puppy was poisoned. That would make it, 19—"

"What was your name back then?"

"Rita."

"It just fits like a hand in a glove! 1915! Exactly one year before! One year before your Rally, Marza. Did Jennifer know?"

"My One," exclaimed Marza excitedly. "Is it feasible that you could have been Jenny's very best friend and neighbor, Rita? I had named my Rally—"

"Of course, Jenny, oh my One, why didn't I make the connection when you were telling your story? Now that my memory has been evoked, I do recall some of those horrible events with you and your dad. I naturally had no idea, though, that you, Marza, had replaced Jen. I do remember hearing everyone saying what a miracle it was that you had lived through that accident. Also, when Jim talked about Rally and happenstance, I should have remembered everything. After all," she said reflectively, "you had named your little guy in honor of my Rally!"

The two women were now standing and tightly hugging each other and calling one another's former names aloud. I spoke only when they had settled down. "How do I tie this in with me in the middle '60s when I got my Rally?"

"You did say that your dog was a guide dog didn't you?" asked Marza with an eccentric sort of smile.

"Yes, but what does that have to do with this mystery?" I asked, feeling a bit perturbed because I had so badly wanted all of the detached pieces of this puzzle fitting together.

"Well, I ask that because as Jenny, my future grandson raised Bouvier des Flandres dogs for many years. He later trained them as guide dogs for the blind, hearing dogs for the deaf, and as rescue dogs."

I had got to my feet and stammered with tremendous feelings of joy, "No, no, it can't be! My Rally was the very first Bouvier trained for guide work!" Excited, I asked, "Why that unusual breed and why was he named Rally?" Smiling at the improbability of this occurring, I quickly asked, "My Rally's trainer was Charley Mandella, was that your—"

"Jim," she said with surprise, "I can't believe it, but you must have had my grandson Charley's very first dog! He only named that one after my beloved Rally who died three years after I had become Jennifer." She paused a minute relishing that thought. "To answer your question about the breed, you have to understand his love of that unique species of dog. He felt that Bouviers were superior to any other breeds. They were becoming extinct in their native country of Belgium. Hence, he started an American club of breeders to prevent this from occurring. Five years later there were more than 500 Bouviers awaiting adoption. He started FADS (First Aid Dog School) so that those intelligent working dogs could be put to good use for worthy purposes."

I looked Gail and Marza straight in the eye while I tried to comprehend the meaning of all this. "As said before, and I paraphrase, 'Things occur during our lives because and for specific reasons.' Gail, what did that lesson about your Rally teach you?"

"I was a very gullible person and I complicated it further by mistrusting my inner most intuition. It also did what being beaten almost daily didn't accomplish; it encouraged me to leave my abusive husband!"

"You, Marza, what were you supposed to learn from your experiences?"

She smiled beneficently, showing her beautiful white teeth. "Being passive is often best. The need of using controlled and creative powers of will are worthy tools. Also, that it was unnecessary to cause greater chaos by fighting."

"Instead of imagining myself a victim, I produced that incident to learn forgiveness," I told them.

"We create all circumstances in our lives for definite and pragmatic reasons," added Rama.

Gail then said profound words that I found myself puzzling over for days: "Stepping beyond the shadows of our karma, we grow in the light of our conquests." Then she gave a short explanation. "We really can't change karma, but we can find reasons for occurrences taking place because of it. Growing from our victory over those difficulties is the sign of our achieving success and overcoming enfites and bad karma."

"I'm not going there right now, Lovie. I do feel rather proud and quite smug about this outcome," I owned up. "Although, I never expected to have this prominent of a closing. Now that it has proven itself true," I said, feeling like a teacher instead of a student, "it clearly demonstrates the power we have in our own lives. We are the architects of our individual existences. We have unique logic and purpose behind the creation of every given moment."

"Like what was said so perfectly before, we are not dumb puppets. How we perform in one act often determines the next," said Marza, before the women sped off to spend the rest of the day reminiscing about beloved dogs, old times, and friends.

"Rama," I said, after noticing the women's preoccupation. "I can see that the women are going to need some time together. How 'bout us two guys getting out for a stretch and a bit of man-to-man conversation?

"Yes. It appears to me that the women are going to be very involved for a considerable period of time," he replied, reaching for his French beret resting under the chair.

We walked to the front of the abode, where three very friendly horses greeted us. They loved the attention that we gave them. After we had scratched and talked to them for a while, we walked to a nearby stone and conversed. "Jim, you and Gail have been making great strides in becoming Clear. Your expanding belief in yourselves and your spirits is a wonderful testimony for all of us bystanders. Every member of the human race creates their own lives to meet specific goals. Life, after all, is a learning tool meant to enrich our views of self. What lessons we fail to learn in one lifetime are brought into the next so that we can grow from them during that following life. As expanding beings, we are tested by loved ones who are giving us difficulties that we've got to overcome. Also diseases, they are testing our endurances. Simply put, that's why there is karma; it's a necessary bridge connecting past with new existences. Without it our very human consciousness wouldn't have a chance of enabling us to recognize our Oneness."

Without a moment's pause, he said, "Between us guys, I expect that in only a few weeks we'll be preparing you both for a rebirth on Earth. I reluctantly use that word 'rebirth' because of its religious connotation. This is especially true in your case since you may not be born again as Christians or babies. You and Gail are going to be replacing departing spirits and we hope to find you young adolescent bodies so that your separation isn't prolonged any more than it has to be. Knowing that your strengths are multiplied when together, we desire that the two of you unite as soon as possible. Then being stronger, continue your conquests over the powers of evil."

"You mean that you can't tell me now how old my wife and I will be, Rama?" I asked with some feelings of apprehension and anxiety. Leaving my Gail and this exquisite setting were a bit unnerving and I wasn't ready to face up to that quite yet. Considering it was intimidating and I wanted to circumvent the discomfort it generated, I avoided further discussion. Weathering this separation was going to be a tough assignment for both Gail and me. How were we to endure without being united? We loved each other and our shared love of this land was so totally powerful. I felt that the concept of leaving all that we knew and loved here was too much for us to deal with right now.

"No need to be disturbed with that matter now," he said confidently. "A total believer has no worries or fears about what future events might ensue. You are very strong in your belief system and you mustn't allow this to disrupt your rapid growth. As you had said to Gail, slighting your teachers and fearing your future only dilutes the spiritual heights gained. Besides, we just saw the two of you in that church, male and female, your ages being nearly the same.

"Marza confronted me with wisdom right after your revelation. Both you and Gail are so gifted with clairvoyance, why not look into your own upcoming futures?"

I smiled and replied with only two words, "Great idea."

"Oh my One," Gail cried, after I had presented Rama's suggestion to her later that night. "Do we have to consider this tonight? I can't bear the thought of having to do without you, and this makes it all too vivid and final!"

"Lovie, I also resent the need of doing without my woman—my woman, my wife! As dismal as this is to the both of us, though, we've been preparing for this moment since our reunion. As much as we both would like, we cannot avoid this quickly approaching separation," I whispered with a few kisses. A second later, I added, "After all we've learned in recent months, we can't contradict our readiness or this worthy cause."

Shaking her head as if to call a truce on her apprehensions, she beamed at me and said the same two words that I had used with Rama. "Great idea." Then, with a little wavering in her voice, she said, "What if we can't—"

"Hush, Gail," I admonished. "We can't have any of that uncertainty if we expect an answer tonight. Making headway depends impart on our having sufficient faith and this information can only aid us as far as that goes."

"Okay," she said. "Hold my hand and let's see what vibes we receive."

We held hands and waited for some kind of guidance. Five minutes passed without any apparent success. I spoke softly and with a deep-seeded feeling of love. "Remove all negativity and fear and replace them with affirmative belief. Now feel yourself," I said for both of our benefits, "becoming less aware of feedback from your senses and mind. Tune into that inner knowing part of your Oneself."

Rather than her receiving clairvoyant sensations as we had envisioned, those words had scarcely exited my mouth when Gail and I simultaneously stepped abruptly into a lucid dream. It was like seeing the usual dream, however, this time we were somehow able to interact. I suddenly found myself a young man of 18 talking with a beautiful female who I immediately knew was my eternal soul mate. "Jim?" she tentatively asked. "Is that you?"

"Yes, Lovie," I elatedly replied. "So we are going to be the same gender as we were in Tesa," I said, after I had stopped kissing her longingly. "Now let's try and remember who and where we are this very minute. Like Angel suggested, we've got to be sure that we come to the same place, at the exact day and year, and know our identities. We can't allow for any misfortunes to waylay our reunion."

Smiling her Mona Lisa smile, this unrecognized, yet familiar, female said, "We met here in Stanford University in California. It is presently 11:00 a.m. on September 29, 2012 in Stanford University's coffee shop," she said a second later.

"Whew," I said, amazed with her mental acuity. "I have absolutely no realization of time, place, or date. I know who we used to be and have a smattering of an idea of who I will be in the future, but nothing else is familiar. How is it possible that you have all of this knowledge?"

"Easy," she replied with a twinkling, shy smile. "It is only three days after my 19th birthday and I've been in Stanford U for a whole year. As far as our past in Tesa, well, like we were taught, I've made it a point to remember and it's all there," she said, tapping her head. "I can even recall every reincarnated life that we had explored while there."

"I can't," I admitted to this gorgeous creature facing me. "I couldn't even tell you what brought me here to this spot at this precise moment. In any case, my name is John Bennett," I said. "That's about all I do remember this instant," I said with frustrating feelings of confusion. There was something about my name to be and it annoyed me that I couldn't recall what was causing this discomfort. We kissed again and, with a few more memories suddenly flooding my mind, I said, "I am almost 18. I work and live a mile from here." As I shifted further into the person that I now embodied, additional memories materialized. "My boss is Professor Jim Winson. After working for him for six months, he told me that I should be attending this university where he teaches philosophy. Dr. Winson's wife passed away and he hired me to care for his only son Mike who is now seven. Noticing my skills at the computer, as a mathematician, and also at sports, he thought that I should get a formal education. After I explained that I hadn't even finished high school, he helped me to earn a GED and got me a full college scholarship." My mind suddenly skipped backwards and I said, "I was 14 when I assumed this body. My One, that's four years without you!"

I quickly realized that I didn't even know this girl's present name and asked, "Hey, I don't know your name or anything. Some personal info 'bout you would be great."

"What happened to your parents?" she asked without answering my query regarding her own history. "Why are you on your own like this?" she asked me directly with a deep frown crisscrossing her forehead. "I remember your having difficulties—"

"I ran off," I responded without embarrassment or remorse. I shook my head trying to clear away the cobwebs that clouded my mind. "I've got to recall everything so that I can avoid this problem in the future when we meet here."

Suddenly I moved into John's past and found myself a young eight year old child. Everything was pitch black around me and it took me a minute to realize that it was because it was late at night. The frightening awareness that someone had silently crept into my bedroom overwhelmed me with heartfelt feelings of fear and dread. I somehow knew what was going to take place and it gave me enormous feelings of anguish. This even darker form stood hungrily above me for some seconds and then I heard, "Johnny, you need new sneakers. Money doesn't grow on trees you know?" When my held breath gave way, he said, "I know you're awake, now stop this childish behavior!" He waited another minute while I, even too petrified to even breathe, lay still. The next thing I knew was that this man who called himself my father was molesting me again.

"No," I unwittingly cried, before perceiving that I was back at Stanford University. "I'm sorry," I said embarrassed. "I just had an awful flashback. In it I found myself being violated by my father." I paused another moment trying to calm myself and recall my age. "I was 8. I was maybe five or six when it began—"

Gail was squeezing me hard; you have to let it go now, John. "Now just release that pain. I am here loving you in this moment. Be fully in this moment."

"Thanks um—"

"Lillian."

"Thanks, Lillian. To answer your question, I just couldn't stay with them after gaining knowledge of his doing those detestable things to his son! I left them about two years after entering this body." Prompting memory, I put the pieces together. "Johnny was five when he began to be physically abused, fourteen when I replaced him, and sixteen when I, the new Johnny, ran away. Sorry," I said, following another short hesitation, "but I don't want to evoke anymore of those pain-filled memories right now. What I'd really like is to stay here in this time frame with you and never depart again!"

"I want you to know that I have heartfelt compassion for you, John, and those years of hell you've experienced." We kissed and like magic I knew only love and enormous desires for this woman. On another note, she wistfully sang out, "Oh, Jim—I mean John, couldn't we please stay here forever?"

"If only we could! Besides, we know that our being here right now is only a vision and might vanish any second," I said, indicating the cafeteria filled with students. I cleared my throat and continued. "I'm afraid that it's too selfish of a detour to make; our worthy cause is primary!"

With a sad downturn of her mouth, she robotically said, "I am Lillian Hanson, 18 years old, and I live—"

Unable to finish her personal data, we reappeared in our home in Tesa. Rama and Marza suddenly materialized and smiled at us. Rama divulged, "We were here with you and know you've once again met with victory." Gail and I nodded in unison and he recommenced, "We'll be back tomorrow."

"In the mean time, rehearse all that you can retain from this experience and do it over and over again," Marza recommended. "When you are reborn on Earth again, recalling all of the facts may be foggy due to your prior being's death, the brain's many new stresses, and changes."

"The new conflicts and onslaughts you will be encountering will hamper your mental ability that much more. That is why it's so imperative that you get these memories implanted deeply into your subconscious."

"Rerunning these events several times daily between now and then will insure preservation of these irreplaceable details."

"Everything hinges on your ability to recall this dimension and what you are learning here," echoed Marza imperatively.

"Rama," I asked, feeling a bit shocked with a piece of a forgotten memory popping suddenly into my head. "The person who I will be succeeding has the same last name as a spoiled and mischievous classmate of mine. We became enemies when I called him down for needling a retarded student in another classroom. Can—"

He smiled and said, "If I am reading you correctly, you want to know if you might be moving into the body of his son or another relative of his?" I nodded affirmatively and he replied, "Attempting to harmonize their own karma, incarnates often purposefully choose familiar people to identify with during their next lifetime. Doing this, they hope to amend prior adversity and/or renew old friendships." With Marza in tow and without another word, he smiled, gave a little wave of his hand, and vanished before our eyes. I was a little sorry because I had wanted to discuss this philosophy further with him, but another desiring part of me was grateful to be left alone with my wife.

Because of our proximity and the heartwarming certainty of our future together, my body was feeling erotic and I began to pant heavily. Her eyes danced with light and joy as I gazed into them. She snuggled up against my shoulder and my heart felt as if it were about to burst with my blissful recognition of an earthly reunion we had just witnessed. All thought and fears of our future life left me and were replaced by a jubilant feeling of success. "Lovie, I can envisage us spending our next life and all of eternity insanely in love," I told her sincerely. Looking down into her shimmering eyes again, I realized how deeply I loved her. The fact that I would have to be without her for four years started to creep into my mind and I quickly abandoned that horrid insight. I began to caress her neck and shoulders, divorcing that deplorable thought from my mind altogether.

"Oh, yes," she whispered with a growing sensuality. Then abruptly opening her eyes wide, she said, "I know that things are going to be difficult especially for you. I'm afraid that love will be an unfulfilled desire of yours for a few years," she said, opening that offensive Pandora's box. "Lacking love from your new parents, being defiled by your father, and not being able to share love with me is going to be tough during the beginning of your next life. Unless, of course, you can transform—"

"That just isn't going to work, Lovie," I revealed frankly. "My running away from my parents because of my inability to tolerate their ridicule, mistrust, loathing, and most of all, fearing dad is a given fact that we both have just learned. As ominous as it is, there isn't any way that we can change or deviate from those details. It is actuality—plain, incontrovertible fact!" I raised my hand, holding her off from disputing me. I was feeling putrid about my future, but felt in my heart that nothing could be done to ratify it. "We did visualize our new setting," I brought out, "and we are going to be lovers. For now, I am not going to think about those years of being without your love!"

"We've been learning that we create our own lives and that time is only a figment of our imagination. Why can't we transform detestable conditions or at least modify them so that they are more tolerable. Maybe," she suggested, "you could just put your foot down and tell your father that if he does it again you will inform your mother, grandparents, police, et cetera."

I pressed my passionate body more urgently against her, wishing that I could gratify all of my future cravings at this time. My next words came in spurts because my stomach was contracting with growing desire. "In this case, we are talking about future events and I don't think that there is much we can do about what will be taking place years from now. We owe this movement everything, Gail. It has enabled us to unite again and that fact alone will mold all of our futures into more fulfilling ones. We can, of course, create our lives differently during the present time that we are in at that moment, but that moment only. We cannot affect past or future history."

"I disagree. That was a revolutionary vision and not set in cement! We should be able to make some adjustments."

I had to think for a moment and spoke as the thoughts came into my mind. "Other than what I just said, John and Lillian are not dead yet," I told her. "We were in their respective bodies, but only in a dream or trance state. Being that they are still alive, they are the directors of their own destinies." I smiled to myself and said, "I feel the same, but for one thing, we don't have the right to alter the future to our specifications.

"But," she protested, "by using the pink light to enhance and even create love, you are altering human conditions!"

"No, we aren't loving them actually, but the One in them. It is that One in them that is improving their conditions. The Earth would be a perfect utopia for everyone if not for gluttonous behavior. We strengthen humanity's inner Oneness with lovenergy and divine harmony, tranquility, and peace are awakened."

My next thoughts were deep and I would have enjoyed discussing them with a more advanced authority like Swuel. "Bear with me, Lovie, while I give voice to my inner thoughts. If this cause hadn't needed us, or if we weren't suitable, we probably wouldn't have met for years—if ever. We would have gone on being unenlightened spirits, our memories deleted every life." I touched her, then myself, and thrust my arm out indicating everything about us. "We wouldn't have ever have experienced this moment or have—"

Insight made her speak her dominant thoughts aloud. "We are going to be lonely and wanting one another for years. Time will inch by for both of us without true love and gladness. How do we endure that painful truth?" she asked me with sadness written clearly in her communicative eyes. "All I know of my future life was glimpsed in seconds while with you in that college. I have no impression now of what it might be like. I'll have to wait until the details are portrayed during that lifetime or perhaps sooner if we revisit our future again," she said optimistically

My heart went out to her and the painful reality of my own soon-to-be-grim life struck me cruelly. "No I won't hear of it!" I moaned aloud. Feeling the reality of my loss deep in my whole being, I said, "I need and want you at my side now and forever! How am I ever going to tolerate our being apart?" I asked with great frustration festering in me. "I'm sorry, but I really can't consider the pain that this is going to produce! If I were to analyze it further, I would be in serious trouble! We have to let it go for now and always live in the moment like you so aptly suggested," I concluded with a shake of my head.

Gail lifted her head and planted a firm kiss on my hungry lips. "I don't want myself always longing for our romance while back on Earth. Nor can I now face the prospect of desiring and needing your presence without being gratified. For our sanity as well as for our spiritual progress, I have to agree with you. We've got to detach ourselves from this very negative and harmful concept. For now, like you just said, let's live in the moment. We are together now and will be unified in our next lifetime. After a few more existences on Earth we will be adjoined for eternity, never having to depart each other again!"

"Jim," she said in a confidential manner, "We do need to be discussing our future while it is still fresh in our minds." Who knows what might happen to those memories if we don't deliberate on them and get them implanted into our memories right now."

After we had recollected every detail possible, even divulging some that hadn't been discovered during that heralding view of our future, we kissed with feelings of triumph and enormous feelings of joy regarding our projected reunion.

We had, by necessity, eluded the fears of our ill-fated and lonely years before giving into the desire that was equally pressuring us both. Feeling excited, I diabolically told Gail, "Sounds to me like we've got to make up for our future love deficiencies." I unbuttoned her blouse, taking in a deep breath and that hateful thought pelted my heart with its anguishing pain. That stubborn thought refused to relinquish its hold on me and I re-experienced the pain of being severed from my beautiful woman again. I silently wondered, *What is insisting on pressing this tormenting feeling deep into my heart, mind, and spirit like this?* Inwardly I cried, *How am I ever going to endure this pain?* I silently agonized as I gazed down at her riveting beauty. A second later, a challenging thought occurred to me and I had to reveal it to Gail. "Why do we have to wait? Why can't we meet before that specific disclosed date?" I asked, feeling delirious with that promising thought. "That might be the date when we will be united in college, but who is keeping us from meeting one another beforehand?"

"Isn't that what I had asked you only moments ago? You told me that we couldn't tailor the future to our whims. You supplanted John Bennett in that vision when he was 14. Immediately afterwards, I had thought to myself, *Since you run away two years later, why can't you relocate to my neighborhood?* In that circumstance, we really wouldn't be converting future events all that much." Slightly out of breath with renewed enthusiasm, she said, "Let's see if we can find out where I will live during my next life."

A pragmatic me realized that we were only playing a game of Make Believe and I continued with that reality in mind. However, I did make perfect sense of it after I said, "I'm sorry, Lovie, I had misunderstood what you were suggesting." The truth hit me hard between the eyes and I replied aloud, "Misreading your meaning, I presumed that you were asking why we couldn't use our powers of will to alter future events? You do," I admitted to the two of us, "bring up a brilliant point. Since we found out that I run away when I am 16, why couldn't we plan to meet earlier?" I paused, having a realization. "Why, though, were we strangers in that meditation? Maybe," I said, attempting to answer my own question, "it's because we were identifying one another from this present perspective?"

"Oh yes, Jim." With a warm smile ingratiating her pleasant face, she said, "I really can't see any harm coming to us by your going to someplace close to me when you run away. You could call me from wherever, and who knows, maybe my own future parents would give you a place to live! Now wouldn't that be spectacular!"

"It sure would, my dear, and it's only a matter of our using our imagination starting now! Though I'm afraid that's asking too much of fate. We really would be remodeling our futures to our specific desires and I doubt that we can realistically change it that drastically. If that were done, what would happen to Professor Jim Winson and his son Mike? We would be constructing the future differently from what we learned only minutes ago."

"It's not happened yet. We are actively, or foolishly inactively, writing our own future life screenplays. Nothing prevents us from creating our next life to our own specifications. As we saw it, John does need Professor Winson in order for you to meet me in the university; you are going to need a job for years, so why couldn't we make him my next door neighbor?"

"Gail?"

With a distinctive twinkle in her eye, she offered, "Why aren't you hearing me?"

I had points that had to be brought up and interrupted her again. "Maybe—"

Laughing, she said, "Maybe nothing. I wish so that you would stop interrupting me like this!" Laughing again at her wit and next brilliant thought, she said, "Heck, why couldn't professor Jim turn out to be a neighbor of Lillian's? Maybe that's how you meet him and learn of his need; so coming to me will be mandatory! Maybe," she suggested, "we will be only taking necessary steps to bring all of those events about."

"You really are becoming the teacher, my dear. Why hadn't I realized the depth of your suggestion when you first spoke of it? The only possible stumbling block that we might encounter has to do with retention of what we have planned. It is going to be up to us to remember our powers and what we've learned here in this last vision. In fact, we've got to start right now, rehearsing our futures to our specifications."

"Right now, imagination is all that is necessary for us to achieve all of our desires. Lets start using our powers of imagination now and the future will be as we desire!" she said with a persuasive voice.

The following day we worked with Rama and Marza for more than four hours and nothing was said about our deliberations of the night before. Our spirit guides were giving us more instruction on how to safely move ourselves in and out of trance states. Before they left us, Marza said, "You are going to need this ability so that you can revisit Tesa for daily instructions and updates."

"I'm sure that you witnessed our unique discussions of our futures—"

"As the time approaches," said Rama, "we will discuss that matter further. For now, let it rest."

"Please answer this, Rama or Marza. "As long as we aren't hurting anyone, are there any other restrictions on what we can imagine and thus create?" Gail asked.

"Like Rama just told you," said Marza, "we will discuss this matter at a later date.

"But we need to know the answer now! You, Rama, and Swuel have told us that altering all conditions is only a matter of our using our imagination. That it is One's ideal desire for all of us to realize our Oneness!"

"My focusing on lovenergy's pink light has transformed me and countless others."

"We are leaving now, we will get into this tomorrow," said Rama as they moved into an undetectable density.

"Why are they avoiding this concept so vehemently?" Gail asked with disturbance reflected in her eyes.

"They can't discuss it. Humanity isn't ready, evil intent still exists."

Our lovemaking moved us both into that peaceful loving place where nothing else intruded. In bed afterwards, I moved myself into a trance. These experiences gave me enormous freedom, even more than the floating or out-of-body experiences had allotted me. Often during the night while my body slept soundly, I explored this pure sphere. Tesa, it turns out, was made up of a lot more levels than first suspected. In another density right in this very spot of our home was also a huge mountain towering thousands of feet above us. In still another I had found an enormous lake filled with prehistoric fish and plant life. In some of these planes there were no signs of human life, unless, of course, they moved in undetectable densities. Densities were like computer windows, one placed over the next on a monitor. Once you had visited and pictured one, you could revisit it again by visualizing it and allowing your spirit to relocate to that window frame. Once in a given space, there was still the option of changing a frame entirely to a different window. When visiting that prehistoric lake, I was there, but in a different frame or proportion, one that included humans, or I should say me.

One was far more than I, still very human, had been able to conceive of being. I had to wonder, though, if it was me or Him that was bringing these different views of life into existence. "He is truly infinite," I heartily proclaimed, but so is my imagination!"

Nights later, I wondered if I would be able to sojourn to other densities when I returned to Earth. I knew that there were people in other realms enjoying their lives on the planet I considered mine. *Could they be as ignorant of humans as we are of them?* I wondered. *Is it possible for beings in one level on Earth to be annihilated, yet not harm those in another? Might their created plane on Earth be as perfect as Tesa and not be negatively affected by humans? In a way, being oblivious to mystical affairs could be blissful!* I pondered while drifting back into awareness.

An unidentifiable voice said, "Becoming One is imagining exactly what you desire; nothing else can be suitable."

Two hours into our teaching session the next day, Marza said, "Using this trance technique will enable you to move in and out of the Cosmic Consciousness Center whenever you are in need of help or counsel. Our spiritual guides there oversee everything that the members of this cause are doing."

"There are millions of people there who can assist you," added Rama.

"Excuse me, Marza, but I am dying to know if we will have as much command of trances during our next earthly existences?" Gail spoke her concern. "Will Jim and I be able to use this technique to at least visit one another during that interminable period of separation?"

"Being able to be in a trance should really give us the capability of meeting and reviewing what we've done here, planning our futures, and aiding us with anything that might crop up unexpectedly," I chimed in.

"Well, guys, I wouldn't put anything over on you. Just as long as you aren't harming yourselves or others," said Rama with a sober smile. "Because you become entirely different people, your present memories will dissipate to some degree. That is why getting this information into your subconscious is so imperative. For a time you may lose total recollection of your current self. We have had some who don't have any such problem, but it occurs far less frequently. Gaining your desires isn't only contingent on these memories, but also on your power of will."

After a minute's reflection, Rama more grimly reported, "From what we saw in your future meeting in college and your private discussion afterwards, I've got to say that it is most unlikely to change as you wish."

"We both concur that you didn't know one another before that meeting, let alone able to plan your futures as you desire." Marza grimaced slightly and added, "Your futures are a reflection of your powers of belief and we've been seeing abnormal proof of your strengths. So please prove us wrong!" she added with a big grin. "This is the time for you to create your futures. Get these new thoughts implanted securely and you could promote your futures prior to moving into them."

"If by chance you do manage to meet while you are in midst of your transformation, from the metaphysical state back to human, you need to know that you will not have any physical abilities. You won't even be able to feel one another hugging," said Rama.

More brightly, Marza added, "You've got to be pleased that you did remember facts about your being here. It shows that you will have memory retention."

"We need to be in contact, even if it is restricted to an OBE," I implored.

"Right now it seems easy to preserve memories of our marriage and everything else that we've learned here," Gail loudly emphasized. "We've spent so much effort—"

"Everything is contingent on your recollection of your experiences here. Even being in communication with us will rely on your ability to sustain your cognitive memories. If you are to competently aid us, it will be essential for you to have memories of your training here."

"You are to expect all of your aptitudes to be reduced to some degree," said Marza. Having to survive in the hostile environment of Earth will cause negativities, which dilute your powers of will, mind, and spirit. Keeping yourselves, now as well as then, in a positive state of mind is so very vital. Don't allow any contrary emotions to enter your minds. Those sensations will only impede your proficiency that much more."

"Especially now while you are progressing so rapidly. You cannot allow any unfavorable emotions to misdirect your powers. You've got to reach Clear before you can advance to your next step of returning to Earth. Until your return there, drill what you are learning here into your minds. That's our purpose for repeating meditations and rehearsing your lessons over and over again. Getting these experiences recorded into your subconscious is our chief objective. Only by relearning the truths can enfites be permanently removed from your minds and future lives."

"The accumulation of enfites is what causes the need for humans to be born over and over again. Only when they are clear of them can they realize their divine Oneness."

"For better meditative reasons, we will be teaching you how to listen to your internal sound of One. Some call this high-pitched whistling and hissing the sound of silence. We know it to be the connective voice of One. You will have to be in full control of your new bodies, minds, and spirits at all times. Concentrating on this inner tone will aid you and bring you more fully into the light and sound during tough times as well as meditative ones."

"I know that sound, but had no idea that it was the sound of One," I said.

"I've also heard it, but it is so weak!"

Marza imparted, "As you become clearer it grows stronger just like the sound of the waterfall we're hearing now. It's the natural mantra of the infinite being of One. It will reside as a part of you at all times. In the beginning, it's only a whisper for most people and you have to be quiet to hear it. It is the true voice of One which verifies everyone's universal union."

I wanted to comprehend this virgin information fully, but Gail intervened with another question. "Marza, can any harm happen to Jim or I if we experiment with trances while we are on this plane? I want to be sure that we can remember this technique when we acquire our new human bodies."

Undoubtedly knowing my nightly excursions, Marza looked me directly in the eyes and said, "I would be careful in the beginning not to get overly attached to it. Because of the sensations of euphoria that accompany trance-like states, people can easily become engulfed with the feelings of ecstasy and thus ignore other important areas of study."

Following another sumptuous meal, Gail and I sat alone on the couch. As usual, I was gently kissing her tender lips. "Oh how I ache to love this creature continuously, never stopping for an instant," I reverently whispered. The feel of her warm, loving body was driving me to distraction and I was preparing for another excursion into Never Never Land. I was suddenly taken away from my sensual anticipation by Gail's unexpected turn toward me and odd request, "Please, Jim, will you join me in returning to the Triple C right now?"

"Huh? Triple C? What pray tell is that?"

"The Cosmic Consciousness Center of course, you silly goose!" she scoffed.

"Whew, why didn't you say that in the first place? You expect me to comprehend your own cockamamie language?" We laughed and I said, "I'd much rather stay right here with you and maybe make—"

"Oh, you men," she said with mocked ridicule. "You've all got one thing on your mind!"

"My dear, I've got three and you also possess three things that I am thinking about right now. Three plus three equals six, so that gives us half a dozen reasons to make love. Not that we need more than one of course!" I said with a laugh. "Besides, Lovie, I don't hear you complaining about all of the pleasures we've been sharing."

"You won't either," she said. "Jim," she beseeched a second later, "something pertaining to our cause or the Triple C has gone wrong. I can feel it in my bones, but can't put my finger on it right here and now."

"Why didn't you say that in the beginning?" I asked with a troubled heart for the unknown woes that we were likely to be facing. "Let's move into a trance and skedaddle." Seconds later we found ourselves in the Triple C where we found the group assembled.

The leader announced, "Welcome, children of the light. Comrades, as you can see, our newlywed eternal soul mates have joined us." Turning from everyone gathered, he said, "You've arrived just in time to hear distressing news; we learned of it only moments ago. Two individuals from our latest group of returnees are encountering great adversities. They are being held hostage in Iraq, and will likely be beheaded soon, unless we can do something to save them."

"How are we going to rescue them?" asked Gail, comprehending the crisis at hand.

Members of this exalted group looked at Gail and me, and I realized that all of them were able to see us in our trance-state bodies. *Does this mean that they can see into every density?* I wondered. It also dawned on me that we were seeing them. Does this mean that, while in a trance, we can visit with beings existing in other levels, too? What is the difference between this and bi-locating?" I wondered.

Looking directly into my eyes, he said, "We see you and you us, but that's because you are in the same density with us. He then replied with a worried look in his eyes. "One has clearly heard us and has brought you here, so let's hear your reasoning? What is your solution to this difficulty?" he asked with a great deal of unrest written in his eyes.

Before Gail had a moment to reply, I started. "Americans are in the area: Iraq, Kuwait, Afghanistan, and other countries. Can't we—"

"Sorry, Jim, unfortunately time is running out for them. We don't have the privilege of negotiating. Armed forces are also unlikely to be able to locate them. Our crusaders were given only 24 hours more of life."

"Couldn't you just zap their inner spirits up and away?" asked Gail.

"As a last resort, we will save them from experiencing severe pain by retrieving them as their bodies are executed," said the reincarnated Buddha. "It's just that we dislike having to take them from their important work again."

"Earthlings everywhere are positively affected by lovenergy. We need only to saturate the area and every living being with pink light. Their captors will release them."

"Yes, they will be freed!" said Gail joyfully. She raised her hand, keeping all of us quiet. There's something else happening. All the people of the area are protesting their country's leaders. Unrest is running rampant and indiscriminate activists are gathering. They want freedom!"

The man who had given Gail and I love and more love during our last visit said, "We were told by your spiritual guides that you were a perfect addition to our team and your perception of this particular crisis and its resolution are prime examples of your wholeness of spirit. I'm glad to see that we had seen your true potential, allowed your union, and welcomed you to stay."

"What would be your procedure, Jim?" asked the leader. "How do we bring your proposal to a victorious conclusion?"

"We get the millions of our fellow comrades projecting lovenergy into this and other troubled areas in the region. We'd all be thrilled to volunteer our service to assist our brothers and sisters in need." I paused again, trying to come up with further basis to assert my reasoning. "Working together on this would also be an uplifting spiritual experience for all of us newcomers. Seeing the immediate effects of our unity of purpose will enhance our dedication to one another and this cause as well."

Looking at his team of masters and getting their nods of approval, he said, "Jim and Gail, we are going to provide you with all of the information we have. As you wisely suggested, we will also get our millions of co-workers cooperating with you. Please," he implored, "promptly arrange this deliverance for our associates!"

"We will begin our quest as soon as we arrive at Tesa," I declared. "I do want even more of us working on this. During my nightly trance travels, I've seen an endless universe filled with unimaginable numbers of love-enhanced beings. Let's reach all of them and get their cooperation. I alone transformed my life and guarantee that with everyone working together, this horror will cease and our comrades will be free real soon." Holding up my own hand, I added, "As far as bringing peace into the whole area, that's going to take longer and require more of a concerted effort, but it will also occur."

With a faraway look in her eyes, Gail more than validated my impression. "Not only will our light workers be released, but also allowed to continue their work throughout that area. They will serve our cause for the enlightenment of mankind for many years to come."

Less than a half-hour later, Gail and I stood before our classmates and their mentors. Every transformed being on every plane of consciousness was listening and aiding our effort. "We have gathered this universal emergency meeting," said Swuel with a deeply furrowed brow, "to solve a life and death dilemma for two of our co-workers. Without further adieu, I present our eternal newlyweds who will give you all of the data regarding this crisis."

Getting some prodding from me, Gail timidly walked to the podium and shyly addressed our comrades. "Just a few minutes ago Jim and I were in the Triple C, as I fondly call the Cosmic Consciousness Center. We learned about this current difficulty and I will let my husband inform you of the remaining details," she quickly added, backing off from the podium.

"Thank you, Lovie," I said, grabbing hold of her hand and stepping forward with her in tow. "My intuitive wife perceived a tragedy taking place on Earth and we went to the Triple C to learn the details. We were told about two of our colleagues in Iraq who have been captured and held for prosecution by a group of Al-Qaeda terrorists." I allowed the news to sink in and then continued. "As you know, the USA will not do any POW bargaining with hostel groups. Unfortunately we've seen these terrorists behead their prisoners and we can't allow that to happen on our watch! These two men are colleagues in our movement and we've got to get them freed. Every person is a necessary component in the mechanism of correction for Earth. We cannot allow a single mishap to occur. We must assist them posthaste! Our Triple C masters believe by all of us transmitting lovenergy to them, that we will get them promptly liberated. In a moment we will need all of you to join with us in projecting pink light onto our captured comrades and their captors."

Also," I beseeched, "we can't discontinue it for any reason. It is imperative that we send One's divine lovenergy to our comrades until they've been delivered into the hands of freedom. My gifted wife has seen them freed and able to continue their important work and that's all the proof I need of our effectiveness in getting them released."

I paused another minute and not getting any retorts or questions, I raised my hands. "Feel the power and great lovenergy of One exiting your hands, foreheads, and hearts. Visualize pink light exiting them, and watch it move toward Earth. Imagine this pink light, One's purest lovenergy, entering through the atmosphere and see it penetrating into everything within existence on Earth. Imagine the soil, stones, trees, and every blade of grass and grain of sand being filled with healing love forces." After giving them time to expand their love to the entire planet, I said, "Now feel One's love being returned to you scores of times more powerfully. Allow this life-altering exchange to fill your hearts, minds, and souls. These powerful sensations of love you that are receiving are so overwhelming that you can hardly contain them." I heard a few of them groan along with me as our feelings of love expanded. "Now, enormously enhanced, you are able to project even more lovenergy toward our constrained comrades. The more love we give, the more love we receive and, therefore, the more we are able to give!" My mouth was open as I breathed deeply in audible sighs, my stomach contracted with orgasms of love. My head rocked from side to side and I opened my arms so that I might welcome, hold, and give even more love. "Pour this enhanced lovenergy into our teammates and their captors in Iraq." The passionate sighs of our assembled group became louder. More than 300 of us in Tesa and possibly millions of our universal colleagues were now transmitting pink light toward our invisible teammates.

Gail whispered, "Jim, the Triple C has more than 780,000,000,000 universal others working with us right now!"

I was aware of conveying love along with them for several minutes more. Then abruptly, without prior thought or intention, I was out of my body and speeding through outer space—enveloped in pink light. Within seconds I approached Earth and quickly entered through her atmosphere aglow with lovenergy. I found myself sitting next to one of the prisoners who was saying, "Do you feel that powerful love which is being showered upon us, Craig?"

"Lou . . . Dr. Hibard," I cried in utter surprise. "You're now Craig?" Even though he was in a different body, I recognized his unique smile and awesome awareness showing in his orb and eyes.

"Hey Jim. What on Earth, or even in the universe, are you doing here? Couldn't you have found a better setting to visit Anthony, Renny, and me? You should have told us you were coming. We would have put on the coffee," he joked. "Who taught you to bilocate like this?"

"Jim, you are bilocating and we and everyone else can see your physical body. If anyone approaches please vanish pronto!" Without another word about my unexpected manifestation, he spoke to Lou and me. "We should soon be hearing a gathering of our transformed terrorists. I expect to be a free man within 10 to 15 minutes. With the abundant love we are receiving we are going to become masters to these people, and they are going to find us innocent of wrongdoings," he said with confidence.

I could sense love coursing its way through every molecule of everything within existence. "Just feel that powerful lovenergy. It will transform even the most criminally minded!" I said excitedly."

Lou exclaimed, "Why are you screaming like that, Jim? You have clearly bilocated and are 100 percent present in this dimension, to use an old incorrect term. We have no trouble seeing or hearing you. Neither will our judges, so please keep it down." With a great sigh, he then said to us both, "Man, love has so much power. If people only used it in place of hate, it would correct any problem that they might be experiencing. They would become powerful magnets and transmitters of love. Things sure would become more pleasant with humans producing love instead of hatred. It would also help to make the world around them more harmonic. As our great teacher Jesus once told us, 'bitterness only generates greater bitterness.' Conversely, he then taught us, 'Love thy neighbor as thyself,'" Lou softly added, "The One in mankind is love and by giving love to our neighbors, we are able to receive greater love."

"Not only would things and people become more pleasant," I softly asserted, "but everyone would now have total feelings of love instead of opposing sensations; love would abolish all negativities. Because only feelings of love would now be prominent, all malicious sensations would be expelled forever. There wouldn't be greed, war, poverty, hunger, or strife of any kind found in a world of always-loving beings."

"You're a noble member of this worthy cause," said Renny, praising me beyond what I deserved. "Informing humans everywhere of this truth you've spoken of so eloquently is a very vital goal. Make it a target for yourself when you return to Earth again." He paused, having heard voices outside the makeshift prison. "However," he quickly added, "that's a tremendous aim. Don't be too hard on yourself if you meet with powerful opposition. Like our teacher Jesus, you are likely to be labeled a fanatic and to be scorned by disbelievers. Evil intenders, in particular, will do everything to discredit you."

"Also, church leaders who feel threatened by your preaching forgiveness and love will label you an anti-Christ!" Lou added.

All three of us then turned our heads in synchrony. "There they are," I announced proudly, "and right on cue like you predicted, Renny." I bid my friends farewell and, before passing through the door, imagined myself becoming undetectable. I saw thousands of people gathered outside the prison room and hundreds more of them faced an impressive building. Pink light permeated everything—even the air seemed to be aglow with it. This structure had large marble columns and stairs with heavy brass railings that resembled coiled snakes. To emphasize my peer's workmanship at Tesa, I directly aimed my lovenergy at this imposing building.

Men of nobility soon exited the palatial building. With great exaltation, they were led and followed by heavily armed guards who walked them straight to the prison door. Then the door was opened and my friends smiled at them with an intense glow of lovenergy.

The influential superiors of this group took a step back as if overpowered by a commanding force from the men facing them. The leader raised his voice and declared in a foreign tongue, "Seeing these men firsthand, I can see that we were wrong to capture and imprison them.

Even though they are not Al-Qaeda, do not follow Islamic law, and do not study the Shariah or Quran as we do, we recognize them as honorable men."

"They are acquitted of the charges against them, and we find them innocent of all accusations," proclaimed another official looking man. "No longer are they required to remain in this prison or are they restricted from teaching in this region. They are free to travel and instruct others wherever they please," he decreed with a great flourish and waving of his arms. The prison guards backed away, and Lou and Renny walked out into the free open air. The crowd cheered loudly. I had understood this Iraqi language as if it were my own.

Because of our profound success, my heart was titillating as I began my return to Tesa. That sensation was embellished even more when I heard Lou and Renny's spiritual voices thanking me. Renny said, "Thank all of our comrades at Tesa for their life saving lovenergy. By the way," he called, "lovenergy is the perfect term for our One and His unconditional forces that comprise all of existence."

"It is the energy of everything, the undetectable gravity-like force that holds existence together," Lou collaborated. He then said, "Glad that you have been unified with your eternal soul mate. Congrats, old man! I knew that One would make sure that everything worked out okay for His chosen people. May His light enlighten your paths of travel and fill you and your mate with eternal love. May it also guide you and your many colleagues at Tesa with undying success. When you become human again, allow One to light your footsteps and they will always fall on fertile land."

"I can feel the magic of love growing in these people," proclaimed Renny joyously. "It is going to make our work easier. Thank everyone for us!"

"Do remember us and these hungry people from time to time with more lovenergy," added Lou seriously "Like all of humanity, these people are starving for it, and your putting us all in it will make things easier and more fulfilling for all concerned!"

"When on Earth again," I promised them, "I will teach very large groups of people how to transmit One's lovenergy. Then with their help we will project it to needy countries and people everywhere. No doubt it will make all undesired world conditions better."

Their words and my feelings were still with me as I returned to my immobilized body in Tesa. I found myself in the same pose and with a tremendous feeling of accomplishment. "We have been successful in getting them released! They are not only found innocent, but free to carry out their work without suppression or censorship." My colleagues loudly cheered the living proof of their effectiveness and the power of lovenergy. When their proclamations had ended, I told them, "As I was leaving their presence I heard Lou and Renny say 'Thank our friends for us Jim, and ask them to keep us and all of our cause in mind and heart.'" Everyone burst into another round of cheers. When they had quieted down again, I said, "I was shocked to learn that these two men had been with us only a few weeks ago. Lou, an old friend of mine from a prior life was one of them. He asked me to thank all of you, saying, and I take the liberty of paraphrasing his words, 'May the light energy of One guide your every footstep for all of eternity.'" I guess because of our marriage," I told them, "Gail and I were oblivious to their leaving you weeks ago. Imagine my surprise when I found my old friend in Iraq?" Smiling into the eyes of all my grinning peers, I said, "Thanks to you and your superior feat, he and Renny are now free to continue their work for our honorable cause."

Gail inched forward and spoke aloud so that everyone could hear. "Our work is not done. All the people in the Middle East need our help. We've got to send them lovenergy as often as we can! People everywhere there are sensing the need to gain their independence, and the dictators are going to oppose them strongly."

Swuel now stepped to the podium and expressed his fervent gratitude. "My dear friends," he began, "we have all been firsthand witnesses to the true power of love. The only alteration or deviation I might have taken would be to first obliterate negativity with the white light of One. I want only to reveal the most effective method of accomplishing your goals. So please," he beseeched, "don't take what I just said as a critique or a belittlement of your measureless mastery. I, as well as my fellow spiritual guides, have been onlookers to an exceedingly convincing behavior modification by your power of love. It was done in a very short time, peacefully and using the lovenergy of One! You all are to be commended for a job well done." He paused for a moment while we once again cheered our promising victory.

Going back to his previous teaching, he raised his hand, took a deep breath, and said, "Can you imagine the effect a large community like a church could make if they were all to transmit the pink light of love to troublemakers? Why, they would transform terrorist groups into peace loving Cub Scouts! We've got to utilize this technique and teach it to everyone via the huge centers of love we establish throughout America and the world. Our objective would be to teach this technique to everyone possible and to create large circles of loving people who would help to manage and transform the world's most poisonous enemies. After witnessing this miracle tonight, I would hazard it a guess that a few million people transmitting pink light could create and maintain worldwide peace. I am going to have to confer with my colleagues about this idea and get their opinions regarding it. I think that it will be a wise thing for us to initiate, and some of you might be the very first to establish such centers in America and other interested countries. Members of our cause could teach it to masses of people there and, with their voluntary support, use it to correct any problems that might crop up in their country or others on Earth." After he had personally thanked all of us again he walked away with a renewed sparkle in his eyes.

Gail and I shook many hands and bid goodnight to our associates and their guides.

"Gail, I've got to ask if you are going to be holding your church service tomorrow?" asked a sizable black woman just as we were attempting to leave."

"I'm sure we will," said Gail, looking over her shoulder at me and getting my affirmation. "Although it hasn't been requested yet, everyone who attends seems to be helped and it is right for us to assist others. My guide Marza told me last week that it was now too large to be held indoors and that we will be using the grounds where our wedding took place."

"Oh, I'm so pleased, Gail. I heard so much about it and I am worried about my husband—"

"No need of putting it off until tomorrow," said Gail generously. She closed her eyes and moved to that inner window that allowed her to view into the normally invisible realm. After a short pause and with a gray look in her eyes, she said, "I'm sorry, Diane, he's—" She cut herself off, unable to complete her commentary because of something she was seeing.

"What? Please—please tell me what you are seeing!" solicited this anxious woman.

"I see him," replied a dismayed Gail, "in bed with another female and they are doing that very private thing—"

"Oh, thank you One for giving him another wife. Bless you, Gail," she said with a warm hug and great sincerity. "I can only be happy for his involvement with another woman. After all," she confided with a female's understanding, "you know how every man needs love, help, understanding, and companionship." The two women giggled at each other conspiratorially and, with genuine camaraderie, slapped each other's shoulders.

"If you women don't mind," I said with a mask of repulsion, "I'd like to get home for some of that close companionship myself and some sleep afterwards since we are getting up early."

After a few more giggles we turned and began to walk away. However, we were quickly halted by petitions of a dozen or more of our cohorts, "We need that service tomorrow," were their urgent pleas.

Others asked, "Can't you hold it now?"

Still another three or four said, "We need your help now. Please come and give us readings."

"I've got a toothache that sure could use some healing!" said a man grabbing at my arm.

A powerfully-built man looked into Gail's eyes and said, "With your assistance we gain knowledge concerning our loved ones at home. It's our only means of intelligence regarding them and it does help us so greatly to hear how they are fairing."

Without saying a word, I sent the man with the toothache healing light. I fear if I hadn't spoken up for ourselves at that point that Gail would have said, 'No need of waiting' to everyone there, and I wanted to circumvent it. "At 10:00 a.m. we will tender another service. Won't we Gail?" I asked, wanting to constrain her eagerness to immediately help everyone.

"Yes, my compassionate husband," she tauntingly complied.

"My toothache is totally gone!" yelled a very happy man.

We made our departure followed by a few jeers, many laughs, and gratitude from everyone there. "Jim," asked Gail as we strolled homeward beneath two nearly full moons, "why didn't you want to stay and help more of our colleagues tonight?"

"Because, my lovely wife," I facetiously answered, "as if I need inform you, we are still honeymooners. In truth, the realization of our too quickly approaching separation adds to my driving need, which I can't put off any longer! If you remember, we were about ready to make love when you correctly felt trouble brewing and stopped me."

"So what does that mean?" she teased me in return.

"If need be, we can establish its significance right here and now," I jeered.

"No thanks," she said. "I'd rather you save that demonstration for home. Besides, we would probably have too many on-lookers here in only minutes."

Directly ahead stood the men's quarters, which was lit up like a Christmas tree. I smiled to myself and said, "You might have something there, Lovie. Most likely the guys will be here in just a few."

A man hidden in the shade of the doorway to the men's dorm suddenly paced forward and stopped our progress. Gail, in fright, shrieked, "Who's that?"

"Sorry, ma'am," said a recoiling Nick. "Didn't mean to startle you. I am in dire straits and you guys are my last rays of hope." Next he nervously said, without giving either of us time to respond, "I've heard about your emotional and physical healing powers and am hoping that you can assist me tonight. I can't control my thinking or actions and, with large portions of my mind deleted, I am being sent back to Earth in the body of a severely retarded child who can't tell anyone about this cause or about the research into alternative sources of power I've discovered. Covering his face with his hands and with an agitated tick of his head, he continued, "I constantly have a battle going on within me. I want to be a member of this crusade, yet it conflicts with another element of me that just won't allow me to participate. This makes me distrust everything I hear."

Being shocked by his past unrestricted mockery of our cause and all of us who were aiding this renowned movement, and especially thinking of the work Swuel and his spirit guide had done, I answered, "I doubt that there is anything else we can do about this situation."

"I can't help it," he supplicated. "Unruly emotions and actions just seem to emerge out of nowhere and they can't be stilled."

"We've all seen that, Nick What can we do to help?" asked Gail sympathetically.

Wanting him to really focus on my next words, I said, "Nick, we are the masters of our own lives and it is up to us to control them! We do, of course, have One who is the head honcho, yet we've got to be in command—"

Unable to allow me to finish, Nick howled in a demonic voice, "No!"

A tinge of guilt hit me and I had a powerful sensation of forgiveness in my heart. A great weight was lifted from me and I learned later that the last of my karma had left me that moment. Someone I adored had scorned me, and the guilt I had held against them had dissolved with my heartfelt desire to help this man.

For a few moments, the three of us stood in total silence below a small-lit streetlight. The full moons and the light of One filled the heavens and the surrounding area with a silvery hue. "I know this man wouldn't have sought us out unless it was an imperative predicament," I told my wife. "Nick, will you please give us some of the details of your tribulations and symptoms?"

"Tell us of the abnormal particularities in each case," asked a perceptive Gail. "First," she interjected, "I've got to know your emotional fortitude. Can you tolerate questioning and the pain of recalling those memories? Some of our questions might be tough for you to answer."

"Nick," I said, putting my attention on him and then my beloved woman who was looking Nick deep in the eyes, "even if it hurts, you've got to listen to both of us and confront all of your anguish. The One has given us gifts and we are now going to share them with you. Please listen and open yourself to the truth."

"Yes," he agreed. "I am already fully cognizant of all of my past lives. My spirit guide and others have made me aware of all of my faults." Then following a brief interval of quiet, he burst out in anger, "There's no excuse for my killing him!"

More than I had witnessed thus far, an intuitive Gail said, "It wouldn't have stopped with the killing of your mother. He would have killed you, your little brother, and three sisters if you hadn't tried defending your mother by jumping on him. He slipped and fell on his knife. By no means did you kill him!"

"I did, and that's why I was born in my next life to a poverty-stricken man from India. I was neglected, begging on the streets from age six till my wanton death at fifteen."

"Excuse me, but unlike my beautiful wife, I don't have psychic abilities right now. Please, will one of you familiarize me with some of the background info?" I had asked that because my mind was in a quandary. For some reason I was feeling apprehensive about this perplexing person. There was something not quite kosher about him. I had learned to distrust him from our few brief encounters. I was feeling paranoid about him talking with my wife, especially now since I heard something about him murdering his own dad.

Gail untangled the puzzle of his past lives as my mind pondered over the known facts and my shameful, biased impressions of him. I abruptly became cognizant of Gail's voice no longer describing his problems. Seconds passed before I ultimately realized that they were waiting for my input. "Well," I commenced, opening myself to him and his obvious need. "It's quite evident that you are justly distraught with some of your past lives," I said, anticipating inspiration. Then suddenly all of the divided fragments miraculously fell into place. "Nick," I said, feeling certain of the reason for my feelings of apprehension, "has anyone told you that you have a powerful belief of an imposed satanic spirit abiding in you? It is provoked by enfites amassed during past disasters, lives, and inaccurate teachings by your religious institutions. They told you that you were sinful right from your birth and, paradoxically, you created this evil in your life so that you could prove them correct."

He instantaneously replied, "Why, yes, of course. A few of my parents took great pride in telling me frequently that I was possessed. You aren't examining that probability, too, are you?" he scorned. Then, after thinking about it for a second, he said, "I won't allow you to charge me with being possessed."

Gail pitched in next. "Nick, it doesn't necessarily mean that you are an evil person. You are merely a victim of circumstances. After lifetimes of troubled lives and incorrect teaching by parents and churches, some souls become corrupted by way of those gruesome and injurious beliefs they've been taught over the years."

"In short, we are One who is only goodness. Nevertheless, you truly believe yourself a demonic spirit," I told him.

"And your believing in that lie has caused you to manifest an evil being in you," added my wife gently.

Concurrently, Gail and I recognized an evil demented man raving before us. "That does it," he ranted. "I am not going to allow you spiritual perverts to commit slander against me any longer!" Terrifying anger shown in his eyes as he said in an unrecognizable voice, "That's it then, let me be eternally damned in hell and barred from joining this cause!" Then, trying to avoid further questioning and perhaps persuading, he quickly turned and ran from us.

"Pour lovenergy on him, Gail!" I cried, chasing after him.

"Is this the Nick who wants to aid our movement or a demonic being trying to escape reality?" yelled a wise and altruistic Gail to his fleeing form.

He then fell to the ground having, what appeared to be, a seizure. Reaching his side, I placed my hands on his head and proclaimed, "In the name and power of One-consciousness, you are free and healed of all afflictions and feelings of unrighteousness. You are One in the name and power of our universal Prime Creator! You are no longer hampered by a belief in an immoral being!" His paroxysm quickly arrested and he lay at rest.

Remembering Swuel's last words about the power of white light, I now saturated him with it. I then loudly declared, "The light of One is reaching into the deepest and darkest place of your soul. All barriers and concepts of evil cannot exist in the pure white light of One. Darkness cannot exist in the purity of our One's unadulterated white light! Darkness, you are enlightened. Now vacate this man at once and to hell with you for eternity!" I said, throwing up my arms in a gesture of releasing its defilement. I was violently knocked backwards by a vile force, and I felt it trying to penetrate unrepentant portions of me. The air became permeated with a stench of rotting waste. "Be gone with you evil darkness!" I yelled above deafening screeching, howling, and grinding earthquakes, wind and fire. "Enter not into man nor beast on this plane or any other. In the name and power of One, I condemn you to annihilation for eternity!"

"Are you alright, Jamie?" Gail asked when the furor had desisted and I had gained awareness. "You sure look awful!" she said, standing by my side.

"Why, what's the matter?" I asked, slowly rising to my feet.

"Well, just look at yourself!" she said with her nose wrinkled. I followed her instructions and looked downward. I was appalled. My clothing was badly scorched and covered with black soot.

We quickly moved to Nick's side and were astonished by the quantity of black ash encasing him. He was absolutely still and, with fear, I fell to my knees and felt for a pulse. It was very weak and, by some inner means, I knew that he was comatose.

Moving to my side, Gail said, "He isn't in his body any longer. He's certainly not dead, but I have no hint of where he might be."

Feeling deep in my heart that it was up to me to locate him, I quickly prepared myself for a search. Instinctively, I knew that with this pulse his body couldn't maintain itself very long. "Please stay here with him and call my name when he has returned or if he should worsen." With all of my power of mind and spirit, I prayed. "Forgive me Swuel and Rama for disobeying your command to not leave this plane. This is an emergency and I've got to search for Nick and bring him back to his body again," I said, looking down at his lifeless form.

I compelled stillness within my mind and body and moved into a trance-like state. I immediately bilocated and began a methodical search for him.

I was surprised to find that I now had a third kind of body. This one was ostensibly spiritual—only a silvery hue. During my exploration of new and awesome planets and spiritual localities, I often found myself desiring the liberty to stay longer. The colors, purity, and peace and quiet of these places were so brilliant and pure that I wanted to share their splendor with my wife. "One day," I said to myself, "Gail and I are going to live on one of these resplendent planes." I had to remind myself to shout out Nick's name every few seconds. I sternly reproved him and told him to return to Tesa.

Passing an especially magnificent orb, my breath was taken away with its resplendence. Only two people resided on this incredible plane. I judged this young man to be 20 and his mate 16. "So what are you doing alone?" called this gorgeous girl. "Where is your eternal soul mate? We were present for your wedding and know your affinity for one another. So we are wondering what you are doing roaming like this on your own?"

"This is our version of paradise," said the tall, thin man. "Of course, there are no forbidden fruits here."

"Please don't leave me—Adam is quickly aging," she said with a loud laugh. With a winning grin, she then said, "Stay eternally young and enjoy the ultimate pleasures of the body and all of existence in the truth and light of One."

"What are we going to do with these flirting women? The male mocked with a loud laugh. "No matter how hard we might try, nor all we do for them, we can't keep them eternally contented!"

"We are cosmic conscious beings and know your mission," said the woman amiably.

"If we can impose, I hope to drop by for tea one of these days soon—with the little woman, of course," I said with a wink.

"Time is only an illusion. It is relative and we've only to live in the moment of eternity," they wisely told me.

I smiled because of my joy at finding these delightful people. Hoping that they could assist in my locating this wayward spirit that I was in search of, I stopped and asked, "Since you are so endowed, where might I find Nick?"

"He is taking in everything," he told me. "One minute he is here and the next somewhere entirely different. He is universal, everywhere at once. He knows that he has to return and wants only to view as much of the universe as he can."

"He is now revisiting the ninth plane of One. No, he is presently heading toward Tesa again. I don't think he even knows where he might be heading next," Eve told me.

We waved goodbye to one another as I passed. In desperation, I commanded, "Now Nick, I want you to return to your body in Tesa right this minute! I have to believe that you wouldn't want me feeling sorry because I had freed you and ultimately caused your death. Your life is in peril—"

A moment later, in the far off distance of an eternal unending universe, I heard Gail calling my name. "Jim, he is in the midst of returning again," she cried.

My heart escalated as I moved in the direction of her voice. The number of densities I had viewed in only minutes astounded me. Earth's best astronomers had no concept of the vastness of this eternal universe. I believe that if I had been able to travel at the speed of light, and had spent all of eternity searching it, I would never realize its unlimited expansiveness. Eternity was an appropriate description, for One's universe was truly endless.

While observing one particular area, I saw new suns and planets being born. It was like watching the largest conceivable sparkler generate billions of them, and each of them ceaselessly creating billions more. I had only encompassed a tiny proportion of its enormity and know that it goes on eternally.

Being a part of the sea of One gives us beings an infinite power of creation. By the power of wanting to experience more, One only creates more of this infinite universe! I realized that all that was necessary was a steadfast belief in the truth found in One. *For having perfect, unwavering faithfulness literally makes us Him.*

With feelings of incredibility, I suddenly comprehended the vast number of believers who decided for themselves that they wanted to remain in their own created plane of consciousness. *One gives equal power of will to all of His believers. Obviously many prefer not to unify and become one with Him.* The evidence of One's acceptance of this fact was all about me. *Maybe,* I thought, *our cause should be putting more effort into persuading more people from these planes to join our crusade?*

This thought had just exited my mind when another thought surfaced. *That's not the way One operates. We all are the creators of our lives and He has cheerfully given us free will to live as we elect. If I had chosen, I could have been a molester and still not have been disgusting to my One, for I am the God of my own choosing. He isn't a taskmaster and we aren't required to be submissive children. Our own goals should be rising to the point of our sharing His consciousness. We are all equal parts of the eternal sea of One and there isn't any division."*

When I returned I found Gail still wiping soot from Nick's ashen face. My bride and I kissed longingly and then watched him for a period of time. He was laying face down and, except for a slight rise and fall of his chest as he breathed shallowly, he did not move. The shimmering moons cast a silvery hue in the empty space between this being and us, and I instinctively knew that we were now separated by even less than moonbeams. He had been aloof and arrogant previously, and I had to wonder what he was going to be like now that he was free of this imposing demonic spirit. Also, I speculated about evil and righteousness. *Do we allow good and evil to enter our lives totally by accident? Or is it because of incorrect teaching, perceptions, deeds, or karma that we become influenced in any of these diverse areas?* I silently hypothesized.

In the light of the two nearly full moons and One's light, Nick's waxen face seemed ghostly, absent of life. Without even so much as a blinking of his eyes, he awoke and began to verbalize. First he addressed my unspoken question, "We are what our minds tell us we are. The world I knew in my pasts was moot and unemotional except for my moments of uncontrollable anger. Then you, or more properly I, freed myself and for an interval I existed on new and exciting planes where time was immeasurable and life was infinitely alluring. All about me, people shown with the purity and love of One. They welcomed me with love! Me—a being that was formerly condemned to a self-imposed hell. With my karma as it was, I would most likely be a black spirit condemned eternally to encircle the Earth when I finally had enough and gave up trying to improve."

"A new and immensely superior Nick was justly welcomed into their paradise. Prior to your intercession, guys," he said sincerely, "I couldn't have fathomed that occurring. I am at last free of that immoral spirit who has made havoc of my own many lives and that of innumerable others. How do I begin to thank you and rectify my harmful past deeds?"

Gail and I smiled at Nick, who was now sitting upright. All I could say was, "It was our duty and pleasure; no thanks are needed. There really isn't any method of our removing harm from pasts," I told him.

A perceptive Gail offered, "You were ready. Enough enfites had been dislodged for our small efforts to have an effect on you. As to your other question, live this new life to the fullest, aid our cause to the best of your ability, and fulfill One's desire of you—to know yourself for who you are: I am He."

Nick then stood and the three of us hugged each other. "Now," he said, realizing his destiny, "I can stay for more training. Eventually when I am prepared enough, I'll make my return to Earth and make amends for all of my past immoral acts. This cause is worthy and I want to help in accomplishing corrective measures for our planet. My primary cause and effect will be further research into humanity using endless and totally non-toxic etheric energy for everything from cars to huge power plants. I had nearly achieved it, but greed . . ."

Gail and I cheered wholeheartedly. At this juncture, I'd like to say that the ground quaked, lightning flashed, and the heavens opened up as Gail and I physically ascended toward Tesa's moons. We did rise toward them, but in another instant we appeared in the Triple C. Swuel, Rama, and Marza were standing in front of us and the seven inhabitants of the Cosmic Consciousness Center were aligned behind them. With a large smile, Swuel exclaimed, "Through your last act of removing a haunting perception of evil and overcoming that last barrier, you both have now reached Clear! All of your past transgressions have been eliminated and you are totally clear of enfites. You are now ready to return to Earth and we will be sending—"

"Please tell us you're not going to send us to Earth and take us away from one another tonight!" said Gail with her hands folded in front of her and her heart-filled passion clearly displayed for everyone to see.

Everyone simultaneously said, "You're clear!" A more sympathetic Marza asked, "Why not tonight, Gail? You both knew that this moment was quickly approaching."

"Primarily because I am not emotionally bolstered enough to leave my husband yet. It's going to be too many years before we are united again and I've got to prepare myself for that reality. As strong as I feel toward this cause now, I know that I've got to ready myself."

"Also," she said with a growing sigh of regret, "comparatively speaking it's a minor issue, but we have promised everyone that we would hold our church service tomorrow. We've got to be there for them and everyone who will be going." Gail's eyes displayed her concern and true feelings about us as well as her regard for our colleagues and the people of Tesa. "We have to assist them before leaving. They need relief from their pain. Especially since this will be our very last chance of helping. We've got to be there for them."

Looking sincerely into everyone's eyes, I added, "There will be many natives of Tesa coming for emotional and physical healing. We simply can't abandon them without any prior notice!"

Swuel smiled appreciatively and replied, "We are pleased with your consideration of your comrades and people of Tesa. We can't ignore your needs of saying goodbye to one another either. For that reason we've decided to permit you to stay in your home for another night. Besides," he said with a knowing smile, "everyone is going to want to bid you farewell, and your service tomorrow will be the perfect time and place for it."

"Directly following your service tomorrow," said Rama, "we will expect you to be ready to depart Tesa. You will then be taken to another location for further preparation prior to your return to Earth."

Everyone was hushed and Gail and I stood expectantly. After a few seconds of complete silence, I asked, "Is this all there is to being Clear? I'm bewildered by the fact that I am not sensing some dissimilarities in my thought processing or sensations."

At my expense, everyone laughed boisterously. Then Rama said, "What did you expect, Jim, fireworks?"

"Pay us no mind. We're only celebrating your fast success," said Swuel with a glimmer of joy in his eyes.

"Swuel, Marza, and I were with you during your search for Nick," said Rama, looking at me somehow more equally. "As you appropriately hypothesized, One has given all humans the right to choose as they like. There aren't any restrictions in His universe. There is no 'have to', 'can't', 'should', or 'should not'. There aren't even goods, wrongs, or evils—it is all self-illusionary. Because the Universal One is perfect, all of His creation is unblemished. However, being that humans become corrupted by society's treacherous teaching and wrong decisions and acts, bad karma is created."

"Imperfection breeds imperfection," said an unseen voice.

"Knock and it shall be opened unto you, seek and ye shall find, believe and create what thou believeth," said another.

"You and Gail felt Nick's corruption and because of your beliefs and his own perceptions, having heard it thousands of times throughout many lives, signs of that evil spirit were made manifest. You were uniformly able to free the perception."

"Become clear, too," added another.

"Nick truly felt his iniquity. It had been building in him for many lifetimes, making him feel repugnantly evil. Honestly it was your concocted impurities that you all released, thus all that soot," finished Rama with applause from his peers.

"One more thing," added Marza. "As well as the peoples of the universe that you explored, earthlings cannot be made to change. You are only to favor them with the truth, not hit them over the head with it. You cannot make them believe in the power of lovenergy, pink light, or their powers of belief; they've got to come to that conclusion themselves. Not believing in their divine Oneness, people everywhere erroneously live from moment to moment as they think they want to live."

"Present them with the concepts of lovenergy and pink light in your book, but don't be too disappointed if its teachings aren't widely accepted," added Swuel. "You may have to offer free classes or something like that to get public attention."

"Make recalling lovenergy a primary goal for yourself when you enter your new life, Jim. Writing a book about the creation of love as soon as possible is going to be enormously fruitful for you and the human race," advised Marza.

"However, change has to be in a person's spiritual plans for themselves," added another person.

In the next room I now noticed a rather large table all festively prepared for a party. Before I could ask about it, a man said to us, "We are exceedingly happy to have two more virtuous and competent spirits fit for their return to Earth. Our cause is in great need of worthy allies. Within only weeks all of your fears and anxieties will be greatly reduced. For now, though, don't feel compelled to remove all negative emotions from your minds. What you focus on, you create. Know that you have taken another giant step in totally eliminating all opposing stresses in your futures. You are still ascending that stairway of purity. You are experiencing Oneness to a fuller extent, now live it!"

"And rejoice in its radiant light of recognition," said another person.

"You have been disciplining your minds with memory of what you have been learning most recently," said Rama with a bona fide smile. "You will have some physical, mental, and emotional maturing to do on Earth before participants in our cause contact you."

"Recollection of your teaching here is going to be a vital element in being prepared for that day when you encounter that member of our crusade. At that precise moment you've got to be able to step in and participate 100% in aiding our cause."

"You both know your calling. While waiting for that contact, get all of the education required for your upcoming vocations. You are not to be worried about this communication from one of us; it will occur at the correct moment," said Swuel with a knowing smile. "Believe and all of your needs shall be met."

Giggling, Gail said, "We are so well-rehearsed that we are feeling like children echoing our alphabet and times tables. What we've learned here should be permanently burned into our minds when we become human beings again."

"Because of your surplus of spiritually gained heights," said Swuel, "you may not encounter difficulties recalling all of your memories. We only want to prepare you for the plausible retention loss that could occur. If you perpetuate your memories as we had done on our return, when you converse with astute people, your vernacular will spontaneously excel. Therefore, be always on guard; you don't want to be too unlike that person who you will be supplanting."

"Drawing attention to a unique personality would most likely disrupt your new lifestyle, and you must fit into your new existence smoothly."

Chapter 7

Serenity

We walked into an extraordinarily decorated sanctuary that was filled with exquisite artistry of all kinds. I saw naked stone statues holding their drinks aloft as if saluting our achievements and one whole side of an elephant's body with his head turned toward the enormous room so that his raised trunk, two tusks, ears, and smiling mouth were extended toward us. In another area all but the tail and hind most part of a lion's legs appeared to be leaping out of the wall at us. A sensual, naked woman was partially out of a raging river; her beautiful figure was in motion with one arm raised to grab hold of a tree branch for support. On one immense wall was carved a meager-sized spaceship resting on a dying planet. Hundreds of alien-appearing beings were fighting for space aboard this ship. All of the art in this room was three-dimensional. Closing my eyes for an odd instant, I wished that I could examine everything by feel. Since feel had been my primary sense for so many years, I wanted to use it now even though I could see. In fact, using both senses would be even better. The art displayed in this room could keep me visually spellbound for days—for months. It suddenly dawned on me that I was fortunate that I had been blind in my last life. I had gotten to perceive and appreciate art from a different perspective. Visually, I could now take the entirety of this complete room in view in only seconds, but being blind it would have taken me months to appreciate. If only time allowed me to now examine the room, not only would I see a face, but with my hands, feel every morsel, every strand of facial or scalp hair, length, width, and tilt of nose, texture of skin, and so on. I knew that in my all-seeing hands as well as eyes, a single flower held the whole world in its beauty.

In the center of the room stood a floor-to-ceiling sized fluid sculpture, which represented a shaft of light. It was the color of the light of One and was covered with tiny carved birds, men, women, hundreds of various insects, and every remembered creature of Earth. There were some that I failed to recognize—most likely prehistoric or extraterrestrial life forms I mentally surmised. Being absorbed in this magnificence, I absent-mindedly walked over to it and closely examined its awesome greatness. On close examination I was dismayed to find that the artist had somehow managed to deposit clear crystal over a shaft of One's pure light. Carved into the crystal were layers of animals atop of other creatures. It was like looking into a transparent sea and seeing different kinds of sea life swimming at diverse depths. There were dragonflies overlaying praying mantises, birds of all varieties outlining winged dinosaurs, and human-like men formed over larger bear-like creatures walking on two legs.

"As you have correctly conceived, this represents One who embodies all of creation," said Marza stepping behind me.

"It's so alive and dynamic," I told her. "I can feel the light and love of One in all of these creatures. His light shines in all of them, yet doesn't hide who or what they might be."

"That's because like you, nature is the reality of One. He is all that they were, are, or will be and that's because, as we've taught you, there is only Onenergy experienced in this moment. One's lovenergy is all there is to existence! Exhibiting His light within yourself only makes a more perfect unity of One."

We all then moved to an elaborately festive table. Rajah raised his glass to us and proclaimed, "Here is to our newest graduating alumni. May your days on Earth be fruitful and joyous for you and all present and future humans." He folded his hands and began to pray, "Almighty One, we ask your blessings on these, your children, and on the food which we are about to eat. May your light shine reverently in our hearts, minds, and eternally grateful spirits."

Not saying another word, we encircled the table and began munching all kinds of delectable foodstuff. "I bet you can't tell that all of this is vegetarian!" I challenged my bride who was at my side.

"Where have I heard that before?" she teased.

"Well, I am consistent." I admitted.

"You mean 'insistent' don't you?"

An hour later we gathered around another table and, following a glass of white wine and many salutations from our enlightened hosts, Swuel handed Gail and I a small, pure white, ivory glass with little carved butterflies etched into its sides. "This drink is a special blended tea from India. It has very unique hypnotic properties, yet it is not a hallucinogenic drug. Since you already know who you will be replacing, a more powerful drug isn't required. This tea will only help you to relax and enable you to display your new identities fully to yourselves and to us. Both of these now-living humans will be functioning normally so you must only be like mirrors, reflecting their emotions and personalities. Their minds, visions, and actions will also be yours, so you have to be on guard not to react or influence them whatsoever," he instructed emphatically. Then with a resourceful grin, he said, "We've got to warn you that because you both will be immersed in your own fill-in's lives, which are naturally separate, you will not be able to see each other's personage. Being forewarned, do not allow this to unnerve you. Remember who you are and what you have learned here. Using your prevailing minds, move into your newly presented lives and placidly observe their sentiment, movement, and emotion. See, think, and feel everything they do. You are to be only detached mirrors, not allowing yourselves to get the least bit involved," he repeated.

One swallow of that majestic potion and I was quickly ascending through densities of space and continuums of time. Within only seconds I had become a tangible segment of the body, mind, and spirit of John Bennett. Thankfully he was fast asleep and I easily got parts of his memory banks open, having only to witness his dreams and probe into them. His now shared memories invaded my tranquility as I saw, felt, and heard appalling episodes of his life. Because I was a part of him, I subliminally suffered the ensuing horrors along with him. Involuntarily, I relived his being repeatedly molested and beaten by his father. He was handicapped by a slight retardation and I observed other kids making fun of him. I became him and felt the kids making fun of me. They as well as my parents called me a retard because I was having difficulties with all of my school subjects due to a reading abnormality. I felt disgusted with my slowness, and felt the ridicule of the girls in high school to be especially hard. They laughed viciously at me, and I personally felt their anguishing sarcasm. Being only a part of his mind at this moment, I was relieved that John was soundly sleeping and didn't have to relive these experiences as I examined his memory bank. Although I did sense that these recollections were causing him discomforts. I experienced his feelings of abandonment and devastating loneliness. He was alienated even more by his handicap than I had been during my years of blindness. I couldn't comprehend how a father could inflict even more pain onto his son. "What an awful added affliction those experiences must be to John," I thought wearily while valiantly trying to keep my emotions at bay.

Only 30 minutes later, which in truth seemed more like years, Gail and I returned to the Triple C. Realizing that I was once again in my body, I allowed myself to feel and express enormous misery. I cried out in a disturbed voice, "How can I cope with entering into that troubled life?" Thinking of John's father, I said, "How could anyone create such upheaval for another person, especially a parent for a child?"

Rajah came to my side and placed his hands on my shoulders. A vibrant green light penetrated through me, and a peaceful feeling over came my anxiety. He gently said, "Jim, surrender those feelings of dejection. You have only perceived the worst of his existence. From the instant you supersede him his life is going to improve. You will not have to continue suffering as John has done all of his life. You will persevere, and your life will fortuitously unfold as his replacement. Live in the moment knowing that the light of the universal spirit of One illuminates all of your current and future paths of travel."

Rama spoke to me in an even-tempered tone. "You will be a mental as well as physical proxy for him. In fact, most likely he'll be dead and gone when you take over his body. In a safe period of time you will totally supplant other's opinions of him and again be able to manifest your true self."

Gail took my hand and, in a conciliatory voice, gave me my first personal psychic reading. "Jim, I told you that you were going to be starved for affection. Please listen to your mentors. There is no law dictating that you live as John. You will be a new and unrestricted person living in his body. His only jurisdiction over you is in name alone!" Following a reviving kiss, she reassuringly said, "My Jamie, you're going to be mentally and physically powerful. Although I know that you are going to have to stand firm in a confrontation with your abusive father, you will overcome all adversities and rise far above them." Lastly she whispered, "You are the master of your fate and the captain of your soul. Know that your life is going to be as fulfilling as a renewed you and only you will create."

"It's only that I love everything so much. Lovenergy has brought me into an expanded perception of love, and this kind of behavior on the part of others causes me so much emotional upheaval!" I said in defense of my outburst. Feeling somewhat calmer and appeased by Gail's encouragement, I replied directly to her. "My saving grace is the fact of our reunion." Our eyes met and I read comprehension written in her unfeigned and shimmering openness.

With an innermost-felt smile, I displayed my prized self-possession to her as well as my masters. "Gail, I know in my heart that after these ordeals have transpired that you and I will be coupled again," I told her with an optimistic feeling of joy. "Knowledge of that future event makes any burden endurable." I kissed her lustfully. To myself, I thought, *Why, oh why, do we have to be separated now? At last I have the woman of my many lives at my side again, and now it's clear that I am going to have to do without her for an arduous period of time!*

Her next horrifying disclosure shot through me like a blast of hell's fire. "No, Gail won't ever be there for you." Then the slyness in her eyes portrayed her cunningness." But Lillian Hanson will be counting the minutes and hours until we are reunited again!" She then gently smiled and implored, "Despite your difficulties ahead, I hope you hold on to the fact that we will be adjoined when in college, and maybe even before that if I know you," she declared proudly.

"My precious Love," I whispered while putting my arm around her shoulders and pulling her closer to me. "The reality of our next union will always sustain me no matter how difficult my new life might become."

I kissed her affectionately and then without warning, like an explosion inside me, my next thought riveted me to a question that I knew had to be answered here and now. "Can we modify our futures to any degree? If we are the creators of our lives, why is waiting necessary? Why can't I locate Gail and move into her neighborhood years earlier when I run away?" I asked, looking everyone in the eye.

The room and its inhabitants had become silent during this interim. Swuel cleared his throat and timidly said, "From the looks of it, your role in your next life is going to be quite chaotic in the beginning, Jim." Then with a warming smile, he said, "Know in your heart, though, that the outcome will be just as grandiose as you desire. Believe and reap what you have sown. Actions create reactions; let all of your actions be services to One and your causes have positive effects." Giving his words time to sink in, he continued, "Now let's answer your important question," he said, pointing at the exquisitely-adorned sculpture that I had scrutinized in the middle of the room. "The light, sound, love, and purity of the Universal One are the center of the universe. Everything is present because He brought it into existence. Life is like a highway that He has produced. Not paying events much mind we often blindly speed through it, allowing anything to befall us. What we have to remember is that we are not constrained to only one lane on this highway. If we distaste what is occurring in a given lifetime, we can change lanes and choose another path. Open yourself to the reality of who you really are: the embodiment of your infinite father One. He created you so that He could experience life in various ways. We are not restricted from making our life as we desire. When you have learned enough from a given lesson, you can release that particular moment and, via your imagination powers, move onto the next."

"Imagine and create," said Rajah.

"Remember that all is a grand illusion presented to you by you, the One," said Rama. As Marza demonstrated in her telling of one of her previous lives, it will be necessary for you to maintain control of your powers. People of

Earth will prosecute and call you a possessed being if you show your mastery too soon," he said with a warning tone in his voice. "You don't want to be crucified, burned at a stake, or end up in some mental institution after all."

Many voices of the group were now heard as they acknowledged his discernment. "That was the case with Jesus Christ. He exhibited his enormous powers of will too fast and far too often for the people of that era," said Rajah, whose eyes held much intrigue in their depths of wisdom. "He died trying to fulfill what had been written and, by his resurrection, showed us that there was no separation between himself and One. 'When you have seen the Father, you have also seen me, for we are as One,' is literally what He had told us. All are equal parts of the wholeness, the Oneness, of Himself and His Father."

"One is the father of imagination, and mankind the seed of that same imagination."

"In the beingness of One, Jesus demonstrated His enormous power of imagination with His resurrection."

"Reap what thou hast sown," came that same unseen voice.

"Why am I getting the feeling that Jesus was one of us?" Gail asked with a look of incredulity in her own very perceptible eyes.

"I guess that you could call Jesus a sincere crusader!" said an obviously amusing man who laughed hard at his own wit. "You must understand, my dear, that the Cosmic Consciousness Center has virtually existed since the creation of mankind, although we weren't known as humans back then. My children," he gently said, "the Triple C still has many who are called ETs. Although we were the originators of earthly intelligence, we are not the origin of humanity."

"Now, God, don't confuse these newcomers like this!" said a more sensitive woman.

Wanting a definitive answer, Gail asserted, "Are you telling us that Jesus was a student here?"

"Yes, my dear. He was my ultimate student," replied Swuel with a whimsical laugh that was soon duplicated throughout the room.

"Jesus was one of us again for a short time. Then he unified himself and became a more brilliant One. Now he is the true essence of One, pure of spirit, light, sound, and love. He told us that his Father's house had many rooms and that he would save one for us. One is in everything, therefore, His rooms are infinite and you are already in one of them. Being of his mind you, my child, are the Christ of today, as is true of all the members of our movement as well as all of mankind. Like One, Jesus, Rajah/Buddha, and all who believe are One and united with all that is present throughout the entirety of the universe. Since we are One, all of us believers can be the masters of our own lives. We can manifest the powers of One seen in wealth, health, fame, and everything we desire. Any phenomenon or miracle that you desire is achievable via your own belief, imagination, and powers of will."

A gentle woman smiled at Gail and then me, "As Jesus said and Brahma repeated twice, 'Reap what you have sown.' Or as has been said, 'Imagine and create.'"

"Being your instructor this long, let me explain it to you, Gail," said a more understanding Marza. "Jesus is now a unified master of our community.

You both have just become Clear. Your next step of mastery, after your next lives, will be earthly guides, better known to humans as angels. At that point you will not be humans, but angelic beings on Earth. After that comes spirit guides. When you have obtained spiritual heights and elect to discontinue your work on Earth, you can come and guide newcomers as Rama and I are doing now. The next advancement is Cosmic Consciousness. If you aspire, you can become a component of this gathering in the Triple C as you so cleverly named it. After Cosmic Consciousness is Unification, and then your spiritual development and succeeding evolution will be complete. Once you have reached the unified level you can decide for yourselves whether or not you want to become one with One, imagine lovenergy into actual substance, continue your work on Earth, go to Tesa to teach, become a sub member of the Triple C, or procure your own plane of consciousness." Her demeanor changed becoming more contemplative, perhaps thinking of her own future. Then with a warm smile she said, "Needless to say, these advancements are only contingent on your remaining fervent in your commitment to spiritual growth. If you don't desire to advance into those stations, you can decide otherwise. It is decisively your option where and how to spend eternity."

"Besides our unified seven masters that we are in the midst of, there are millions of other unified members of this close-knit society who remain here because they want to remain active participants," said Rama. "They freely choose to remain here assisting wherever needed. As you know, while you and your collaborators in Tesa were projecting pink light, all of the million-plus members of the Triple C adjoined you in that noble effort. "

"Earthlings are ignoring global warming. This negligence will only make your planet more intolerable and soon destructive to all life. So, Jim, it is going to be imperative that you teach everyone to love Mother Earth as well as loving one another," urged Rajah.

"This fact is especially sad since many humans deny the concept of global warming."

"And to also start efforts to reverse it before it's too late!"

"Humans only need to realize their powers of mind and to believe in the spirit of One."

"Also to unify and rectify this profound ending of humanity."

"Just collectively believe in your Oneness and Earth will be perfectly healthy and mankind will enable her to be as they deem," said Swuel with a knowing smile.

"I saw millions of beings living on their own created planes of consciousness during my search for Nick," I told my masters. "I've got to wonder why we aren't trying harder to get those millions of extra beings working with us members of this worthy cause?"

Marza said, "They choose to live in and on their own planes of consciousness, but they are still included amongst us. They are awakened and kept abreast of all developments. If needed, they do assist us in whatever way necessary."

"The One has given us free will and will never infringe on this gift."

"He is infinite and in our reactions to various stimuli, He is deriving a more distinctive view of Himself through our existences."

A beautiful blond declared in a pleasant voice, "I can tell that you will enjoy your future technique of learning. Everything that has ever been written or will be written in the future will be available to you. It is already stored on computers in the library of Tesa. This is possible because time after all is only an illusion of the moment, which is an eternal present. Believe in now, for the future and past are only parts of this reality. Because the viewpoints and concepts are constantly evolving in humans, we have people whose job it is to make changes in the records so that you can stay up to date."

Favoring us with a gracious smile, Swuel then said, "As Syena just alluded to, during your ensuing life you will need to travel nightly to Tesa. Start this as soon as you become conscious of who you are and once you realize that you are members of our cause. While your bodies are in a trance, project your eternal souls to Tesa where you can access this data."

"There you will be learning manifold things. You will be given a room equipped with a computer terminal. Using it you will be able to access all of the newest and past writings. This arrangement is done for all of our workers, but will be even better for you specifically."

"This is true because of your vocation's need of authentic truth written by masters over the ages. When your church has been established, you will be communicating with thousands of people who are all searching for enlightenment. You've got to furnish them with true facts. These facts will not be limited in any fashion."

Looking into my wife's sparkling eyes, Marza said, "You will have foreknowledge of events in case you are too busy and unable to psychically forecast them."

"In your clairvoyant moments, what you are often really doing is subconsciously tapping into your masters here in the Triple C and accessing data from them."

Looking at both of us, Swuel then said, "On your computer monitors at Tesa you will be able to read of current and future earthquakes, hurricanes, volcano eruptions, and all other global catastrophes. You will even be able to forewarn humans of terrorist acts, plane crashes, and just about anything else that might befall them. You can advise your parishioners of personal problems, accidents and sicknesses—preventing them when they choose to take your words to heart."

"How is it that you can have prior knowledge of earthly events?" asked Gail, looking at both Swuel and Syena.

"The fifth dimension, time continuum, which is many years ahead of Earth's time," answered Syena before Swuel could respond."

"The further you get ahead of Earth's moment it is enduring, the more into her future you see," Swuel finished for her.

"So, you are giving facts rather than predictions," Syena said with a giggle.

"It is Einstein's relativity. Gail, you will be given all of the facts in time, for now let that suffice," suggested Marza.

As I deliberated over this mind-boggling information, all of the seven masters stood as Swuel approached us. "We send you off with a prayer," he announced. After all of the hands in the room were coupled, he prayed, "As You have requested, One, we have prepared these two individuals for a return to Earth. May they be resourceful in their efforts of restoring Earth to its just-created perfection. Reformation, religious revival, and human reformation of behavior are going to be tremendously important and difficult assignments. Please be with them and guide their every footstep. As they demonstrated earlier tonight, may they be continuously successful in winning over perceptions of evil and bringing lost souls into your eternal light of truth and wisdom."

"Father One," said Rajah, "you helped me to be an enlightened Buddha, Nam-myoho-renge-kyo, blessings on cause and effect. Our latest SGI students demonstrated true cause and effect via their usage and teaching of lovenergy, blessings on them."

Our arms were wrapped tightly around each other as Gail and I soared upwards out of the Triple C and headed home for a quick goodbye to one another and Tesa. Our hearts were heavy with remorse and great reluctance of leaving each other and this superb plane of consciousness. Replacing John Bennett was going to be an enormous ordeal for me, and having to do without Gail was only going to make it that much more unendurable.

The moons were full again and were showing directly above the house as we gently settled on the front lawn of our beloved homestead. Their combined light and the light of One permitted us to see the lake shimmering in the not-too-far-off distance. I silently wished that we could ride to it now and enjoy our lovemaking in our favorite place. Turning slowly to face me, she whispered as if in a trance, "I am going to miss this beautiful mansion. It is my ideal of a perfect home: friendly horses, privacy, and unlimited miles of pure open land." Putting her arms around me, she said with the same rapture that I was feeling, "Oh my One, being your wife, living here with you, reliving our pasts, and enjoying our incredible lovemaking are all so difficult for me to relinquish."

Her body shook gently as she silently cried. My own passions coursed through me, and my erroneous feeling of masculinity was the only thing that prevented me from crying along with her. "Oh, Lovie," I said through clenched teeth, "I, too, am going to miss this setting. It has been especially incredible since we've shared this splendor together," I said, kissing her tear-moistened cheeks. I am going to be yearning for our mutually-shared love until the very day when I can once again hold you in my arms." With a painful admission of truth, I said, "I am feeling as if I've lost my Claire all over again! Withstanding living without you again . . ." My kisses quickly became more ardent. ". . . is excruciating!"

"Oh, Jim," she said with desperation in her voice. "Because of my powerful clairvoyant skill, I know now that a new Lillian Hanson will have to isolate herself from schoolmates and family. I will be afraid of having insights and having to confront them with the truths. I wish so that there was some way for us to at least communicate—"

"Email! We can communicate over the net!" Joyously, I guided her indoors. "I'll use lovenergy in my Email address so you only need to search for lovenergy@whatever . . ."

Feeling very sure of our being able to communicate just as soon as we realized who we were, I took her to our bedroom. "After helping her to lay down on our bed, I whispered as I unbuttoned her blouse, "Believe with me, Lovie, that what we find on the other side of this new bridge we are approaching is going to be even more spectacular than what we have discovered thus far. Also, believe with me that we will procure all of our personal goals, including almost immediate contact via the Internet!"

"Yes, you're right. I can see and feel it now!"

"Surrender your mind, body, and spirit to this moment and time. Now is only a continuation of the past, present, and future of eternity itself. This very moment is all we've ever had or, for that matter, will ever have. Rejoice in the moment," I said after a few more gentle caresses. "You know how precious this very moment is for the both of us. Celebrate it fully with me," I urged.

Although we were elated about future Email communications, our night was spent with trying to fulfill each other's needs for the lonely years ahead. I found Gail's body, heart, and mind more desirable and at the same time, more receptive than ever before. "Oh my, Jim," she cried out early in the morning as I lay at her side panting heavily for the third time. "We've only been together now for a few months at best. We won't be meeting again for so many despairing years! I can't possibly live without our shared love for that long!"

"Lovie," I whispered trying to bolster her feelings, "we are not sure of the present Earth date. For all we know, it could even be when we meet in college!"

"Oh my One, if only that was the case. I could easily live with that," she mused. "Jim," she wistfully asked a second later, "would it be improper for me to believe that it is already year 2008?"

"Lovie," I said with alarm, "we have no idea what havoc our powers of belief might bring about in that situation. Can you possibly imagine the chaos that would be generated if you caused a modification of the time sequence for every human?"

"Not really," she replied. "Only you and I need to know the real date."

I began to laugh, but somehow managed to say between my spurts of joviality, "I'm afraid, Lovie, it doesn't work that way. I will, though, keep that concept in mind. It will enable me to better withstand our separation."

"Why?" she innocently asked with a giggle in response to my mirth," can't I really make it that year?"

"Reality on Earth doesn't perform in that manner. It would be an unheard of phenomenon for time to pass without events occurring. For example, I left Earth November of year 2000, only days after George W. Bush's election. So, there will be another election day almost four years before we meet in the university, and another less than two months following our reunion. We mustn't even ponder ideas that drastic."

"We've been told over and over again that with the power of belief and imagination . . . Besides, only hours ago Marza and Syena mentioned time continuum . . ."

"Jim," she said with a wry grin, "we're going to be different people and unable to reveal ourselves to our old family. It's going to be awful difficult staying away from our loved ones and not going to our old homes to pay them a visit."

"Wow, you've got that right!"

"Lovie," I said after looking at the clock, "it is already 5:00 a.m. and I think we better get some sleep. Our church service is only five hours away."

Wordlessly, she turned and I pressed my body against hers and held her tightly. Two thoughts drifted into mind before I fell into a deep sleep. *How am I going to survive without this woman in my life?* A deep intake of air and I mused, *I'm so glad that I found that computer in my room here! I learned how we will be able to communicate.*

Three hours later we rose, showered, and, following our last definitive lovemaking for one knows how many years, ate a quick but adequate breakfast. We longingly stood holding hands on our front porch wanting only to prolong our departure from this perfect plane and each other. The sun was high and the panorama was so bright and colorful that it took my breath away. Before I could comment on it or express the feelings in my heart, Gail said with appreciation, "It's so peaceful and beautiful here! Why are we humans abusing Earth?"

"Oh, Jim," she whimpered a moment later. "I wish that Earth didn't so desperately need our help! We have to forsake what is so dear to us now and just because irresponsible humans have all but destroyed her."

"Gail, I have the same sentiment exactly," I told her with heartfelt regret. "Unfortunately Earth's restoration is partly dependent on our abilities, rather than the billions who are now living there. It is grossly unfair, but after all, someone has to show them their errors and thereby enable them to reform their unwholesome ways." A breath later I had an after thought and voiced it wholeheartedly. "To be honest, though, Lovie, I am grateful that they are being so fool-hearted. It has allowed me to discover you again and One knows that this opportunity makes up for any pain we are experiencing for Earth and especially for ourselves!"

We kissed longingly and as we parted, Gail moaned sorrowfully, "Oh my One, look!" Pointing at our horses that stood far to the side of the house with their heads gloomily lowered, she said, "I think they must know that we are leaving them today."

We walked to them and they pressed their noses against our faces and stood dejectedly at our sides. "Gail, they are truly saddened because we are leaving without them and they do know it, too, don't they," I said with sorrow in my heart for them.

"Jim," she anxiously asked with her hands clapping in front of her. "I know that it isn't far to Tesa, but couldn't we please ride them to church this morning? It would be a fantastic way of saying goodbye to them and this plane we love so much."

Before I had a chance to reply to her question our mounts began to prance gaily around us. "Sure thing, Lovie," I answered, feeling happy that I could satisfy her and them by granting this simple request. At the same time, I realized it pleased me just as much to be riding them another time.

"Since we don't have far to travel, let's just ride them bareback, okay?" she begged with her hands folded again. Those words scarcely out of her mouth and Gail's favorite spotted horse fell to her knees directly in front of her. "Look, she knows what I want!" said Gail with a broad grin.

"Maybe it's you, honey, who knows what she wants," I said with a resourceful laugh of my own.

We rode toward Tesa, Gail on her mount and I on mine with a hand draped over the neck of the third horse. "Oh, Jim, remember how fun we had there?" said Gail reflectively as we rode toward the lake.

We paused to view our lake and reminisce. I inhaled the sweet fragrant perfume of the overhanging honeysuckle. "Boy, oh boy, do I remember that day when you drove me nearly crazy with lustful desires!"

"It was only a moment ago, yet we're talking as if they are aloof memories of a distant past," said Gail sadly. "I am very grateful for these wonderful memories. They are going to have to suffice until we can relive them on Earth years from now. Oh, Jim," she rhapsodized. "We are going to be tenderly recalling every moment that we have shared here, and for such a long time, too!"

My heart recoiled with the reality of her words. "Oh, my lovely wife," I moaned. "You are going to be in my every waking moment when we've returned to Earth again. I will be cherishing every email message." I bent over our mounts and kissed her voraciously.

As we approached Tesa I became aware of the sound of distant voices. When we topped the hill we were climbing, the sight below caused me to gasp aloud. "Look, Gail!" There were many thousands of people waiting for us and the sight of them reminding me of our wedding. I felt two contesting emotions: thrilled and simultaneously fearful that we would say or do something wrong. This was all so new to us that it made me ask, "Will we ever be competent enough to handle this number of people without trepidation?"

"Oh my One, I can't talk in front of all of them!" she cried. "I get petrified just talking in front of a handful of our friends. How am I ever going to handle this?" she responded without further need of answering my question.

"I'm sure," I said trying to reassure the two of us, "that they know that this is our last day here. It's most probable that most of them are attending this service only to bid us goodbye."

We dismounted and with her arms enveloping her horse, I heard Gail weeping farewells. Beating some of the dust from our trip off her pony, she said, "I love you, Dusty."

The horse, whose head was draped over her mistress's shoulder, picked up her head and looked Gail straight in the eye. With a short whinny, she said her farewell. "Jim," said Gail with amazement, "she must recognize that name. It wouldn't surprise me that during our last visit to Tesa, I had called her Dusty."

As if to prove her recognition of the name, the horse snickered again and put her nose against Gail's cheek.

Following a few more strokes of our reliable horses, I said to my trusty steed, "Okay, Buddy, take 'em straight home with you." To my absolute astonishment he did to me exactly what Dusty had done to Gail. Moving between us, the third horse whinnied his farewell. The sun shown in his eyes and I said, "Goodbye, Sunny." He pressed his nose against my cheek and moaned almost human-like. When we reached the bottom of the decline we looked back and noticed that our mounts were standing immobile and looking sadly down at us. In unison they whinnied their goodbyes as we waved to them. Taking the clue, Buddy turned and led the others off in a gallop.

As we moved closer to the mass of people waiting for us, their cheers intensified. I was dismayed to see so many disabled members among the crowd. There were handicapped citizens in wheelchairs, on stretchers, standing with the aid of crutches, carrying white canes, and many others that we were unable to classify. "Gail," I said, distraught by the visible number of handicapped people, "how can I ever heal that many individuals? Why it would take me days just to lay my hands on all of them!"

"The same way Jesus fed thousands of people with only two fishes and five loaves of bread. He believed and manifested enough to feed them all."

With a laugh I said, "You can still say that after our all-nighter?"

Standing to the left of the chapel I saw Swuel, Rama, and Marza waiting for us. Behind them I noticed an elegant garden. The colorful flowers were exquisitely adorned in every possible color of the rainbow. I remembered hearing that every plant, bush, and tree in it was watered by a lavish natural spring. This spring I saw was shooting a thin stream of water a hundred feet high into the air. It returned to the ground like a misty rainfall. Placed in a spherical position around it were gorgeously-carved, marble, naked girls. Some of them were catching water in their cupped hands and others had their arms raised and folded above them as if trying to shelter themselves from the falling water.

"He also made wine out of water, didn't he? With the power of One, I will give this geyser healing properties," I said, walking toward it.

Having endowed the spring with the healing powers of One, I felt exuberant about these events unfolding before me. I ran to a nearby man whose body was grotesquely deformed. His contorted face was shrunken into a head that was disfigured and hideous to all observers. Because of its huge size, he was unable to support it and he had to wear a thick neck brace. His arms and chest were also shrunken. His baggy pants likely concealed deformity in his lower body.

"For healing purposes, do you mind getting a little wet?" I asked him.

In reply, he made a short guttural sound and rotated his head slightly to one side, which I inferred to be his way of saying no. I then took his hand and personally helped him into the curative drizzle. His transformation was immediate and apparent to all of us. His countenance was changed, and he became handsome and all but princely. His head, arms, and chest were suddenly balanced with the rest of his body.

"Look!" people trumpeted. "By the water falling on him he is made whole!"

"He now looks as normal as we are!" other voices cried out.

"Look," cried an ancient woman whose voice was just audible above the voices of the mass of onlookers. "My son's body is now completely made whole and he is so handsome, too!"

"Mom," he said with an natural sounding voice, "come in, it'll cure your rheumatism for you!" Not only did his mother approach, but hundreds of people stampeded toward the healing spring. Beautiful plants and bushes forgotten. Crippled people in wheelchairs, on stretchers, and on crutches were taken into the falling water and were instantly cured. Everyone was soon crying with joy as they were healed of their disabling infirmities.

I found Gail in a trance and giving readings to a group of people gathered around her. I began to move in her direction, but was cut off by Rama. "Jim," he said out of breath, "you have made this geyser into a place of healing."

"No, I only asked One to assist me and He gifted these people with healing."

For many years to come people will be coming here to have their health restored," Rama finished.

Marza who had joined us, quickly added, "Look, the trampled plants are restored! We will most likely have to hold classes for interested residents of Tesa and other planes as well. This place will induce a lot more people to come here and to enroll into our training classes, which will subsequently aid our cause enormously!"

Swuel, Nick, and his spiritual guide advanced toward us. "Sorry to intrude, Marza," said Swuel who had heard her talking, "but I want to thank Jim and Gail for their intercession in regards to Nick. Following his evaluation we find him perfectly suited for our cause. In fact, he will be a great asset when he is reinstated on Earth." I shook my head and was about to tell him that no thanks were needed when he continued. "Nick here has come to me with an exciting request," he said tapping Nick's shoulder. With a genuine grin, Swuel asked, "Why don't you tell us about it, Nick?"

"Besides my journalistic skills, I've been doing a ton of research into alternative sources of power. I was hot into tapping etheric energy when my human body died from a cardiac arrest. Now that I have been cleared of my demonic greed for wealth and fame, I am ready to proceed with my incomplete work in this field. No longer will I be working for the wealth and recognition it will render me. Now my motive is to aid our quest to supply Earth with a very inexpensive and totally endless source of energy.

"Nick asked me to allow him to return to Earth in the body of a 25 to 40 year old adult," announced Swuel to the 30 or more of us who were gathered around them. "In that way, no time would be wasted waiting for him to mature. Because of the healing he has received from our eternal soul mates, he is now equipped spiritually and mentally to attend classes again. Along with dedicated members of our crusade, corrective solutions to the obstacles that face Earth's future survival will be greatly aided by his presence."

I noticed Gail raising her hand to stifle the crowd gathered around us. When everyone was quiet she spoke in a monotone voice as if from another place and time. Even her facial expression had changed noticeably. "Nick, in year 2012 you will win the Nobel award. It will be given to you for your breakthrough in alternative power. A year after that you will get another award for your research into utilizing etheric energy. Your conversion formulas were precisely calculated before your death, and if you had only lived months longer you would have had an eye-opening breakthrough. It was lucky for mankind that you hadn't lived longer. With your avaricious greed at that time, you would have charged too much to make it a viable option for humanity. On your return to Earth, terminate all other avenues of exploration. Concentrate all of your efforts into generating One's etheric energy. This zero-point energy is lovenergy. The source energy Einstein wrote about in 1917. As you correctly surmised, it is the infinite energy commonly known as gravity."

"Without it nothing would exist," said Nick softly.

Gail's hand was still raised so everyone around remained quiet. "There is a man who has been trying to pilfer your research." She hesitated for another moment then revealing his name said, "Raymond Knight was a colleague in your exploration team. As yet he hasn't succeeded in finding the method of modifying the conductivity of etheric energy, zero-point energy, and One's divine lovenergy—the energy of everything, and what holds everything together." Lastly, she said, "How you will maneuver around this dangerous man should be a serious concern. Since your death, he has replaced your name with his own on all of your vast experimentation files. He will undoubtedly feel intimidated when you begin methodically researching your past subject of study. Your only saving grace will be the new, unrecognized body you will inhabit. Nevertheless, caution is necessary, he will stop at nothing."

I could see apprehension written in Nick's eyes. He shifted his weight uneasily from one foot to another. "Ray was a good trusty friend," he said with grief. "Why would he betray me and pirate all of my research papers like this? I had nearly put my name on completed formulas. He has evidently squandered years of my exhausting work and for naught, too! I can't figure why he hasn't brought this to a victorious conclusion by now. I wonder what link he is missing?" he said more to himself than the rest of us. "Heck, a blind man could have seen that missing link!"

Nick's eyes once again resumed that unique peaceful look of inner wisdom, which had temporarily been displaced by disappointment. "I hope that I am privileged enough to meet the two of you again on Earth," he said with sincerity shining in his eyes. "My work sure would be more enjoyable and prosperous with people like you around me. We've got to see if we can somehow correlate our efforts. Now that I've got it from a good authority that my premises were correct, I know where I am to work and I won't have to waste time doing unproductive research. The whole human race owes you a great thank you for those time savers!" he said, smiling into Gail's face. "This worthy movement and I have to thank you and Jim for your unselfishness. I wouldn't be standing here with you now if you hadn't been so patient and forbearing."

Chapter 8

Homeward Bound

When Gail and I finally completed our goodbyes to many of the thousands of people scattered around Tesa, we were taken into the chapel. The interior of this tabernacle with which we were moderately acquainted had a totally different image. Now there were paintings depicting large cities in America as well as other cities on Earth and statues of familiar earthling heroes, Greek gods, and mythical beings. Even the stained glass windows had been replaced with new ones. Passing through the library section, Swuel stopped before a massive statue of Hercules. "When you are traveling from Earth in your spiritual bodies, you will enter your designated study area which is beneath this chapel. Directly underneath this particular sculpture you will find a corridor that takes you to your study area. Your names will be on the door of your individual rooms. Like I've told you, you will be in your spiritual bodies and you are not to try locating each other. You are righteous beings right now and you must shield yourselves against becoming defiled by immoral desires."

"Rama told us that we wouldn't be able to even feel one another! "So tell me how that could lead to uncontrollable acts of passion?" asked Gail with a deeply furrowed forehead.

"Believe me," said Swuel with concern. "Your eternal affiliation would cause discomfort if you were to communicate in some capacity. Your full attention has to be centered on this cause alone; anything that might distract you from your work will be detrimental. For your own peace of mind, heart, and spirit endure your separation and do nothing that could put yourselves at risk of dereliction of duty or inner peace. Also, as Jesus once told us, and I am taking the liberty of paraphrasing, 'Thinking of adultery and having lustful desires is like committing the act itself.'"

Sensing uneasiness, Gail asked, "What is it Marza?"

Rama's eyes were touching something distinctive, yet imperceptible deep inside me. Uneasy feelings overran my sensibility and I blurted out, "What is the unresolved predicament?"

The place of reverence remained silent as we anxiously awaited some kind of response from one of our masters. Having to be the arbitrator, Swuel said, "I am afraid to inform you that the two of you are going to have to be separated here and now. This will be your last moment together until you are reunited on Earth again. We know your abhorrence of this moment and we are most reluctant to separate you. Nevertheless, this occasion has risen and it is necessary for you to depart these familiar paths and enter onto your new Earthbound ones."

While my eyes were pathetically focused on Gail, I noticed that tears seeped from the mirrors of her soul. "Couldn't we have just an hour alone?" I asked, equally sharing her tormented anguish. I was more infatuated with this woman than I had thought it possible for me to experience. Shrinking into myself I realized that I was about to lose the most precious treasure of my lives. Only hours ago we had been totally enthralled with each other and now our lovemaking seemed to be light years away.

"I dislike disappointing you," said Swuel in reply to my anxious question about giving us a little more time alone, "but we've already given you an extra night to say your goodbyes. This must be the last you will see of each other until your reunion. You are now entering the final stage of your training and time is an essential that can't be expanded anymore than it has been."

Totally disregarding our companions, I enfolded Gail in a desiring embrace. "Oh, my intimate love," I whispered with fervent love in my voice, mind, and heart, "how I wish that we could be eternally united and not ever have to be secluded from one another!" My arms ached with the feel of her body in them and I desired to hold onto her forever. Putting all of my strength into it I squeezed her hard and quickly withdrew my agonizing body from hers.

"I resent goodbyes," she bravely said with tears discoursing down sallow cheeks. "One, oh my One," she remorsed. "I can't bare the thought of being without you a single day, let alone for years!" Her tears were now cascading from her eyes in torrents, portraying the truth of her words. "I can't help it," she cried with tremendous agony in her voice. "This reality of being without you is tearing me apart."

"Oh, Lovie," I said as Swuel, Rama, and Marza turned glowing green hands toward us, "how can I possibly eliminate or at least ease this emotional despair? This time is going to pass so interminably slow. I am going to be yearning for that day when I can once again gather you in my arms and love you, and this time for eternity!"

"Please hold me tighter and kiss away my pain," she said fervently. Moments later, placated by the hands of Swuel and our spiritual guides and along with my ardent kisses and desiring embrace, Gail regained her composure.

The late morning sun abruptly shifted and shown into the chapel through two colorful stained glass windows and their life-sized reflections were displayed on a vacant wall opposite them. This spectacle took away my breath and had made it impossible for me to speak. Observing my intent gaze behind her, Gail turned and gasped admirably at the portrayals revealed to all of us. "It's a sign from One," she said appreciatively.

I stood totally still and spellbound by the enormous beauty and magnitude they symbolized. One of them portrayed a man and woman who just happened to have our present appearances. They were sitting in a sailboat adrift in space and the variations of the sun gave animation to the sailboat as we watched spellbound. It seemed as if we were actually passing planets and spheres of all colors, sizes, and shapes. The light of One encircled our metaphysical forms. Everything we could now see was through His purity and perfection of spirit. "You are currently afloat in the truth of One," replied Swuel, pointing at that particular window's image. "Imminently, whether together or isolated from one another, you must remain coupled in the truth of One's uniting Love-Energy/Life-Energy/One-Energy."

The second stained glass window manifestation was filled with brown, black, and gray cocoons. Each of them exhibited brilliantly colorful butterflies in different levels of emergence. A few of them only had a portion of one wing exposed, others had all of one wing showing, and still others had nearly extricated themselves from their sheaths of ignorance. "Your old bodies and differing degrees of misconception are represented there," he said, reflectively pointing to the cocoons and the partially emerging butterflies mirrored on the wall. "The liberated, colorful butterflies signify your new birth in the enlightenment of One." He pointed out two gorgeous butterflies, which flew freely in a blue sky. "Now that you have been in the light, love, and truth of One, they portray unconstrained belief. The light of One envelops them entirely, and as long as you stay within the wholeness of His light you will be protected from any debilitating errors of perception. May you always remain in His light and love, and may His light always brighten your futures."

Silence prevailed as all of us were in awe of the wonderment and beauty of the universality of One. Marza was the first to articulate, following this period of reflection. She moved to Gail's side and conferred privately with her. Gail nodded and dutifully followed through. Turning to me, with fresh tears trickling down her cheeks and in a suppressed voice she said, "It's time for us to depart, Jim. We've got to venture onward into new avenues of thought and feelings and to undertake new objectives."

Not wanting to confound an already nonplus problem, I conceded with an affirmative nod of my head. We kissed fervently once more then I heard thunder, saw streaks of lightning, and felt a tremor as if I was experiencing an earthquake. I realized afterwards that all of these sensations occurred within my own body. I had actually created them out of my emotional turmoil. With sorrow in my heart, I wailed, "Goodbye," and a prolonged, "Gaaailllllllll." I was then physically whisked away from her and Tesa.

Still quivering throughout my body, I took shape on an altogether new plane of consciousness. "Jim," said Rama, materializing before me, "you are now on Authentis, the final phase before your soul's next evolution on Earth. This is the final plane of reckoning before rebirths on Earth. For all of you who are working in this crusade, it's a place for training, then re-emergence."

We stood in a rather ordinary looking room. There were several comfortable looking chairs, two large couches, and an antique desk with a young blonde-haired woman behind it. She wore a headphone and was occupied with listening and closely observing a monitor. As we turned toward her she abstractly tilted her head to her right and said, "In conference room H, Rama." She looked up at a clock and added, "They're in the midst of a meditation session right now, so you know what to do."

"I'll show you around later, John," he said to me rather nonchalantly.

Baffled by his use of another name, I stammered, "Huh?" Then it dawned on me that he was using my future name. Feeling awkwardly inept, I lingered affixed to my spot a moment too long.

"Are you going to stand there gaping all day? Come on, follow me." I followed him into a very long hallway with doors on either side. We rapidly maneuvered our way down it, walking mute save for the slight clicking sounds of our shoes. We passed an open room and looking in, I noticed three people in the prone position with wires attached to their heads. I was about to ask Rama the purpose for it when he replied without further explanations, "Our encephalogram room, John." Before I had the opportunity of prevailing on him for more information, we reached the end of the wing and stopped at a door marked with an H. With a slight incline of his head, a reserved smile, and two hardly perceptible taps on the door, Rama and I entered the conference room.

In a moderately-sized room I noticed a dozen overstuffed chairs, two large well-cushioned couches, and four cots. Half of this sitting area was occupied with meditating men. This comfortable room was so explicitly tranquil that a pin being dropped could have been clearly heard. Two men, who were reclining behind a desk, sedately stood and signaled silence. One of them pointed to an office-like area to his right and indicated that we should ensue him there. The soundproofed interior provided us with a locality where we could talk freely without intruding upon the silent inhabitants of the meditation room.

After we had seated ourselves in comparatively unyielding chairs and he had quietly closed the door, the gentlemen who had followed us in, candidly spoke aloud, "Welcome to you, the future John Bennett. This is the last facility you'll have to attend in your long arduous journey of enlightenment." He smiled warmly and winked conspiratorially at me. "I've heard that you have unearthed your eternal soul mate and that the two of you have made miraculous strides toward a more perfect future for yourselves and succeeding generations of earthlings. Congratulations on that and your fast attainment of Clear, your necessary step to another earthly existence." He once again smiled warmly. Then in a partially repressed voice, said, "Although this is going to be primarily a test of your emotional endurance, the mental as well as physical stresses of this last mission will clearly epitomize your fortitude and allegiance to our noble cause." His amiable style of talk had reduced the jittery sensation I was feeling in my stomach. Previous to my becoming Clear I would have been uncontrollably anxious being in an interview similar to this. Now I was comparably at peace with myself, even though this was an unfamiliar experience.

He was quiet for a long time and not receiving a response from either Rama or me, he eventually resumed, "I'm sorry, but I purposefully declined to introduce myself until now. I don't quite know how to convey this to you, but I do have to prelude my introduction with a warning." Now he really had my full attention. I puzzled over the extent or necessity of his warning. I had already lost the love of my life and wondered what other mishap could befall me now. "John," he began after another short pause, "as you know, we are all reincarnates of the human race." Even though I was suddenly aware of some disquiet in his voice, I remained silent. "John," he started indecisively, "this laborious task—" He tried once more. "As difficult as it is, I've got to inform you . . ." Some undesired stress started to show itself in my stomach as I began to feel an unwanted apprehension about this man. However, I wasn't prepared for the bomb that he was about to drop. "John," he feebly started again, "my name is Neil Rios-nino." Vigorously nodding his head up and down, he conveyed an unbelievable truth to me. "But you knew me better as Daddy. It was previous to your last lifetime."

Wanting to refrain myself from shrieking my revulsion aloud, I instinctively clasped my hand over my mouth. When I had finally repossessed my composure enough, I more evenly asked, "How could you possibly have done that to mom and me?"

He curiously smiled and said, "I assure you that it was the only option I had, Jose."

Feeling my past emotions broiling within me because of all of the pain he had caused my mother and me by his selfish actions, I wanted to reproach him for his deed. The first thing that stopped me was his using my childhood name during that period; he had somehow brought the two of us closer. This man who had caused mom and me so much sorrow and so many difficulties was now confronting me with fresh felt grief. Rama's strong hand and gentle words halted my heartfelt reaction, "Give Neil an opportunity to explain his reasons," he advised.

"Believe me, John," he said in a dejected manner, "there was no other recourse that I could take. I had a terminal disease and its prescribed therapy would have devoured all of our savings and put you and your mother in irretrievable debt. Despite its spiritual reduction along with the emotional pain that I knew it would mean for you both, I felt that it was my only option. I'm sorry, but back then I wanted you and your mother to have the financial benefit that I had worked so diligently to give you—"

This man before me had been my beloved dad, had committed suicide to provide for mom and me, and was now facing me with the truth. Without further contemplation, I pulled away from Rama and reached out to the father I had hardly known. We embraced and slapped each other's shoulders fondly.

What I had been aching inwardly suddenly poured out. "My daddy, why did you have to leave me so early? Oh how I missed all the fun we used to have! Mom was always good to me, but you know girls can't play ball right. Oh, my daddy! I missed and cried for you for weeks after you vanished from our lives."

Then holding me out at arms-length, Neil said, "I am so grateful to One for giving me the opportunity to apologize to you, for allowing me to feel, and for you to release your feelings like this. My cherished son, Jose! I am so proud of you and your steadfast spiritual growth. I am honored to be assisting you in procuring this next fulfilling step in your life. It is an immense tribute to your achievements and enlightenment that you have been accepted into this crusade and now reached Clear so quickly."

With a slight nod of our respected achievements, I said, "Father-like son!"

Following a short burst of relieving laughter, Neil and I talked about that former life as if in present times rather than past. It seemed as if it were only a few years ago that I had lost him. Closing my eyes, I could see him, my mother, and I fishing in a nearby pond. I even sensed the sentiment and significance of the period. "Do you remember when you caught your first big trout in Indian Pond?" he asked enthusiastically. "You talked about him for days, giving him a name and all. Smokey Joe you had called him."

We talked for another 20 minutes about our shared experiences. I was pleased that he honored my undeniably strong longing to call him dad. He seemed to enjoy hearing it and I freely used it. I suddenly tuned into what he was saying about my then mother. "My love for you and your mom were enormous, Jose. An agonizing and uncontrollably horrendous disease was torturing my mind, body, heart, and spirit. During the last six weeks of my life my doctors were constantly telling me that I should immediately be having that costly operation. Nevertheless, I was planning for—"

"Dad," I cried, getting to my feet again, "but you may have been cured if you had only—"

"No, my son," he said irrefutably. "There was no chance of recovering from colon and abdominal cancer back then. All they could have done was to keep removing the new growth. Two or three times a year I'd have to undergo that overpriced procedure. It would have stopped only when life finally decided to relinquish its hold on me or when our cash reserves ran out. Neither of these alternatives were permissible to me, especially the latter!"

Then he raised his hand and as if he hadn't digressed, he resumed, "Like I've said, I am enormously proud of your excellence and impressive spiritual augmentation, John. You and your eternal soul mate have clearly demonstrated your dedication to our cause. Your own power of will shows us what you both are capable of performing in your shared futures. We are grateful for your assistance in helping us gain this moral duty, which we have all taken upon ourselves." Clearing his throat, he added, "We've already gotten living proof of your value and can't wait to see your achievements in your coming life as John and Lillian Bennett."

"You're awake and sleep brain-waves must be calibrated today. This recording is necessary merely so that we know the differences of your brain fluctuations. Tomorrow begins your submersion training. In no more than three days it will be required that you are not only familiarized with the technique of mental immersion, but are prepared to commence." Taking a deep breath, he resumed. "You will become an eminent component in your future name sake's life. Once you have become an implant in his mind, you will sense everything he feels and does. You will have instantaneous and total access to all of his memories."

At that point I had to interrupt his dialogue. "Excuse me, but I can't believe what you are saying. Are you actually telling me, Neil, that I am going to be inside his head in only three days?"

"If simplification is essential, John, you will legitimately be inside his brain and part of his conscious and subconscious minds. In rudimentary terms, for many hours a day you will be feeling, smelling, tasting, hearing, seeing, and thinking everything your host does. You will even experience his most intimate behavior and thought processes. What could be even more stressful for you, though, is what others might do to the real John. Remember, not even in extreme situations are you to react in the slightest way. No circumstances will allow you to run interference in his life."

Noticing the astonishment on my face, Rama cleared his throat and said, "That's the real purpose of my asking Marza to tell you her story about her abusive father when she was existing in Jennifer."

"Rally?"

Rama nodded and fervently looking into my eyes, said, "In your vernacular, you are to be only an eavesdropper. Even if you were to witness his father doing something malicious to him, you are not to intervene. Marza was far more spiritually advanced when she had that encounter with Jenny's father. Besides she had already totally replaced Jennifer."

"For now, you are only to witness John's life as if it were a movie."

Not responding further to Rama's input, I asked, "What will I derive from this? What purpose can my being a part of him like this attain?"

Neil smiled at me and I recognized cunningness in his eyes that I hadn't taken notice of previously. "Good question, John. At the end of his existence, you must have already acquired all of John's memories. To accomplish this, you must become an intrinsic observer of his life. You've got to be an eyewitness to as many events as possible occurring in his waking hours. You will also more efficiently learn how to open his memory banks so that during his sleeping time you can observe his past and familiarize yourself with people and events that have taken place throughout his life."

"You're giving a whole new meaning to eavesdropping," I said with a smile. After the three of us had finished giggling, I asked, "But won't I have any power—"

Rama and Neil jumped to their feet and Neil was the first to speak, "No, John! Like I told you, you are not to have any authority over him or anyone else in his life. You cannot assert yourself in any fashion." After saying this, the two men sat heavily in their respective chairs. "He is not to be the least bit aware of your presence."

Rama looked passionately into my eyes and said, "Like I've told you, you are to be only a spectator. Even if you were molested while in him, you are not to intervene. Keeping your feelings out of him, only watch, listen, and view what is going on."

"How can I continuously restrain myself? If his conduct or someone he is familiar with disgusts me, how do I inhibit my natural feelings of repulsion?" I asked, feeling a bit anxious about my ability of not responding in a desperate predicament.

Neil held up four fingers and lowering each in turn, replied, "In simple words, John, meditation, control, willpower, and remembering that all of his feelings and experiences are only illusionary for you. Don't let that agitate you now. During this training phase, you will be learning special stress reduction techniques. Besides," he said congenially, "while absent from your body, your brain waves are constantly monitored. The minute you show any unbearable distress you will be separated from the cause of irritation. We realize since his father has sexually violated John, that we are going to need to keep an especially vigilant eye on you."

"That's relieving to know," I said half aloud and half to myself. "I had thought after achieving Clear that I'd be forever free of feeling any stress whatsoever."

"Sorry to disillusion you, John," said Neil compassionately. "Only when reaching USC, Universal One Clear, also known as GC for God Consciousness, will you be absolutely free of being victimized by troublesome stresses. Rationally, though, you could more quickly obtain tangible tranquility if you remained in an even-tempered atmosphere. As you can imagine, moving back onto Earth will generate a different parable. It will, in fact, cause you to lose your temporary Clear. Months, perhaps even years will have to pass before you will obtain your present level of serenity again. As you now realize, anxiety, tension, and stress are undeviating elements of human existences. In spite of these unremitting issues, when you again acquire Clear your life will be free of overwhelming pressures and obtaining USC should be quite easy for you. In the meanwhile, we want you to know that thanks to your being clear, whatever problems may arise, no matter how severe the crisis, you will never collapse or have a mental breakdown."

After checking the time, he said, "In two minutes the intermediaries outside this office will be completing their prescribed meditation apportionment. When they are stirring around, you and Rama will be escorted to the EEG, electroencephalogram, room for a complete brainwave analysis of you while you're awake, asleep, and under stress ." He paused for a deep breath, and then asked, "Do you have any other unresolved questions or problems that are still bothering you, John? This is the moment to get them resolved if you are still feeling any uncertainties."

"Only one, Neil," I reluctantly replied. "Will I be residing within him for long periods of time?"

"You do have to thoroughly memorize the names of his friends, schoolmates, and family. You also have to acquaint yourself with various facts, learn the area sufficiently, and know millions of odd bits and pieces of his life. You will be in your astral body, which means that some of this probing will be done during his sleeping hours as you already know. Because he is moderately retarded, his memories might be reduced, but we don't know to what degree."

Rama said, "After you disclosed his name, we checked in Tesa for time of birth and death, and you've got a bit more than six days."

"Less than a week? And I've got to witness his killing himself?"

"Yes, John, you do."

I began to notice dreadful feelings of apprehension creeping into every aching bone in my body. "I've got only days? When I've taken over for him, can't we blame any lack of memory on his retardation?"

"Imagination is far more powerful than you know, and what you focus on you create. Imagine that you are happy/sad, angry/loving, forgetful/mindful, or what-have-you. You will manifest those things in your life. You shouldn't ever limit your knowledge or abilities in any manner!" After taking a sip of water, he offered, "He will most likely be entirely brain-dead when you take over. So as soon as you enter, jumpstart his heart and immediately begin healing his brain and body."

Rama spoke with a grimace wrinkling his brow. He gazed straight into my eyes and asked, "Why are you allowing confusion to fog your perceptions, John? This is not the same you who I've grown to know and love over the past few months. You are creating these conflicts in your present life; expel them now and don't allow them to manifest again. Know in your heart that this rebirth is going to be a simple procedure, and don't impede progress with negative thoughts. Don't oppose this simple transformation with negativity. Acknowledge your fears to yourself and you create them if too often repeated. You know better than most that what you focus on you create!"

"Now, John," said Neil after my EEG, "listen to this and do just as it advises. Do not deviate from it whatsoever, nor allow yourself to be immersed into his life just yet," he said, handing me an mp3 player. "There is a very fine line between being yourself and John. Therefore, be aware of your thoughts and body at all times so that you won't go beyond that point. This is going to be your meditation room for listening and learning how to immerse yourself into John's life," he said, indicating a small well-lit and ventilated area adjacent to the conference room. "You have 24 hours to learn this particular technique and after you have accomplished it, we will move you to the EEG room for the next phase. Only when you have engulfed yourself into him and his life, learned most of his acquaintances, and even his deepest secrets, will you be prepared to replace him."

Although I had thought about my next question several times, I hadn't asked until now. "How will you know that he will need to be replaced and when it is to take place?"

"Birth and death records of every soul are kept in Tesa." Because of your rapid expansion of spirit and viewing of your futures, you and Gail have personally shown us who you are to supplant. This knowledge allowed us to quickly uncover details of their birth and death. Generally, this maneuver means months of inadvertent research for a special team. Since you have disclosed this information we were able to skip that step, which allowed you to spend more time together in Tesa. Time is an essential issue that we can't prolong. "

"We had your, Jim's, previous personal birth and death dates stored in the record book at Tesa. So once we had concluded that you would be joining us, we had to prepare the person who would be succeeding you. Not having the facts of your death too far in advance meant that he was less suitably equipped to replace you. This hindrance caused him not to heal his brain, which was damaged slightly from the car accident that killed you. This damage made him partially numb and explained why he was so suddenly unable to read Braille."

I wanted to ask him more about this spirit who had been an indistinct part of me for a time before my leaving, but his next disclosure drove that thought from my mind. Pausing only a second, he looked me in the eye and revealed, "In four nights, John will succumb to the mounting pressures. On June 11th, we will remove you from his body the moment you begin showing abnormal agitation. Awaiting the point of his spiritual evacuation, you will immerse yourself into his body. You will then ensue, becoming a new and better John Bennett."

After learning the emersion technique, the following days were experienced in John, an expanding version of my new self. I found that my recurrent transporting between Earth and the deceptive time of where my metaphysical body resided caused an absence of time and space awareness. Despite a precarious and stormy beginning, my slow progress into this separate person's life went rather smoothly and I was happy as were my teachers.

Only an hour after my first impressions of his world, his father came into the room. I was immediately taken from the scene when I realized his father's malicious intent.

"What's wrong, John?" asked an anxious Rama that first time. "Your EEG just went off the chart! You've only been in him for 90 minutes, what could be wrong?"

"Sorry, Rama," I said, still feeling a little shaky from my first encounter with John's father. "His dad turned out to be a barbarous schoolmate of mine. I guess that I overreacted when faced with that fact, and then the realization of what he was planning on doing to me . . . um, John . . . hit me."

Days later Rama remotely called my name. "John, time has nearly arrived. Things ought to be happening any minute now. You are going to be re-experiencing life as a human again."

Two minutes later the recognition of John's intent brought me into a panic. I knew this was the hour. He had opened the door leading from his bedroom and listened closely. The house was quiet; only the sound of a TV downstairs and the whispering whir of his mother's sewing machine from the closed den across from where he stood could be heard. He tiptoed into his parent's bedroom and went into his father's top dresser drawer. There his hand fell onto his father's revolver and he extracted it with a victorious feeling deep within his heart and mind. At this juncture I became too agitated and was removed from his body and brought into the EEG room. In the growing distance I heard his voice fade as he whispered, "Oh dad, how I wish I could use this on you-oooo!"

Rama, who I had rarely seen in recent times, was instantaneously at my side. "John," he murmured, "it is time for your rebirth on Earth!"

"He has gotten his father's gun!"

"This is where your metaphysical body becomes human again," he jubilantly told me. "One week from tonight I will meet with you in your learning room beneath the Herculean statue. Immediately on entering his body, bring the healing light of One into every cell of your quickly expanding brain. Being the great healer of your future, start healing yourself as soon as you enter him," he said with a pat on my back and a winning smile, which warmed my heart. "We have been expecting and training you for this very moment. Now let's get down there and supplant him immediately as his spirit leaves him."

"Remember that he will have more serious brain damage from this suicide attempt, so demand total healing as soon as possible. Because of your efforts, do expect total healing. The body you are substituting will have some tardiness so you've got to be extra diligent and do it continuously until you are totally healed. In the beginning you will be a very alive spirit in a basically dead body. Like you've been told, you have to consciously make your heart beat, lungs breath, and brain cells reproduce."

After we had hugged one another appreciatively, Rama and I headed for Earth. We reached John's bedroom just moments before he pulled the trigger. "I'm sorry, Mommy," he screamed as loud as possible. He placed the barrel of the gun between his eyes and prayed fervently, "Forgive me, God, but he won't stop unless—" The explosion produced a marble-sized hole in the front of his skull and a much larger one in the back. I heard his mother's startled scream coming from the den, and seconds later John made a prolonged exhaling noise. His spirit ascended perpendicularly from his body and vanished from view.

Rama said. "Now, John!" and I instantaneously assumed his departing spirit's place. My ethereal body merged and became him. As if from miles away, I intuitively heard Rama say, "Don't forget to jumpstart your heart and start breathing." Begin your healing immediately and don't stop until you have totally recovered."

Through his partially closed eyes, I saw his . . . my mother run fearfully into my newly acquired bedroom, and on seeing me she screamed a prolonged, "Johhhn!" and collapsed unconsciously to the floor.

I found it very difficult to induce heartbeat, but finally got the body's necessary organ pumping again. At first I feared that I was going to be unable to revive him and fail the cause that I had worked so diligently for. The thought of my waiting eternal soul mate divorced that concept from my mind and I concentrated fully on healing myself with my heart being the first focal point. My body was still blue from a lack of oxygen when I heard my father running up the stairs—two or three at a time.

When he saw his wife lying in the doorway, he bellowed at my still slightly blue body, "You S.O.B! What have you done now?" He gave me the finger. After seeing the hole in my head, he quickly went into his room where he called 911. He returned to my room after leaving our street address with the operator and stepped over his prostrate wife. "You misbegotten bastard, I hope you rot in hell," he angrily proclaimed after spitting in my paralyzed frozen face. I could hear him searching through my namesake's papers on the small office desk where John had often done his homework. "Good," he grunted a minute later. "I don't see any suicide notes. After all, we don't need some nosy ass cop sticking his nose into our private affairs anymore than they will be doing now." Never looking at me again, he backed out of the room stepping over my still prone mother and went downstairs to await the police and ambulance.

I tried for the longest time to wipe his spit from my face, but was totally unable to move a single muscle and finally gave up, concentrating all efforts on healing my brain.

"When I first saw this boy in emergency," reported the doctor an hour later, "I thought for sure he would expire within minutes. To be completely frank with you, I don't know what is keeping his body alive. This is highly abnormal; there is so much brain damage . . ." His voice faded away to nothing. "However," he said a moment later with surprise, "by some grace of God he is hanging in there." Viewing the MRI and X-rays that were just taken, he said, "I can see that he has lost a massive portion of his brain matter. If he somehow manages to live . . . well, I honestly can't make an optimistic prognosis. I have to be frank; if he does survive I'm afraid that he is only going to be a vegetable. Most likely he will be living on a respirator and dependent on artificial life support mechanisms until his body has defeated his exceptional powers of will and allows him to die."

My mother, with her hands clasped in front of her, cried, "You've got to do everything you can to save him!" Then with tears running down her cheeks and her voice coming out hoarsely, she said, "I won't hear anymore of this negative talk!"

"Face it, babe, he's as good as dead," declared my father almost optimistically. Turning to the doctor, he demanded, "In any regard, we don't want him living on those damn machines. Remove them now."

"No," cried mom in a strong voice.

Ignoring this anxious man who considered himself my father, the doctor shook his head and less dubiously said, "At this point I presume nothing. He is only at a very high risk of dying. Right now, Mr. and Mrs. Bennett, I recommend that you leave him be. He might never regain consciousness again, yet God only knows. In any regard, you are enormously stressed, and I will not remove him from these life support machines without both of you approving that final step.

I was fully cognizant of everything around me, even seeing through inner eyes some call astral. I found myself suspended in an unmoving concrete-like shell. I wasn't even adequately able to breathe on my own; I was grateful that a nearby respirator was aiding me with this bodily function. I was totally paralyzed from head to toe. Since entering his body I had been working on keeping his lungs functioning and reproducing new brain cells. It seemed to me that my healing powers were defective; my body just wasn't cooperating as I desired. I scolded myself for thinking negatively, knowing full well that what I believed in would inevitably come true. *Therefore*, I imparted, *I assume perfect health!* From that moment on I concentrated all of my efforts and thoughts on reconstructing my brain to utter perfection. *I am one with One and in no way can He be impaired*, I kept repeating to myself while focusing on healing my injured brain.

My parents signed papers for an exploratory operation. When the doctor spoke to them afterwards, his prognosis was glum and disheartening. "Unfortunately the damage to his brain is as extensive as it had appeared on the MRI."

He smiled slightly and reported, "Now for a bit of good news. His EEG taken last night was totally flat, but today it is showing activity. This indicates that his brain is trying to mend itself. Although in truth, there isn't that much that it can do on its own, and God knows there is nothing we can do to help him. Nevertheless, this boy is showing enormous powers of will and I wouldn't put him down for the count just yet." With a catch in his throat, he said, "That bullet has destroyed any chance of him having usable sight or mental ability. There isn't any way that we can repair his brain damage to any degree necessary for his prognosis to be more promising. We all concur that he won't even be able to return home with you. He most likely will have to remain bedridden for the balance of his life," he proclaimed, shaking his head regrettably.

"Why the hell allow him to live like this," questioned my father. "Disconnect this apparatus, we've got to let him go!"

"No, I won't permit you to do that to our son," cried my mother. "We've got to give him every opportunity to live. He is diligently fighting and we won't give up on him like that!"

Without a word, my heartless dad walked over and pulled the power cord to the respirator. I gasped and was pleased to find that I was now breathing without having to depend on a machine to do this vital function for me. Inasmuch as I was now breathing on my own, I really didn't know if my body could produce sound yet. I only knew that I desired to scream, "You would like me dead wouldn't you, Dad? That way I couldn't squeal on you and inform mom and authorities about what you've been doing to me for so many years."

"He's breathing!" exclaimed mom triumphantly, quickly followed by the doctor.

What this same surprised doctor had defined a minute before assaulted me next and I thought to myself, *No, I am not going to be blind in this lifetime, too. I will be totally functional and even better than what normal is considered to be. This cause is far too great for me to be hampered in any fashion. I am the perfection and strength of One and he and I are one, and He is flawlessly whole.*

I doubled my healing efforts, putting my full energy into my total recuperation. It actually created feelings of ecstasy in my mind, heart, and body. "I know that I am going to be absolutely normal again," I inwardly asserted.

Throughout the night in the ICU, my mother sat at my side muttering prayers for my recovery. Desiring to give her hope and to also test my healing powers, I purposefully focused on whispering, "Mommy, I'm sorry." I was extremely happy when those same words actually escaped my lips. She jumped up screaming for the doctor.

After he had given me a superficial examination, which included examining the EEG printout and showing undetectable lights into my eyes, a stand-in doctor proclaimed, "His brain activity has improved remarkably. He might even regain consciousness, perhaps even as soon as morning. To prevent his body from waking too soon and putting more pressure on his brain, I am going to prescribe medication that will put him into a drug induced coma."

"No, please," begged my joyous mother. "I want you to let him alone. We can't hamper his healing spirit!"

"I've got to warn you, though," he said calmly, "I have no idea of what his mental capacity is going to be. Because of the brain damage, there are overwhelming probabilities of severe paralysis and cognitive limitations. Right now there are no fluctuations in the pupils of either eye, which tells me that he is blind, as we surmised from the MRI and surgery." After my mother had moaned aloud, he added, "When we had first examined his X-rays, we strongly doubted that he would even survive for a few hours. He has proven us wrong thus far; let's hope that he will continue doing it again. Your son is showing enormous corrective powers of healing. Like you desire, I'm not going to hamper his powers." We had honestly thought that you would never hear John articulate again," he said hoarsely

He was studying the EEG and absent-mindedly said, "This clearly demonstrates his strong curative powers." This may sound odd coming from a doctor, but I wouldn't put any limitations on his ability to cure himself. For his EEG to be improved to this extent, he's got to be miraculously generating millions of new brain cells! Hell," he said, awed by what he was seeing. "At this rate, this boy might even produce new optic nerves!" and a gaffer escaped his lips.

Like the previous hours, I focused on the now and didn't allow myself to sleep a minute. Achieving total healing was my objective. I ceaselessly focused blue revitalizing light in my two eyes and head. I repeatedly felt my brain producing millions of new cells.

Right on cue, two nights later, when my mother had returned to my side from the facility room, I tried to speak again. "Is this heaven or hell?"

"No! No, you're very much alive, Johnny," said my very excited mother. "You're in the hospital ICU ward."

Speaking as if I were far away, I said, "I'm sorry, Mommy." A moment later, I asked, "Water. May I please have some water Mommy?"

I waited a moment then whispered a tad louder, "Mommy?"

"Yes, I'm getting the doctors!" she said from a ways off.

"I'm extremely thirsty, Mommy. I need some water please." I turned my head from side to side while she was away from my bed. To my rejoicing heart

I noticed normal movement in my neck and a slight glimmer of light in both of my eyes.

By late afternoon that very day, I was seeing shadows and was able to move every desired part of my body. After the doctor had discovered normal movement in my body and two optic nerves, he told us with great surprise in his voice, "I've seen remarkable and rapid recoveries during my practice, but never as swift nor as revitalizing as this one! To be completely forthright," he told me, "like I told your parents only days ago, John, I expected you to be living in a vegetative state and to be totally blind for the rest of your life—at very best. Not only are you seeing, but you have no paralysis or striking advancement in your retardation, and that's utterly astonishing to me and our staff." Putting his attention on my mom as well as me, he said, "I am so glad that your son has proven all of us so indisputably wrong."

"God has been kind to us, John," Mom said, looking my father straight in the eye. Then looking more lovingly at me, she smiled joyfully. "I don't mean to rush your procedures, but when do you think it will be safe for us to take our son home?" she asked the doctor, emphasizing the word "our".

With a far-off look in his eyes, my still utterly stunned doctor said, "Why, I suspect that it will be safe for you to take him home in a few days. First, though, he needs a thorough neurological examination. We need to test his motor, visual, and mental faculties to determine at what capacity he will be able to function normally. We will remove him from ICU right away and put him into a room in our neurological wing. We will get those tests started immediately on his arrival. Also, I'll get our best PT people getting him started on a stringent Physical Therapy workup. Then work on areas that are showing slower, weaker, or needed assistance."

To my chagrin I noticed some slow response time during the tests. It showed both in my mental and motor skills. I fervently prayed that this didn't mean permanent mental or physical disabilities, although my only true stumbling block came when I was asked the date. I had actually lost track of time. Being totally indecisive, I muttered, "Hmm . . . sorry, but being that I was catatonic for a time, I don't know the exact date. The date of my suicide attempt was June 11th, if that will suffice." Then I realized that I had conversed with them intellectually instead of the simpleton that I should have been portraying. "I've got to be more cautious when talking with others like this," I warned myself.

"The correct date is June 15th," said the examining neurologist while jotting a note on my chart.

"Four days later, that's all, huh?"

Except for that one negligible time ebb and a very slight reflex slowdown, my body functioned quite well and I was pleased. I could also see my two doctor's amazement as the tests progressed. "You're correct, Graham," decreed the neurologist to my medical doctor. "This is an amazing case. The magnitude of that injury should have killed him. If he had managed to stay alive, like you, I would have expected him to be a living vegetable at best. For him to have almost normal reflexes, an IQ of an intelligent boy, virtually a photographic memory and total recall, a hardly discernible tardiness in his dexterity, and 20/20 vision is an outright miraculous feat!"

Agreeing, my medical doctor said, "We've got to record this enormous feat of healing! He's got to have the strongest inner healing powers of any person alive!" Scratching his head, he declared with surprise, "He has actually grown new optic nerves, produced a new pituitary gland, and billions and billions of brain cells!" Turning to me, he said, "John, you should see if you can apply some of your healing powers to others. I've got a lot of needy patients I'd like you to work on. Just let me know when you can get started."

"I've got army men with injuries less severe than yours who are totally disabled; they need you, too!" announced the other doctor.

> Note to reader:
> At this writing, I am wishing that I had immediately taken Dr. Thomas up on his offer. It would have likely changed events enormously. However, it is likely that I would not have run away, met the professor, gone to college, etc. One only knows the outcome of drastic changes like that.

The next afternoon I was discharged with only these instructions, "For the coming days don't exert yourself too much. Your body has been under enormous stress so eat, sleep, and drink as much as your body desires. I will see you in two weeks to remove those stitches in your head, although, they appear to be minimal now. Until that visit, I don't want you to even go to school; you don't need that extra strain. Your body has gone through an extraordinary transition so I want you to call me if any peculiar sensations or symptoms should arise," he instructed Mom and me.

I smiled to myself while thinking, "Doctor, you wouldn't believe how much my body has altered. You might even say that I am a whole new person!"

"There is one more delicate subject you have to understand," he said with a worried frown. "Because you attempted to take your life you must come here twice weekly to the Mental Health Clinic. Your first appointment is with Dr. Rafique, who is a fine psychiatrist. Have your mother and father with you Monday morning at 9:30. I believe that Dr. Rafique will want to talk first with your parents, then with the three of you, and finally with you privately for the remainder of that time period."

John had been an introvert, which I found to be difficult to parrot. Because he had attempted suicide, I was not left entirely alone. As a result, I got to know my parents even faster and more thoroughly than previously expected. During the initial weeks of close observation, I had found John's mother to be a very patient and caring person. Living as John now, I had wanted to inform her of my molesting dad, but wanting to shield her from that perplexing truth, I resisted. I didn't want her to misconstrue my words or to disbelieve me, so I sat on that knowledge for the time being. Also, there was a selfish reason for my silence; because I needed her alliance so imperatively and was concerned about breaking it, I didn't broach that topic with her. If he dared to do something to me, I would go to my mother immediately and then to the hospital, if necessary, to prove molestation. If absolutely essential, I would even go to court with the evidence.

Other than following my doctor's orders to eat, drink, and sleep as much as my body required, my day was filled with reading newspapers, magazines, and books. I had an insatiable drive to catch up with the past and also to learn everything possible. I was going to be a doctor as well as a minister of some sorts; Gaining knowledge became a significant part of my present life.

Four days after my discharge, Mom was out filling my reading needs in the local library. Having rested more than I liked, I decided to sit down at the piano and play some of my favorite compositions. I wondered how my new body would act for me, being that John had disliked playing the piano. Since this new body of mine hadn't ever really played, I had doubts that I would physically be able to play any of my old pieces. I had just gotten into the Moonlight Sonata when my mother made a surprise return. "Johnny," she said, startling me because I hadn't heard her approach. "Since when do you play like that? You had hardly ever touched that piano. How'd you ever get that talented? You weren't gifted either, but where else could this evident skill come from? You never allowed us to give you lessons so how on Earth did you ever accomplish your capacity for playing like that?"

I simulated a trance and replied as if in a daze, "I didn't know I could. It's just automatically coming out of me, Mom. I think of something that I would like to play and boom, just like that, I'm playing it!"

"Since when do you like classical music?" she shrewdly asked.

Luckily for me, resting on the piano directly in front of me was a large book of classical music. I remembered her playing this particular piece one night while I was a bystander in John. "I was just looking through that book, Mom. You played this piece only weeks ago," I said, pointing at the book in front of me. "I was bored and decided that I'd try playing something. I always admired how superbly you'd render everything within its covers." With an afterthought, I asked, "You perform so magnificently, why hadn't you become a classical pianist, Mom?"

"I told you that your dad came along while I studied in Julliard and we fell madly in love. My pregnancy was unexpected, and I decided to give up my dreams of becoming an accomplished pianist so that I could put all of my efforts into raising and loving you." Smiling sagaciously into my eyes, she turned the pages of the music book and paused when she had found her desired selection. Pointing at Chopin's Revolutionary, she said, "Johnny, this is my favorite piece and I really couldn't do it justice unless I were to practice it daily for weeks. Oh Johnny, will you please play it for me?"

Although I had tried to get it during my just past life, this fabulous piece had never been put into Braille music. I wondered what I was going to do and then I recalled Rama telling me that after I had reached Clear, I could call on the best musicians and composers to play via my body. "Mom, please close the book, and give me a second. I've got to get into a trance again," I said, no longer puzzling about how to solve this predicament that I had gotten myself into. With my eyes gently closed, I asked Chopin to enter and to play his outstanding piece through my body. A few seconds later, I raised my amateur hands to the piano and played his masterpiece perfectly. It actually gave me chills to hear it flowing out of me onto the piano.

"Oh my God," cried Mom with tears streaming down her cheeks, "I had never heard it executed that splendidly!" It was absolutely flawless, too, I'm sure."

"Well, Mom," I said with verified feelings, my eyes shut and tears dripping. "It had to be exact, after all, Chopin himself performed it for the both of us."

Two days later, I sat in the visitor's sitting room, waiting for my parents who were talking with my psychiatrist. "I've, as you know, just talked with your parents," said Dr. Rafique after coming out of his office for me. "The three of us will now discuss troublesome areas of your more perplexing life. You have become a different person since you attempted suicide. Your mother is puzzled about you," he said after we had taken our seats. "She says that it seems like there is a different person in your body since that drastic moment. Your neurologist wrote a comment in your chart that we can't ignore. 'Since this boy isn't displaying any of his previous retardation symptoms, I've got to wonder curiously if another being had replaced him?' John, can you account for these changes of your personality and abilities? She has heard you play the piano, telling your dad and me that you render classical pieces like a professional lifetime musician. She told me that you played some of the most complex pieces without ever even looking once at the music, not that it would help since you can only read the names of the pieces."

"I couldn't read music if I tried," I told him frankly. "The only suggestion I can offer is maybe it's me giving up my old self. After all, my old brain had been blown out of me Doc, and somehow I created another in place of it. Although I don't understand what she's alluding to really, I am not perceiving anything unconventional about myself other than an obvious intellectual enhancement," I replied with bewilderment in my voice.

"Your using words like 'alluding', 'perceiving', and 'unconventional' are thoroughly unlike your old manner of speech," Mom promptly announced.

With a sly grin, doctor Rafique said, "Your medical records and parents told me that you had been excuse the expression if it discomforts you, but slightly retarded previously. Since you've gotten home your vocabulary has vastly improved, you now have great musical abilities where formally you could scarcely play 'Mary Had A Little Lamb.' Your mother also told me that you suddenly have a veracious appetite for reading, and that you hated all kinds of literature before your suicidal attempt. Your dad even told me that he has been shooting baskets with you and watching you shoot them more accurately than the old you who didn't show any interest in any sports previously. The old you was not very good at sports and really didn't make any effort to practice. Now he sees you shooting baskets daily, how do you explain these variations in your mental acuity and improved physical abilities?"

I sat baffled for a minute trying to come up with a plausible answer that all of them would buy. Finally I fixed on my stratagem and opened all barriers to gaining a dazzling future for myself. Looking my parents and Dr. Rafique in the eyes I said, "I don't want any of you to get the wrong idea or to think me mad, but seconds after I had shot myself I exited my body. After moving through a long dark tunnel I spent an interval in what we regard as heaven. While there I received total healing from an angelic appearing person. He told me that I'd be a spiritual master and a medical doctor in my future. He also informed me that I'd have an omnipotent craving for reading all kinds of literature; especially mind expanding, spiritual enlightening and medical publications. Also he told me that since I had desired to be able to play music, that I could request spirits of the most renowned composers and musicians to play through me. He was right too wasn't he mom?" Still looking my mother in the eyes as she nodded affirmatively I told her, "After years of listening to you play the piano so sensationally, I desired that gift. Well now, thanks to that angel and his healing gifts, all of my desires will be fulfilled. I am no longer illiterate, disabled by mental restrictions or past ineptitudes. The world is an open oyster to me, and its pearl is mine to claim as my own. I am presently who I desire to be, and my future is an unrestricted pearl of belief. I was instructed that all I need to do is believe, and it will inevitably be mine."

"You, a doctor or a church minister? What the hell kind of church are we talking anyhow? You're not talking about being a priest . . . and you a scholar . . ." said my dad sarcastically. "Now that's a real laugh! God help your students, patients and parishioners!"

I noticed Dr. Rafique shaking his head and waited for him to speak. "John, do you really expect us to believe these prevarications?" he asked me with another shake of his head.

Shaking my own head I smugly said, "Well Doctor Rafique, mom and dad, I guess I've been found out. The plain and simple truth of the matter is, although everything is an illusion, that I sold my soul to the devil!" I jumped to my feet and in a raspy voice and a wry toothy smile I screeched, "And now he's mine for eternity!"

"Oh Johnny, what am I going to do with you?" asked my mother who was broadly smiling.

"Mr. and Mrs. Bennett," asked my doctor, "would you please leave so that John and I can speak privately?" With only a smile at me and a nod to Dr. Rafique from mom, my parents stood and exited.

"Suppose we really get down to the truth about this?" he asked me after my parents had left closing the door behind them. "How do you explain these enormous dissimilarities between you of the present and your past?"

Acting like a smart-aleck I impudently answered, "Well Doc, if you had asked my mother what was the first book that I had requested her to get for me, she'd tell you that it was 'Out-of-Body Experiences.' Now you tell me why I would want to read that book first, especially if I hadn't had that eccentric episode outside my body?"

"So you still insist that you really had an out of body experience?" he asked me with an unfeigned grin of intrigue. He gave me only time to nod my head yes and then spoke again." No doubt you and I could discuss that for the rest of the hour. First, though, we've got to confront your reason for your suicidal attempt."

I shrank back into the chair and wondered, *Is this the Pandora's Box opening for me? Is it already the right time for me to tell all? Should I talk about these molestations of this new body that I was now inhibiting? John's father had to pay for his cruelty to his son, but was this the right time and place?*

The End

Appendix

Applying the Lovenergy Technique

There is nothing that you have to do. What I am writing now comes from my heart. In the next few paragraphs I will give you the truths that will transform your lives and all of your undesired living conditions.

You need only to repeat and deeply feel the phrases I have written below. Even if you are severely depressed, by the time you finish these next few lines you will no longer be feeling that way. That, my friends, is my solemn promise to all of you.

When you repeat these words and feel them in your hearts, they will transform your lives 100%. I was once suicidal and wanted desperately to be dead. I was in and out of hospitals on suicidal watch. My beloved, this simple method will transform your lives profoundly, as it did mine. It surely is our next step to absolute enlightenment. It works magically, but it is not magic. After a very short period of time, you will find that only five to ten minutes of daily use are essential. This time is required so that what you have learned will remain with you for life. I almost didn't learn this truth, so please don't do what I almost did and stop. Continue no matter what your head might tell you. You will soon be feeling so good that you will probably think that you no longer need it, but you do. Everyone who sees the differences in you will be begging for you to tell them your secret. Do it with my love.

Now, for the real magic of your lives, say the following aloud:

I am unconditional love.

I feel this love expanding within every cell of my body.

I am real genuine lovenergy.

Joy is filling every cell of my body, heart, and mind.

Now with all of the powers of your will, imagine enormous waves of love pouring through you. Notice that these feelings are so strong that they nearly take your breath away.

Say the following aloud:

I am loving others and being loved more in return.

This is true expansion and I feel love awakening in me.

I love life and everything about it.

My life is improving because I am more loving.

All is divine because I am divine.

Now feel your stomachs contracting with unrestrained passion. That is your proof of this method's effectiveness. Take a deep breath and feel the power of love increase beyond measure.

Say the following aloud:

I am perfect unconditional love.

I feel it expanding my whole horizon.

The more love I give the more love I receive.

I am real divine love as it is meant to be for all of humanity.

This love is real and it is mine!

How grand to be loving others like this and for them to be loving me.

This is real and I can feel it moving all through me.

I am becoming more and more loving every minute.

I am alive in love and it is alive in me.

It is perfect and I am becoming more perfect in its divinity.

Feel yourselves having more of those stomach contractions and notice them so powerful that it is almost hard to keep breathing. Life is so delightfully fulfilling.

Now, louder and with more feeling, say the following aloud:

Now that I am creating greater love, my life is becoming much more fulfilling and affluent.

The more I give the more is given back.

I am becoming more and more wealthy every minute.

All of my heartfelt desires are being gratified.

I have more riches than I will ever need!

The more money, love, and joy I give the more I receive.

I love everyone and everyone loves me, too!

Oh, this life is so perfect!

It just is impossible to need or want more!

I have far more than I could ever need!

Everything in my life is so abundantly divine.

I daily feel love growing in my mind, heart, and spirit.

The more love I give, the more love is given back and the more I can hold.

Now you have the basic tools. Use and expand them however you desire. If you still feel in need, you know what to do. Just keep saying those phrases. For variety, make up your own slogans and say them for as long as you need to. I guarantee you that in only weeks you will need only a few minutes of some of your favorites.

Now get out there and put it to work for yourselves!

> If sincere love existed, how could someone who felt it toward you impose his or her will upon you? What many people feel for and from others is not love but manipulation and neediness. We need each other for whatever reason, and too often we force those needs on those we know, strangers, beloved, or even disliked others.
>
> Joe Tolve

We are the actors, play writers, scene designers, and directors of our own lives. It's about time we learn how to create them the way we desire rather than just accepting them the way they happen. What I have honestly experienced and am writing in this book is true. If you want to experience some of what I've written—especially about how you can activate feeling genuine love within yourself and having it amplify itself over and over in others—I guess that it will be up to you to determine truth from fiction. Although it honestly doesn't matter, for all is One and that, my beloved, is the truth! Experiencing growth via passion-filled love is the reason for our very existence!

> Love is not what you want; it is what you are. It is very important to not get these two confused. If you think that love is what you want, you will go searching for it all over the place. If you think love is what you are, you will go sharing it all over the place.
>
> Neal Donald Walsch

> Love is misunderstood to be an emotion; actually, it is a state of awareness, a way of being in the world, a way of seeing oneself and others.
>
> David Hawkins

In essence, we are all made of the same stuff: LovEnergy/LifEnergy/OnEnergy. That's why we combine those words. After all, there is only One energy.

We are all One perceived as many. We are all Light.

Light is the essential quality of stars. The moment we realize our light, we can shine like the stars we truly are. If our individual and collective light or brilliance is not fully shining, it is not because it doesn't exist as strongly; it is simply because we are not fully aware or connected to its enormity.

In the pages of this book you have learned how to ignite your light via a powerful and simple method of activating your unconditional lovenergy within. This is our gift to the world, our very reason for being here and aiding you now. First, humanity needs to know of their Oneness with the universal spirit of God/One, and then how to activate this equalizing lovenergy for all of humanity. You have learned this revitalizing truth in this book.

99.9% of the members of our cause exist in the fourth dimension/density.

The rest of us are with you now—expanding by aiding you in countless ways. Know that you are each One's expression of lovenergy. Through this uniquely powerful method of creating love through yourselves and everyone on earth, you will all live peacefully in this world. You need only to realize your absolute Oneness. In truth, we are universal sparks of OnEnergy/LifEnergy/LovEnergy, which is all there is to existence. There is after all only Onenergy, which is found throughout existence. In 1917 Einstein called it Source Energy.

Knowing ourselves as lovenergy/One's Light allows us to move from the culture of tolerance—mind oriented—to the culture of Love—heart oriented. It allows us to shift our focus of dualism (diversity) to the true belief in our divine Oneness.

The challenge is that activating lovenergy cannot be taught in an intellectual way. Love resides within and must be awakened through realization and experiences that touch us at a heart level. We can refer to these experiences as "Aha Moments". "Aha Moments" will be spontaneous once you have learned our Love Energizing technique.

These enlightening moments seem to happen rarely in our lives. However, they will be part of your daily life if you apply our transforming method, which will change you AND all of your living conditions.

> As a result, you will shine in the world like the brilliant star that you truly are.
>
> Joe Tolve

> Being deeply loved by someone gives you strength while loving someone deeply gives you courage.
>
> Lao Tzu

Infinite Being is The One and The All. We can see the infinite variety of The All in the external world, but, at the deepest level of consciousness, each individual part of The All is The One.

At the deepest level, you are not a part of the One within a being nor the outer, but you are a part of the wholeness of One. There are no separate parts. There is no division within the One—you are the One. You are Infinite Being. If this were not so, then at that deepest level of awareness, there would be both The One and you. That would make two, and that is not what is there at that deepest level of consciousness. Only The One exists in that ultimate state. Therefore, you are The One, as is everyone else. Infinite Being is The One and The All.

We are Infinite Being. So, The great paradox of Infinite Being is this: While you appear to be one of infinite parts of The All, at the deepest level of awareness you are not a separate part, you are, instead, simply The One.

The reason for the paradox is that we live in an existence that creates the illusion of separation. Deep down we're all the same—we are One. But for the sake of being able to experience all the drama and excitement that life in this world has to offer, the appearance of separation into the All was created. This was done so that One can observe itself from an infinite variety of viewpoints. That includes your unique viewpoint, my unique viewpoint, and everyone else's unique viewpoints of their Oneness or less-desired individuality.

Courtesy of Owen Waters at www.InfiniteBeing.com and modified by Joe Tolve:

There are two basic motivating forces: fear and love. When we are afraid, we pull back from life. When we are in love, we open to all that life has to offer with passion, excitement, and acceptance.

We need to learn to love ourselves first, in all our glory and our imperfections. If we cannot love ourselves, we cannot fully open to our ability to love others or our potential to create.

Evolution and hopes for a better world rest in the fearlessness and the open-hearted vision of people who embrace life.

> It matters not who you love, where you love, why you love, when you love, or how you love, it matters only that you love.
>
> John Lennon

TRANSFORMATION

> The man who removes a mountain begins by carrying away small stones.
> William Faulkner

Longing for a miracle that will transform your life? Miracles happen, and if we don't want that magic to disappear on us, we need to learn from each epiphany—to integrate it, apply it, and build on it so we can permanently shift to a new level of being.

The real key to fulfillment lies in ONGOING transformation: building our awareness of daily opportunities to change our perceptions and raise our consciousness. Life is about dissolving the old and creating anew. The more we open to accepting and learning from every life experience, the more our lives transform.

> Enlightenment must come little by little—otherwise it would overwhelm.
> Idries Shah

WHAT IFS

The universe is full of magical things patiently waiting for us to accept them as our own. What if you were to pretend that you were perfectly healthy, wealthy, wise, and that life was as fulfilling in every way imaginable? What if you were to decide to be loving no matter what your perceived living conditions were like? Take the power of "What if..." seriously and you will grasp the power to create a world of your own design. Everything—and I mean everything—begins in your imagination. Put it to work constructively for you. The greatest discovery in my life is that a human being can alter his life perceptions by altering his attitudes.

Aren't you tired of arguments, being hurt by loved ones, disappointed and ignored by children, and feeling hopeless and ready to give up? It is now time you take command of those emotions and your life!

In the pages of this book you have learned an effective method of creating unconditional lovenergy for yourself and others. Within only weeks of 10 to 20 minutes of daily practice, you will transform your life and, like magic, see others change, too. Remember that WE are the One, and so is everyONE else you perceive. Be ye the lovenergy of One, and be number ONE in your own lives!

> The kind of love you will develop with this technique will transform your life entirely. If alone, you will find your special mate, if married, you will enhance your relationship. Even addictions, yes all of them including overeating, alcoholism, anger, fear, hatred, molesting, hunger, greed, poverty, and drug dependency will be corrected, and your paradise will come into being. Be ye the One in love.
>
> Joe Tolve

> What a curious phenomenon it is that you can get men to die for the liberty of the world who will not make the little sacrifice that is needed to free themselves from their own individual bondage.
>
> Bruce Barton

GRATITUDE

As you project pink light on others, feel the divine lovenergy of One pouring into your whole being. Feel your stomach contracting in orgasms of pleasure as One in them is unconditionally loving you in return. Thank Him with the unity of your Oneness, and be grateful for His perfect, unselfish love.

The more you love, the more you are being loved. You are the sea of God/One. Unlike Him/Her your sea of Oneness is empty. However, by sharing your lovenergy with others your sea is being filled. Feel your heart expanding every moment of loving, for you are becoming the perfection of One. Feel love intensifying and know its flawlessness in your heart, mind, and very spirit of One.

"Be ye the Oneness of I am."

About the Author

Joseph "Joe" L. Tolve, Jr. lived in Mamaroneck, NY for the first 23 years of his life. He lost his sight at 12 and spent years in a school for the blind learning Braille and other necessities that enabled him to live a very fulfilling life. He worked as a freelance tennis racket stringer and ran his own private stringing business, yet he still felt an isolation and reservation from people due to his disability. This triggered a powerful longing in his heart to find a remedy that would dissolve the barriers between all individuals. This magic fixer turned out to be as simple as love. God answered his prayers and gave him a gift that not only removed the obstructions in his life, but opened floodgates of love for him and everyone in his life.

Within only eight weeks his life was transformed by his lovenergy technique and he no longer felt ignored by society. At 67, Joe's life is just beginning. He has written two books and continues to write.

Watch for Joe and his lovenergy technique on TV and radio.

"We are all equal and what works for me will also work for you. Use it and allow unconditional love to reign in your life as it does in mine. I pray that you will give it a thorough try. Try it you'll like it!"

Joseph L. Tolve